P9-CSH-463

International Management

International Management

Insights from Fiction and Practice

Edited by Sheila M. Puffer
Foreword by Dane A. Bedward

M.E.Sharpe
Armonk, New York
London, England

Copyright © 2004 by M.E. Sharpe, Inc.

While every effort was made to contact copyright holders of the materials reprinted here (specifically, readings 4.2, 6.3, 8.2, 8.5, 9.1, 13.1), we apologize for any inadvertent omissions. If any acknowledgment is missing, it would be appreciated if the publisher were contacted so that this can be rectified in any future edition.

All rights reserved. No part of this book may be reproduced in any form without written permission from the publisher, M.E. Sharpe, Inc., 80 Business Park Drive, Armonk, New York 10504.

Library of Congress Cataloging-in-Publication Data

International management : insights from fiction and practice / edited by Sheila M. Puffer.
    p. cm.
    ISBN 0-7656-0970-3 (cloth : alk. paper) ISBN 0-07656-0971-1 (pbk. : alk. paper)
    1. International business enterprises—Management—Case studies. 2. Business communication—Cross-cultural studies. 3. Intercultural communication. I. Puffer, Sheila M.
HD62.4.I5643 2004
658′.049—dc22

2003019172

Printed in the United States of America

The paper used in this publication meets the minimum requirements of
American National Standard for Information Sciences
Permanence of Paper for Printed Library Materials,
ANSI Z 39.48-1984.

∞

| BM (c) | 10 | 9 | 8 | 7 | 6 | 5 | 4 | 3 | 2 | 1 |
| BM (p) | 10 | 9 | 8 | 7 | 6 | 5 | 4 | 3 | 2 | 1 |

ACC Library Services
Austin, Texas

For my dear neighbors,
with appreciation for the bonds we have formed—
The Wise Women of Winchester Book Club
and The Transfer Station Band

CONTENTS

FOREWORD

Lord Palmerston once wrote in defending his foreign policy in the British House of Commons that: "We have no eternal allies, and we have no perpetual enemies. Our interests are eternal and perpetual, and those interests it is our duty to follow." These words are not only true for countries, but also for companies that have products and services that are marketable worldwide. Expansion beyond your own country is mandatory for continued growth, and globalization of your business better ensures long-term financial and competitive strength.

In the face of the increasing facility of companies to do business across borders, a need exists for personnel and processes that take into account the differences of one country or region from another. The enlightened global manager is hard to find. Diverse points of view about the essence of management exist as you move from culture to culture. Culture is a filter through which business issues are viewed, and it determines how they are handled. Global managers of international organizations must be able to recognize these differences and modify their approaches in order to maximize returns in all markets.

When I started writing this foreword, I was flying at 30,000 feet above southern Brazil. I had just left a conference in Porto Alegre (a key city in the State of Rio Grande de Sul, Brazil), one of the countries covered by two short stories in this book. I was on my way to Buenos Aires, Argentina, via Montevideo, Uruguay. It was June, winter in South America. From this southern vantage point, the weather gets warmer the farther north you go. South is the direction you take toward the snow and ice of the Antarctic. It is amazing how many travelers I meet who have very little knowledge of basic geography. However, through books and short stories they can gain some insight related to foreign lands. In the past six months my work has taken me to Canada, England, Chile, Mexico, Argentina, and Brazil. Before this year is through I will have revisited these countries at least once, and I will have visited Colombia, Venezuela, Italy, Spain, and France. The cultures of each of these countries are very different even though their roots lie in some common ancestry. My responsibilities as Vice President and General Manager, Americas, for Genzyme Corporation result in travel within my region as well as into other regions of the world to ensure that we use appropriate best practices as we grow our business and our industry. Sensitivity to the particular local requirements has allowed for accelerated growth of our company. I do not try to export the American way but modify my approach to meet local needs.

Genzyme Corporation is a global biotechnology company driven by a commitment to patients. Since our founding more than two decades ago, we have dedicated our efforts to making a positive impact on the lives of people with serious diseases and medical conditions. This commitment has driven innovation in treating both widespread diseases and rare genetic conditions, in providing leading diagnostic tests and services, in bringing the benefits of biotechnology to the practice of surgery, and in developing novel approaches to combating cancer. Today our nearly 6,000 employees worldwide serve patients in more than seventy-five countries. Globalization is a must for us as we are dedicated to meeting these unmet medical needs regardless of where the patients are located. We understand the uniqueness of the diseases we treat and the need for local management to be versed in the norms of the countries that they service. To ensure that we have the production capacity to support the growth of current and new products, we are expanding globally. This strategy has served us well.

I was privileged in my early career to be with Johnson and Johnson, a company that moved me to international assignments and had the experience to know that an expatriate needs to be provided with training in local business practices and cross-cultural issues prior to an assignment. Their consultants explained to me the same truths that are found in the stories in this book. Sheila Puffer and her business students at Northeastern University have worked with our Genzyme International Group to help managers understand a particular part of the world in which they were involved. Through their research and selected short stories and management readings, the students summarized the particularities of the cultures and business practices in these parts of the world, thus clarifying gray areas and misconceptions.

I, like most businesspeople, read a number of newspapers, books, and journals and watch CNN, Fox, BBC, and the local stations in the countries that I visit. But this is not enough. Professor Puffer's novel approach to business writing combined with short stories simplifies the task of understanding other cultures while giving the reader a feeling for the milieu in which business is conducted. By reading this book you will have an opportunity to take a step further toward understanding the context in which individuals in other parts of the world think and operate—their own culture.

Dane A. Bedward
Senior VP and General Manager, Americas
Genzyme Corporation

INTRODUCTION

More and more companies, large and small, are conducting business in a worldwide context, entering new markets and seeking reliable and cost-effective suppliers around the world. Competitive pressures for high quality and low prices, as well as ever-shorter product life cycles, drive many companies into the global marketplace for survival and growth. As a result, increasing numbers of working people find themselves in contact with people from other cultures. Some people travel to other countries for short periods, while others live abroad for several years. Some individuals work in multicultural environments in their home countries, while others communicate with customers, suppliers, and other employees around the world without ever leaving home.

SHORT STORIES AS A VEHICLE FOR CROSS-CULTURAL INSIGHTS IN MANAGEMENT

The diversity of cultures and different business practices around the world, if not well understood, can pose serious obstacles to business success. But in today's fast-paced and resource-scarce business environment, it is difficult to find the time and the means to learn about doing business in other cultures. This book offers a collection of business articles and international short stories that can be read and enjoyed in a small time frame and with little expenditure of resources. The collection could also be made part of a more extensive cross-cultural training program.

Although the pairing of business articles and fictional pieces may seem an unlikely combination at first glance, the two writing approaches actually complement each other. The business articles provide practical guidelines and concrete examples, while the short stories convey cultural subtleties and shades of meaning that cannot be transmitted as richly in a clear, concise business article. The short stories can serve a similar purpose as traditional business case studies—specific, concrete situations that lend themselves to discussion and analysis of management concepts and incidents. The business articles can be used to analyze management issues and to suggest solutions for issues raised in the stories. This combination has the additional benefit of improving communication skills through a richer, more descriptive vocabulary and writing style than is typically found in technical management writing.

Selections represent a variety of countries and business situations and cover humorous as well as serious topics. Authors from around the world are included, providing cultural and managerial insights from an insider's perspective. Developing cultural sensitivity and global managerial skills is a continuous process. The stories and management readings contained in this volume can help make the process enjoyable and enlightening.

STRUCTURE OF THE BOOK

This is the third volume of short stories and management readings that I have compiled in the past decade. The first, *Managerial Insights from Literature,* was published in 1991 and contains primarily American and British short stories and management readings. The second, *Management Across Cultures: Insights from Fiction and Practice,* was published in 1996 and presents stories and management readings from around the world.

The current book is organized into four parts reflecting specific aspects of managing in cross-cultural and international contexts. Part I discusses phases of cross-cultural experience, Part II emphasizes values and ethics, Part III examines power and group dynamics, and Part IV explores various aspects of doing business together. Each section begins with an overview of the contents and purpose. Subsections of short stories are then organized by international management topics, and a concluding section contains related management readings.

The management readings can be paired with stories in various sections in addition to those listed. For instance, "Building Competitive Advantage from *Ubuntu*: Management Lessons From South Africa," included in Section 10, provides background for understanding "The Zulu and the Zeide" in Section 13, in addition to "Government by Magic Spell" in Section 8. Similarly, "Leadership Made in Germany: Low on Compassion, High on Performance," which is included in Section 10, can be used to discuss "The Awful German Language" in Section 1, in addition to "Welcoming the Board of Directors" in Section 8 and "Action Will Be Taken" in Section 9. Other pairings can be made with stories and readings about the same country. Stories and readings having similar themes can also be matched; for example, "Navigating the Hostile Maze: A Framework for Russian Entrepreneurship" in Section 7 is useful for analyzing "A New Customer" and "A Brief History of Capitalism" in Section 12.

Several new features are offered in this book. First, many stories have been included that were not published in my two previous collections. Also, all of the management readings are new to this book and were published from 1999 to 2002. Part IV has been added to reflect new topics in international and cross-cultural management. These include multicultural workplaces, customer service, and teams and alliances. Most of the management readings are excerpted from articles recently published in *The Academy of Management Executive*. Having been the editor from 1999 through 2001, I find the articles to be highly relevant for practicing managers and solidly grounded in the latest management theories and concepts.

WHO CAN BENEFIT FROM THIS BOOK?

This book is intended for students in a variety of programs and courses focusing on cross-cultural issues and international management. In business schools and training programs the book can be useful in international business, cross-cultural management, and international human resources management courses. It is also relevant for courses in business and organizational communication, managing diversity, English across the curriculum, and English as a second language. The book can be the main text in a course or used as a supplement to traditional textbooks, and can be used in courses ranging from those at community colleges through undergraduate, MBA, and executive education. Business practitioners engaged in or planning to do business internationally or in multicultural workplaces can also find insights in the selections that they may consider in their work settings.

For over a decade, many students in the College of Business Administration at Northeastern University have taken my courses in management across cultures through literature. Class discussions at all academic levels, including the undergraduate, MBA, and Executive MBA programs, have been highly engaging. Different interpretations emerge of each story, and management readings are applied to the stories in creative ways. Coming from different cultures and circumstances from all over the world, many students find that the stories make them feel comfortable discussing in an uninhibited way their personal experiences living in their own cultures as well as in adapting to other cultures. Students find many interesting short stories and management readings on their own to complete course papers. They connect with the business community by interviewing managers and other employees working in international settings. They select short stories and management readings for these colleagues, analyze the stories and readings, and offer recommendations for working effectively in these cultures.

WITH THANKS

I am grateful to the dedicated and skillful MBA students who worked as research assistants on this book. Jianfang Pei from China, and Miglena Patarinska and Denitsa Bekova from Bulgaria, expertly managed the complex copyright permissions process and copied, electronically scanned, and proofread the hundreds of pages of text that are included in the book. Thanks are also due to the students and guest speakers in my executive, graduate, and undergraduate classes for their engaging and insightful discussions of the stories and readings. And I am grateful to the managers in various Boston-area organizations, including Genzyme Corporation, the Boston World Trade Center, and Eaton Consulting Group, who collaborated with students on applying the stories and readings to their work. I also appreciate the support of my colleagues at M.E. Sharpe, especially editor Harry Briggs, who championed the book, Elizabeth Granda, and all those who saw it through to production.

Sheila Puffer
Boston, 2004

International Management

PART I

PHASES OF
CROSS-CULTURAL EXPERIENCE

SECTION 1. CULTURAL AND COMMUNICATION CHALLENGES

The images we create in our minds of life in other cultures can be intriguing, exotic, or curious but not necessarily well informed or accurate. Even with careful preparation and keeping an open mind, the actual experience of other cultures can be confusing and can hold many surprises. In "Name Six Famous Belgians," a well-intentioned Philadelphia couple take a vacation in Europe in search of "a certain degree of insulation from the abrasions of life." Instead, they encounter a series of bewildering and irritating situations. Compounding their confusion and distaste are unpleasant past experiences that keep them from seeing other cultures in a positive light.

"American Dreams" recounts a young Australian boy's fantasizing about America, "because we all have dreams of the big city, of wealth, of modern houses, of big motor cars: American dreams, my father has called them." In contrast, "for our town, my father says, we have nothing but contempt." Life changes dramatically when the town becomes a tourist attraction that Americans come en masse to visit.

Language is a key to understanding and functioning in a culture. Written by an English instructor, "English as a Second Language" is a testimony to the fortitude and determination of immigrants coming to America to build a new life. For them, learning English is a matter of survival. The story portrays immigrants who practice their new language skills by recounting incidents from their lives of extreme hardship and violent conditions in the developing world. One of them, Maria Perez from Guatemala, "is an inspiration to her classmates. Not only has she learned to read and write in her new language, but she initiated an oral history project in which she taped and transcribed interviews with other students, who have told their stories from around the world."

"The Awful German Language" is a playful account by a famous frustrated language student, the American humorist Mark Twain. Attempting to learn German more than a century ago, he drolly complains, "Surely there is not another language that is so slipshod and systemless, and so slippery and elusive to the grasp." Rather than make the effort to master its complexities, Twain declares that the German language needs reforming and offers eight suggestions to simplify it.

SECTION 2. SETTLING INTO NEW SURROUNDINGS

Living abroad is often a family affair, with adjustment to the new culture being difficult for both accompanying family members as well as the employee on a foreign assignment. In "Saree of the Gods," a young Indian couple tries to adapt to life in New York City by inviting two American couples for dinner. The husband's objective is to build closer relationships with his work colleagues, but his newly arrived wife has difficulty accepting the cultural differences. An accident that damages her prized dress causes her to resent the guests and blame her husband for "lavishing food and liquor that they could scarcely afford on the people that were yet to be called friends."

"How to Be an Expatriate" is written in a no-nonsense style that reads like a how-to manual of practical advice for people about to embark on an international assignment. In fact, it is a diary of the ups and downs of a young British man who leaves home for a year to study in Boston, with his anxious parents trying not to interfere. He stays in the United States for several years, making occasional trips home, and questions his identity when "your best friend tells you you've changed."

SECTION 3. COMING HOME

An overseas assignment is a life-changing experience, and coming home can be traumatic in its own way. Exposure to another culture alters a person's perspective and prompts questions about one's own culture. In "Yard Sale," the culture of Polynesia "clearly got into the bones" of a young Peace Corps volunteer in Samoa. Returning to Cape Cod after a two-year assignment, he nearly drives his aunt to distraction with incessant stories about how life in Samoa is better than life in the United States. Greater sensitivity to his aunt's point of view would have helped smooth the young man's reentry and made her more receptive to his experiences.

In "Letter from Gaza," a young student explains to his friend who moved to California that he is declining the opportunity to study civil engineering at the University of California. Instead, he has decided to stay at home after visiting his thirteen-year-old niece who has been wounded. He vows, "No, I'll stay here, and I won't ever leave." He then asks, "What is this ill-defined tie we had with Gaza which blunted our enthusiasm for flight?"

SECTION 4. MANAGERIAL INSIGHTS

As the stories "Name Six Famous Belgians" and "American Dreams" illustrate, beginning the cross-cultural experience can be daunting and confusing. With little information to guide us, we often rely on imperfect stereotypes of another culture. It can be puzzling, however, when people do not behave according to these stereotypes. In such cases, cultural paradoxes arise. "Beyond Sophisticated Stereotyping: Cultural Sensemaking in Context" provides a model for identifying the sources of cultural paradoxes and for understanding how certain cultural values take precedence over others in specific situations.

Learning a foreign language requires patience, practice, and a willingness to make mistakes. "English as a Second Language" and "The Awful German Language" touch on the pitfalls of expressing oneself in another tongue. Although English is the major international language of business, "'Englishes' in Cross-Cultural Business Communication" points out that many variations of English exist that are accepted as standard in different parts of the world. Miscommunication can occur because of differences in English usage and misunderstanding of cultural meanings. Tips are offered to reduce the incidence of bypassing in cross-cultural communication.

The family members of expatriates described in "Saree of the Gods" and "How to Be an Expatriate" might have fared better in their new surroundings had they benefited from the findings reported in "When Managing Expatriate Adjustment, Don't Forget the Spouse." A key to successful adjustment of spouses is how well the spouse can reestablish his or her identity in the new culture. Surprisingly, spouses who believed they had good social skills were actually somewhat less likely to adjust successfully.

Maintaining loyalty to both the home office and operations abroad is a delicate balance for managers in international assignments. "Adapting to a Boundaryless World: A Developmental Expatriate Model" identifies the stressors and coping responses in the various stages of expatriate life. Accepting the paradox of two cultural identities is an essential coping mechanism. The characters in all the stories in this section exhibit various stressors and coping responses that can be analyzed with this reading.

Section 1
———— Cultural and Communication Challenges ————

1.1   NAME SIX FAMOUS BELGIANS
David R. Slavitt

What they give you when you check into the Villa Igiea is a little card to carry with you—but not in your wallet, presumably—to certify that you are a guest in the hotel and that you are insured. The pamphlet that comes with the card explains the insurance policy the hotel carries that covers you in case your pocket is picked, your wallet stolen, your purse snatched, or even worse. If you have a mind to, you can read through the impressive document until you get to the clause about how, if you are hospitalized, your next of kin will be brought to Palermo from anywhere in the world. Or about how, if you are killed, your body will be shipped home at no charge to your estate.

Bad as it is back in Philadelphia, it has not yet come to this. But then Palermo has had a couple of millennia headstart.

With a straight face, Harry thanked the desk clerk, but when they got up to their room, he and Joan made nervous jokes about it. Out through the double doors of their balcony they could see the glassy Mediterranean, more pacific than the Pacific. They simply couldn't believe it—not that there could be such lawlessness as the insurance company's document implied, but that it could be so taken for granted. Harry supposed it was remotely possible that this could be a gesture the management made to give the tourists a pleasant frisson of fear, to suggest without seriously inconveniencing anyone the depredations either of the Mafia or merely of the desperately poor. It would be going too far to subject their guests to the disagreeable business of an actual mugging.

Far from the center of town, the Villa Igiea is secluded in its own gardened enclave. From the balcony of their room, Harry and Joan could look left to the open sea. A little to the right, they could see a couple of giant cranes of the port. The city itself, though, was out of sight, even farther to the right and behind them. Harry's idea had been that a certain degree of insulation from the abrasions of life in a strange and poor city would be a good thing, especially on the first days of their visit when they were still acclimating themselves not only to local customs but also to the water and the time of day. Recovering from jet lag, they wanted at least the possibility of respite from assaults by Sicilian exuberance.

And it looked as though it would work out just as they'd hoped. The only trouble was that, being a little way out of town, they had to drive to do any sight-seeing or to eat anywhere except in the hotel dining room, and the map Avis had given them was almost useless. It did not show one-way streets, which was essential in a place like Palermo. Navigation was further complicated by the absence of any systematic posting of street signs. It was one thing to find a street on a map, but quite another to find it out in the real world. This was Joan's job, and she complained a lot. Harry complained, too, about the stick shift of the underpowered and overgeared Fiat Uno they'd been given and the erratic driving habits of the Sicilians, who slowed down for red lights but did

From *Short Stories Are Not Real Life* (Baton Rouge, LA: Louisiana State University Press, 1991), 43–57. Copyright © 1991 David R. Slavitt. Reprinted with permission of Louisiana State University Press.

not feel obligated to come to anything as deferential as a full stop. And people on motor scooters wove through the traffic in a demonstration of a death wish, the fulfillment of which was occasionally celebrated by a blare of sirens from ambulances and police cars, which in their haste contributed to the excitement and general sense of peril.

It was in an attempt to circumvent the busy center of town and save themselves a little time and stress that they got lost on the morning of their second day. And perhaps they were a little crabby with each other, too. Joan kept insisting that Harry pull over and stop so that she could find where they were on the wretched Avis map. Eventually he did so, but gracelessly. He stared through the windshield, making no effort to hide his impatience with her. Hers was an easier job, after all, and if he could do the driving, then she ought to be able to keep track of where they were and where they wanted to go. He waited while she pored over the tiny print of the map on her lap, and then quite suddenly she screamed. Harry turned toward her, not yet thinking anything, but shocked, this being an excessive display of her frustration with the map and with him. He was startled and puzzled, and not quite certain that he'd seen what he thought he'd seen—the blur of a disappearing hand.

"He tried to grab my purse," Joan said. Her voice was high, not shrill but unnaturally thin.

Harry's head turned further. Through the back window, he could see—no question now— the would-be purse snatcher, straddling a bicycle perhaps six feet behind the car, and ready to flee if they should try to pursue him. He might have been thirteen or so. He looked even younger, maybe eleven, but then Sicilians are small, and the diet of the poorest of them must be very meager indeed.

"Drive!" Joan commanded through clenched teeth, her voice still strained. "Let's get out of here."

He drove. They rolled the windows up until they were almost closed and checked the door locks. They kept going until they found an unfrightening part of town and a place where they could park and go into a bar for a coffee. It had been an invasion, of course, a terrible intrusion, and what had kept the boy from getting the purse was the seatbelt that had covered the shoulder strap of Joan's purse, securing it. They'd left their passports and most of their traveller's checks back at the hotel. And for the first time they had been wearing their moneybelts, light navy-blue nylon articles that they had strapped on that morning after breakfast, feeling a little silly. And, Harry reminded Joan, there was that insurance policy the hotel carried!

She laughed, a single sardonic snort. No harm had been done. Still, the idea of the thing was nasty, the disesteem it implied that one human being should have for another. That the thief had been only a child made it worse, if anything. Youngsters are supposed to be innocent and only later to fall from grace as they are called by the necessities of survival to compromise their original principles of fairness and decency. (This was the fiction to which they pretended to subscribe most of the time, if only because the alternative was so uncomfortable: what kind of a world would it be in which such risks and violences are normal?)

The carping about the driving and the map reading stopped, now that something more serious had intruded upon them. With a studied determination—so as not to admit to themselves or each other that they had been defeated or even much affected by this small, nasty incident—they pushed on with their search for the road to Monreale, found it, made their pilgrimage, and even managed to enjoy the extraordinary cathedral with its dazzling mosaics and the cloister next door with that wonderfully various colonnade.

By that evening the incident had been all but forgotten. Neither of them at any rate made mention of it. It is possible, of course, that one or the other of them might have found this omission just a bit peculiar, might have wondered at the other's diffidence, but for her part she might have been reluctant to probe at what was perhaps a tender place. And he might have attributed to her silence a solicitude that was at once welcome and intolerable—because he hated to be condescended to or treated as other than healthy and sane. The closest they'd come to that kind of therapeutic attention had been her asking him, back home in the dark, when neither had to look at the other's facial expression or body language, if he was sure he wanted to go to Italy.

"It's Magna Graecia we're going to see," he had said, "Greek ruins and a few Norman churches and some Bourbon buildings."

"I know," she had said, "but still . . ."

"It's okay," he'd told her.

How far beyond that could she have pushed?

And here he was, and even after what had happened, he seemed to be okay.

For the next few days, it was okay. He was, or it was. Nobody else in Palermo tried to rob them or mug them or kill them. And they drove out, heading east toward Cefalù, with memories of good food and fine buildings and some memorable statuary in the archaeological museum. And most of the good stuff was still to come: Taormina, the mosaics in the remains of the Imperial Villa at Piazza Armerina, and the avenue of temples in Agrigento. And their mood was okay—good enough at least so that at the worst each was, for the sake of the other, putting up a good front. But as each of them knew, to be able still to do that is to be in reasonable shape.

They both had the feeling that they deserved a good time. For one thing they hadn't taken a vacation in almost two years. For another, they'd spent all those evenings planning this trip, working out the sights they wanted to see, and the distances, and the hotels where it would be fun to stay. One of the high points was going to be Agrigento, which was perhaps grounds for a certain skepticism. To have excessive expectations is to be vulnerable to disappointment. Still, there was a picture of the Temple of Concord on the cover of their *Blue Guide* showing between the inner and outer colonnades a narrow swath of sky, and one could see the rough texture of the caramel-colored marble stucco of the columns, which had been baking in the Sicilian sun for a couple of millennia. That the editors had put this on the cover meant it had to be good, didn't it? That was an accolade even greater than its three stars in the text and its bold print in the index.

They were wary, but it was impossible for them never to let their hopes off the leash. And as it turned out, they were astonished, absolutely delighted when the Villa Athena porter, having shown them to their room, drew back the curtains, opened the shutters of the French windows that gave onto their patio, and stood back to reveal, just outside and up a little rise, the avenue of the temples. Directly in front of them was the Temple of Concord, in such a remarkable state of preservation that it looked theatrical. It was odd, certainly, so that Harry laughed, not at the temple or even at himself and his wariness, but just because a thing like that could be in the world, could be real, let alone so close. It was like an exotic bird that had lit on a branch right outside their window, an unlooked-for grace. Joan reacted in much the same way but didn't laugh, because she didn't want to scare it away.

There was no point in going anywhere or doing anything. They didn't have to discuss it. They decided just to stay where they were, drink things from the Frigo-bar, and look at the temple. Later they'd go out, climb up to it, and walk around it, but that could keep a while, until the cool of the afternoon. For now, it was more than enough that they could just stare at it, try to grasp it, try to let it soak in. Joan put on her bathing suit and went out to the terrace with a book so that she could sun herself, reading a sentence or two but then looking up every now and again for another confirmation that, yes, it was still there, presiding over its quarter of the sky. Inside, Harry lay down on the bed and watched television, not because he was interested in dubbed American soap operas but for the contrast between the familiarly tacky program and what was there outside the room, unfamiliar and untacky, and available to him without his even having to turn his head. All he had to do was adjust his eyeballs ever so slightly and there it was, not a figment of his imagination, but real, actual, substantial. The program changed to something called "Dada-Oompah," just as dumb but Italian. The building did not go away.

"Okay?" he called out.

"Terrific!" she answered. And then, after a beat, she ventured to ask, "Happy?"

"Oh, yeah!"

The terrace, it turned out, was not theirs alone but was shared with the room across the hall, which was why there was a row of planters down the middle. Late that afternoon, Harry and Joan walked over to inspect the Temple of Herakles, the Temple of Hera, the Temple of Zeus, and their own—they actually thought of it that way now—Temple of Concord. When they got back to their room, they found that their neighbors had established themselves on the terrace, as of course it was their right to do. They were a slightly younger couple, in their early forties maybe, English as it turned out. He was an investment banker. She was in publishing. She was Dotty. He was Paul.

It wasn't as bad as it might have been. In fact, there was a kind of advantage to small talk with the English couple much like the benefit of having the television set turned on. One could talk about ordinary things, exchange trivial information—that *nespolle,* for instance, those unimpressive little fruits they had been seeing on restaurant dessert carts, were the medlars Giovanni Verga mentioned in his title, or that Luigi Pirandello had been born down there, between the new city and the sea. And then one could glance again at the ridge and see the Temple of Concord, still there, still gorgeous, or perhaps even slightly more gorgeous, those earth-brown tones having deepened now as the sun sank toward the horizon.

The two couples sat there on either side of their planter-divider, drinking Campari and soda from their Frigo-bars and keeping watch on the temple. Paul said that the great event at the hotel was sitting in the outdoor dining pavilion and watching the temple disappear into the darkness and then reemerge abruptly when they turned the arc lights on. It was a good idea to plan to eat around eight in order to catch this. Harry thanked him. There was a delicate moment in which each considered making the suggestion that the four of them dine together, but nobody said anything. Perhaps each had been waiting for one of the others to make the overture that never came. At any rate, the moment passed. They finished their drinks and wished one another a good evening.

But when Harry and Joan went down to dinner, they saw that almost all the tables were occupied. A bus had deposited a crowd of tourists, Germans mostly, who weren't staying at the hotel but were eating there, perhaps for that dramatic moment of the illumination Paul had talked about. Harry and Joan had already resigned themselves to waiting, but the head waiter came back to ask if they would like to share the far table with the couple there who had suggested that they join them. They looked to see Paul and Dotty waving encouragingly.

"Shall we?" Harry asked.

"We can't not," Joan said.

They followed the head waiter to Paul and Dotty's table, thanked them, and sat down. The English couple had arrived just a few moments earlier and had not yet ordered. Harry suggested champagne as the only appropriate way to toast that temple off to the south. Or the closest local equivalent, which was Asti Spumanti.

It was a pleasant dinner, and, yes, there was a moment when the lights switched on and the temple, a dimmed shape, sprang back into a sudden and almost garish clarity. After their meal, they went into the bar for coffee and exchanged itineraries and stories. At one point, Paul mentioned an odd custom Dotty had heard of when she'd gone to the Frankfurt Book Fair. Some of the London publishers take the ferry across to Ostend and then drive to Frankfurt because it's cheaper that way, he said. And as they make their way through Belgium, the game is to name six famous Belgians before they get to the German border. "And the wonderful thing," he said, "is that it can't be done."

"Can't it?" Harry asked, though not combatively. "Leopold and Beaudoin, for starters. And Paul-Henri Spaak."

"Yes, but then it gets tough," Paul said, grinning.

"I guess it does. Glière, maybe. His people were Belgian, anyway."

"Doubtful, but okay."

"Hercule Poirot?" Joan asked.

"He's fictional. He doesn't count, I'm afraid," Dotty said, shaking her head. "People always try him when they get desperate enough."

"Okay, okay," Joan agreed.

"Maybe that's a good thing, though," Harry said. "I mean, that it's so tough. I like the idea of ordinary people leading ordinary lives."

"And eating good food. The food in Brussels is wonderful," Paul said.

"Famous people," Harry said, "are frequently villains."

There was a moment, but the conversation resumed, and there were suggestions about their all getting together again one day, in New York, maybe, or in London. They actually exchanged addresses before they went up to their hallway to separate and retire for the night.

"Nice people," Joan said, once the door was closed.

"Yes, they were," Harry said.

"Well, they still are, aren't they?"

"I suppose so, yes," he admitted. And then, as an afterthought, "Funny about the Belgians. I can't think of any more."

"Neither can I."

They did get swindled once. They discovered it only when they were back in Palermo waiting for the ferry to take them up to Naples. They went into a little place on the Via Cavour for iced coffee, and at the cashier's desk, Harry peeled off what he thought was the right amount of Italian money, only to be told that one of the bills he'd offered, a five-hundred-lire note, was no good. These had been recalled more than a year ago. There was a coin now for that denomination—which was worth at the time maybe thirty-three cents. Harry shook his head, realizing that he'd been taken, that only tourists would be ignorant enough to be victimized this way, and put the worthless note back into his wallet. But he didn't seem really upset. Joan observed all this and was encouraged. And she began to relax, now that Sicily was mostly behind them.

They took the Tirrenia, which got them to Naples at six in the morning. Their plans were to spend a few days in Naples, going down to Pompeii and Herculaneum, and then to take a *rapido* up to Rome to do some shopping and be entertained by some of Harry's old friends. The trip, Joan thought, had gone well enough. Not only had they not had a bad time, they'd enjoyed an affirmatively good one. And when they got to Naples, Harry again seemed no more than wryly amused by the petty thievery of the cab driver who had charged so exorbitantly for a ride of only a few blocks from the dock to their hotel on the Via Partenope, claiming surcharges because it was Sunday morning, because it was not yet seven so the night rates were still in effect, and because they had baggage and he'd been obliged to open the trunk. Harry groused that he'd thought he was hiring the entire cab, trunk included, but he paid and he even smiled.

So Joan thought she could relax. She took only the precautions any prudent American tourist tries to remember to take, always walking so that Harry was on the street side and taking care that her bag was clutched tightly under her arm. And in Naples they never came any closer to getting robbed than they had on that second day in Palermo. Their net loss to crime on the whole trip was that thirty-three cents, the value of that recalled note.

The assault—if it was an assault—came from a different and altogether unexpected quarter, from the soccer madness that gripped the nation and especially caught up the Neapolitans. The World Cup matches were going on in Mexico, and all over Naples there were Italian flags hanging out of apartment windows, the official red-white-and-green tricolor or homemade banners with "Forza Italia" lettered in those colors. Sometimes they stretched across streets from one building to another, on lines that were ordinarily used to hang laundry.

Harry and Joan went out to dinner one night at a little pizzeria they'd found a few blocks from the hotel. It had looked lively enough when they'd first spotted it, crowded and inviting, but this evening it was almost deserted. And the waiter spent most of his time in the back room, watching the Italian team struggle with the South Koreans in an effort not to get eliminated. Evidently, all of Naples was engaged in this effort half a world away, for whenever the Italian team did something good, there would be an encouraging blast of automobile horns from the cars outside. It was all right if they wanted to enjoy themselves that way, but the waiter's inattention was irksome. Harry had to get up and find him to ask for the bill.

"Didn't you want coffee?" Joan asked.

"Yes, but not there. Let's go someplace else. Someplace nice—where they care about the customers. This is nuts."

"It's sports. You like sports."

"This is worse than that. It's nationalism. It's madness. What the hell difference will it make to anybody in Naples if the Italian team beats the South Koreans?"

"It takes their minds off their troubles," she suggested, not wanting to argue.

"What minds? It lets them reveal their true character. That's what it really does. And that's ugly."

Joan could have answered him in a number of ways. He'd been the one who had insisted on Italy, for God's sake! And she'd once asked him, point-blank, "Are you sure you want to do this?" But he'd looked at her and nodded, as if to say that he wasn't going to be deprived of Italy, too.

As if to say that it was not significant that the thug who had broken into his mother's house to burglarize it, whom his mother had confronted, and who had bludgeoned her to death happened to be Italian. Two years later, Harry had been talking about Italy, about Sicily in particular, and how he'd never been there. It made perfect sense, but Joan was shrewd enough to distrust sense. She'd seen Harry piece himself back together, a crude patching job like that of a child mending a sugar bowl he had dropped, gluing the shards together as well as he could.

She'd asked him that, but only once. Because when he reacted, it was unpredictable whether he would lash out or just collapse inwardly. And in neither event was it good to be close by.

They walked from the pizzeria back past their hotel and on toward the Piazza del Martiri, the district of chic shops where they had noticed a flossy coffee bar and gelateria with outside tables. There were plenty of empty tables now, and there were a couple of waiters standing ready to bring ice cream or coffee. They weren't inside, huddled around some television set. Harry seemed satisfied, and he and Joan sat down and ordered—coffee ice cream for her and *zuppa inglese* ice cream for him. The waiter brought their order right away.

And then, in Mexico City, the Italians came from behind to beat the South Koreans, and in Naples, everybody went wild. They bolted from their apartments, jumped into their cars or onto their motorcycles or scooters, unfurled their enormous flags and banners, and raced through the streets yelling and blowing their horns. The street, which had been quiet a moment before, was alive with people now, swarming with traffic, loud, blaring, grating, triumphant, frenzied, insisting on the wonderfulness of their being Italians, their national pride and ebullience bubbling up and spewing forth.

She watched Harry retreating into himself, watched his color drain, the muscles along his jaw twitch, the tears well up in his eyes and spill down his cheeks. What they were insisting upon was exactly what he could not bear, what he hated: the barbarousness that was the verso of their culture, their potentiality for cruelty and violence, the thuggish nastiness they could assume when they assembled into crowds for a Mussolini to harangue, passionate oafs ready to be seduced by villains and clowns.

"You want to go?" she asked.

He couldn't speak. He only nodded.

He threw a few thousand lire onto the table. He hesitated. Then he threw that worthless five-hundred-lire note onto the pile with it.

They started back toward the hotel, a matter of five blocks or so, but they were a long five blocks, and there were wide streets to cross, dangerous in the Mezzogiorno at the best of times and utterly intimidating now. There was a couple on a Vespa, a young man with a young woman behind him, and they had a dog running along beside them on a leash, and the dog was struggling to keep up. Joan saw it and saw that Harry saw it, noting his grimace of pain and rage . . . and she could do nothing.

Back at the hotel, their bed had been turned down. The shutters were closed and the heavy draperies pulled closed, but they could still hear the blare of horns, that mindless mechanical braying as tireless as it was inescapable. The best they could do was to undress and go to bed. Harry took a long pull of brandy from the bottle they carried with them, got into bed, and put his head under a pillow that could not possibly have blocked out the noise but maybe muffled it a little.

Joan turned on the television set, found a channel that was broadcasting something other than the gloating interviews about the soccer victory—an old "Mission Impossible" episode, actually—and turned up the volume. There was no response from Harry, but at least he didn't object. Eventually, she supposed, he'd fall asleep. And eventually he did.

In the morning they were subdued, like people with hangovers, but they did what they'd planned to do. They went over to Capri for the day, didn't like it, came back, packed, and took the train to Rome early the next morning.

Rome was all right. "River City," one of their American friends who lived there called it. They were there for three days, during which Joan kept looking surreptitiously at her watch, counting the hours until they could make their way through Da Vinci's impressive array of guards and inspectors and board the plane heading home.

For those first few weeks after their return, friends in Philadelphia asked them about their vacation and where they'd gone. The first time it happened, Harry surprised Joan, lying badly and outrageously. "Belgium," he said, absolutely straight-faced.

"Oh? And how was it?" they asked, politely.

Harry let Joan tell them. It was, at last, something she could do, something he could let her do for him.

"Wonderful," she said. "Very peaceful. A wonderful country."

"The whole time? In Belgium?"

"Oh, yes," Harry said, glancing at her in a quick look of acknowledgment that was like an embrace. "It's a fine place. The food in Brussels is wonderful."

1.2 AMERICAN DREAMS
Peter Carey

No one can, to this day, remember what it was we did to offend him. Dyer the butcher remembers a day when he gave him the wrong meat and another day when he served someone else first by mistake. Often when Dyer gets drunk he recalls this day and cusses himself for his foolishness. But no one seriously believes that it was Dyer who offended him.

But one of us did something. We slighted him terribly in some way, this small meek man with the rimless glasses and neat suit who used to smile so nicely at us all. We thought, I suppose, he was a bit of a fool and sometimes he was so quiet and grey that we ignored him, forgetting he was there at all.

When I was a boy I often stole apples from the trees at his house up in Mason's Lane. He often saw me. No, that's not correct. Let me say I often sensed that he saw me. I sensed him peering out from behind the lace curtains of his house. And I was not the only one. Many of us came to take his apples, alone and in groups, and it is possible that he chose to exact payment for all these apples in his own peculiar way.

Yet I am sure it wasn't the apples.

What has happened is that we all, all eight hundred of us, have come to remember small transgressions against Mr. Gleason who once lived amongst us.

My father, who has never borne malice against a single living creature, still believes that Gleason meant to do us well, that he loved the town more than any of us. My father says we have treated the town badly in our minds. We have used it, this little valley, as nothing more than a stopping place. Somewhere on the way to somewhere else. Even those of us who have been here many years have never taken the town seriously. Oh yes, the place is pretty. The hills are green and the woods thick. The stream is full of fish. But it is not where we would rather be.

For years we have watched the films at the Roxy and dreamed, if not of America, then at least of our capital city. For our own town, my father says, we have nothing but contempt. We have treated it badly, like a whore. We have cut down the giant shady trees in the main street to make doors for the school house and seats for the football pavilion. We have left big holes all over the countryside from which we have taken brown coal and given back nothing.

The commercial travelers who buy fish and chips at George the Greek's care for us more than we do, because we all have dreams of the big city, of wealth, of modem houses, of big motor cars: American Dreams, my father has called them.

Although my father ran a petrol station he was also an inventor. He sat in his office all day drawing strange pieces of equipment on the back of delivery dockets. Every spare piece of paper in the house was covered with these little drawings and my mother would always be very careful about throwing away any piece of paper no matter how small. She would look on both sides of any piece of paper very carefully and always preserved any that had so much as a pencil mark.

I think it was because of this that my father felt that he understood Gleason. He never said as much, but he inferred that he understood Gleason because he, too, was concerned with similar problems. My father was working on plans for a giant gravel crusher, but occasionally he would become distracted and become interested in something else.

From *The Fat Man in History* (London and Boston: Faber and Faber, 1980). Copyright © 1974, 1979 Peter Carey. Reprinted with permission.

There was, for instance, the time when Dyer the butcher bought a new bicycle with gears, and for a while my father talked of nothing else but the gears. Often I would see him across the road squatting down beside Dyer's bicycle as if he were talking to it.

We all rode bicycles because we didn't have the money for anything better. My father did have an old Chev truck, but he rarely used it and it occurs to me now that it might have had some mechanical problem that was impossible to solve, or perhaps it was just that he was saving it, not wishing to wear it out all at once. Normally, he went everywhere on his bicycle, and when I was younger, he carried me on the cross bar, both of us dismounting to trudge up the hills that led into and out of the main street. It was a common sight in our town to see people pushing bicycles. They were as much a burden as a means of transport.

Gleason also had his bicycle, and every lunchtime he pushed and pedalled it home from the shire offices to his little weatherboard house out at Mason's Lane. It was a three-mile ride and people said that he went home for lunch because he was fussy and wouldn't eat either his wife's sandwiches or the hot meal available at Mrs. Lessing's cafe.

But while Gleason pedalled and pushed his bicycle to and from the shire offices everything in our town proceeded as normal. It was only when he retired that things began to go wrong.

Because it was then that Mr. Gleason started supervising the building of the wall around the two-acre plot up on Bald Hill. He paid too much for this land. He thought it from Johnny Weeks, who now, I am sure, believes the whole episode was his fault, firstly for cheating Gleason, secondly for selling him the land at all. But Gleason hired some Chinese and set to work to build his wall. It was then that we knew that we'd offended him. My father rode all the way out to Bald Hill and tried to talk Mr. Gleason out of his wall. He said there was no need for us to build walls. That no one wished to spy on Mr. Gleason or whatever he wished to do on Bald Hill. He said no one was in the least bit interested in Mr. Gleason. Mr. Gleason, neat in a new sportscoat, polished his glasses and smiled vaguely at his feet. Bicycling back, my father thought that he had gone too far. Of course we had an interest in Mr. Gleason. He pedalled back and asked him to attend a dance that was to be held on the next Friday, but Mr. Gleason said he didn't dance.

"Oh well," my father said, "any time, just drop over."

Mr. Gleason went back to supervising his family of Chinese labourers on his wall.

Bald Hill towered high above the town and from my father's small filling station you could sit and watch the wall going up. It was an interesting sight. I watched it for two years, while I waited for customers who rarely came. After school and on Saturdays I had all the time in the world to watch the agonizing progress of Mr. Gleason's wall. It was as painful as a clock. Sometimes I could see the Chinese labourers running at a jog-trot carrying bricks on long wooden planks. The hill was bare, and on this bareness Mr. Gleason was, for some reason, building a wall.

In the beginning people thought it peculiar that someone would build such a big wall on Bald Hill. The only thing to recommend Bald Hill was the view of the town, and Mr. Gleason was building a wall that denied that view. The top soil was thin and bare clay showed through in places. Nothing would ever grow there. Everyone assumed that Gleason had simply gone mad and after the initial interest they accepted his madness as they accepted his wall and as they accepted Bald Hill itself.

Occasionally someone would pull in for petrol at my father's filling station and ask about the wall and my father would shrug and I would see, once more, the strangeness of it.

"A house?" the stranger would ask. "Up on that hill?"

"No," my father would say, "chap named Gleason is building a wall."

And the strangers would want to know why, and my father would shrug and look up at Bald Hill once more. "Damned if I know," he'd say.

Gleason still lived in his old house at Mason's Lane. It was a plain weatherboard house with a rose garden at the front, a vegetable garden down the side, and an orchard at the back.

At night we kids would sometimes ride out to Bald Hill on our bicycles. It was an agonizing, muscle-twitching ride, the worst part of which was a steep, unmade road up which we finally pushed our bikes, our lungs rasping in the night air. When we arrived we found nothing but walls. Once we broke down some of the brickwork and another time we threw stones at the tents where the Chinese labourers slept. Thus we expressed our frustration at this inexplicable thing.

The wall must have been finished on the day before my twelfth birthday. I remember going on a picnic birthday party up to Eleven Mile Creek and we lit a fire and cooked chops at a bend in the river from where it was possible to see the walls on Bald Hill. I remember standing with a hot chop in my hand and someone saying, "Look, they're leaving!"

We stood on the creek bed and watched the Chinese labourers walking their bicycles slowly down the hill. Someone said they were going to build a chimney up at the mine at A. 1 and certainly there is a large brick chimney there now, so I suppose they built it.

When the word spread that the walls were finished most of the town went up to look. They walked around the four walls, which were as interesting as any other brick walls. They stood in front of the big wooden gates and tried to peer through, but all they could see was a small blind wall that had obviously been constructed for this special purpose. The walls themselves were ten feet high and topped with broken glass and barbed wire. When it became obvious that we were not going to discover the contents of the enclosure, we all gave up and went home.

Mr. Gleason had long since stopped coming into town. His wife came instead, wheeling a pram down from Mason's Lane to Main Street and filling it with groceries and meat (they never bought vegetables, they grew their own) and wheeling it back to Mason's Lane. Sometimes you would see her standing with the pram halfway up the Gell Street hill. Just standing there, catching her breath. No one asked her about the wall. They knew she wasn't responsible for the wall and they felt sorry for her, having to bear the burden of the pram and her husband's madness. Even when she began to visit Dixon's hardware and buy plaster of paris and tins of paint and water-proofing compound, no one asked her what these things were for. She had a way of averting her eyes that indicated her terror of questions. Old Dixon carried the plaster of paris and the tins of paint out to her pram for her and watched her push them away. "Poor woman," he said, "poor bloody woman."

From the filling station where I sat dreaming in the sun, or from the enclosed office where I gazed mournfully at the rain, I would see, occasionally, Gleason entering or leaving his walled compound, a tiny figure way up on Bald Hill. And I'd think "Gleason," but not much more.

Occasionally strangers drove up there to see what was going on, often egged on by locals who told them it was a Chinese temple or some other silly thing. Once a group of Italians had a picnic outside the walls and took photographs of each other standing in front of the closed door. God knows what they thought it was.

But for five years between my twelfth and seventeenth birthdays there was nothing to interest me in Gleason's walls. Those years seem lost to me now and I can remember very little of them. I developed a crush on Susy Markin and followed her back from the swimming pool on my bicycle. I sat behind her in the pictures and wandered past her house. Then her parents moved to another town and I sat in the sun and waited for them to come back.

We became very keen on modernization. When coloured paints became available the whole town went berserk and brightly coloured houses blossomed overnight. But the paints were not of good quality and quickly faded and peeled, so that the town looked like a garden of dead flowers. Thinking of those years, the only real thing I recall is the soft hiss of bicycle tyres on the main street. When I think of it now it seems very peaceful, but I remember then that the sound induced in me a feeling of melancholy, a feeling somehow mixed with the early afternoons when the sun went down behind Bald Hill and the town felt as sad as an empty dance hall on a Sunday afternoon.

And then, during my seventeenth year, Mr. Gleason died. We found out when we saw Mrs. Gleason's pram parked out in front of Phonsey Joy's Funeral Parlour. It looked very sad, that pram, standing by itself in the windswept street. We came and looked at the pram and felt sad for Mrs. Gleason. She hadn't had much of a life.

Phonsey Joy carried old Mr. Gleason out to the cemetery by the Parwan Railway Station and Mrs. Gleason rode behind in a taxi. People watched the old hearse go by and thought, "Gleason," but not much else.

And then, less than a month after Gleason had been buried out at the lonely cemetery by the Parwan Railway Station, the Chinese labourers came back. We saw them push their bicycles up the hill. I stood with my father and Phonsey Joy and wondered what was going on.

And then I saw Mrs. Gleason trudging up the hill. I nearly didn't recognize her, because she didn't have her pram. She carried a black umbrella and walked slowly up Bald Hill and it wasn't until she stopped for breath and leant forward that I recognized her.

"It's Mrs. Gleason," I said, "with the Chinese."

But it wasn't until the next morning that it became obvious what was happening. People lined the main street in the way they do for a big funeral but, instead of gazing towards the Grant Street corner, they all looked up at Bald Hill.

All that day and all the next people gathered to watch the destruction of the walls. They saw the Chinese labourers darting to and fro, but it wasn't until they knocked down a large section of the wall facing the town that we realized there really was something inside. It was impossible to see what it was, but there was something there. People stood and wondered and pointed out Mrs. Gleason to each other as she went to and fro supervising the work.

And finally, in ones and twos, on bicycles and on foot, the whole town moved up to Bald Hill. Mr. Dyer closed up his butcher shop and my father got out the old Chev truck and we finally arrived up at Bald Hill with twenty people on board. They crowded into the back tray and hung on to the running boards and my father grimly steered his way through the crowds of bicycles and parked just where the dirt track gets really steep. We trudged up this last steep track, never for a moment suspecting what we would find at the top.

It was very quiet up there. The Chinese labourers worked diligently, removing the third and fourth walls and cleaning the bricks, which they stacked neatly in big piles. Mrs. Gleason said nothing either. She stood in the only remaining corner of the walls and looked defiantly at the townspeople who stood open-mouthed where another corner had been.

And between us and Mrs. Gleason was the most incredibly beautiful thing I had ever seen in my life. For one moment I didn't recognize it. I stood open-mouthed, and breathed the surprising beauty of it. And then I realized it was our town. The buildings were two feet high and they were a little rough but very correct. I saw Mr. Dyer nudge my father and whisper that Gleason had got the faded "U" in the BUTCHER sign of his shop.

I think at that moment everyone was overcome with a feeling of simple joy. I can't remember ever having felt so uplifted and happy. It was perhaps a childish emotion but I looked up at my father and saw a smile of such warmth spread across his face that I knew he felt just as I did. Later he told me that he thought Gleason had built the model of our town just for this moment, to let us see the beauty of our own town, to make us proud of ourselves and to stop the American Dreams we were so prone to. For the rest, my father said, was not Gleason's plan and he could not have foreseen the things that happened afterwards.

I have come to think that this view of my father's is a little sentimental and also, perhaps, insulting to Gleason. I personally believe that he knew everything that would happen. One day the proof of my theory may be discovered. Certainly there are in existence some personal papers, and I firmly believe that these papers will show that Gleason knew exactly what would happen.

We had been so overcome by the model of the town that we hadn't noticed what was the most remarkable thing of all. Not only had Gleason built the houses and the shops of our town, he had also peopled it. As we tip-toed into the town we suddenly found ourselves. "Look," I said to Mr. Dyer, "there you are."

And there he was, standing in front of his shop in his apron. As I bent down to examine the tiny figure I was staggered by the look on its face. The modelling was crude, the paintwork was sloppy, and the face a little too white, but the expression was absolutely perfect: those pursed, quizzical lips and the eyebrows lifted high. It was Mr. Dyer and no one else on earth.

And there beside Mr. Dyer was my father, squatting on the footpath and gazing lovingly at Mr. Dyer's bicycle's gears, his face marked with grease and hope.

And there was I, back at the filling station, leaning against a petrol pump in an American pose and talking to Brian Sparrow who was amusing me with his clownish antics.

Phonsey Joy standing beside his hearse. Mr. Dixon sitting inside his hardware store. Everyone I knew was there in that tiny town. If they were not in the streets or in their backyards they were inside their houses, and it didn't take very long to discover that you could lift off the roofs and peer inside.

We tip-toed around the streets peeping into each other's windows, lifting off each other's roofs, admiring each other's gardens, and, while we did it, Mrs. Gleason slipped silently away down the hill towards Mason's Lane. She spoke to nobody and nobody spoke to her.

I confess that I was the one who took the roof from Cavanagh's house. So I was the one who found Mrs. Cavanagh in bed with young Craigie Evans.

I stood there for a long time, hardly knowing what I was seeing. I stared at the pair of them for a long, long time. And when I finally knew what I was seeing I felt such an incredible mixture of jealousy and guilt and wonder that I didn't know what to do with the roof.

Eventually it was Phonsey Joy who took the roof from my hands and placed it carefully back on the house, much, I imagine, as he would have placed the lid on a coffin. By then other people had seen what I had seen and the word passed around very quickly.

And then we all stood around in little groups and regarded the model town with what could only have been fear. If Gleason knew about Mrs. Cavanagh and Craigie Evans (and no one else had), what other things might he know? Those who hadn't seen themselves yet in the town began to look a little nervous and were unsure of whether to look for themselves or not. We gazed silently at the roofs and felt mistrustful and guilty.

We all walked down the hill then, very quietly, the way people walk away from a funeral, listening only to the crunch of the gravel under our feet while the women had trouble with their high-heeled shoes.

The next day a special meeting of the shire council passed a motion calling on Mrs. Gleason to destroy the model town on the grounds that it contravened building regulations.

It is unfortunate that this order wasn't carried out before the city newspapers found out. Before another day had gone by the government had stepped in.

The model town and its model occupants were to be preserved. The minister for tourism came in a large black car and made a speech to us in the football pavilion. We sat on the high, tiered seats eating potato chips while he stood against the fence and talked to us. We couldn't hear him very well, but we heard enough. He called the model town a work of art and we stared at him grimly. He said it would be an invaluable tourist attraction. He said tourists would come from everywhere to see the model town. We would be famous. Our businesses would flourish. There would be work for guides and interpreters and caretakers and taxi drivers and people selling soft drinks and ice creams.

The Americans would come, he said. They would visit our town in buses and in cars and on the train. They would take photographs and bring wallets bulging with dollars. American dollars.

We looked at the minister mistrustfully, wondering if he knew about Mrs. Cavanagh, and he must have seen the look because he said that certain controversial items would be removed, had already been removed. We shifted in our seats, like you do when a particularly tense part of a film has come to its climax, and then we relaxed and listened to what the minister had to say. And we all began, once more, to dream our American Dreams.

We saw our big smooth cars cruising through cities with bright lights. We entered expensive night clubs and danced till dawn. We made love to women like Kim Novak and men like Rock Hudson. We drank cocktails. We gazed lazily into refrigerators filled with food and prepared ourselves lavish midnight snacks which we ate while we watched huge television sets on which we would be able to see American movies free of charge and forever.

The minister, like someone from our American Dreams, reentered his large black car and cruised slowly from our humble sportsground, and the newspaper men arrived and swarmed over the pavilion with their cameras and notebooks. They took photographs of us and photographs of the models up on Bald Hill. And the next day we were all over the newspapers. The photographs of the model people side by side with photographs of the real people. And our names and ages and what we did were all printed there in black and white.

They interviewed Mrs. Gleason but she said nothing of interest. She said the model town had been her husband's hobby.

We all felt good now. It was very pleasant to have your photograph in the paper. And, once more, we changed our opinion of Gleason. The shire council held another meeting and named the dirt track up Bald Hill "Gleason Avenue." Then we all went home and waited for the Americans we had been promised.

It didn't take long for them to come, although at the time it seemed an eternity, and we spent six long months doing nothing more with our lives than waiting for the Americans.

Well, they did come. And let me tell you how it has all worked out for us.

The Americans arrive every day in buses and cars and sometimes the younger ones come on the train. There is now a small airstrip out near the Parwan cemetery and they also arrive there, in small aeroplanes. Phonsey Joy drives them to the cemetery where they look at Gleason's grave and then up to Bald Hill and then down to the town. He is doing very well from it all. It is good to see someone doing well from it. Phonsey is becoming a big man in town and is on the shire council.

On Bald Hill there are half a dozen telescopes through which the Americans can spy on the town and reassure themselves that it is the same down there as it is on Bald Hill. Herb Gravney sells them ice creams and soft drinks and extra film for their cameras. He is another one who is doing well. He bought the whole model from Mrs. Gleason and charges five American dollars admission. Herb is on the council now too. He's doing very well for himself. He sells them the film so they can take photographs of the houses and the model people and so they can come down to the town with their special maps and hunt out the real people.

To tell the truth most of us are pretty sick of the game. They come looking for my father and ask him to stare at the gears of Dyer's bicycle. I watch my father cross the street slowly, his head hung low. He doesn't greet the Americans any more. He doesn't ask them questions about colour television or Washington, D.C. He kneels on the footpath in front of Dyer's bike. They stand around him. Often they remember the model incorrectly and try to get my father to pose in the wrong way. Originally he argued with them, but now he argues no more. He does what they ask. They push him this way and that and worry about the expression on his face, which is no longer what it was.

Then I know they will come to find me. I am next on the map. I am very popular for some reason. They come in search of me and my petrol pump as they have done for four years now. I do not await them eagerly because I know, before they reach me, that they will be disappointed.

"But this is not the boy."

"Yes," says Phonsey, "this is him alright." And he gets me to show them my certificate.

They examine the certificate suspiciously, feeling the paper as if it might be a clever forgery. "No," they declare. (Americans are so confident.) "No," they shake their heads, "this is not the real boy. The real boy is younger."

"He's older now. He used to be younger." Phonsey looks weary when he tells them. He can afford to look weary.

The Americans peer at my face closely. "It's a different boy."

But finally they get their cameras out. I stand sullenly and try to look amused as I did once. Gleason saw me looking amused but I can no longer remember how it felt. I was looking at Brian Sparrow. But Brian is also tired. He finds it difficult to do his clownish antics and to the Americans his little act isn't funny. They prefer the model. I watch him sadly, sorry that he must perform for such an unsympathetic audience.

The Americans pay one dollar for the right to take our photographs. Having paid the money they are worried about being cheated. They spend their time being disappointed and I spend my time feeling guilty that I have somehow let them down by growing older and sadder.

1.3 ENGLISH AS A SECOND LANGUAGE
Lucy Honig

Inside Room 824, Maria parked the vacuum cleaner, fastened all the locks and the safety chain and kicked off her shoes. Carefully she lay a stack of fluffy towels on the bathroom vanity. She turned the air conditioning up high and the lights down low. Then she hoisted up the skirt of her uniform and settled all the way back on the king-sized bed with her legs straight out in front of her. Her feet and ankles were swollen. She wriggled her toes. She threw her arms out in each direction and still her hands did not come near the edges of the bed. From here she could see, out the picture window, the puffs of green treetops in Central Park, the tiny people circling along the paths below. She tore open a small foil bag of cocktail peanuts and ate them very slowly, turning each one over separately with her tongue until the salt dissolved. She snapped on the TV with the remote control and flipped channels.

The big mouth game show host was kissing and hugging a woman playing on the left-hand team. Her husband and children were right there with her, and *still* he encircled her with his arms. Then he sidled up to the daughter, a girl younger than her own Giuliette, and *hugged* her and kept *holding* her, asking questions. None of his business, if this girl had a boyfriend back in Saginaw!

"Mama, you just don't understand." That's what Jorge always said when she watched TV at home. He and his teenaged friends would sit around in their torn bluejeans dropping potato chips between the cushions of her couch and laughing, writhing with laughter while she sat like a stone.

Now the team on the right were hugging each other, squealing, jumping up and down. They'd just won a whole new kitchen—refrigerator, dishwasher, clothes washer, microwave, *everything!* Maria could win a whole new kitchen too, someday. You just spun a wheel, picked some words. She could do that.

She saw herself on TV with Carmen and Giuliette and Jorge. Her handsome children were so quick to press the buzzers the other team never had a chance to answer first. And they got every single answer right. Her children shrieked and clapped and jumped up and down each time the board lit up. They kissed and hugged that man whenever they won a prize. That man put his hands on her beautiful young daughters. That man pinched and kissed *her,* an old woman, in front of the whole world! Imagine seeing *this* back home! Maria frowned, chewing on the foil wrapper. There was nobody left at home in Guatemala, nobody to care if a strange man squeezed her wrinkled flesh on the TV.

"Forget it, Mama. They don't let poor people on these programs," Jorge said one day.

"But poor people need the money, they can win it here!"

Jorge sighed impatiently. "They don't give it away because you *need* it!"

It was true, she had never seen a woman with her kids say on a show: My husband's dead. Jorge knew. They made sure before they invited you that you were the right kind of people and you said the right things. Where would she put a new kitchen in her cramped apartment anyway? No hookups for a washer, no space for a two-door refrigerator . . .

She slid sideways off the bed, carefully smoothed out the quilted spread, and squeezed her feet

From *The Truly Needy and Other Stories* (Pittsburgh: University of Pittsburgh Press, 1999). Copyright © 1999 University of Pittsburgh Press. Reprinted with permission.

into her shoes. Back out in the hall she counted the bath towels in her cart to see if there were enough for the next wing. Then she wheeled the cart down the long corridor, silent on the deep blue rug.

Maria pulled the new pink dress on over her head, eased her arms into the sleeves, then let the skirt slide into place. In the mirror she saw a small dark protrusion from a large pink flower. She struggled to zip up in back, then she fixed the neck, attaching the white collar she had crocheted. She pinned the rhinestone brooch on next. Shaking the pantyhose out of the package, she remembered the phrase: the cow before the horse, wasn't that it? She should have put these on first. Well, so what. She rolled down the left leg of the nylons, stuck her big toe in, and drew the sheer fabric around her foot, unrolling it up past her knee. Then she did the right foot, careful not to catch the hose on the small flap of scar.

The right foot bled badly when she ran over the broken glass, over what had been the only window of the house. It had shattered from gunshots across the dirt yard. The chickens dashed around frantically, squawking, trying to fly, spraying brown feathers into the air. When she had seen Pedro's head turn to blood and the two oldest boys dragged away, she swallowed every word, every cry, and ran with the two girls. The fragments of glass stayed in her foot for all the days of hiding. They ran and ran and ran and somehow Jorge caught up and they were found by their own side and smuggled out. And still she was silent, until the nurse at the border went after the glass and drained the mess inside her foot. Then she sobbed and screamed, "Aaiiiee!"

"Mama, stop thinking and get ready," said Carmen.
"It is too short, your skirt," Maria said in Spanish. "What will they say?"
Carmen laughed. "It's what they all wear, except for you old ladies."
"Not to work! Not to school!"
"Yes, to work, to school! And Mama, you are going for an award for your English, for all you've learned, so please speak English!"
Maria squeezed into the pink high heels and held each foot out, one by one, so she could admire the beautiful slim arch of her own instep, like the feet of the American ladies on Fifth Avenue. Carmen laughed when she saw her mother take the first faltering steps, and Maria laughed too. How much she had already practiced in secret, and still it was so hard! She teetered on them back and forth from the kitchen to the bedroom, trying to feel steady, until Carmen finally sighed and said, "Mama, quick now or you'll be late!"

She didn't know if it was a good omen or a bad one, the two Indian women on the subway. They could have been sitting on the dusty ground at the market selling corn or clay pots, with the bright-colored striped shawls and full skirts, the black hair pulled into two braids down each back, the deeply furrowed square faces set in those impassive expressions, seeing everything, seeing nothing. They were exactly as they must have been back home, but she was seeing them *here,* on the downtown IRT from the Bronx, surrounded by businessmen in suits, kids with big radio boxes, girls in skin-tight jeans and dark purple lipstick. Above them, advertisements for family planning and TWA. They were like stone-age men sitting on the train in loincloths made from animal skins, so out of place, out of time. Yet timeless. Maria thought, they are timeless guardian spirits, here to accompany me to my honors. Did anyone else see them? As strange as they were, nobody looked. Maria's heart pounded faster. The boys with the radios were standing right over them and never saw them. They were invisible to everyone but her: Maria was utterly convinced of it. The spirit world had come back to life, here on the number 4 train! It was a miracle!

"Mama, look, you see the grandmothers?" said Carmen.

"Of course I see them," Maria replied, trying to hide the disappointment in her voice. So Carmen saw them too. They were not invisible. Carmen rolled her eyes and smirked derisively as she nodded in their direction, but before she could put her derision into words, Maria became stern. "Have respect," she said. "They are the same as your father's people." Carmen's face sobered at once.

She panicked when they got to the big school by the river. "Like the United Nations," she said, seeing so much glass and brick, an endless esplanade of concrete.

"It's only a college, Mama. People learn English here, too. And more, like nursing, electronics. This is where Anna's brother came for computers."

"Las Naciones Unidas," Maria repeated, and when the guard stopped them to ask where they were going, she answered in Spanish: to the literacy award ceremony.

"English, Mama!" whispered Carmen.

But the guard also spoke in Spanish: take the escalator to the third floor.

"See, he knows," Maria retorted.

"That's not the point," murmured Carmen, taking her mother by the hand.

Every inch of the enormous room was packed with people. She clung to Carmen and stood by the door paralyzed until Cheryl, her teacher, pushed her way to them and greeted Maria with a kiss. Then she led Maria back through the press of people to the small group of award winners from other programs. Maria smiled shakily and nodded hello.

"They're all here now!" Cheryl called out. A photographer rushed over and began to move the students closer together for a picture.

"Hey Bernie, wait for the Mayor!" someone shouted to him. He spun around, called out some words Maria did not understand, and without even turning back to them, he disappeared. But they stayed there, huddled close, not knowing if they could move. The Chinese man kept smiling, the tall black man stayed slightly crouched, the Vietnamese woman squinted, confused, her glasses still hidden in her fist. Maria saw all the cameras along the sides of the crowd, and the lights, and the people from television with video machines, and more lights. Her stomach began to jump up and down. Would she be on television, in the newspapers? Still smiling, holding his pose, the Chinese man next to her asked, "Are you nervous?"

"Oh yes," she said. She tried to remember the expression Cheryl had taught them. "I have worms in my stomach," she said.

He was a much bigger man than she had imagined from seeing him on TV. His face was bright red as they ushered him into the room and quickly through the crowd, just as it was his turn to take the podium. He said hello to the other speakers and called them by their first names. The crowd drew closer to the little stage, the people standing farthest in the back pushed in. Maria tried hard to listen to the Mayor's words. "Great occasion . . . pride of our city . . . ever since I created the program . . . people who have worked so hard . . . overcoming hardship . . . come so far." Was that them? Was he talking about them already? Why were the people out there all starting to laugh? She strained to understand, but still caught only fragments of his words. "My mother used to say . . . and I said, Look, Mama . . . " He was talking about *his* mother now; he called her Mama, just like Maria's kids called *her.* But everyone laughed so hard. At his mother? She forced herself to smile; up front, near the podium, everyone could see her. She should seem to pay attention and understand. Looking out into the crowd she felt dizzy. She tried to find Carmen among all the pretty young women with big eyes and dark hair. There she was! Carmen's eyes met Maria's; Carmen waved. Maria beamed out at her. For a moment she felt like she belonged there, in this crowd. Everyone was smiling, everyone was so happy while the Mayor of New York stood at the podium telling jokes. How happy Maria felt too!

"Maria Perez grew up in the countryside of Guatemala, the oldest daughter in a family of 19 children," read the Mayor as Maria stood quaking by his side. She noticed he made a slight wheezing noise when he breathed between words. She saw the hairs in his nostrils, black and white and wiry. He paused. "Nineteen children!" he exclaimed, looking at the audience. A small gasp was passed along through the crowd. Then the Mayor looked back at the sheet of paper before him. "Maria never had a chance to learn to read and write, and she was already the mother of five children of her own when she fled Guatemala in 1980 and made her way to New York for a new start."

It was her own story, but Maria had a hard time following. She had to stand next to him while he read it, and her feet had started to hurt, crammed into the new shoes. She shifted her weight from one foot to the other.

"At the age of 45, while working as a chambermaid and sending her children through school, Maria herself started school for the first time. In night courses she learned to read and write in her native Spanish. Later, as she was pursuing her G.E.D. in Spanish, she began studying English as a Second Language. This meant Maria was going to school five nights a week! Still she worked as many as 60 hours cleaning rooms at the Plaza Hotel.

"Maria's ESL teacher, Cheryl Sands, says—and I quote—'Maria works harder than any student I have ever had. She is an inspiration to her classmates. Not only has she learned to read and write in her new language, but she initiated an oral history project in which she taped and transcribed interviews with other students, who have told their stories from around the world.' Maria was also one of the first in New York to apply for amnesty under the 1986 Immigration Act. Meanwhile, she has passed her enthusiasm for education to her children: her son is now a junior in high school, her youngest daughter attends the State University, and her oldest daughter, who we are proud to have with us today, is in her second year of law school on a scholarship."

Two older sons were dragged through the dirt, chickens squawking in mad confusion, feathers flying. She heard more gunshots in the distance, screams, chickens squawking. She heard, she ran. Maria looked down at her bleeding feet. Wedged tightly into the pink high heels, they throbbed.

The Mayor turned toward her. "Maria, I think it's wonderful that you have taken the trouble to preserve the folklore of students from so many countries." He paused. Was she supposed to say something? Her heart stopped beating. What was folklore? What was preserved? She smiled up at him, hoping that was all she needed to do.

"Maria, tell us now, if you can, what was one of the stories you collected in your project?"

This was definitely a question, meant to be answered. Maria tried to smile again. She strained on tiptoes to reach the microphone, pinching her toes even more tightly in her shoes. "Okay," she said, setting off a high-pitched ringing from the microphone.

The Mayor said, "Stand back," and tugged at her collar. She quickly stepped away from the microphone.

"Okay," she said again, and this time there was no shrill sound. "One of my stories, from Guatemala. You want to hear?"

The Mayor put his arm around her shoulder and squeezed hard. Her first impulse was to wriggle away, but he held tight. "Isn't she wonderful?" he asked the audience. There was a low ripple of applause. "Yes, we want to hear!"

She turned and looked up at his face. Perspiration was shining on his forehead and she could see by the bright red bulge of his neck that his collar was too tight. "In my village in Guatemala," she began, "the mayor did not go along—get along—with the government so good."

"Hey, Maria," said the Mayor, "I know exactly how he felt!" The people in the audience laughed. Maria waited until they were quiet again.

"One day our mayor met with the people in the village. Like you meet people here. A big crowd in the square."

"The people liked him, your mayor?"

"Oh, yes," said Maria. "Very much. He was very good. He tried for more roads, more doctors, new farms. He cared very much about his people."

The Mayor shook his head up and down. "Of course," he said, and again the audience laughed.

Maria said, "The next day after the meeting, the meeting in the square with all the people, soldiers come and shoot him dead."

For a second there was total silence. Maria realized she had not used the past tense and felt a deep, horrible stab of shame for herself, shame for her teacher. She was a disgrace! But she did not have more than a second of this horror before the whole audience began to laugh. What was happening? They couldn't be laughing at her bad verbs? They couldn't be laughing at her dead mayor! They laughed louder and louder and suddenly flashbulbs were going off around her, the TV cameras swung in close, too close, and the Mayor was grabbing her by the shoulders again, holding her tight, posing for one camera after another as the audience burst into wild applause. But she hadn't even finished! Why were they laughing?

"What timing, huh?" said the Mayor over the uproar. "What d'ya think, the Republicans put her here, or maybe the Board of Estimate?" Everyone laughed even louder and he still clung to her and cameras still moved in close, lights kept going off in her face and she could see nothing but the sharp white poof! of light over and over again. She looked for Carmen and Cheryl, but the white poof! poof! poof! blinded her. She closed her eyes and listened to the uproar, now beginning to subside, and in her mind's eye saw chickens trying to fly, chickens fluttering around the yard littered with broken glass.

He squeezed her shoulders again and leaned into the microphone. "There are ways to get rid of mayors, and ways to get rid of mayors, huh Maria?"

The surge of laughter rose once more, reached a crescendo, and then began to subside again. "But wait," said the Mayor. The cameramen stepped back a bit, poising themselves for something new.

"I want to know just one more thing, Maria," said the Mayor, turning to face her directly again. The crowd quieted. He waited a few seconds more, then asked his question. "It says here 19 children. What was it like growing up in a house with 19 children? How many *bathrooms* did you have?"

Her stomach dropped and twisted as the Mayor put his hand firmly on the back of her neck and pushed her toward the microphone again. It was absolutely quiet now in the huge room. Everyone was waiting for her to speak. She cleared her throat and made the microphone do the shrill hum. Startled, she jumped back. Then there was silence. She took a big, trembling breath.

"We had no bathrooms there, Mister Mayor," she said. "Only the outdoors."

The clapping started immediately, then the flashbulbs burning up in her face. The Mayor turned to her, put a hand on each of her shoulders, bent lower and kissed her! Kissed her on the cheek!

"Isn't she terrific?" he asked the audience, his hand on the back of her neck again, drawing her closer to him. The audience clapped louder, faster. "Isn't she just the greatest?"

She tried to smile and open her eyes, but the lights were still going off—poof! poof!—and the noise was deafening.

"Mama, look, your eyes were closed *there,* too," chided Jorge, sitting on the floor in front of the television set.

Maria had watched the camera move from the announcer at the studio desk to her own stout form in bright pink, standing by the Mayor.

"In my village in Guatemala," she heard herself say, and the camera showed her wrinkled face close up, eyes open now but looking nowhere. Then the mayor's face filled the screen, his forehead glistening, and then suddenly all the people in the audience, looking ahead, enrapt, took his place. Then there was her wrinkled face again, talking without a smile. ". . . soldiers come and shoot him dead." Maria winced, hearing the wrong tense of her verbs. The camera shifted from her face to the Mayor. In the brief moment of shamed silence after she'd uttered those words, the Mayor drew his finger like a knife across his throat. And the audience began to laugh.

"Turn it off!" she yelled to Jorge. "Off! This minute!"

Late that night she sat alone in the unlighted room, soaking her feet in Epsom salts. The glow of the television threw shadows across the wall, but the sound was off. The man called Johnny was on the screen, talking. The people in the audience and the men in the band and the movie stars sitting on the couch all had their mouths wide open in what she knew were screams of laughter while Johnny wagged his tongue. Maria heard nothing except brakes squealing below on the street and the lonely clanging of garbage cans in the alley.

She thought about her English class and remembered the pretty woman, Ling, who often fell asleep in the middle of a lesson. The other Chinese students all teased her. Everyone knew that she sewed coats in a sweatshop all day. After the night class she took the subway to the Staten Island Ferry, and after the ferry crossing she had to take a bus home. Her parents were old and sick and she did all their cooking and cleaning late at night. She struggled to keep awake in class; it seemed to take all her energy simply to smile and listen. She said very little and the teacher never forced her, but she fell further and further behind. They called her the Quiet One.

One day just before the course came to an end the Quiet One asked to speak. There was no reason, no provocation—they'd been talking informally about their summer plans—but Ling spoke with a sudden urgency. Her English was very slow. Seeing what a terrible effort it was for her, the classmates all tried to help when she searched for words.

"In my China village there was a teacher," Ling began. "Man teacher." She paused. "All children love him. He teach mathematic. He very—" She stopped and looked up toward the ceiling. Then she gestured with her fingers around her face.

"Handsome!" said Charlene, the oldest of the three Haitian sisters in the class.

Ling smiled broadly. "Handsome! Yes, he very handsome. Family very rich before. He have sister go to Hong Kong who have many, many money."

"*Much* money," said Maria.

"Much, much money," repeated Ling thoughtfully. "Teacher live in big house."

"In China? Near you?"

"Yes. Big house with much old picture." She stopped and furrowed her forehead, as if to gather words inside of it.

"Art? Paint? Pictures like that?" asked Xavier.

Ling nodded eagerly. "Yes. In big house. Most big house in village."

"But big house, money, rich like that, bad in China," said Fu Wu. "Those year, Government bad to you. How they let him do?"

"In *my* country," said Carlos, "government bad to you if you got *small* house, *no* money."

"Me too," said Maria.

"Me too," said Charlene.

The Chinese students laughed.

Ling shrugged and shook her head. "Don't know. He have big house. Money gone, but keep big house. Then I am little girl." She held her hand low to the floor.

"I *was* a little girl," Charlene said gently.

"I *was*," said Ling. "Was, was." She giggled for a moment, then seemed to spend some time in thought. "We love him. All children love—all children did loved him. He giving tea in house. He was—was—so handsome!" She giggled. All the women in the class giggled. "He very nice. He learn music, he go . . . he went to school far away."

"America?"

Ling shook her head. "Oh no, no. You know, another. . . west."

"Europa!" exclaimed Maria proudly. "Espain!"

"No, no, another."

"France!" said Patricia, Charlene's sister. "He went to school in France?"

"Yes, France," said Ling. Then she stopped again, this time for a whole minute. The others waited patiently. No one said a word. Finally she continued. "But big boys in more old school not like him. He too handsome."

"Oooh!" sang out a chorus of women. "Too handsome!"

"The boys were jealous," said Carlos.

Ling seized the word. "Jealous! Jealous! They very jealous. He handsome, he study France, he very nice to children, he give tea and cake in big house, he show picture on wall." Her torrent of words came to an end and she began to think again, visibly, her brow furrowing. "Big school boys, they . . ." She stopped.

"Jealous!" sang out the others.

"Yes," she said, shaking her head "no." "But more. More bad. Hate. They hate him."

"That's bad," said Patricia.

"Yes, very bad." Ling paused, looking at the floor. "And they heat."

"Hate."

"No, they heat. "

All the class looked puzzled. Heat? Heat? They turned to Cheryl. The teacher spoke for the first time. "Hit? Ling, do you mean hit? They hit him?" Cheryl slapped the air with her hand.

Ling nodded, her face somehow serious and smiling at the same time. "Hit many time. And also so." She scooted her feet back and forth along the floor.

"Oooh," exclaimed Charlene, frowning. "They kicked him with the feet."

"Yes," said Ling. "They kicked him with the feet and hit him with the hands, many many time they hit, they kick."

"Where this happened?" asked Xavier.

"In the school. In classroom like . . ." She gestured to mean their room.

"In the school?" asked Xavier. "But other people were they there? They say stop, no?"

"No. Little children in room. They cry, they . . ." She covered her eyes with her hand, then uncovered them. "Big boys kick and hit. No one stop. No one help."

Everyone in class fell silent. Maria remembered: they could not look at one another then. They could not look at their teacher.

Ling continued. "They break him, very hurt much place." She stopped. They all fixed their stares on Ling, they could bear looking only at her. "Many place," she said. Her face had not changed, it was still half smiling. But now there were drops coming from her eyes, a single tear down each side of her nose. Maria would never forget it. Ling's face did not move or wrinkle or frown. Her body was absolutely still. Her shoulders did not quake. Nothing in the shape or motion of her eyes or mouth changed. None of the things that Maria had always known happen when you cry happened when Ling shed tears. Just two drops rolled slowly down her two pale cheeks as she smiled.

"He very hurt. He *was* very hurt. He blood many place. Boys go away. Children cry. Teacher break and hurt. Later he in hospital. I go there visit him." She stopped, looking thoughtful. "I went there." One continuous line of wetness glistened down each cheek. "My mother, my father say don't go, but I see him. I say, 'You be better?' But he hurt. Doctors no did helped. He alone. No doctor. No nurse. No medicine. No family." She stopped. They all stared in silence for several moments.

Finally Carlos said, "Did he went home?"

Ling shook her head. "He go home but no walk." She stopped. Maria could not help watching those single lines of tears moving down the pale round face. "A year, more, no walk. Then go."

"Go where?"

"End."

Again there was a deep silence. Ling looked down, away from them, her head bent low.

"Oh, no," murmured Charlene. "He died."

Maria felt the catch in her throat, the sudden wetness of tears on her own two cheeks, and when she looked up she saw that all the other students, men and women both, were crying too.

Maria wiped her eyes. Suddenly all her limbs ached, her bones felt stiff and old. She took her feet from the basin and dried them with a towel. Then she turned off the television and went to bed.

1.4   THE AWFUL GERMAN LANGUAGE
Mark Twain

> A little learning makes the whole world kin.
> —*Proverbs xxxii, 7*

I went often to look at the collection of curiosities in Heidelberg Castle, and one day I surprised the keeper of it with my German. I spoke entirely in that language. He was greatly interested; and after I had talked awhile he said my German was very rare, possibly a "unique"; and wanted to add it to his museum.

If he had known what it had cost me to acquire my art, he would also have known that it would break any collector to buy it. Harris and I had been hard at work on our German during several weeks at that time, and although we had made good progress, it had been accomplished under great difficulty and annoyance, for three of our teachers had died in the meantime. A person who has not studied German can form no idea of what a perplexing language it is.

Surely there is not another language that is so slipshod and systemless, and so slippery and elusive to the grasp. One is washed about in it, hither and thither, in the most helpless way; and when at last he thinks he has captured a rule which offers firm ground to take a rest on amid the general rage and turmoil of the ten parts of speech, he turns over the page and reads, "Let the pupil make careful note of the following *exceptions*." He runs his eye down and finds that there are more exceptions to the rule than instances of it. So overboard he goes again, to hunt for another Ararat and find another quicksand. Such has been, and continues to be, my experience. Every time I think I have got one of these four confusing "cases" where I am master of it, a seemingly insignificant preposition intrudes itself into my sentence, clothed with an awful and unsuspected power, and crumbles the ground from under me. For instance, my book inquires after a certain bird—(it is always inquiring after things which are of no sort of consequence to anybody): "Where is the bird?" Now the answer to this question,—according to the book,—is that the bird is waiting in the blacksmith shop on account of the rain. Of course no bird would do that, but then you must stick to the book. Very well, I begin to cipher out the German for that answer. I begin at the wrong end, necessarily, for that is the German idea. I say to myself, "*Regen* (rain) is masculine—or maybe it is feminine—or possibly neuter—it is too much trouble to look now. Therefore, it is either *der* (the) Regen, or *die* (the) Regen, or *das* (the) Regen, according to which gender it may turn out to be when I look. In the interest of science, I will cipher it out on the hypothesis that it is masculine. Very well—then *the* rain is *der* Regen, if it is simply in the quiescent state of being *mentioned,* without enlargement or discussion—Nominative case; but if this rain is lying around, in a kind of a general way on the ground, it is then definitely located, it is *doing something*—that is, *resting* (which is one of the German grammar's ideas of doing something—that is, resting (which is one of the German grammar's ideas of doing something), and this throws the rain into the Dative case, and makes it *dem* Regen. However, this rain is not resting, but is doing something *actively,*—it is falling,—to interfere with the bird, likely,—and this indicates *movement,* which has the effect of sliding it into the Accusative case and changing *dem* Regen into *den* Regen." Having completed the grammatical horoscope of this matter, I answer up confidently and state in German that the bird is staying in the blacksmith shop "wegen

From *A Tramp Abroad* (London: Chatto &Windus [imprint of Random House], 1880).

(on account of) *den* Regen." Then the teacher lets me softly down with the remark that whenever the word "wegen" drops into a sentence, it *always* throws that subject into the *Genitive* case, regardless of consequences—and that therefore this bird staid in the blacksmith shop "wegen *des* Regens."

N. B. I was informed, later, by a higher authority, that there was an "exception" which permits one to say "wegen *den* Regen" in certain peculiar and complex circumstances, but that this exception is not extended to anything *but* rain.

There are ten parts of speech, and they are all troublesome. An average sentence, in a German newspaper, is a sublime and impressive curiosity; it occupies a quarter of a column; it contains all the ten parts of speech—not in regular order, but mixed; it is built mainly of compound words constructed by the writer on the spot, and not to be found in any dictionary—six or seven words compacted into one, without joint or seam—that is, without hyphens; it treats of fourteen or fifteen different subjects, each enclosed in a parenthesis of its own, with here and there extra parentheses which re-enclose three or four of the minor parentheses, making pens within pens: finally, all the parentheses and reparentheses are massed together between a couple of king-parentheses, one of which is placed in the first line of the majestic sentence and the other in the middle of the last line of it—*after which comes the* VERB, and you find out for the first time what the man has been talking about; and after the verb—merely by way of ornament, as far as I can make out,—the writer shovels in *"haben sind gewesen gehabt haben geworden sein,"* or words to that effect, and the monument is finished. I suppose that this closing hurrah is in the nature of the flourish to a man's signature—not necessary, but pretty. German books are easy enough to read when you hold them before the looking-glass or stand on your head,—so as to reverse the construction,—but I think that to learn to read and understand a German newspaper is a thing which must always remain an impossibility to a foreigner.

Yet even the German books are not entirely free from attacks of the Parenthesis distemper—though they are usually so mild as to cover only a few lines, and therefore when you at last get down to the verb it carries some meaning to your mind because you are able to remember a good deal of what has gone before.

Now here is a sentence from a popular and excellent German novel,—with a slight parenthesis in it. I will make a perfectly literal translation, and throw in the parenthesis-marks and some hyphens for the assistance of the reader,—though in the original there are no parenthesis-marks or hyphens, and the reader is left to flounder through to the remote verb the best way he can:

"But when he, upon the street, the (in-satin-and-silk-covered-now-very-unconstrainedly-after-the-newest-fashion-dressed) government counsellor's wife *met,*" etc., etc.[1]

That is from "The Old Mamselle's Secret," by Mrs. Marlitt. And that sentence is constructed upon the most approved German model. You observe how far that verb is from the reader's base of operations; well, in a German newspaper they put their verb away over on the next page; and I have heard that sometimes after stringing along on exciting preliminaries and parentheses for a column or two, they get in a hurry and have to go to press without getting to the verb at all. Of course, then, the reader is left in a very exhausted and ignorant state.

We have the Parenthesis disease in our literature, too; and one may see cases of it every day in our books and newspapers: but with us it is the mark and sign of an unpracticed writer or a cloudy intellect, whereas with the Germans it is doubtless the mark and sign of a practiced pen and of the presence of that sort of luminous intellectual fog which stands for clearness among these people. For surely it is *not* clearness,—it necessarily can't be clearness. Even a jury would have penetration enough to discover that. A writer's ideas must be a good deal confused, a good deal out of line and sequence, when he starts out to say that a man met a counsellor's wife in the street, and then right in the midst of this so simple undertaking halts these approaching people and makes them stand still until he jots down an inventory of the woman's dress. That is manifestly absurd. It reminds a person of those dentists who secure your instant and breathless interest in a tooth by taking a grip on it with the forceps, and then stand there and drawl through a tedious anecdote before they give the dreaded jerk. Parentheses in literature and dentistry are in bad taste.

The Germans have another kind of parenthesis, which they make by splitting a verb in two and putting half of it at the beginning of an exciting chapter and the *other half* at the end of it. Can any one conceive of anything more confusing than that? These things are called "separable verbs." The German grammar is blistered all over with separable verbs; and the wider the two portions of one of them are spread apart, the better the author of the crime is pleased with his performance. A favorite one is *reiste ab,*—which means *departed.* Here is an example which I culled from a novel and reduced to English:

"The trunks being now ready, he DE- after kissing his mother and sisters, and once more pressing to his bosom his adored Gretchen, who, dressed in simple white muslin, with a single tuberose in the ample folds of her rich brown hair, had tottered feebly down the stairs, still pale from the terror and excitement of the past evening, but longing to lay her poor aching head yet once again upon the breast of him whom she loved more dearly than life itself, PARTED."

However, it is not well to dwell too much on the separable verbs. One is sure to lose his temper early; and if he sticks to the subject, and will not be warned, it will at last either soften his brain or petrify it. Personal pronouns and adjectives are a fruitful nuisance in this language, and should have been left out. For instance, the same sound, *sie,* means *you,* and it means *she,* and it means *her,* and it means *it,* and it means *they,* and it means *them.* Think of the ragged poverty of a language which has to make one word do the work of six,—and a poor little weak thing of only three letters at that. But mainly, think of the exasperation of never knowing which of these meanings the speaker is trying to convey. This explains why, whenever a person says *sie* to me, I generally try to kill him, if a stranger.

Now observe the Adjective. Here was a case where simplicity would have been an advantage; therefore, for no other reason, the inventor of this language complicated it all he could. When we wish to speak of our "good friend or friends," in our enlightened tongue, we stick to the one form and have no trouble or hard feeling about it; but with the German tongue it is different. When a German gets his hands on an adjective, he declines it, and keeps on declining it until the common sense is all declined out of it. It is as bad as Latin. He says, for instance:

SINGULAR.
Nominative—Mein gut*er* Freund, my good friend.
Genitive—Mein*es* gut*en* Freund*es,* of my good friend.
Dative—Mein*em* gut*en* Freund, to my good friend.
Accusative—Mein*en* gut*en* Freund, my good friend.
PLURAL.
N.—Mein*e* gut*en* Freund*e,* my good friends.
G.—Mein*er* gut*en* Freund*e,* of my good friends.
D.—Mein*en* gut*en* Freund*en,* to my good friends.
A.—Mein*e* gut*en* Freund*e,* my good friends.

Now let the candidate for the asylum try to memorize those variations, and see how soon he will be elected. One might better go without friends in Germany than take all this trouble about them. I have shown what a bother it is to decline a good (male) friend; well this is only a third of the work, for there is a variety of new distortions of the adjective to be learned when the object is feminine, and still another when the object is neuter. Now there are more adjectives in this language than there are black cats in Switzerland, and they must all be as elaborately declined as the examples above suggested. Difficult?—troublesome?—these words cannot describe it. I heard a Californian student in Heidelberg say, in one of his calmest moods, that he would rather decline two drinks than one German adjective.

The inventor of the language seems to have taken pleasure in complicating it in every way he could think of. For instance, if one is casually referring to a house, *Haus,* or a horse, *Pferd,* or a dog, *Hund,* he spells these words as I have indicated; but if he is referring to them in the Dative case, he sticks on a foolish and unnecessary *e* and spells them Hause, Pferde, Hunde. So, as an added *e* often signifies the plural, as the *s* does with us, the new student is likely to go on for a month making twins out of a Dative dog before he discovers his mistake; and on the other hand, many a new student who could ill afford loss, has bought and paid for two dogs and only got one of them, because he ignorantly bought that dog in the Dative singular when he really supposed he was talking plural,—which left the law on the seller's side, of course, by the strict rules of grammar, and therefore a suit for recovery could not lie.

In German, all the Nouns begin with a capital letter. Now that is a good idea; and a good idea, in this language, is necessarily conspicuous from its lonesomeness. I consider this capitalizing of nouns a good idea, because by reason of it you are almost always able to tell a noun the minute you see it. You fall into error occasionally, because you mistake the name of a person for the name of a thing, and waste a good deal of time trying to dig a meaning out of it. German names almost always do mean something, and this helps to deceive the student. I translated a passage one day, which said that "the infuriated tigress broke loose and utterly ate up the unfortunate fir-forest" *(Tannenwald).* When I was girding up my loins to doubt this, I found out that Tannenwald in this instance, was a man's name.

Every noun has a gender, and there is no sense or system in the distribution; so the gender of each must be learned separately and by heart. There is no other way. To do this one has to have a memory like a memorandum book. In German, a young lady has no sex, while a turnip has. Think what overwrought reverence that shows for the turnip, and what callous disrespect for the girl. See how it looks in print—I translate this from a conversation in one of the best of the German Sunday-school books:

"*Gretchen.* Wilhelm, where is the turnip?

"*Wilhelm.* She has gone to the kitchen.

"*Gretchen.* Where is the accomplished and beautiful English maiden?

"*Wilhelm.* It has gone to the opera."

To continue with the German genders: a tree is male, its buds are female, its leaves are neuter; horses are sexless, dogs are male, cats are female,—Tom-cats included, of course; a person's mouth, neck, bosom, elbows, fingers, nails, feet, and body, are of the male sex, and his head is male or neuter according to the word selected to signify it, and *not* according to the sex of the individual who wears it,—for in Germany all the women wear either male heads or sexless ones; a person's nose, lips, shoulders, breast, hands, hips, and toes are of the female sex; and his hair, ears, eyes, chin, legs, knees, heart, and conscience, haven't any sex at all. The inventor of the language probably got what he knew about a conscience from hearsay.

Now, by the above dissection, the reader will see that in Germany a man may *think* he is a man, but when he comes to look into the matter closely, he is bound to have his doubts; he finds that in sober truth he is a most ridiculous mixture; and if he ends by trying to comfort himself with the thought that he can at least depend on a third of this mess as being manly and masculine, the humiliating second thought will quickly remind him that in this respect he is no better off than any woman or cow in the land.

In the German it is true that by some oversight of the inventor of the language, a Woman is a female; but a Wife *(Weib)* is not,—which is unfortunate. A Wife, here, has no sex; she is neuter; so, according to the grammar, a fish is *he,* his scales are *she,* but a fishwife is neither. To describe a wife as sexless may be called under-description; that is bad enough, but over-description is surely worse. A German speaks of an Englishman as the *Engländer;* to change the sex, he adds *inn,* and that stands for Englishwoman,—*Engländerinn.* That seems descriptive enough, but still it is not exact enough for a German; so he precedes the word with that article which indicates that the creature to follow is feminine, and writes it down thus: *"die Engländerinn,"*—which means "the *she-Englishwoman."* I consider that that person is over-described.

Well, after the student has learned the sex of a great number of nouns, he is still in a difficulty, because he finds it impossible to persuade his tongue to refer to things as *"he"* and *"she,"* and *"him"* and *"her,"* which it has been always accustomed to refer to as *"it."* When he even frames a German sentence in his mind, with the hims and hers in the right places, and then works up his courage to the utterance-point, it is no use,—the moment he begins to speak his tongue flies the track and all those labored males and females come out as *"its."* . . .

I suppose that in all languages the similarities of look and sound between words which have no similarity in meaning are a fruitful source of perplexity to the foreigner. It is so in our tongue, and it is notably the case in the German. Now there is that troublesome word *vermählt:* to me it has so close a resemblance,—either real or fancied,—to three or four other words, that I never know whether it means despised, painted, suspected, or married; until I look in the dictionary, and then I find it means the latter. There are lots of such words and they are a great torment. To increase the difficulty there are words which *seem* to resemble each other, and yet do not; but they make just as much trouble as if they did. For instance, there is the word *vermiethen* (to let, to lease, to hire); and the word *verheirathen* (another way of saying to *marry).* I heard of an Englishman who knocked at a man's door in Heidelberg and proposed, in the best German he could command, to "verheirathen" that house. Then there are some words which mean one thing when you emphasize the first syllable, but mean something very different if you throw the emphasis on the last syllable. For instance, there is a word which means a runaway, or the act of glancing through a book, according to the placing of the emphasis; and another word which signifies to *associate* with a man, or to *avoid* him, according to where you put the emphasis,—and you can generally depend on putting it in the wrong place and getting into trouble.

There are some exceedingly useful words in this language. *Schlag,* for example; and *Zug.* There are three-quarters of a column of Schlags in the dictionary, and a column and a half of Zugs. The word Schlag means Blow, Stroke, Dash, Hit, Shock, Clap, Slap, Time, Bar, Coin, Stamp, Kind, Sort, Manner, Way, Apoplexy, Wood-Cutting, Enclosure, Field, Forest-Clearing. This is its simple and *exact* meaning,—that is to say, its restricted, its fettered meaning; but there are ways by which you can set it free, so that it can soar away, as on the wings of the morning, and never be at rest. You can hang any word you please to its tail, and make it mean anything you want to. You can begin with *Schlag-ader,* which means artery, and you can hang on the whole dictionary, word by word, clear through the alphabet to *Schlag-wasser,* which means bilge-water,—and including *Schlag-mutter,* which means mother-in-law.

Just the same with *Zug.* Strictly speaking, Zug means Pull, Tug, Draught, Procession, March, Progress, Flight, Direction, Expedition, Train, Caravan, Passage, Stroke, Touch, Line, Flourish, Trait of Character, Feature, Lineament, Chess-move, Organ-stop, Team, Whiff, Bias, Drawer,

Propensity, Inhalation, Disposition: but that thing which it does *not* mean,—when all its legitimate pendants have been hung on, has not been discovered yet.

One cannot over-estimate the usefulness of Schlag and Zug. Armed just with these two, and
the word *Also,* what cannot the foreigner on German soil accomplish? The German word *Also* is
the equivalent of the English phrase "You know," and does not mean anything at all,—in *talk,*
though it sometimes does in print. Every time a German opens his mouth an *Also* falls out; and
every time he shuts it he bites one in two that was trying to *get* out.

Now, the foreigner, equipped with these three noble words, is master of the situation. Let him
talk right along, fearlessly; let him pour his indifferent German forth, and when he lacks for a
word, let him heave a *Schlag* into the vacuum; all the chances are that it fits it like a plug, but if it
doesn't let him promptly heave a *Zug* after it; the two together can hardly fail to bung the hole; but
if, by a miracle, they *should* fail, let him simply say *Also!* and this will give him a moment's chance
to think of the needful word. In Germany, when you load your conversational gun it is always best
to throw in a *Schlag* or two and a *Zug* or two, because it doesn't make any difference how much the
rest of the charge may scatter, you are bound to bag something with *them.* Then you blandly say
Also, and load up again. Nothing gives such an air of grace and elegance and unconstraint to a
German or an English conversation as to scatter it full of "Also's" or "You-knows."

In my note-book I find this entry:

July I.—In the hospital yesterday, a word of thirteen syllables was successfully removed from
a patient,—a North-German from near Hamburg; but as most unfortunately the surgeons had
opened him in the wrong place, under the impression that he contained a panorama, he died. The
sad event has cast a gloom over the whole community.

That paragraph furnishes a text for a few remarks about one of the most curious and notable
features of my subject,—the length of German words. Some German words are so long that they
have a perspective. Observe these examples:

Freundschaftsbezeigungen.

Dilettantenaufdringlichkeiten.

Stadtverordnetenversammlungen.

These things are not words, they are alphabetical processions. And they are not rare; one can
open a German newspaper any time and see them marching majestically across the page,—and if
he has any imagination he can see the banners and hear the music, too. They impart a martial thrill
to the meekest subject. I take a great interest in these curiosities. Whenever I come across a good
one, I stuff it and put it in my museum. In this way I have made quite a valuable collection. When
I get duplicates, I exchange with other collectors, and thus increase the variety of my stock. Here
are some specimens which I lately bought at an auction sale of the effects of a bankrupt bric-a-
brac hunter:

GENERALSTAATSVERORDNETENVERSAMMLUNGEN.

ALTERTHUMSWISSENSCHAFTEN.

KINDERBEWAHRUNGSANSTALTEN.

UNABHAENGIGKEITSERKLAERUNGEN.

WIEDERERSTELLUNGSBESTREBUNGEN.

WAFFENSTILLSTANDSUNTERHANDLUNGEN.

Of course when one of these grand mountain ranges goes stretching across the printed page, it
adorns and ennobles that literary landscape,—but at the same time it is a great distress to the new
student, for it blocks up his way; he cannot crawl under it, or climb over it, or tunnel through it. So
he resorts to the dictionary for help, but there is no help there. The dictionary must draw the line

somewhere,—so it leaves this sort of words out. And it is right, because these long things are hardly legitimate words, but are rather combinations of words, and the inventor of them ought to have been killed. They are compound words with the hyphens left out. The various words used in building them are in the dictionary, but in a very scattered condition; so you can hunt the materials out, one by one, and get at the meaning at last, but it is a tedious and harassing business. I have tried this process upon some of the above examples. "Freundschaftsbezeigungen" seems to be "Friendship demonstrations," which is only a foolish and clumsy way of saying "demonstrations of friendship." "Unabhaengigkeitserklaerungen" seems to be "Independencedeclarations," which is no improvement upon "Declarations of Independence," so far as I can see. "Generalstaatsverordnetenversammlungen" seems to be "Generalstatesrepresentativesmeetings," as nearly as I can get at it,—a mere rhythmical, gushy euphemism for "meetings of the legislature," I judge. We used to have a good deal of this sort of crime in our literature, but it has gone out now. We used to speak of a thing as a "never-to-be-forgotten" circumstance, instead of cramping it into the simple and sufficient word "memorable" and then going calmly about our business as if nothing had happened. In those days we were not content to embalm the thing and bury it decently, we wanted to build a monument over it.

But in our newspapers the compounding-disease lingers a little to the present day, but with the hyphens left out, in the German fashion. This is the shape it takes: instead of saying "Mr. Simmons, clerk of the county and district courts, was in town yesterday," the new form puts it thus: "Clerk of the County and District Court Simmons was in town yesterday." This saves neither time nor ink, and has an awkward sound besides. One often sees a remark like this in our papers: "*Mrs.* Assistant District Attorney Johnson returned to her city residence yesterday for the season." That is a case of really unjustifiable compounding; because it not only saves no time or trouble, but confers a title on Mrs. Johnson which she has no right to. But these little instances are trifles indeed, contrasted with the ponderous and dismal German system of piling jumbled compounds together. I wish to submit the following local item, from a Mannheim journal, by way of illustration:

"In the daybeforeyesterdayShortlyaftereleveno'clock Night, the inthistownstandingtavern called 'The Wagoner' was downburnt. When the fire to the onthedownburninghouseresting Stork's Nest reached, flew the parent Storks away. But when the bytheraging, firesurrounded Nest *itself* caught Fire, straightway plunged the quickreturning Mother Stork into the Flames and died, her Wings over her young ones outspread."

Even the cumbersome German construction is not able to take the pathos out of that picture,—indeed, it somehow seems to strengthen it. This item is dated away back yonder months ago. I could have used it sooner, but I was waiting to hear from the Father-Stork. I am still waiting.

"*Also!*" If I have not shown that the German is a difficult language, I have at least intended to do it. I have heard of an American student who was asked how he was getting along with his German, and who answered promptly: "I am not getting along at all. I have worked at it hard for three level months, and all I have got to show for it is one solitary German phrase,—'*Zwei glas,*'" (two glasses of beer). He paused a moment, reflectively; then added with feeling:

"But I've got that *solid!*"

And if I have not also shown that German is a harassing and infuriating study, my execution has been at fault, and not my intent. I heard lately of a worn and sorely-tried American student who used to fly to a certain German word for relief when he could bear up under his aggravations no longer,—the only word in the whole language whose sound was sweet and precious to his ear and healing to his lacerated spirit. This was the word *Damit*. It was only the *sound* that helped him, not the meaning;[2] and so, at last, when he learned that the emphasis was not on the first syllable, his only stay and support was gone, and he faded away and died.

I think that a description of any loud, stirring, tumultuous episode must be tamer in German than in English. Our descriptive words of this character have such a deep, strong, resonant sound, while their German equivalents do seem so thin and mild and energyless. Boom, burst, crash, roar, storm, bellow, blow, thunder, explosion; howl, cry, shout, yell, groan; battle, hell. These are magnificent words; they have a force and magnitude of sound befitting the things which they describe. But their German equivalents would be ever so nice to sing the children to sleep with, or else my awe-inspiring ears were made for display and not for superior usefulness in analyzing sounds. Would any man want to die in a battle which was called by so tame a term as a *Schlacht*? Or would not a consumptive feel too much bundled up, who was about to go out, in a shirt collar and a seal ring, into a storm which the bird-song word *Gewitter* was employed to describe? And observe the strongest of the several German equivalents for explosion,—*Ausbruch*. Our word Toothbrush is more powerful than that. It seems to me that the Germans could do worse than import it into their language to describe particularly tremendous explosions with. The German word for hell,—Hölle,—sounds more like *helly* than anything else; therefore, how necessarily chipper, frivolous, and unimpressive it is. If a man were told in German to go there, could he really rise to the dignity of feeling insulted?

Having now pointed out, in detail, the several vices of this language, I now come to the brief and pleasant task of pointing out its virtues. The capitalizing of the nouns I have already mentioned. But far before this virtue stands another,—that of spelling a word according to the sound of it. After one short lesson in the alphabet, the student can tell how any German word is pronounced without having to ask; whereas in our language if a student should inquire of us, "What does B, O, W, spell?" we should be obliged to reply, "Nobody can tell what it spells when you set it off by itself; you can only tell by referring to the context and finding out what it signifies,—whether it is a thing to shoot arrows with, or a nod of one's head, or the forward end of a boat."

There are some German words which are singularly and powerfully effective. For instance, those which describe lowly, peaceful, and affectionate home life; those which deal with love, in any and all forms, from mere kindly feeling and honest good will toward the passing stranger, clear up to courtship; those which deal with outdoor Nature, in its softest and loveliest aspects,—with meadows and forests, and birds and flowers, the fragrance and sunshine of summer, and the moonlight of peaceful winter nights; in a word, those which deal with any and all forms of rest, repose, and peace; those also which deal with the creatures and marvels of fairyland; and lastly and chiefly, in those words which express pathos, is the language surpassingly rich and effective. There are German songs which can make a stranger to the language cry. That shows that the *sound* of the words is correct,—it interprets the meanings with truth and with exactness; and so the ear is informed, and through the ear, the heart.

The Germans do not seem to be afraid to repeat a word when it is the right one. They repeat it several times, if they choose. That is wise. But in English, when we have used a word a couple of times in a paragraph, we imagine we are growing tautological, and so we are weak enough to exchange it for some other word which only approximates exactness, to escape what we wrongly fancy is a greater blemish. Repetition may be bad, but surely inexactness is worse.

There are people in the world who will take a great deal of trouble to point out the faults in a religion or a language, and then go blandly about their business without suggesting any remedy. I am not that kind of a person. I have shown that the German language needs reforming. Very well, I am ready to reform it. At least I am ready to make the proper suggestions. Such a course as this might be immodest in another; but I have devoted upwards of nine full weeks, first and last, to a careful and critical study of this tongue, and thus have acquired a confidence in my ability to reform it which no mere superficial culture could have conferred upon me.

In the first place, I would leave out the Dative Case. It confuses the plurals; and, besides, nobody ever knows when he is in the Dative Case, except he discover it by accident,—and then he does not know when or where it was that he got into it, or how long he has been in it, or how he is ever going to get out of it again. The Dative Case is but an ornamental folly,—it is better to discard it.

In the next place, I would move the Verb further up to the front. You may load up with ever so good a Verb, but I notice that you never really bring down a subject with it at the present German range,—you only cripple it. So I insist that this important part of speech should be brought forward to a position where it may be easily seen with the naked eye.

Thirdly, I would import some strong words from the English tongue,—to swear with, and also to use in describing all sorts of vigorous things in a vigorous way.[3]

Fourthly, I would reorganize the sexes, and distribute them according to the will of the Creator. This as a tribute of respect, if nothing else.

Fifthly, I would do away with those great long compounded words; or require the speaker to deliver them in sections, with intermissions for refreshments. To wholly do away with them would be best, for ideas are more easily received and digested when they come one at a time than when they come in bulk. Intellectual food is like any other; it is pleasanter and more beneficial to take it with a spoon than with a shovel.

Sixthly, I would require a speaker to stop when he is done, and not hang a string of those useless "haben sind gewesen gehabt haben geworden seins" to the end of his oration. This sort of gew-gaws undignify a speech, instead of adding a grace. They are, therefore, an offense, and should be discarded.

Seventhly, I would discard the Parenthesis. Also the re-parenthesis, the re-re-parenthesis, and the re-re-re-re-re-re-parentheses, and likewise the final wide-reaching all-enclosing King-parenthesis. I would require every individual, be he high or low, to unfold a plain straightforward tale, or else coil it and sit on it and hold his peace. Infractions of this law should be punishable with death.

And eighthly and last, I would retain *Zug* and *Schlag*, with their pendants, and discard the rest of the vocabulary. This would simplify the language.

I have now named what I regard as the most necessary and important changes. These are perhaps all I could be expected to name for nothing; but there are other suggestions which I can and will make in case my proposed application shall result in my being formally employed by the government in the work of reforming the language.

My philological studies have satisfied me that a gifted person ought to learn English (barring spelling and pronouncing) in thirty hours, French in thirty days, and German in thirty years. It seems manifest, then, that the latter tongue ought to be trimmed down and repaired. If it is to remain as it is, it ought to be gently and reverently set aside among the dead languages, for only the dead have time to learn it.

NOTES

1. "Wenn er aber auf der Strasse der in Sammt und Seide gehüllten jetz sehr ungenirt nach der neusten mode gekleideten Regierungsrathin begegnet."

2. It merely means, in its general sense, *"herewith."*

3. *"Verdammt,"* and its variations and enlargements, are words which have plenty of meaning, but the *sounds* are so mild and ineffectual that German ladies can use them without sin. German ladies who could not be induced to commit a sin by any persuasion or compulsion, promptly rip out one of these harmless little words when they tear their dresses or don't like the soup. It sounds about as wicked as our "My gracious." German ladies are constantly saying, "Ach! Gott!" "Mein Gott!" "Gott in Himmel!" "Herr Gott!" "Der Herr Jesus!" etc. They think our ladies have the same custom, perhaps; for I once heard a gentle and lovely old German lady say to a sweet young American girl: "The two languages are so alike—how pleasant that is; we say 'Ach! Gott!' you say '*Goddam.*'"

Section 2
——— Settling into New Surroundings ———

2.1   SAREE OF THE GODS
G.S. Sharat Chandra

One of the things that Prapulla had insisted was to have a place waiting for them in New York where other Indian immigrants lived. She had worried a great deal over this sudden change in her life. First, there was her fear of flying over Mount Everest, a certain intrusion over Lord Shiva's territory which he did not approve of for any believing Hindu. Then the abrupt severance of a generation of relationships and life in a joint family. She had spent many a restless night. In daylight, she'd dismiss her nightmares as mere confusions of a troubled mind and set herself to conquer her problems as she faced them, like the educated and practical woman that she was. If anything happened to the transgressing jet, she would clutch her husband and child to her breasts and plummet with at least a partial sense of wholeness, to whatever ocean the wrath of the god would cast her. She would go down like those brave, legendary sea captains in the history books and movies. But moving over to the West, where you lived half the year like a monk in a cave because of the weather, was something she was unable to visualize. Besides, how was she going to manage her household without the maid-servant and her stalwart mother-in-law? To be left alone in a strange apartment all day while Shekar went to work was a recurring fear. She had heard that in New York City, even married women wore mini-skirts or leather slacks and thought nothing of being drunk or footloose, not to mention their sexual escapades in summer in parks or parked automobiles. But cousin Manjula who had returned from the States was most reassuring:

"All that is nonsense! Women there are just like women here! Only they have habits and customs quite different from ours. There are hundreds of Indian families in New York. Once you've acclimatized yourself to the country, you'll find it hard to sit and brood. You may run into families from Bangalore in the same apartment house, who knows!"

Prapulla liked the apartment house as soon as she saw some sareed women in the lobby. It was Shekar who looked distraught at the Indian faces. In the time it took for them to arrive from the airport to the apartment, he had seen many of his brown brethren on the city streets, looking strange and out of place. Now he dreaded being surrounded by his kind, ending up like them building little Indias in the obscure corners of New York. He wasn't certain what Prapulla thought about it. She was always quiet on such subjects. Back in India, she was a recluse when it came to socializing and on the few occasions they had entertained foreigners at the firm, she would seek the nearest sofa as a refuge and drop her seven yards of brocade at anchor. She left the impression of being a proper Hindu wife, shy, courteous and traditional.

En route to New York on the jumbo, Shekar had discreetly opened up the conversation about what she'd wear once they were in America. At the mention of skirts she had flared up so defiantly he had to leave the seat. For Prapulla, it was not convenience but convention that made the

---

From *Saree of the Gods: Stories* (Minneapolis, MN: Coffee House Press, 1998). Copyright © 1998 G.S. Sharat Chandra. Reprinted with permission of Coffee House Press.

difference. She had always prized her sarees, especially the occasions she wore her wedding saree with its blue handspun silk and its silver border of gods. There were times she had walked into a crowded room where others were dressed differently and had relished the sudden flush of embarrassment on their faces at her exquisite choice of wear.

The first day of their new life went quite smoothly. When Shekar returned from the office, she was relieved to hear that all had gone well and he had made friends with two of his American colleagues. Shekar described them. Don Dellow was in the firm for fifteen years and was extremely pleasant and helpful. Jim Dorsen and his wife Shirley had always wanted to visit India and shared great interest in the country and its culture.

"I bought them lunch at the corner deli, you know, and you should've seen their faces when I asked for corned beef on rye!" Shekar chuckled. It was during that weekend that Shekar suggested they ought to invite the Dellows and the Dorsens for dinner so she could meet and get to know the wives. Prapulla shrugged her shoulders. It was so soon. She was still unaccustomed to walking into the sterilized supermarkets where you shopped like a robot with a pushcart, led on to the products by where they lay waiting like cheese in a trap, rather than having them beseech you like the vendors and merchants in the bazaars and markets in her country. Besides, everything had a fixed price tag. The frozen vegetables, the canned fruits and spices, the chicken chopped into shapes that were not its own but of the plastic, all bothered her. But Shekar had not complained about her cooking yet. He was so busy gabbing and gulping, she wasn't even sure he knew what was on the plate. Then Shekar walked in from the office Thursday and announced he had invited his friends for dinner on Saturday.

"They both accepted with great delight. It's rather important I develop a strong bond with them."

Prapulla pulled out a pad and started making the shopping list. Shekar was about to ask her what she'd wear but changed his mind.

The Dorsens arrived first. Shirley Dorsen introduced herself and immediately took a liking to Prapulla. The Dellows, caught in traffic, came late. Judy Dellow was a lean Spanish woman in her late twenties. She wore a velvet dress with lace cuffs and asked for bourbon. The living room filled with the aroma of spices. In the background, Subbalakshmi recited on the stereo.

"What sort of music is this?" Jim asked, looking somewhat sullen. He had just finished his drink. Shirley was on her fourth.

"Karnatak music," explained Prapulla. "Subbalakshmi is the soprano of South Indian music. She sings mostly devotional songs and lyrics."

"Sounds rather strange and off key to me," said Jim nodding his head in dismay. He sang for the church choir on Sundays.

Shekar announced dinner. He had set the wine glasses next to the handloomed napkins like he had seen in *Good Housekeeping*. As soon as everyone was seated, he abruptly got up. "Gee! I forgot to pour the wine!" he despaired. When he returned, he held an opaque bottle with a long German name.

"What kind of wine is it?" asked Jim.

"The best German riesling there is!" replied Shekar with authority.

"My, you do know your liquor!" said Shirley, impressed.

"Like a book!" quipped Prapulla.

"It's a misconception," Shekar continued hastily, "that French wines are the best. Germans actually mastered the art of wine making long before the French. Besides, you can't beat a German riesling to go with Indian food."

"Excellent!" said Jim. Shekar filled the glasses apologizing again for not having filled them beforehand. "You see, good wine has to be chilled right," he added avoiding Prapulla's unflinching stare. They began to eat. Shirley attacked everything, mumbling superlatives between mouthfuls. Shekar kept a benevolent eye on the plates and filled them as soon as they were empty. Prapulla sat beaming an appropriate smile. When everyone had their fill, Prapulla got up for dessert.

"Is it going to be one of the exotic Indian sweets?" Shirley asked.

"Of course," butted Shekar.

Prapulla returned from the kitchen with Pepperidge Farm turnovers. "Sorry, I had an accident with the jamoons," she said meekly.

"Don't worry dear. Turnovers do perfectly well," said Shirley, giving her an understanding look.

Shekar had placed a box of cigars on the coffee table. As they all sat, he offered it to his guests who waved it away in preference to their own crumpled packages of Salem. Don and Jim talked about a contract the firm had lost. A junior engineer from Bombay who used to work for the firm had bungled it. They asked Shekar if he knew the man. Shekar had already stiffened in the chair but he pressed for details. But they veered the conversation away from the topic to compliment him on his choice of brandy.

Prapulla entered with a tray of coffee mixed with cream and sugar, just like back home. Subbalakshmi coughed, cleared her throat and strummed the veena in prayer.

Judy raved about Prapulla's saree. Prapulla, momentarily saved from embarrassment over the coffee, began to explain the ritual importance of the wedding saree. She pulled the upper part from her shoulder and spread it on the table. The silver border with the embroidered legend of the creation of the universe, the different avatars of Lord Shiva and the demons he killed while on earthly mission gleamed under the light. Her favorite one depicted Shiva drinking the poison emitted by the sea serpent with which the universe was churned from the ocean. The craftsman had even put a knot of gold at Shiva's neck to indicate the poison the god had held in his throat. A sheer triumph of skill.

"With the exception of Shiva as the begging ascetic, the sareemaker has woven all the other avatars. This blank space on the border perhaps is the space left to challenge our imagination!" mused Prapulla. Shirley, with a snifterful of brandy, leaned from her chair for a closer look. The brandy tipped. "Oh no!" screamed everyone. Judy ran into the kitchen for a towel but the alcohol hissed like a magical serpent over the saree spreading its poisonous hood. The silver corroded fast and the avatars, disfigured or mutilated, almost merged. Prapulla sat dazed, just staring at her saree. The silence was unbearable. Jim puffed on his pipe like a condemned man. Judy, after trying valiantly to wipe the brandy, bent her head over her hand. Shirley looked red, like she was either going to scream or giggle. Shekar came to the rescue:

"Don't worry. I know a way I can lift the smudges. It's nothing!" No one believed him. Prapulla abruptly got up and excused herself.

"I guess we should better be leaving," said Don looking at his watch. "I've to drive the babysitter home and she lives three traffic jams away!"

Shekar hurried to the closet for their coats. "I hope you enjoyed the dinner!" he said meekly, piling up the coats over his shoulder. Prapulla appeared at the door in a different saree. She seemed to have recollected herself and felt bad about everyone leaving so soon. "You know, my husband is right. I've already dipped the saree border in the lotion. It'll be as good as new by morning," she said. They shook hands and Shirley hugged Prapulla and rocked her. "I'll call you dear, let me know how it comes off!" she whispered drunkenly and backed into her coat like an animal perfectly trained.

Prapulla stood at the door with one hand on her stomach, and as the guests disappeared down the elevator, she banged the door shut and ran into the bedroom. She remembered the day she had shopped for the saree. It was a week before her wedding. The entire family had gone to the silk bazaar and spent the day looking for the perfect one. They had at last found it in the only hand-spun saree shop in the market. The merchant had explained that the weaver who had knitted the god into its border had died soon after, taking his craft with him. This was his last saree, his parting gift to some lucky bride. "You modern young people may not believe in old wives tales, but I know that he was a devotee of Shiva. People say the Lord used to appear for him!" the merchant had said.

She sobbed into her shoulders. Where was she going to find a replacement? How was she ever going to explain the tragedy to her family? A wedding saree, selected by the bride became her second self, the sail of her destiny, the roof that protected her and her offspring from evil. She rushed to Ratri's room to make sure that no mythical serpent or scorpion had already appeared over her daughter's head.

She could hear Shekar washing the dishes in the kitchen and turning the sinkerator that gurgled like a demon with its gulletful of leftovers. She fought the impulse to make sure that Shekar had not fallen into it. It was not really Shirley's fault. It was the brandy that her "Americanized" husband kept pouring into her glass. He was so imitative and flippant, lavishing food and liquor that they could scarcely afford on people that were yet to be called friends. He had drunk more than he should have as if to prove that he held his liquor well enough to win points for promotion! Who really discovered brandy? Shekar had brackishly turned the picture of Napoleon on the bottle toward his guests, but surely it must have been a demon who despised her or was sent to convey the god's displeasure at her mixed company, her expatriatism.

She grew tired of her mind's hauntings. There was no way to change the events or turn back now. When Ratri grew up, she would cut the saree and make a dress for her. She'd write to her mother-in-law and send money for a special puja at the temple.

In her dream, it was her funeral. Four priests carried her on bamboo. The family walked behind. Shekar, dressed in traditional dhoti walked ahead with the clay vessel of hot coals with which he'd kindle the first spark of fire. The procession moved briskly to the crematory grounds. A pyre was built and her corpse decked with her favorite flowers was laid on top. Someone tied the border of the saree firmly to a log. The bereaved went around chanting the necessary hymns and the priests sprinkled holy water over her. Suddenly she was ablaze. She felt nothing but an intense heat around her. The flames did not seem to touch her. She pinched herself. She was not on the pyre but was standing with her family. It was her wedding saree wrapped around a giant bottle of brandy that was burning! Inside the bottle a demon danced, spitting fire. The avatars slowly uncurled from the silver border like an inflated raft and ascended the smoke. They were all in miniature, fragile in their postures and luminous. The brandy in the bottle foamed and swirled like an ocean. The demon raved in its ring of fire. Prapulla screamed. One of the uncles gently touched her on the arm and said:

"Do not be alarmed. The demon points its tongue upwards. The gods have flown to their proper heaven."

When she woke herself from the nightmare, Shekar was soundly snoring on the bedside. The sky outside hung in a spent, listless grayness. She could see a haze of light back of a skyscraper. Dawn would soon brim the horizon of her new world with neither birds nor the song of priests in the air. She sat in the dark of the living room with the saree on her lap, caressing its border absentmindedly. A brittled piece broke and fell.

2.2   HOW TO BE AN EXPATRIATE
Peter Ho Davies

Go to America. You love the books, the TV shows, the movies. Tell people you're tired of being a tourist and you want to live in a foreign country for a few months. You know, really live there. Tell your mother it's what you've always wanted. Remind your father how often he's said you should get out of England if you have the chance. Say it's only a master's degree. In American lit. One year.

Pack two suitcases and give away your guitar to a friend who plays it better than you anyway. Give away your TV and your tennis racket. Sit in the pub on your last night home and wish for any excuse—fire, flood, earthquake—not to go.

At Heathrow your father slips you five hundred dollars in cash that he's changed at the bank that morning. Then he warns you to look out for muggers. Give them the money, he says. Everyone has a gun over there. Your mother wants to make sure you've got your tickets and your passport. You say yes. She makes you show them to her. You are an only child, and sometimes you think your family takes this to mean you're only a child.

Tell your parents on the phone how much you like Boston. How friendly everyone is. The size of the portions in restaurants. Tell them you're happy, so they won't worry about you. Hear the worry in your mother's voice. Marvel at how clear the line is. And how cheap international calls are from the U.S. Promise to call every week. Tell your father that you miss football. Tell him, "They call it soccer here." In the post the next week, receive a week's worth of cuttings from the sports pages of English newspapers. "What else do you miss?" your mother wants to know. Tell her you can't get English marmalade, but by the time some arrives in the post (which you now call the mail) you've found a little store in Faneuil Hall that stocks it. Don't tell her and continue to get a new jar of marmalade every month.

At night, lie awake listening to sirens—the distinctive American wail—and wonder if they're from the street or your neighbor's TV.

Walk the Freedom Trail. See the sites of historic importance. Realize you don't know any of the important history. Get bored and stop halfway. Go to Filene's Basement and the Bull and Finch Pub, the one *Cheers* is based on. The Bull and Finch doesn't look much like *Cheers* inside and doesn't feel like a real pub to you. You haven't been asked your age in a pub for years and you don't have a driving license and you don't feel safe carrying your passport everywhere. Have a Coke. Explain to your mother on the phone that they only use the outside of the pub on TV. Learn to call pubs bars. When you feel homesick, eat at McDonald's or Burger King or Kentucky Fried Chicken, just like at home. Think if anyone ever invents teleport booths, they should all be placed in fast-food joints around the globe to minimize the effects of immediate culture shock.

In the supermarket find jars of Coleman's mustard, Cross and Blackwell pickled onions, Lea and Perrin's Worcestershire sauce. Feel the tang of homesickness. Defend English food to your fellow students. Explain what Yorkshire pudding is. Complain that you can't get a decent curry in Boston.

Work out how much everything is in pounds. Phone calls are cheaper. Food is cheaper. Gas is cheaper than petrol.

From *Equal Love: Stories* (Boston: Houghton Mifflin, 2000). Copyright © 2000 Peter Ho Davies. Reprinted with permission of Houghton Mifflin. All rights reserved.

At parties, people come up to you and ask you to say *weekend* or *schedule* or *Scottie Pippen*. Discover you can bring the house down by saying, "Whatchoo talking about, Willis?"

Drink a lot. American beer is weaker, and the bars stay open all night. Get a reputation as a drinker. Completely fail to explain to people why Budweiser was once fashionable in England. Smoke pot for the first time. Amaze your new friends with the fact that it's your first time. One of your fellow graduate students refuses to believe you. She lived in England for six months and she says she smoked pot. Be slightly annoyed that this person is telling you about your own country. Wonder how well you know your own country. She says words like *chemist* and *dustbin* and you share a taxi home with her. She is from New York, and you can hardly believe you're sleeping with a New Yorker. In bed you tell her you hear it's a wonderful town. "The Bronx is up," she observes, lifting the covers and sliding under them, "and the Battery down." Afterward, she lays her head on the pillow next to yours, whispers, "If you can make it there, you can make it anywhere."

"Do you have *Oprah*?" someone asks you, and you say, "Yes, we have *Oprah*. And *Cosby* and *L.A. Law* and *Baywatch*. And electricity and microwaves and indoor plumbing too. Just no guns and drugs." Get into stupid arguments. Insist that the movie *Glory* is a western, "maybe not geographically, but generically."

There is an election. You follow it with interest. It seems like a grand thing to be in another country during an election. When Bill Clinton wins, you feel slightly superior to your friends in England, with John Major for prime minister. When they call or write and ask you how you like America, think of that map on election night. Say you like Boston fine but you don't know enough about the rest of America to judge: "It's like asking someone in London what they think of Vienna." Feel like an experienced traveler when you say this.

At Thanksgiving, call your parents and tell them, "It's Thanksgiving." Explain that it's just like Christmas, "except without presents or a tree." Spend the day with the family of the New Yorker. Her mother tells you she loves your accent. She knew a girl from England who was evacuated to the U.S. during the war. Maureen Johnson was her name. You nod, not that you know her, but as though you *might* know her. They ask you all about England, what you think of the Queen, Princess Di, Northern Ireland. Form some opinions. They tell you how much they admire Margaret Thatcher. You compliment the pumpkin pie. No, they don't have pumpkin pie in England. You tell your parents all this on the phone, and your mother says, "Americans are very hospitable, aren't they? I'm so glad they took you into their home." Feel suddenly like a refugee receiving charity.

You tell your parents that you're not coming home for Christmas. You want to experience an American Christmas. Break up with the New Yorker, just too late to buy a ticket home. On Christmas Day, spend forty bucks on the phone to your parents. Tell them how much you like America, so they won't worry. Listen to your father tell you how much your mother misses you. Listen to your mother tell you how much your father misses you. "All we want is for you to be happy," your mother says. Microwave the Christmas pudding they've sent you. Hope your father liked the Red Sox cap you sent him.

Discover that you're more popular with women than you ever thought. Ask them what they see in a bloke like you and make them laugh. You think they like your accent, these graduate students, and then you decide there's just a more mature approach to sex in the U.S. And then you realize it's because they're expecting you to leave the country in a few months. You're just a holiday romance. Sleep with them anyway.

Between girlfriends, when you are lonely, do a lot of academic work and in the spring get offered a Ph.D. place and a full ride. Fly home at the start of the summer to explain your decision to your parents. Bring live lobsters from Logan. Your mother says you look tired. Your father asks when you're going to get a job. "I thought you were only going for one year," he says. Take a deep breath. Tell them you don't want to fight. You're only home for a fortnight, shouldn't they make the most of it? In the silence afterward, listen to your lobsters scratching against their cardboard box.

In the days that follow, notice that instant coffee is undrinkable and that the service in Britain is terrible.

Back in the U.S., call and write to your parents, inviting them to visit. Tell them, "You don't have to wait for me to come there." Your mother says she'd like to, "but you know what your father's like." Call in the middle of the day with the news that you've had an article accepted for publication in a journal. "That's nice," she says, and tells you about her garden.

Go to an American football game. Tell your friends at the tailgate party how everyone in England admires American sports crowds because they're not hooligans. Your friends have brought something called a suitcase of beer, and you take turns smoking pot in the portable toilet. Get into the stadium and realize that you've never seen a crowd of drunker people in your life, but marvel at the absence of violence. Have this revelation: there's no crowd violence at American sports because there are only home fans. The country's just too big for fans to travel to away games. That's why so many sports are decided by series. Think, this is the kind of deep insight you came to the U.S. for.

Watch the Oscars live for the first time.

Manchester United, the soccer team you've supported since you were a kid, wins the Premiere League Championship for the first time in twenty-five years. You tell your American friends and they say, "Cool."

In the spring go to your first basketball game. In the summer go to your first baseball game. Nod your head knowledgeably about the Celtics and the Red Sox and the Patriots. Say, "So that's what a raincheck is." Learn to call them the Celts and the Sox and the Pats.

At the end of your second year, go home for Christmas. Sit in the departure lounge at Logan and feel oddly embarrassed for all the English people and then suddenly shy about your own accent. Sit in the pub at home and tell your friends about American girls, every British boy's fantasy. New York, California—these words in an English pub sound like sex. Let slip words like *fall* and *soccer* and have them make fun of you. Apparently you don't even sound like you anymore. Hear the way your tone goes up at the end of a sentence? Feel the anxiety of influence. Listen to them talk about bands and politicians and TV shows and sportsmen you've never heard of. When they say you look tired, say it's jet lag. Try to sound more English, and wonder if you're starting to talk like the Artful Dodger. Gor' blimey! Stone the crows! Lor' luv a duck!

Your best friend tells you you've changed. He tries to sound pleased, as if he told you so, but he looks at you as if it's a betrayal. Tell him, you should hope so. Tell him, didn't you go to the U.S. to change? Wasn't that the point? But later wish you'd asked him how you've changed. Wish you could be sure yourself.

In the pub on your last night home, call your friends "mates" and tell them, "Cheerio."

Meet a girl from California. Sleep with her and think, "She's from California." On your first date, she makes you wait in line for a table at a pizzeria in the North End. You'd never queue this long for fish and chips, but she says it's the best pizza in the world and you nod and listen to her tell you how the Mafia makes the North End safe by running off muggers and junkies. This makes about as much sense to you as queuing for pizza.

At the end of the summer, take her home to meet your parents. "Tell us about California," they say. They like her. She likes England. Wouldn't mind living there one day. This seems terribly attractive to you. Fall in love. Marry her. When your parents get off the plane to come to your wedding, they look smaller and older than you've ever seen them. They tell you your wife is lovely. They're really happy for you. They look scared in all the photographs.

Take your wedding album to the immigration interview. Tell the INS inspector how you met. Melt her heart. Get your green card and discover that it's pink. Your wife comes out of the interview looking a little pale. She says, how strange to think that her government could deny her something and she wouldn't have any rights. As if it weren't her own country. She is trembling slightly. Tell her everything's okay now. At the party to celebrate your new permanent-resident status, someone asks if you'll take citizenship. Say no. Say you can't imagine yourself swearing allegiance to any country. Tell your parents you're a legal alien. Never use the words *permanent resident* to them.

Lose track of how many months you've been in the U.S. Say eighteen months when it's been two years. Argue about it with your friends on the phone. Do well in your Ph.D. program. Have your parents tell you they're very proud. Explain your achievements to them carefully. Understand that to them, every success you have in your new country keeps you from going home. Have your professor write a glowing recommendation for a tenure-track position. Go out for jobs, even though you're still writing up and the chances are slim. Talk with your wife about moving back to Britain and getting a job. Remind her that she'd like to live there one day. What about her mother? she says.

Get a position in the U.S. In Wisconsin. Think about it for about two seconds. Accept it. Call your parents with the good news. "All we want is for you to be happy," your mother says. "I thought you were only going for one year," your father says. Call your best friend to give him the news. Have him tell you he's marrying his fiancée of two years, whom you realize you've never met.

Point out to your new academic colleagues wryly that *The Bridges of Madison County* was initially a flop in Britain, when it was published as *Love in Black and White*. But then, of course, it was reissued with a lot of hype and became a big hit. Wonder what your point is.

Realize one day that you haven't had any good marmalade in the mail for months.

Develop an interest in all things British. See every Anthony Hopkins movie ever made. Reread Forster and Austen. Watch the Monty Python marathon. Quote from all these sources occasionally. Disagree with all the anglophile articles in *The New Yorker* but read them avidly. At Christmas your wife buys you a subscription to the foreign edition of a British newspaper. Your mother sends you a Manchester United shirt, which you put in your closet. Which you used to call a wardrobe. Write articles about Britain and the British. Say you had to leave to really understand your home.

Buy a car with a hood and a trunk rather than a bonnet and a boot. Say to your wife, "Do you call it a windshield or a windscreen?" Once when you've had a little too much to drink, swing onto the wrong side of the road. Your wife screams at you and you pull back. There's no real danger and you feel oddly elated.

Tell your wife you've noticed you're spelling words like *realize* with a z. Stare at her blankly when she says, "A zee? You mean a zed. A zee!" Ask her if she thinks you're losing your accent. Hear her say, "I don't *think* so."

When people ask you where you're from, start to say, "Originally?"

Be wary of other British people. Avoid them at parties. Feign surprise when your colleagues introduce you to their British graduate students. Say, "Oh, hello." They look pale and half starved. Notice how bad their teeth are.

Clinton's second election comes around and your wife goes to a rally. Remember how you used to be more political. How every little thing—roadworks, the homeless, Benny Hill—made you despair of Britain. Things like that in the U.S. are someone else's problem. Get a call from the Democrats. Can they count on your vote? Explain that you don't have a vote, that you're not a citizen. Besides, you're not a democrat. You're a socialist. It sounds so exotic. Forget to register for a postal vote in the upcoming British general election.

The Patriots make the playoffs. Say, "That kid Bledsoe—nothing but bullets." It makes people laugh at parties.

Your mother calls and tells you she's clearing out the attic. Do you want to keep any of your old schoolbooks? Say no, you don't think so. Not any? she says. Why not keep a couple? Say all right. Your father comes on the other extension and tells you he's sold your bicycle. You had been meaning to ship it over. Ask him why. He says it was in the way, underfoot. "Clutter," he says. Ask him what he got for it and get angry when he says, "Twenty quid." It's only four years old and you paid over two hundred for it. "I'm only kidding," he says quickly. "It's still here. But it's getting rusty. There's nothing I can do about that." Next time he comes on the phone he pretends he's sold your books. Next time he jokes about taking in a lodger in your old room. Next time he says they're thinking of selling the house and buying something smaller. Tell him, very funny. Tell him you're not laughing. "Only teasing," he says.

When your mother calls, take the phone from your wife and say, "How ya doing?" and feel like you've just slapped her in the face. When your father calls, say, "What's up?" and groan inwardly.

Lose track of how many years you've been in the U.S. Work it out by administrations. Lose track of how many kids your best friend has. Teach students Shakespeare. They look at you as though you're an expert with your accent, although you know their accents are closer to the Bard's. You call home every week and write every couple of weeks. More often than any of your old friends in England, you're sure. There isn't enough news for all these letters and phone calls. On the phone your mother tells you she and your father have fights about you. "He doesn't understand," she says. Tell her that you know what you're doing. That they shouldn't worry about you. Ask, is it because they miss you? Hear her say, "Oh, no." They're both busy and active, enjoying their retirement. She says it's not your fault. They'll have to get used to it. "I tell him, perhaps I should have had another child," she says. Neither of you speaks for a long moment. "I mean a *second* child," she says at last.

Cheat on your wife. She tells you one night you are losing your accent and it makes you feel like you're losing your hair. "Going, going, gone," she says. Cheat on her with a gifted student from your class. Cheat on her with less gifted students from your class. Talk to your oldest friend from England late at night on the phone. He's jealous of your affairs. "I could never do that," he says. You wonder if you could if you were there. "Have you been drinking?" he asks, and when you say "No!" he says, "Only it's six A.M. here."

A Starbucks opens around the corner from you, and you tell your wife, "Conformity. That's what I love about this country," and she calls you an asshole. Tell her you're an arsehole and watch her not laugh. Have a harassment suit filed against you by one of the students you didn't sleep with. Your wife wants a separation. She says, "Don't look so miserable. We've been together more than two years." She means that even if you divorce, you'll get to keep your pink green card.

"You've changed," she tells you, and you say, "I had to change to stay."

"You've changed," she says, and you ask, "How? Tell me how I used to be."

You've changed, and you wonder, too much or not enough?

Look at old photos. Reread letters. Wish you'd kept a diary. Think, you chose this. You're an expatriate, not an exile. It's what you always wanted.

At Christmas, after your wife leaves you, fly home for the first time in two years. You've spent winters in Boston when the Charles River froze solid and the snow was piled on street-corners into April, but you feel cold to your bones at Gatwick. Yes, you think, but it's a damp cold. The atrocious fucking coffee costs a fortune. Your parents have preserved your old room like a shrine for six years. They're delighted to have you home for Christmas. Your father slaps you on the back, and your mother's eyes fill with tears at the airport. "It's good to have you home," they say, although they insist they haven't missed you.

At night you lie awake in your old bed in your old room in your old home and you wonder how everything could have changed so much.

Section 3
——— Coming Home ———

3.1   YARD SALE
Paul Theroux

As things turned out, Floyd had no choice but to spend the summer with me in East Sandwich. To return home to find his parents divorced was awkward; but to learn that they had already held their yard sale was distinctly shaming. I had been there and seen my sister's ghastly jollity as she disposed of her old Hoover and shower curtains and the chair she had abandoned caning; Floyd senior, with a kind of hostile generosity, turned the whole affair into a potlatch ceremony by bestowing his power tools on his next-door neighbor and clowning among his junk with the word "freebie." "Aunt Freddy can have my life jacket," he crowed. "I'm not your aunt," I said, but I thanked him for it and sent it via the local church to Bangladesh, where I hoped it would arrive before the monsoon hit Chittagong. After the yard sale, they made themselves scarce—Floyd senior to his Boston apartment and his flight attendant, my sister to the verge of a nervous breakdown in Cuttyhunk. I was glad to be deputized to look after little Floyd, and I knew how relieved he would be, after two years in the Peace Corps in Western Samoa, to have some home cooking and the sympathetic ear of his favorite aunt. He, too, would be burdened and looking for buyers.

At Hyannis Airport, I expected a waif, an orphan of sorts, with a battered suitcase and a heavy heart. But Floyd was all smiles as he peered out of the fuselage, and when the steps were lowered and he was on them, the little plane actually rocked to and fro: Floyd had gained seventy-five pounds. A Henry Moore moppet of raw certainty, he was dark, with hair like varnished kapok and teeth gleaming like Chiclets. He wore an enormous shirt printed with bloated poppies, and the skirtlike sarong that Margaret Mead tells us is called a *lava-lava*. On his feet were single-thong flip-flops, which, when he kicked them off—as he did in the car, to sit cross-legged on the bucket seat—showed his toes to be growing in separate directions.

"Wuppertal," he said, or words to that effect. There was about him a powerful aroma of coconut oil and a rankness of dead leaves and old blossoms.

"Greetings," I said.

"That's what I just said."

"And welcome home."

"It doesn't seem like home anymore."

We passed the colonial-style (rough-hewn logs, split-rail fence, mullion windows) Puritan Funeral Home, Kopper Krafts, the pizza joints, and it occurred to me that this part of Route 132 had changed out of all recognition. I thought: Poor kid.

The foreknowledge that I would be led disloyally into loose talk about his father's flight attendant kept me silent about his parents' divorce. I asked him about Samoa; I was sure he was

---

From *World's End and Other Stories* (Boston: Houghton Mifflin, 1980), 39–49. Copyright © 1979 Paul Theroux. Used with permission of Wylie, Aitken & Stone.

aching to be quizzed. This brought from him a snore of approval and a native word. I mentioned his sandals.

He said, "My mother never wears sandals. She's always barefoot!"

I determined upon delicacy. "It's been a hard year."

"She says the craziest things sometimes."

"Nerves."

Here was the Hyannis Drive-In Movie. I was going to point out to him that while he had been away, they had started holding drive-in church services on Sunday mornings—an odd contrast to Burt Reynolds in the evenings, the sacred and profane in the same amphitheater. But Floyd was talking about his father.

"He's amazing, and what a sailor! I've known him to go out in a force-nine gale. He's completely reckless."

Aren't the young downright? I thought. I did not say anything about the life jacket his old man had given me; I was sure he had done it out of malice, knowing full well that what I really coveted was the dry pinewood sink lost in the potlatch.

"Floyd," I said, with a shrill note of urgency in my voice—I was frantic to drag him off the topic I knew would lead him to his parents' fractured marriage—"what about Samoa?"

"Sah-moa," he said, moving his mouth like a chorister as he corrected my pronunciation. So we have an emphatic stammer on the first syllable, do we? I can take any amount of well-intentioned pedantry, but I draw the line at condescension from someone I have laboriously diapered. It was so difficult for me to mimic this unsayable word that I countered with "And yet, I wonder how many of them would get Haverhill right?"

Floyd did not move from his Buddha posture. "Actually, he's wicked right-wing, and very moralistic about things. I mean, deep down. He hates change of any kind."

"You're speaking of—?"

"My father."

Your psychiatrists say grief is a great occasion for rationalizing. Still, the Floyd senior I knew was indiscernible through this coat of whitewash. He was the fiery engine of change. Though my sentence was fully framed, I didn't say to his distracted son, That is a side of your father I have not been privileged to observe.

"Mother's different."

"How so?"

"Confident. Full of beans. Lots of savvy."

And beside herself in Cuttyhunk. Perhaps we do invent the friends and even the parents we require and yet I was not quite prepared for what Floyd said next.

"My sister's pretty incredible, too. I've always thought of myself as kind of athletic, but she can climb trees twice as fast as me."

This was desperate: he had no sister. Floyd was an only child. I had an overwhelming desire to slap his face, as the hero does in B movies to bring the flannel-mouthed fool to his senses.

But he had become effusive. "My sister . . . my brother . . . my grandmother"—inventing a fictitious family to make up for the one that had collapsed in his absence.

I said, "Floyd dear, you're going to think your old auntie is horribly literal-minded, but I don't recognize your family from anything you've said. Oh, sure, I suppose your father *is* conservative—the roué is so often a puritan underneath it all. And vice versa. Joseph Smith? The Mormon prophet? What was it, fifty wives? 'When I see a pretty girl, I have to pray,' he said. His prayers were answered! But listen, your mother's had a dreadful time. And, um, you don't actually have any brothers or sisters. Relax. I know we're under a little strain, and absolutely bursting with Samoa, but—"

"In Samoa," he said, mocking me with the half sneeze of its correct pronunciation, "it's the custom to join a local family. You live with them. You're one of them."

"Much as one would join the Elks around here?"

"It's wicked complicated."

"More Masonic—is that it?"

"More Samoan. You get absorbed kind of. They prefer it that way. And they're very easygoing. I mean there's no word for bastard in Samoan."

"With so little traffic on the roads, there's probably no need for it. Sorry. I see your point. But isn't that taking the extended family a bit far? What about your parents?"

"He thatches roofs and she keeps chickens."

"Edith and Floyd senior?"

"Oh, them," was all he said.

"But you've come home!"

"I don't know. Maybe I just want to find my feet." Was it his turn of phrase? I dropped my eyes and saw a spider clinging to his ankle. I said, "Floyd, don't move—there's a creature on your foot."

He pinched it lovingly. "It's only a tattoo."

That seemed worse than a live spider, which had the merit of being able to dance away. I told him this, adding, "Am I being fastidious?"

"No, ethnocentric," he said. "My mother has a mango on her knee."

"Not a banjo?" When I saw him wince, I said, "Forgive me Floyd. Do go on—I want to hear everything."

"There's too much to tell."

"I know the feeling."

"I wouldn't mind a hamburger," he said suddenly. "I'm starving."

Instead of telling him I had a cassoulet waiting for him in East Sandwich, I slowed down. It is the fat, not the thin, who are always famished; and he had not had a hamburger in two years. But the sight of fast food woke a memory in him. As he watched the disc of meat slide down a chute to be bunned, gift-wrapped, and clamped into a small Styrofoam valise, he treated me to a meticulous description of the method of cooking in Samoa. First, stones were heated, he said, then the hot stones buried in a hole. The uncooked food was wrapped in leaves and placed on the stones. More hot stones were piled on top. Before he got to the part where the food, stones, and leaves were disinterred, I said, "I understand that's called labor intensive, but it doesn't sound terribly effective."

He gave me an odd look and excused himself; taking his little valise of salad to the drinking fountain to wash it.

"We always wash our food before we eat."

I said, "Raccoons do that!"

It was meant as encouragement, but I could see I was not doing at all well.

Back at the house, Floyd took a present out of his bag. You sat on it, this fiber mat. "One of your miracle fibers?" I said. "Tell me more!" But he fell silent. He demurred when I mentioned tennis, and at my suggestion of an afternoon of recreational shopping he grunted. He said, "We normally sleep in the afternoon." Again I was a bit startled by the plural pronoun and glanced around, half expecting to see another dusky islander. But no—Floyd's was the brotherly folk "we" of the native, affirming the cultural freemasonry of all Polynesia. And it had clearly got into his bones. He had acquired an almost catlike capacity for slumber. He lay for hours in the lawn hammock, swinging like a side of beef, and at sundown entered the house yawning and complaining of the cold. It was my turn to laugh: the thermometer on the deck showed eighty-one degrees.

"I'll bet you wish you were at Trader Vic's," I said over the cassoulet, trying to avert my ethnocentric gaze as Floyd nibbled the beans he seized with his fingers. He turned my Provençal cuisine into a sort of astronaut's pellet meal.

He belched hugely, and guessing that this was a ritual rumble of Samoan gratitude, I thanked him.

"Ironic, isn't it?" I said. "You seem to have managed marvelously out there in the Pacific, taking life pretty much as you found it. And I can't help thinking of Robert Louis Stevenson, who went to Samoa with his sofas, his tartans, his ottoman, and every bagpipe and ormolu clock from Edinburgh in his luggage."

"How do you know that?" he asked.

"Vassar," I said. "There wasn't any need for Stevenson to join a Samoan family. Besides his wife and his stepson, there were his stepdaughter and her husband. His wife was a divorcée, but she was from California, which explains everything. Oh, he brought his aged mother out, too. She never stopped starching her bonnets, so they say."

"Tusitala," said Floyd.

"Come again?"

"That was his title. 'Teller of tales.' He read his stories to the Samoans."

"I'd love to know what they made of 'Weir of Hermiston.'" It was clear from Floyd's expression that he had never heard of the novel.

He said gamely, "I didn't finish it."

"That's not surprising—neither did Stevenson. Do much reading, Floyd?"

"Not a lot. We don't have electricity, and reading by candlelight is really tough."

"'Hermiston' was written by candlelight. In Samoa, it would be an act of the greatest homage to the author to read it that way."

"I figured it was pointless to read about Samoa if you live there."

"All the more reason to read it, since it's set in eighteenth-century Scotland."

"And he was a *palagi*."

"Don't be obscure, Floyd."

"A white man."

Only in the sense that Pushkin was an octoroon and Othello a soul brother, I thought, but I resisted challenging Floyd. Indeed, his saturation in the culture had made him indifferent to the bizarre. I discovered this when I drew him out. What was the food like after it was shoveled from beneath the hot stones? On Floyd's report it was uninspired: roots, leaves, and meat, sweated together in this subterranean sauna. What kind of meat? Oh, all kinds; and with the greatest casualness he let it drop that just a week before, he had eaten a flying fox.

"On the wing?" I asked.

"They're actually bats," he said. "But they call them—"

"Do you mean to tell me that you have eaten a bat?"

"You act as if it's an endangered species," he said.

"I should think that Samoans are if that's part of their diet."

"They're not bad. But they cook them whole, so they always have a strange expression on their faces when they're served."

"Doesn't surprise me a bit. Turn up their noses, do they?"

"Sort of. You can see all their teeth. I mean, the bats'."

"What a stitch!"

He smiled. "You think that's interesting?"

"Floyd, it's matchless."

Encouraged, he said, "Get this—we use fish as fertilizer. Fish!"

"That's predictable enough," I said, unimpressed. "Not far from where you are now, simple folk put fresh fish on their vegetable gardens as fertilizer. Misguided? Maybe. Wasteful? Who knows? Such was the nature of subsistence farming on the Cape three hundred years ago. One thing, though—they knew how to preach a sermon. Your agriculturalist is so often a God-fearing man."

This cued Floyd into an excursion on Samoan Christianity, which sounded to me thoroughly homespun and basic, full of good-natured hypocrisy that took the place of tolerance.

I said, "That would make them—what? Unitarians?"

Floyd belched again. I thanked him. He wiped his fingers on his shirtfront and said it was time for bed. He was not used to electric light: the glare was making him belch. "Besides, we always go to bed at nine."

The hammering some minutes later was Floyd rigging up the hammock in the spare room, where there was a perfectly serviceable double bed.

"We never do," I called.

Floyd looked so dejected at breakfast, toying with his scrambled egg and sausage, that I asked him if it had gone cold. He shrugged. Everything was hunky-dory, he said in Samoan, and then translated it.

"What do you normally have for breakfast?"

"Taro."

"Is it frightfully good for you?"

"It's a root," he said.

"Imagine finding your roots in Samoa!" Seeing him darken, I added, "Carry on, Floyd. I find it all fascinating. You're my window on the world."

But Floyd shut his mouth and lapsed into silence. Later in the morning, seeing him sitting cross-legged in the parlor, I was put in mind of one of those big lugubrious animals that look so homesick behind the bars of American zoos. I knew I had to get him out of the house.

It was a mistake to take him to the supermarket, but this is hindsight; I had no way of anticipating his new fear of traffic, his horror of crowds, or the chilblains he claimed he got from air conditioning. The acres of packaged foods depressed him, and his reaction to the fresh-fruit department was extraordinary.

"One fifty-nine!" he jeered. "In Samoa, you can get a dozen bananas for a penny. And look at that," he said, handling a whiskery coconut. "They want a buck for it!"

"They're not exactly in season here on the Cape, Floyd."

"I wouldn't pay a dollar for one of those."

"I had no intention of doing so."

"They're dangerous, coconuts," he mused. "They drop on your head. People have been known to be killed by them."

"Not in Barnstable County," I said, which was a pity, because I felt like aiming one at his head and calling it an act of God.

He hunched over a pyramid of oranges, examining them with distaste and saying that you could buy the whole lot for a quarter in a village market he knew somewhere in remote Savai'i. A tray of mangoes, each fruit the rich color of old meerschaum, had Floyd gasping with contempt: the label stuck to their skins said they were two dollars apiece, and he had never paid more than a nickel for one.

"These cost two cents," he said, bruising a grapefruit with his thumb, "and they literally give these away," he went on, flinging a pineapple back onto its pile. But his disbelief was nothing compared to the disbelief of shoppers, who gawped at his *lava-lava*. Yet his indignation at the prices won these people over, and amid the crashing of carts I heard the odd shout of "Right on!"

Eventually I hauled him away, and past the canned lychees ("They grow on trees in China, Floyd!") I became competitive. "What about split peas?" I said, leading him down the aisles. "Scallops? Indian pudding? Dreft? Clorox? What do you pay for dog biscuits? Look, be reasonable. What you gain on mangoes, you lose on maple syrup!"

We left empty-handed. Driving back, I noticed that Floyd became even gloomier. Perhaps he realized that it was going to be a long summer. I certainly did.

"Anything wrong, Floyd?"

He groaned. He put his head in his hands. "Aunt Freddy, I think I've got culture shock."

"Isn't that something you get at the other end? I mean, when the phones don't work in Nigeria or you find ants in the marmalade or the grass hut leaks?"

"Our huts never leak."

"Of course not," I said. "And look, this is only a *palagi* talking, but I have the unmistakable feeling that you would be much happier among your own family, Floyd."

We both knew which family. Mercifully, he was gone the next day, leaving nothing behind but the faint aroma of coconut oil in the hammock. He never asked where I got the price of the Hyannis-Apia airfare. He accepted it with a sort of extortionate Third Worlder's wink, saying, "That's very Samoan of you, Aunt Freddy." But I'll get it back. Fortunately, there are ways of raising money at short notice around here.

3.2 LETTER FROM GAZA
Ghassan Kanafani

Dear Mustafa:

I have now received your letter, in which you tell me that you've done everything necessary to enable me to stay with you in Sacramento. I've also received news that I have been accepted in the department of Civil Engineering in the University of California. I must thank you for everything, my friend. But it'll strike you as rather odd when I proclaim this news to you—and make no doubt about it, I feel no hesitation at all, in fact I am pretty well positive that I have never seen things so clearly as I do now. No, my friend, I have changed my mind. I won't follow you to "the land where there is greenery, water and lovely faces" as you wrote. No, I'll stay here, and I won't ever leave.

I am really upset that our lives won't continue to follow the same course, Mustafa. For I can almost hear you reminding me of our vow to go on together, and of the way we used to shout: "We'll get rich!" But there's nothing I can do, my friend. Yes, I still remember the day when I stood in the hall of Cairo airport, pressing your hand and staring at the frenzied motor. At that moment everything was rotating in time with the ear-splitting motor, and you stood in front of me, your round face silent.

Your face hadn't changed from the way it used to be when you were growing up in the Shajiya quarter of Gaza, apart from those slight wrinkles. We grew up together, understanding each other completely, and we promised to go on together till the end. But . . .

"There's a quarter of an hour left before the plane takes off. Don't look into space like that. Listen! You'll go to Kuwait next year, and you'll save enough from your salary to uproot you from Gaza and transplant you to California. We started off together and we must carry on. . . ."

At that moment I was watching your rapidly moving lips. That was always your manner of speaking, without commas or full stops. But in an obscure way I felt that you were not completely happy with your flight. You couldn't give three good reasons for it. I too suffered from this wrench, but the clearest thought was: why don't we abandon this Gaza and flee? Why don't we? Your situation had begun to improve, however. The Ministry of Education in Kuwait had given you a contract though it hadn't given me one. In the trough of misery where I existed you sent me small sums of money. You wanted me to consider them as loans, because you feared that I would feel slighted. You knew my family circumstances in and out; you knew that my meagre salary in the UNRWA schools was inadequate to support my mother, my brother's widow and her four children.

"Listen carefully. Write to me every day . . . every hour . . . every minute! The plane's just leaving. Farewell! Or rather, till we meet again!"

Your cold lips brushed my cheek, you turned your face away from me towards the plane, and when you looked at me again I could see your tears.

Later the Ministry of Education in Kuwait gave me a contract. There's no need to repeat to you how my life there went in detail. I always wrote to you about everything. My life there had a gluey, vacuous quality as though I were a small oyster, lost in oppressive loneliness, slowly struggling with a future as dark as the beginning of the night, caught in a rotten routine, a spewed-out combat with time. Everything was hot and sticky. There was a slipperiness to my whole life, it was all a hankering for the end of the month.

From *Men in the Sun and Other Palestinian Stories,* trans. Hilary Kirkpatrick (Washington, DC: Three Continents Press, 1988). Copyright © 1988 Anni Kanafani. Reprinted with permission of Lynne Reinner.

In the middle of the year, that year, the Jews bombarded the central district of Sabha and attacked Gaza, our Gaza, with bombs and flame-throwers. That event might have made some change in my routine, but there was nothing for me to take much notice of: I was going to leave this Gaza behind me and go to California where I would live for myself, my own self which had suffered so long. I hated Gaza and its inhabitants. Everything in the amputated town reminded me of failed pictures painted in grey by a sick man. Yes, I would send my mother and my brother's widow and her children a meagre sum to help them to live, but I would liberate myself from this last tie too, there in green California, far from the reek of defeat which for seven years had filled my nostrils. The sympathy which bound me to my brother's children, their mother and mine would never be enough to justify my tragedy in taking this perpendicular dive. It mustn't drag me any farther down than it already had. I must flee!

You know these feelings, Mustafa, because you've really experienced them. What is this ill-defined tie we had with Gaza which blunted our enthusiasm for flight? Why didn't we analyse the matter in such a way as to give it a clear meaning? Why didn't we leave this defeat with its wounds behind us and move on to a brighter future which would give us deeper consolation! Why? We didn't exactly know.

When I went on holiday in June and assembled all my possessions, longing for the sweet departure, the start towards those little things which give life a nice, bright meaning, I found Gaza just as I had known it, closed like the introverted lining of a rusted snail-shell thrown up by the waves on the sticky, sandy shore by the slaughterhouse. This Gaza was more cramped than the mind of a sleeper in the throes of a fearful nightmare, with its narrow streets which had their peculiar smell, the smell of defeat and poverty, its houses with their bulging balconies . . . this Gaza! But what are the obscure causes that draw a man to his family, his house, his memories, as a spring draws a small flock of mountain goats? I don't know. All I know is that I went to my mother in our house that morning. When I arrived my late brother's wife met me there and asked me, weeping, if I would do as her wounded daughter, Nadia, in Gaza hospital wished and visit her that evening. Do you know Nadia, my brother's beautiful thirteen-year-old daughter?

That evening I bought a pound of apples and set out for the hospital to visit Nadia. I knew that there was something about it that my mother and my sister-in-law were hiding from me, something which their tongues could not utter, something strange which I could not put my finger on. I loved Nadia from habit, the same habit that made me love all that generation which had been so brought up on defeat and displacement that it had come to think that a happy life was a kind of social deviation.

What happened at that moment? I don't know. I entered the white room very calm. Ill children have something of saintliness, and how much more so if the child is ill as a result of cruel, painful wounds. Nadia was lying on her bed, her back propped up on a big pillow over which her hair was spread like a thick pelt. There was a profound silence in her wide eyes and a tear always shining in the depths of her black pupils. Her face was calm and still but eloquent as the face of a tortured prophet might be. Nadia was still a child, but she seemed more than a child, much more, and older than a child, much older.

"Nadia!"

I've no idea whether I was the one who said it, or whether it was someone else behind me. But she raised her eyes to me and I felt them dissolve me like a piece of sugar that had fallen into a hot cup of tea. Together with her slight smile I heard her voice.

"Uncle! Have you just come from Kuwait?"

Her voice broke in her throat, and she raised herself with the help of her hands and stretched out her neck towards me. I patted her back and sat down near her.

"Nadia! I've brought you presents from Kuwait, lots of presents. I'll wait till you can leave your bed, completely well and healed, and you'll come to my house and I'll give them to you. I've bought you the red trousers you wrote and asked me for. Yes, I've bought them."

It was a lie, born of the tense situation, but as I uttered it I felt that I was speaking the truth for the first time. Nadia trembled as though she had had an electric shock, and lowered her head in a terrible silence. I felt her tears wetting the back of my hand.

"Say something, Nadia! Don't you want the red trousers?"

She lifted her gaze to me and made as if to speak, but then she stopped, gritted her teeth and I heard her voice again, coming from far away.

"Uncle!"

She stretched out her hand, lifted the white coverlet with her fingers and pointed to her leg, amputated from the top of the thigh.

My friend . . . Never shall I forget Nadia's leg, amputated from the top of the thigh. No! Nor shall I forget the grief which had moulded her face and merged into its traits for ever. I went out of the hospital in Gaza that day, my hand clutched in silent derision on the two pounds I had brought with me to give Nadia. The blazing sun filled the streets with the colour of blood. And Gaza was brand new, Mustafa! You and I never saw it like this. The stones piled up at the beginning of the Shajiya quarter where we lived had a meaning, and they seemed to have been put there for no other reason but to explain it. This Gaza in which we had lived and with whose good people we had spent seven years of defeat was something new. It seemed to me just a beginning. I don't know why I thought it was just a beginning. I imagined that the main street that I walked along on the way back home was only the beginning of a long, long road leading to Safad. Everything in this Gaza throbbed with sadness which was not confined to weeping. It was a challenge; more than that, it was something like reclamation of the amputated leg!

I went out into the streets of Gaza, streets filled with blinding sunlight. They told me that Nadia had lost her leg when she threw herself on top of her little brothers and sisters to protect them from the bombs and flames that had fastened their claws into the house. Nadia could have saved herself, she could have run away, rescued her leg. But she didn't.

Why?

No, my friend, I won't come to Sacramento, and I've no regrets. No, and nor will I finish what we began together in childhood. This obscure feeling that you had as you left Gaza, this small feeling must grow into a giant deep within you. It must expand, you must seek it in order to find yourself, here among the ugly debris of defeat.

I won't come to you. But you, return to us! Come back, to learn from Nadia's leg, amputated from the top of the thigh, what life is and what existence is worth.

Come back, my friend! We are all waiting for you.

Section 4
—————— Managerial Insights ——————

4.1   BEYOND SOPHISTICATED STEREOTYPING: CULTURAL SENSEMAKING IN CONTEXT
Joyce S. Osland and Allan Bird

If U.S. Americans are so individualistic and believe so deeply in self-reliance, why do they have the highest percentage of charitable giving in the world and readily volunteer their help to community projects and emergencies?

In a 1991 survey, many Costa Rican customers preferred automatic tellers over human tellers because "at least the machines are programmed to say 'good morning' and 'thank you.'" Why is it that so many Latin American cultures are noted for warm interpersonal relationships and a cultural script of *simpatía* (positive social behavior), while simultaneously exhibiting seeming indifference as service workers in both the private and public sectors?

Based on Hofstede's value dimension of Uncertainty Avoidance, the Japanese have a low tolerance for uncertainty while Americans have a high tolerance. Why then do the Japanese intentionally incorporate ambiguous clauses in their business contracts, which are unusually short, while Americans dot every i, cross every t, and painstakingly spell out every possible contingency?

Many people trained to work in these cultures found such situations to be paradoxical when they first encountered them. These examples often contradict and confound our attempts to neatly categorize cultures. They violate our conceptions of what we think particular cultures are like. Constrained, stereotypical thinking is not the only problem, however. The more exposure and understanding one gains about any culture, the more paradoxical it often becomes. For example, U.S. Americans are individualistic in some situations (e.g., "the most comprehensive of rights and the right most valued is the right to be left alone") and collectivist in others (e.g., school fundraising events).

Long-term sojourners and serious cultural scholars find it difficult to make useful generalizations since so many exceptions and qualifications to the stereotypes, on both a cultural and individual level, come to mind. These cultural paradoxes are defined as situations that exhibit an apparently contradictory nature.

Surprisingly, there is little mention of cultural paradoxes in the management literature. Our long-term sojourns as expatriates (a combined total of 22 years), as well as our experience in teaching cross-cultural management, preparing expatriates to go overseas, and doing comparative research, have led us to feel increasingly frustrated with the accepted conceptualizations of culture. Thus, our purpose is to focus attention on cultural paradoxes, explain why they have been overlooked and why they exist, and present a framework for making sense of them. Our intent is

Excerpted from *The Academy of Management Executive* 14, no. 1 (February 2000): 65–77. Copyright © 2000 Academy of Management Executive. Reprinted with permission.

Table 1

Common Cultural Dimensions

Subjugation to nature	Harmony	Mastery of nature
Past	Present	Future
Being	Containing and controlling	Doing
Hierarchical relationships	Group	Individualistic
Private space	Mixed	Public
Evil human nature	Neutral or mixed	Good
Human nature as changeable		Human nature as unchangeable
Monochronic time		Polychronic time
High-context language		Low-context language
Low uncertainty avoidance		High uncertainty avoidance
Low power distance		High power distance
Short-term orientation		Long-term orientation
Individualism		Collectivism
Masculinity		Femininity
Universalism		Particularism
Neutral		Emotional
Diffuse		Specific
Achievement		Ascription
Individualism		Organization
Inner-directed		Outer-directed
Individualism (competition)		Group-organization (collusion)
Analyzing (reductivist)		Synthesizing (larger, integrated wholes)

Sources: Hall, E.T., and M.R. Hall. 1990. *Understanding Cultural Differences.* Yarmouth, ME: Intercultural Press; Hofstede, G. 1980. *Culture's Consequences: International Differences in Work Related Values.* Beverly Hills: Sage; Kluckhohn, F., and F.L. Strodtbeck. 1961. *Variations in Value Orientations.* Evanston, IL: Row, Peterson; Parsons, T., and E. Shils. 1951. *Toward a General Theory of Action.* Cambridge: Harvard University Press; Trompenaars, F., and C. Hampden Turner. 1993. *The Seven Cultures of Capitalism.* New York: Doubleday.

Note: The dimensions are bipolar continua, with the first six containing midpoints.

to initiate a dialogue that will eventually provide teachers, researchers, and people who work across cultures with a more useful way to understand culture.

A look at the comparative literature reveals that cultures are described in somewhat limited terms. There are 22 dimensions commonly used to compare cultures, typically presented in the form of bipolar continua, with midpoints in the first examples, as shown in Table 1. These dimensions were developed to yield greater cultural understanding and allow for cross-cultural comparisons. An unanticipated consequence of using these dimensions, however, is the danger of stereotyping entire cultures.

SOPHISTICATED STEREOTYPING

In many parts of the world, one hears a generic stereotype for a disliked neighboring ethnic group—"The (fill in the blank) are lazy, dirty thieves, and their women are promiscuous." This is a low-level form of stereotyping, often based on lack of personal contact and an irrational dislike of people who are different from oneself. Professors and trainers work very hard to dispel such stereotypes. Rarely, however, do we stop to consider whether we are supplanting one form of stereotyping for another. For example, when we teach students and managers how to perceive the

Israelis using Hofstede's cultural dimensions, they may come to think of Israelis in terms of small power distance, strong uncertainty avoidance, moderate femininity, and moderate individualism. The result is to reduce a complex culture to a shorthand description they may be tempted to apply to all Israelis. We call this sophisticated stereotyping, because it is based on theoretical concepts and lacks the negative attributions often associated with its lower-level counterpart. Nevertheless, it is still limiting in the way it constrains individuals' perceptions of behavior in another culture.

Do we recommend against teaching the cultural dimensions shown in Table 1 so as to avoid sophisticated stereotyping? Not at all. These dimensions are useful tools in explaining cultural behavior. Indeed, cultural stereotypes can be helpful—provided we acknowledge their limitations. They are more beneficial, for example, in making comparisons between cultures than in understanding the wide variations of behavior within a single culture. . . .

The limitations of sophisticated stereotyping become most evident when we confront cultural paradoxes. This is the moment we realize our understanding is incomplete, misleading, and potentially dangerous. Perhaps because cultural paradoxes reveal the limitations in our thinking, they are often left unmentioned, even though virtually anyone with experience in another culture can usually identify one or two after only a moment's reflection.

WHY DON'T WE KNOW MORE ABOUT CULTURAL PARADOXES?

. . .

Perceptual Schemas

. . . Expatriates and researchers alike tend to focus first on cultural differences and make initial conclusions that are not always modified in light of subsequent evidence. Proactive learning about another culture often stops once a survival threshold is attained, perhaps because of an instinctive inclination to simplify a complex world. This may lead us to seek black-and-white answers rather than tolerate the continued ambiguity that typifies a more complete understanding of another culture.

One of the best descriptions of the peeling away of layers that characterizes deeper cultural understanding is found in a fictionalized account of expatriate life written by an expatriate manager, Robert Collins. He outlines ascending levels on a Westerner's perception scale of Japanese culture that alternate, in daisy-petal-plucking fashion, between seeing the Japanese as significantly different or not really that different at all:

> The initial Level on a Westerner's perception scale clearly indicates a "difference" of great significance. The Japanese speak a language unlike any other human tongue . . . they write the language in symbols that reason alone cannot decipher. The airport customs officers all wear neckties, everyone is in a hurry, and there are long lines everywhere.

> Level Two is represented by the sudden awareness that the Japanese are not different at all. Not at all. They ride in elevators, have a dynamic industrial/trade/financial system, own great chunks of the United States, and serve cornflakes in the Hotel Okura.

> Level Three is the "hey, wait a minute" stage. The Japanese come to all the meetings, smile politely, nod in agreement with everything said, but do the opposite of what's expected. And they do it all together. They really are different.

But are they? Level Four understanding recognizes the strong group dynamics, common education and training, and the general sense of loyalty to the family—which in their case is Japan itself. That's not so unusual, things are just organized on a larger scale than any social unit in the West. Nothing is fundamentally different.

Level Five can blow one's mind, however. Bank presidents skipping through streets dressed as dragons at festival time; single ladies placing garlands of flowers around huge, and remarkably graphic, stone phallic symbols; Ministry of Finance officials rearranging their bedrooms so as to sleep in a "lucky" direction; it is all somewhat odd. At least, by Western standards. There is something different in the air.

And so on. Some Westerners, the old Japan hands, have gotten as far as Levels 37 or 38.

The point of Collins's description is that it takes time and experience to make sense of another culture. The various levels he describes reflect differing levels of awareness as more and more pieces of the puzzle are put into place. Time and experience are essential because culture is embedded in the context. Without context it makes little sense to talk about culture. Yet just as its lower-order counterpart does, sophisticated stereotyping tends to strip away or ignore context. Thus, cognitive schemas prevent sojourners and researchers from seeing and correctly interpreting paradoxical behavior outside their own cultures. . . .

SOURCES OF PARADOX IN CULTURAL BEHAVIOR

Behavior that looks paradoxical to an expatriate in the initial stages of cultural awareness may simply reflect the variance in behavioral norms for individuals, organizational cultures, subcultures, as well as generational differences and changing sections of the society. In addition, expatriates may also form microcultures with specific members of the host culture. The cultural synergy of such microcultures may not be reflective of the national culture. These false paradoxes need to be discarded before more substantive paradoxes can be evaluated.

Based on an analysis of all the paradoxes we could find, we have identified six possible explanations for cultural behaviors that appear truly paradoxical. They are:

- the tendency for observers to confuse individual with group values
- unresolved cultural issues
- bipolar patterns
- role differences
- real versus espoused values
- value trumping, a recognition that in specific contexts certain sets of values take precedence over others.

Confusing individual with group values is exemplified by the personality dimension labeled allocentrism versus idiocentrism, which is the psychological, individual-level analog to the individualism-collectivism dimension at the level of culture. Allocentric people, those who pay primary attention to the needs of a group, can be found in individualistic cultures, and idiocentric people, those who pay more attention to their own needs than to the needs of others, in collectivist cultures. What we perceive as cultural paradox may not reflect contradictions in cultural values, but instead may reveal the natural diversity within any culture that reflects individual personality and variation.

Unresolved cultural issues are rooted in the definition of culture as a learned response to problems. Some paradoxes come from problems for which there is no clear, happy solution. Cultures may manifest a split personality with regard to an unresolved problem. As a result, they shuttle back and forth from one extreme to the other on a behavioral continuum. U.S. Americans, for example, have ambivalent views about sex, and, as one journalist recently noted: "Our society is a stew of prurience and prudery." Censorship, fears about sex education, and sexual taboos coexist uncomfortably with increasingly graphic films and TV shows and women's magazines that never go to press without a feature article devoted to sex. This melange is more than a reflection of a diverse society that has both hedonists and fundamentalists with differing views of sex; both groups manifest inconsistent behaviors and attitudes about sex, signaling an enduring cultural inability to resolve this issue.

Bipolar patterns make cultural behavior appear paradoxical because cultural dimensions are often framed, perhaps inaccurately, as dualistic, either-or continua. Cultures frequently exhibit one of these paired dimensions more than the other, but it is probable that both ends of the dimensions are found in cultures—but only in particular contexts. For example, in Latin America, ascribed status, derived from class and family background, is more important than its polar opposite, achieved status, which is based on talent and hard work. When it comes to professional soccer, however, achieved status trumps class and ascription.

Often some groups and roles appear to deviate from cultural stereotypes. For example, in the United States, autocratic behavior is frequently tolerated in CEOs, even though the United States is characterized as an egalitarian culture. Such behavior may also be an example of a high power distance context in a low power distance culture: We accept that CEOs possess an unequal degree of power and that they will behave in a different manner than most U.S. Americans.

There is also a difference between real versus espoused values. All cultures express preferences for ideal behaviors—for what should be valued and how people should act. Nevertheless, people do not always act consistently with ideal behaviors and values. For example, U.S. Americans may simultaneously pay lip service to the importance of equality (an espoused value), while trying to acquire more power or influence for themselves (a real value).

A final possible explanation of cultural paradoxes derives from a holistic, contextual view of culture in which values co-exist as a constellation, but their salience differs depending on the situation. Using the Gestalt concept of figure-ground, at times a particular value becomes dominant (figure), while in other circumstances, this same value recedes into the background (ground). In India, for example, collectivism is figural when individuals are expected to make sacrifices for their families or for the larger society—such as Hindu sons who postpone marriage until their sisters marry, or daughters who stay single to care for their parents. In other circumstances, however, collectivism fades into the background and individualism comes to the fore and is figural when Indians focus more upon self-realization—for example, elderly men who detach themselves from their family to seek salvation. Taking the figure-ground analogy a step further, depending on the context, one cultural value might trump another, lessening the influence another value normally exerts. For example, we find it useful to view culture as a series of card games in which cultural values or dimensions are individual cards. Depending on the game, previous play, and the hand one is dealt, players respond by choosing specific cards that seem most appropriate in a given situation. Sometimes a particular card trumps the others; in another round, it does not. In a given context, specific cultural values come into play and have more importance than other values. To a foreigner who does not understand enough about the cultural context to interpret why or when one value takes precedence over another, such behavior looks paradoxical. Members of the culture learn these nuances more or less automatically. For example, children learn in what context a socially acceptable white lie is more important than always telling the truth. A true understanding of the logic of another culture includes comprehending the interrelationships among values, or how values relate to one another in a given context.

A MODEL OF CULTURAL SENSEMAKING

To make sense of cultural paradoxes and convey a holistic understanding of culture, we propose a model of cultural sensemaking. . . . Cultural sensemaking is a cycle of sequential events:

• *Indexing context.* The process begins when an individual identifies a context and then engages in indexing behavior, which involves noticing or attending to stimuli that provide cues about the situation. For example, to index the context of a meeting with a subordinate, we consider characteristics such as prior events (recent extensive layoffs), the nature of the boss-subordinate relationship within and without work (golfing partner), the specific topic under discussion (employee morale), and the location of the interaction (boss's office).

• *Making attributions.* The next step is attribution, a process in which contextual cues are analyzed in order to match the context with appropriate schema. The matching process is moderated or influenced by one's social identity (e.g., ethnic or religious background, gender, social class, organizational affiliation) and one's history (e.g., experiences and chronology). A senior U.S. American manager who fought against the Japanese in World War II will make different attributions about context and employ different schema when he meets with a Japanese manager than will a Japanese-American manager of his generation, or a junior U.S. manager whose personal experience with Japan is limited to automobiles, electronics, and sushi.

• *Selecting schema.* Schemas are cultural scripts, "a pattern of social interaction that is characteristic of a particular cultural group." They are accepted and appropriate ways of behaving, specifying certain patterns of interaction. From personal or vicarious experience, we learn how to select schema. By watching and working with bosses, for example, we develop scripts for how to act when we take on that role ourselves. We learn appropriate vocabulary and gestures, which then elicit a fairly predictable response from others.

• *The influence of cultural values.* Schemas reflect an underlying hierarchy of cultural values. For example, people working for U.S. managers who have a relaxed and casual style and who openly share information and provide opportunities to make independent decisions will learn specific scripts for managing in this fashion. The configuration of values embedded in this management style consists of informality, honesty, equality, and individualism. At some point, however, these same managers may withhold information about a sensitive personnel situation because privacy, fairness, and legal concerns would trump honesty and equality in this context. This trumping action explains why the constellation of values related to specific schema is hierarchical.

• *The influence of cultural history.* When decoding schema, we may also find vestiges of cultural history and tradition. Mindsets inherited from previous generations explain how history is remembered. For example, perceptions about a colonial era may still have an impact on schemas, particularly those involving interactions with foreigners, even though a country gained its independence centuries ago.

SOME ILLUSTRATIONS OF SENSEMAKING

Sensemaking involves placing stimuli into a framework that enables people "to comprehend, understand, explain, attribute, extrapolate, and predict." Let's analyze each of the cultural paradoxes presented in the introduction using the sensemaking model. In the United States, when a charity requests money, when deserving people are in need, or when disaster hits a community (indexing contexts), many U.S. Americans (e.g., religious, allocentric people making attributions) respond by donating their money, goods, or time (selecting schema). The values underlying this schema are humanitarian concern for others, altruism, and collectivism (cultural values). Thus, individualism (a sophisticated stereotype) is moderated by a communal tradition that has its roots in religious and cultural origins (cultural history).

Fukuyama writes that U.S. society has never been as individualistic as its citizens thought, because of the culture's relatively high level of trust and resultant social capital. The United States "has always possessed a rich network of voluntary associations and community structures to which individuals have subordinated their narrow interests." Under normal conditions, one should take responsibility for oneself and not rely on others. However, some circumstances and tasks can overwhelm individual initiative and ingenuity. When that happens, people should help those in need, a lesson forged on the American frontier (cultural history). To further underscore the complexity of culture, in the same contexts noted above, the tax code and prestige associated with philanthropy (cultural history) may be the primary motivations for some citizens (e.g., idiocentric, upwardly ambitious people making attributions) to act charitably (selecting schema), but the value underlying the schema would be individualism.

The Costa Rican example is illustrated in Figure [1]. When bank tellers interact with clients (indexing context), many of them (e.g., members of various in-groups, civil servants making attributions) do not greet customers and make eye contact, but concentrate solely on their paperwork (selecting schema). The values that underlie this schema are in-group-out-group behavior and power (cultural values). In collectivist cultures such as Costa Rica, members identify strongly with their in-group and treat members with warmth and cooperation. In stark contrast, out-group members are often treated with hostility, distrust, and a lack of cooperation. Customers are considered as strangers and out-group members who do not warrant the special treatment given to in-group members (family and friends). One of the few exceptions to *simpatía* and personal dignity in Costa Rica, and Latin America generally, is rudeness sometimes expressed by people in positions of power. In this context, the cultural value of high power distance (the extent to which a society accepts the fact that power in institutions and organizations is distributed unequally) trumps *simpatía*. Whereas *simpatía* lessens the distance between people, the opposite behavior increases the distance between the powerful and the powerless. Unlike many other contexts in Costa Rica, bank telling does not elicit a cultural script of *simpatía*, and state-owned banks did not have a history of training employees in friendly customer service (cultural history) at this time.

In the third cultural example, when Japanese business people make contracts (indexing context), they (e.g., business people making attributions) opt for ambiguous contracts (selecting schema). The dominant value underlying this schema is collectivism (cultural value). In this context, collectivism is manifested as a belief that those entering into agreement are joined together and share something in common; thus, they should rely on and trust one another. Collectivism trumps high uncertainty avoidance (sophisticated stereotype) in this context, but uncertainty avoidance is not completely absent. Some of the uncertainty surrounding the contract is dealt with upstream in the process by carefully choosing and getting to know business partners, and by using third parties. An additional consideration is that many Japanese like flexible contracts,

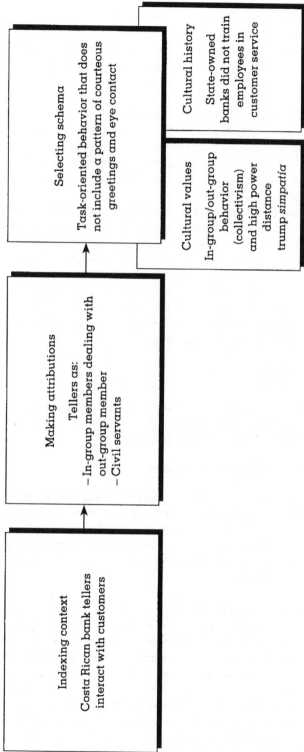

Figure 1   **Making Sense of Paradoxical Behavior: Seemingly Indifferent Customer Service in a Culture Characterized by Positive, Warm Relations**

Indexing context

Costa Rican bank tellers interact with customers

Making attributions

Tellers as:
– In-group members dealing with out-group member
– Civil servants

Selecting schema

Task-oriented behavior that does not include a pattern of courteous greetings and eye contact

Cultural history

State-owned banks did not train employees in customer service

Cultural values

In-group/out-group behavior (collectivism) and high power distance trump *simpatía* because they have a greater recognition of the limits of contracts and the difficulties of foreseeing all contingencies (cultural history). Even though U.S. Americans are typically more tolerant of uncertainty (sophisticated stereotype), they value pragmatism and do not like to take unnecessary risks (cultural values). If a deal falls through, they rely on the legal system for a resolution (cultural history).

WORKING FROM A SENSEMAKING APPROACH

Sophisticated stereotypes are useful in the initial stages of making sense of complex behaviors within cultures. However, rather than stereotyping cultures somewhere along a continuum, we can advance understanding by thinking in terms of specific contexts that feature particular cultural values that then govern behavior. . . .

If we accept that cultures are paradoxical, then it follows that learning another culture occurs in a dialectical fashion—thesis, antithesis, and synthesis. Thesis entails a hypothesis involving a sophisticated stereotype; antithesis is the identification of an apparently oppositional cultural paradox. Synthesis involves making sense of contradictory behavior—understanding why certain values are more important in certain contexts. Behavior appears less paradoxical once the foreigner learns to index contexts and match them with the appropriate schemas in the same way that members of the host culture do. Collins's description of the Westerner's Perception Scale in comprehending Japanese culture illustrates one form of dialectical culture learning, an upwardly spiraling cycle of cultural comprehension.

USING THE MODEL

Because this cultural sensemaking model provides a more complex way of understanding culture, it has clear implications for those who teach culture, for those who work across cultures, and for organizations that send expatriates overseas.

Teaching About Cultural Understanding

Sophisticated stereotyping should be the beginning of cultural learning, not the end, as is so often the case when teaching or learning about culture. Recognition of a more complex, holistic, sensemaking model of culture allows us to respond more effectively when students or trainees provide examples of paradoxes that seem to contradict cultural dimensions. The model also requires a somewhat different teaching approach. We have developed a sequential method that has been effective in our teaching:

• *Help students understand the complexity of their own culture.* To acquaint students with the vast challenge of comprehending culture, we begin with a thorough understanding of the internal logic of one's own culture and its socioeconomic, political, and historical roots. We add complexity by pointing out paradoxes as well as identifying regional, ethnic, religious, organizational, and individual variations in behavior. For example, when Thai students describe their culture as friendly, we ask the following series of questions: "Are all Thais friendly? Are Thais always friendly? Under what circumstances would Thais not exhibit friendly behavior? Why?"

• *Give students cultural dimensions and values as well as sophisticated stereotypes as basic tools.* These dimensions, including the values listed in Table 1, can then be used to explain contrasting behavior from two or more different cultures (e.g., what can sample obituaries from the

United States and Mexico reveal about cultural values? What is the typical response of businesses in both countries when a member of an employee's family dies?). Students practice recognizing cultural dimensions in cross-cultural dialogues and cases and learn sophisticated stereotypes. This helps them gain conceptual knowledge about different cultures so they can make between-culture distinctions.

• *Develop students' skills in cultural observation and behavioral flexibility.* One of the difficulties expatriates confront in making sense of a new culture is the contradiction between the expected culture, the sophisticated stereotype taught in predeparture training or gleaned from others, and the manifest culture, the one actually enacted in a situation. To help students become skilled at observing and decoding other cultures, teach them to think more like anthropologists and give them practice in honing observational and interpretive skills. To help students develop the behavioral flexibility needed to adapt to unanticipated situations, role-playing and videos of cross-cultural interactions can be used.

• *Have students do an in-depth study or experience with one culture.* To go beyond sophisticated stereotypes, students learn the internal logic and cultural history of a single culture. They acquire attributional knowledge from cultural mentors and/or cultural immersion, in addition to extensive research.

• *Focus on learning context-appropriate behavior in other cultures and developing cultural hypotheses and explanations for paradoxical behavior.* Once students have mastered the preceding steps, the emphasis changes to learning schemas for different contexts. For example, student teams are instructed to deliberately demonstrate incorrect behavior; they ask others to point out the mistakes and then replay the scene using correct behavior. To model the crucial behavior of asking for help in understanding cultural mysteries, students use cultural mentors to explain situations they choose to learn about (e.g., "How do managers in _____ encourage employees to perform at high levels? Why does that work for them?"). The variation in the mentors' answers ("Some managers are successful doing this while others . . .") and the qualified answers ("This seems to work unless . . .; it depends on . . .") helps students develop more complex understandings of the other culture. To highlight the message of moving beyond cultural stereotypes, use language that focuses on forming and testing hypotheses about contextual behavior: "What are your hypotheses about why a French employee behaves this way in this situation? How can you find out if these hypotheses are correct?"

Sensemaking for Individuals Working Across Cultures

After the training program, and once on assignment in a new culture, this cultural sensemaking approach has other practical implications.

• *Approach learning another culture more like a scientist who holds conscious stereotypes and hypotheses in order to test them.* One of the key differences between managers who were identified by their fellow MBA students as the "most internationally effective" and the "least internationally effective" is that the former changed their stereotypes of other nationalities as they interacted with them while the latter did not.

• *Seek out cultural mentors and people who possess attributional knowledge about cultures.* Perhaps one of the basic lessons of cross-cultural interaction is that tolerance and effectiveness result from greater understanding of another culture. Making sense of a culture's internal logic and decoding cultural paradoxes is easiest with the aid of a willing and knowledgeable informant.

• *Analyze disconfirming evidence and instances that defy cultural stereotypes.* Even people with a great deal of experience in another culture can benefit from analyzing cultural paradoxes. For instance, the question, "In what circumstances do Latin Americans fail to exhibit *simpatía?*" led to a more complex cultural understanding for one of the authors, who had already spent nine curious years in that region. Once expatriates can function reasonably well in another culture, it is easy for them to reach plateaus in their cultural understanding and mistakenly assume that they comprehend the entire puzzle. This presents a danger when expatriates inadvertently pass on inaccurate information about the local culture, or make faulty, and even expensive, business decisions based on partial understandings.

• *Learn cultural schemas that will help you be effective.* Knowing how to act appropriately in specific cross-cultural settings results in self-confidence and effectiveness. One cannot memorize all the rules in another culture, but understanding the values that underlie most schemas can often prevent us from making serious mistakes.

How Multinational Organizations Can Use the Sensemaking Model

The cultural sensemaking model also has practical implications for multinational organizations.

• *Use cognitive complexity as a selection criterion for expatriates and people in international positions.* Avoid black-and-white thinkers in favor of people who exhibit cognitive complexity, which involves the ability to handle ambiguity and multiple viewpoints. This skill is better suited to a thesis-antithesis approach to understanding the paradoxical nature of culture.

• *Provide in-country cultural training for expatriates that goes beyond factual and conceptual knowledge.* Predeparture cultural training is complemented by on-site training, which has the advantage of good timing. In-country culture training takes place when expatriates are highly motivated to find answers to real cultural dilemmas and when they are ready for greater complexity.

• *Gauge the cultural knowledge possessed by expatriates within a country.* The accuracy and depth of one's cultural understanding is not always linked to the time one has spent in another country; it depends on the degree of involvement with the other culture as well as cultural curiosity and desire to learn. Nevertheless, when companies determine the optimum length of overseas assignments, they should consider how much time is generally necessary to function effectively in a particular culture. If a firm's expatriates stay abroad for only two years, it is less likely that a deep understanding of the culture will be shared among them than if they were to stay for longer periods. As long as the longer-term expatriates do not stop at a low-level plateau of cultural learning, mixing short-term (2–3 years) with longer-term expatriates (6–7 years) with permanent expatriates could produce more shared organizational learning about the culture. It is also essential to recognize that expatriates working for the same organization may be at different levels of cultural understanding.

• *Act like learning organizations with regard to cultural knowledge.* Multinationals benefit from formal mechanisms to develop a more complex understanding of the cultures where they do business through such methods as cultural mentors and in-country cultural training. There should also be mechanisms for sharing cultural knowledge. For example, having returned expatriates give formal debriefing sessions in which they report what they learned in their assignment increases the company's collective cultural knowledge and eases the expatriates' transition home by helping them make sense of a highly significant experience.

4.2 "ENGLISHES" IN CROSS-CULTURAL BUSINESS COMMUNICATION
Naoki Kameda

"Send us your message again in English!" This was a stern telex reply from the headquarters of a multinational firm in The Hague to their subsidiary in Paris. The Paris secretary had sent a telex in her mother tongue, French. The headquarters' reply must surely have hurt the pride of the French workers, who are known for loving their own language. This one example, a true story, heard from the Tokyo subsidiary, illustrates two interesting facts:

1. English is prescribed as a common language within many multinational firms for their internal communications. In some multinational firms, there is an unwritten law that each subsidiary must use English for its communications with other subsidiaries and with headquarters.
2. In one known multinational firm, neither the Netherlands where it has its headquarters nor France where it has a subsidiary has English as its mother tongue. However, English is the international language used.

In the business world today non-native speakers use English primarily to communicate with other non-native users—for example, Japanese with Koreans, Koreans with Taiwanese, Taiwanese with Indonesian, Indonesian with Greek, Greek with Portuguese, etc. The president of a Swiss company, who is German, visits the Far East twice a year with an executive director of his French subsidiary, who is French, for purchasing products from Asia. The problem is neither can speak his counterpart's language. Each must use English all the time to communicate with each other. Their business language when doing business with their Asian suppliers is of course English.

Chinese business people, often called overseas Chinese, must resort to English to communicate with other Chinese people when the two parties are from different places because each one's own Chinese is mutually unintelligible when spoken, due to the influence of dialect.

It is said English has emerged over the last 40 years as the world's premier international language. It is even said English has in essence become a world language, the common property of all cultures. But, is it really so?

Tables 1–5 give some interesting insights about English as an international language.

The number of people around the world who speak the English language is considerable. Over 300 million people speak it as a mother tongue or first language, another 300 million use it as a second language, and between 100 million and 300 million speak it as a foreign language. In total, between 700 million and 1 billion people speak English. The latter figure represents one fifth of the world's population.

WIDESPREAD USE OF ENGLISH: REASONS

Some factors have been already introduced by scholars to explain the spread of English—such as English usage in science and technology, English usage by developing countries, the structure of the language, etc.

From *The Bulletin of the Association for Business Communication* (March 1992): 3–8.

Table 1

The World's Major Mother Tongues

	Speakers (in millions)	% of world population
Chinese (Han)	1,031.3	20.6
English	309.9	6.2
Spanish	246.0	4.9
Hindi	219.0	4.4
Bengali	166.8	3.3
Russian	166.0	3.3
Arabic	160.2	3.2
Portuguese	149.3	3.0
Japanese	122.5	2.4
French	84.7	1.7
Total	2,655.7	53.0

Table 2

Countries with the Largest Number of English Mother Tongue Users

	English first language speakers (in millions)	Total population (in millions)	% English first language speakers
USA	216.18	243.77	88.7
UK	53.00	56.87	93.3
Canada	15.84	25.85	61.3
Australia	13.80	16.18	85.3
Irish Republic	3.38	3.56	94.9
New Zealand	3.12	3.34	93.4
South Africa	1.85	34.97	5.3
Zimbabwe	0.69	8.64	8.0
Jamaica	0.64	2.37	27.0
Liberia	0.35	2.35	15.0
Others	12.88		
Total	321.81		

Source: Britannica World Data Book, 1988.
Note: "Others" includes English Creole and English bilingual speakers.

Whatever the reasons may be, it is an indisputable fact that the number of countries where people speak English as their mother tongue or official language and the number of people who speak it far exceed those of other languages.

The actual structure of the language itself is also contributing to the spread of English as a world language. English is relatively easy to pronounce. The basic syntax is fairly straightforward, as is the fact that English has dispensed with gender systems and has less inflection and declension than most other languages such as French and German possess.

Because of this easy structure and accessibility, English has gained the position of the first foreign language for those who can't make themselves understood in their mother tongue when communicating with foreigners.

As the name suggests, the operations of a multinational firm are spread over many countries.

Table 3

Geographic Locations Where English Is Both the Official and the Majority First Language Used

Location	% of population using English as first language
Anguilla	100.0
Antigua and Barbados	95.8
Australia	85.3
Bermuda	93.0
British Virgin Isles	91.6
Canada	61.3
Cayman Isles	100.0
Falkland Isles	100.0
Grenada	96.0
Guam	35.0
Guernsey	100.0
Irish Republic	94.9
Isle of Man	100.0
Jersey	100.0
Montserrat	100.0
New Zealand	93.4
Norfolk Isles	100.0
St. Helena	100.0
Turks and Caicos Isles	100.0
UK	93.3
USA	88.7
U.S. Virgin Isles	81.0
Western Samoa	52.0

Source: Britannica World Data Book, 1988.

Table 4

Estimated Population of Countries Where English Is Used as an Official or Second Language (in millions)

Total population of countries where English is an official language	222.0
Other Commonwealth countries	14.2
Pakistan	10.6
Total	246.8

Sources: Britannica World Data Book, 1988; and McCallen, B. 1989. "English: A World Commodity. The International Market for Training in English as a Foreign Language." Special Report No. 1166. In *The Economist Intelligence Unit*, 1–25. London: The Economist Intelligence Unit Ltd.

Table 5

Estimated Number of ESL Speakers (in millions)

Population of countries where English is spoken as a first or second language	246
Mother tongue speakers	32
Non-mother tongue speakers	214
Estimated ESL speakers	30
Non-English speakers	184

Source: McCallen, B. 1989. "English: A World Commodity. The International Market for Training in English as a Foreign Language." Special Report No. 1166. In *The Economist Intelligence Unit*, 1–25. London: The Economist Intelligence Unit Ltd.

The mother tongues of the senders and the receivers of the firm's internal communications are all different. If, therefore, they were to be allowed to use their own languages, the whole operations system of the firm might collapse; time and money involved with translation work would be enormous and cause considerable loss to the firm.

One of the big ten trading companies in Japan has been using English for their telex communications with their Warsaw office. The reasons given were as follows:

1. To meet the requirements of the Polish Import and Export Agency, which officially prescribes that the language to be used for negotiations with them must be either Polish or English.
2. To make the local employees feel like "first string" members of the firm. They may lose their interest and will to work if the day's telex messages are not understandable to them.
3. To avoid misunderstanding instructions from the headquarters in Tokyo and details of negotiations with the Agency or details of negotiations forwarded from the Warsaw office to the head office in Tokyo.
4. To eliminate the need for translation, thus keeping at a minimum the work load of the Japanese representatives at the Warsaw office.

In the special report *English: A World Commodity*, Brian McCallen writes, "Many linguists are beginning to reject the notion of a blanket unaccountable noun 'English' with its suggestion of a relatively homogeneous language and suggest instead the term 'Englishes.' The key issue here is that each country which speaks the language can inject aspects of its own culture into the usage. Though differences in grammar, syntax, and pronunciation may result, the language still remains comprehensive to speakers of the 'standard' variety." This remark implies that English has become not just a national language used internationally, but rather a true international language.

NONSTANDARD "ENGLISHES" USAGE: SAMPLES

To identify Nonstandard "Englishes," one must first have knowledge of Standard English. In their *International English: A Guide to Varieties of Standard English,* Peter Trudgill and Jean Hannah define Standard English as one of the different variants of modern English written and spoken by educated native speakers. It naturally includes different varieties of English known as "English as a Foreign Language," or EFL, and "English as a Second Language," or ESL, both being taught to the students of English at schools in foreign countries. They take two major varieties of English as Standard English: British English written and spoken by educated native speakers in England, Wales, Scotland, North Ireland, the Republic of Ireland, Australia, New Zealand, and South Africa; and North American English which educated people in the States and Canada use for writing and speaking. These varieties can be categorized as United States English and Canadian English respectively.

All other varieties of English can be defined as Nonstandard English. Some examples of Nonstandard English collated from Nigeria, India, Singapore, and the Philippines, countries using English as their official or joint official language, are as follows:

1. Ramesh said he will be coming here soon, isn't it?
2. Patricia has left the company, is it?
3. We are here since yesterday.

4. When you will receive our L/C, please advise us.
5. I wonder where is he.
6. I can't got it, too.
7. He is not around.
8. He suggested me to meet with you in Bombay.
9. She hasn't had no idea, also.
10. Hasn't he come back yet?
    Yes = he hasn't come back yet.
    No = he has come back already.
11. Don't you mind my smoking?
    Yes = Please go ahead. I don't mind at all.

These are just a few of the patterns and expressions often seen and heard when communicating with non-natives. Listed are only those whose usage is accepted in a given local speech community—not a single person's misuse.

These expressions would be marked by a teacher of English as incorrect usage or mistakes. But, with these expressions in actual use, non-native speakers are doing business with their foreign counterparts. It is interesting to note that number 10 is one from Nigeria and number 11 is from the Philippines. "Yes, no" mistakes are not a birthmark nor a patent of Japanese.

BYPASSING IN CROSS-CULTURAL BUSINESS COMMUNICATION

Many businessmen from countries other than the ten whose mother tongue is Standard English are doing business with the Englishes cited. In their business communication, however, such minor grammatical errors, or what could perhaps be called divergent forms of Standard English, hardly cause misunderstanding. The actual misunderstanding in their business communication takes place outside the scope of the style of Englishes.

It is the misunderstanding caused by bypassing. As Haney (1979) observes, "Bypassing is the name for the miscommunication pattern which occurs when the *sender* (speaker, writer, and so on) and the *receiver* (listener, reader, and so forth) *miss each other with their meanings*" (p. 285).

The following examples obtained from business experience illustrate bypassing. The first is an exchange of telexes between the import manager of a German company in Munich and a Tokyo office. (R stands for "Received" and S stands for "Sent.")

(R) RE OUR CONTAINER: PLS ADVISE BY RTN TLX TIME OF DEPARTURE, E.T.A. AND VESSEL USED.
(S) M.S. CHEVALIER PAUL IS TO LEAVE TOKYO ON FEB 12 AND ARRIVE AT HAMBURG ON MARCH 12.
(R) PLS ADVISE TIME OF DEPARTURE, E.T.A. AND VESSEL.
(S) RCVD UR TLX N WISH TO ADVISE U ALL INFO WAS ALREADY GIVEN TO U ON JAN 26. MS CHEVALIER PAUL IS LEAVING ON FEB 12 N ARRIVING AT HAMBURG ON MARCH 12.
(R) WHERE IS OUR CONTAINER???
(R) MR. CHEVALIER PAUL WILL HE VISIT US IN MUNICH? IF SO, PLS ADVISE SO I CAN MEET HIM. PLS ALSO EXPLAIN WHAT HIS POSITION IS.

(S)   UR CONTAINER CHEVALIER PAUL IS SOMEWHERE ON THE HIGH SEA OF THE INDIAN OCEAN N EXPECTED TO ARRIVE AT HAMBURG ON OR ABOUT MARCH 12. M.S. STANDS FOR MOTOR SHIP NOT FOR MONSIEUR IN FRENCH.

(R)   EVERYTHING IS CLEAR REGARDING MR-MS CHEVALIER PAUL. WE ALL HAD A GOOD LAUGH HERE. WILL PLACE A NEW ORDER ABOUT 14–21 DAYS AFTER RECEIPT OF CONTAINER.

This example precisely illustrates bypassing. The words of issue are M-S and M-R. It was thought that the import manager who had used the trade term ETA (Estimated Time of Arrival) was familiar with the abbreviation MS for Motor Ship as used in export and import practice.

A second example occurred recently when products were shipped to Portugal under the requested payment terms C.A.D. Experience of shipment under this payment condition to a Greek customer had been previously mutually accepted to be the same as D/P (Documents against Payment) at sight because it is Cash Against Documents. In the usual case, D/P is always with an at sight condition. If the terms are wanted with usance, it should be changed to D/A (Documents against Acceptance). Goods were shipped and the bill and shipping documents were negotiated at the bank for cash. A month passed and the bank advised that the payment was not yet settled and wanted the buyer coerced for payment. The representative in Lisbon responded that payment would definitely be made when the goods were ready for custom clearance, but as yet the goods had not arrived.

The reason for the misunderstanding was the simple letter "D." The buyer, from the beginning, meant this "D" as "Delivery," that is, local delivery of the goods, as Cash Against Delivery. The seller took "D" to mean "Documents," the interpretation of C.A.D. based on the standard usage of the payment terms prevailing in Europe.

The word "Delivery" used in the international trade practice is interchangeable with "Shipment" unless otherwise specified such as "Deliver to (place of delivery) in Sydney by 30 September 1989." The Sale of Goods Act, 1893, Section 32, gives such a definition as—(1) Delivery to carrier.—Where, in pursuance of a contract of sale, the seller is authorized or required to send the goods to the buyer, delivery of the goods to a carrier, whether named by the buyer or not, for the purpose of transmission to the buyer, is *prima facie* deemed to be a delivery of the goods to the buyer.

Not everyone who does international business knows this definition. A known American buyer in Los Angeles has his own definitions on several trade terms that often appeared in correspondence. To him "Delivery" meant delivery to his store in the States. "September" delivery meant that he expects products to be delivered to his store in September.

CAUSES OF BYPASSING

The causes of these three bypassing cases can be classified roughly into the following three factors:

1.   The absence of general agreement
2.   Egocentric interpretation
3.   Self-conceited conception

If there were general agreements between the two parties in each case on the words such as M.S., C.A.D., and Delivery, they could have easily avoided such a miscommunication. However, individuals are selfish and apt to think that they know what they know because they know what they know. It is often forgotten that people have different cultures, customs, values, etc. and understandably give different meanings to words.

People give their own meanings to words they perceive. Words do not "mean" at all. Only people "mean." And, people give entirely different meanings to words, meanings which they have acquired through experience which is completely different from that of others. In Athens a few years ago, a local businessman took an international visitor to a hilltop near his office for lunch. The visitor saw an old building that looked like a monastery in the distance. He said, "Look! That's a nice OLD monastery down there." The amazed businessman replied, "Old? You said it's an old building? It's still a new construction, built in 16th century." For the Greek people a monastery built in 16th century is still a new building. Meanings are really in people not in words.

When a Japanese traveller was in India some 20 years ago, there was a turmoil in Bombay; a large group of local Indian people started rioting against Chinese people living there. Many Chinese people were threatened. The local Japanese society held a committee meeting and were discussing how their members and their families could be free from the Indians' possible attack on them. They were about to decide each family should put a large Hinomaru rising-sun mark on the door of each house to tell Indian people "We are Japanese not Chinese." Only the Japanese traveller objected to the idea. He said that there was no guarantee that Indian people knew that the sign of a round red mark on a white background signified Japan's national flag. "Instead, simply write down 'Not Chinese' because Indian people can read English," he said.

This anecdote condenses the causes of bypassing or the three factors mentioned: the absence of general agreement, egocentric interpretation, and self-conceited conception.

The Hinomaru or a rising-sun flag is nothing but just a piece of cloth or paper if there isn't national and governmental general agreement that it signifies the national flag and the symbol of Japan. It must be realized, however, that the span of the scope in which the general agreement works is not limitless. There is a limit beyond which it doesn't work at all. Had the Japan Society's committee members been more astute, they would have realized that not everyone can identify the Japanese flag.

Another example is one easily overlooked. Many authors of English literature, or even those of business English textbooks, suggest students should not write, "He is tall," which is only a subjective opinion. "He stands six feet four" allows no misconception, but another problem arises. Suppose the reader is not American, not familiar with measurement in feet and inches, and does not know the average height of American men. Can such a reader give a judgement, accurate or vague, whichever it may be? Can the reader tell, with this bit of information, that the man in question is tall? Unfortunately he can't.

To follow what the authors suggest, one must write "He's got 165 square meters of land in Ginza" instead of "He is rich." But, the number of people who can associate the land with the man's richness is limited. For those who have no knowledge of the Ginza's extraordinary land prices, the sentence only means a man's possession of relatively small land in a place called Ginza.

This may be one of the most difficult aspects of cross-cultural communication. In order to convey a message across the boundary of a cultural sphere to the receiver, some additional information must be given to complete the message. "He stands six feet four and is tall in our society," or "He has a land of 165 square meters in Ginza. One tsubo (3.3 m^2) costs roughly US$500,000 down there."

Yamamoto Takashi of Tokyo University says in *Language and Communication,* "In order to make the transmission of an idea by language or communication possible, it is not enough that the sender (speaker, writer) and the receiver (listener, reader) share the knowledge of the language used. To make such an utterance as 'Challenger has exploded' transmitted, the sender and the receiver must be able to share their empirical knowledge that 'Challenger' refers to a spaceship.

"If the receiver has no such knowledge, the sender must explain to the receiver, 'You know, Challenger is an American space shuttle.' The reason why communication between races or ethnic groups and between different generations doesn't go smoothly is that the sender and the receiver share fewer ways of thinking, such as customs, systems, traditions, cultures—the criteria necessary for verbal communication."

THE MESSAGE IS THE MESSAGE RECEIVED

Much failure to communicate is due to lack of imagination, a failure to put oneself into the position of the other person, a lack of empathy. We must not assume that our readers know as much about the topic in our message as we do. Be considerate of readers and put yourself in their places and in their situations, and most of the communication problems will be solved.

Once there was a good passage full of empathy to readers of an English newspaper in Japan. It went like this ". . . the high school textbooks are scheduled to go into use next April, *when the school year begins.*" The writer of the article put himself in the shoes of his readers from other countries in which the school year does not always start in April, even though it would sound redundant to Japanese readers. Additional information or expansion of your message is thus important.

When communicating across societies and cultures in Englishes, attention should be paid to the following:

1. Assume the receiver of your message may not interpret the words you used in the same way as you intended.
2. Do not assume the receiver knows as much about the topic or the new words in the message as yourself.
3. Assume, when you are the receiver, the sender of the message you have received might have given another meaning to the words which may be quite different from yours.

Some suggestions to help make communication more comprehensive are:

1. Have your secretary, colleagues, superiors, or any other third party read what you have written before you pass it on to a typist or telex/fax operator.
2. Expand your message by adding as much information as possible so that the receiver may not receive too little information. Ask yourself what he needs to know in order to comprehend the message, and give him what you think he should know, thereby making what you know what he knows.
3. Do not try to interpret the message you receive by giving your own meaning to it when you find it difficult to understand the message. Ask the sender immediately to restate it in other words.

"Be considerate of others and put yourself into the position of the other person." This is the teaching of *You-Consideration* advocated by late Professor Ozaki and the key to successful human-centered communication in Englishes across business and cultures.

REFERENCES

Haney, W.V. 1979. *Communication and Interpersonal Relations*. New York: Irwin.
McCallen, B. 1989. *English: A World Commodity. The International Market for Training in English as a Foreign Language*. Special Report No. 1166. London: The Economist Intelligence Unit.
Trudgill, P., and J. Hannah. 1985. *International English: A Guide to Varieties of Standard English*. London: Arnold.
Yamamoto, T. 1988. *Language and Communication*. Tokyo: Tokyo University Press.

4.3 WHEN MANAGING EXPATRIATE ADJUSTMENT, DON'T FORGET THE SPOUSE

Talya N. Bauer and Sully Taylor

How can firms maximize the success of expatriate assignments? Thanks to globalization, many companies continue to send increasing numbers of expatriates abroad to manage their burgeoning foreign operations. Of course, expatriates represent a potential competitive advantage for international corporations. But expatriates also represent a big financial drain for companies, especially when they fail. And failing can have serious negative consequences for expatriates' careers.

In recent years, companies have improved the cross-cultural training offered to expatriates. But the spouses who relocate with them are often overlooked and given little or no training and support. This is a major oversight, since poor adjustment by a spouse is a key reason why expatriates return early from their assignments. What's staggering is the potential scope of this complex problem. Companies that ignore spouse adjustment may contribute to the alienation experienced by the more than one million spouses who take part in international relocations.

One possible reason why spouses often are overlooked is that the factors that relate to their adjustment have received almost no research attention and aren't well understood. On top of that, what we know about expatriate adjustment isn't very useful for understanding the adjustment challenges that a spouse often faces. For example, spouses typically interact more extensively with the local community than expatriates.

Margaret A. Shaffer, a researcher from the Hong Kong Baptist University, and David A. Harrison, a researcher from Pennsylvania State University, undertook a two-part study to better understand spouse adjustment and the processes involved. First, they conducted in-depth interviews with the spouses of expatriates who had returned from a variety of countries. Shaffer and Harrison included spouses who had adjusted well and those who had experienced significant adjustment difficulties.

After analyzing the interviews and previous research, they concluded that spouse adjustment consists of three dimensions: how well the spouse builds relationships with host-country nationals, how well the spouse adjusts to local customs and the culture in general, and the extent to which the spouse has a sense of becoming part of or feeling at home in the foreign country (a more inwardly focused dimension of personal adjustment). Shaffer and Harrison believe that achieving successful adjustment in all three dimensions depends on whether the spouse can reestablish his or her identity in the new culture. When we enter a new culture, our self-concept is often challenged because our normal ways of reinforcing identity don't work, such as how we interact socially.

Next, Shaffer and Harrison sent surveys to 221 expatriate couples to see if the factors that help establish these different identities led to better adjustment of the spouse. The expatriates worked for 10 different U.S. multinationals in 37 countries. Obtaining the views of the expatriates themselves helped corroborate the spouse's adjustment from another source. Their results showed that foreign-language skill was the factor that most influenced the ability to rebuild a personal sense of identity and, as a result, achieve greater adjustment. Having foreign-language skills has also

From *The Academy of Management Executive* 15, no. 4 (November 2001): 135–138. Copyright © 2001 Academy of Management Executive. Reprinted with permission.

been found to be very helpful for expatriates. Interestingly, Shaffer and Harrison found that a change in employment status (e.g., the spouse's giving up a job to go overseas) had no impact on adjustment. But the researchers noted that they had little information about the spouse's previous employment history or career stage. Paradoxically, spouses who go into a foreign environment feeling that they have good social skills are actually somewhat less likely to adjust successfully. Perhaps some spouses became frustrated when their normally effective social behaviors fell short abroad.

The survey also revealed that the greatest impact on adjustment comes from the spouses' ability to reestablish a social sense of themselves. Family was particularly important in that regard, but in an unexpected way. Spouses with strong extended families adjusted poorly, perhaps because they focused on family members left back home. Likewise, children played a key role, but their impact varied by age. In families with young children, spouses were better adjusted than in families with no children or school-age children. This may be the case because spouses with young children are carrying out the same family responsibilities that they would at home. Consequently, they experience less disruption in this part of their social identities. An expatriate's adjustment also affects his or her spouse. Indeed, a negative spiral can occur, with each person's problems creating more adjustment difficulties for their partner.

Another surprising finding was that greater certainty about the length of the foreign assignment did not improve adjustment. Knowing how long it will be until they can reunite with their extended families or resume their careers could have a calming effect on spouse anxiety. But when the spouse was living in a culture not too dissimilar from that of the home country, and when the living conditions were at least as good as those at home, adjustment was better regardless. According to previous research, this finding for spouses holds true for expatriate employees as well.

Shaffer and Harrison's model is an extremely useful way of conceptualizing how spouses can successfully adjust to a foreign environment. By viewing the spouse as having various identities that are challenged abroad, both companies and expatriate families can better prepare themselves, more clearly understand what is happening to them, and take proactive steps to successfully adjust. Especially encouraging is the support found for several of the factors thought to affect identity and adjustment.

Because the model was developed from a limited a..nount of previous research and a fairly small set of 10 interviews, it needs to be tested and examined in different contexts. Likewise, only five percent of the spouses were male. Since dual-career couples are increasingly likely to be sent overseas, we need to better understand any differences in the adjustment process between male and female spouses. Several results also need to be examined more closely before any practical applications are developed. In particular, it is premature to say that a change in employment does not affect a spouse's adjustment. We simply need to know more.

In the end, what is especially fascinating about these results is that many of the assets spouses believe they have going into a relocation context (e.g., perceived social skills) were often of no help, or actually worked against their successful adjustment. The implications are crystal clear. First, companies should give realistic job previews to spouses both prior to and during relocation. This will help spouses accurately identify the challenges they will face as well as the personal assets they can bring to bear.

Companies should also take steps to ensure that spouses learn language skills, build good social networks, and establish a new social identity if they want to increase the odds of expatriate success. While some spouses may naturally form new social identities on their own, firms that help facilitate this process by offering programs such as social events with host-country nationals, cultural counselors, pre-relocation training, and cultural education are doing themselves a favor. That is a small price to pay for avoiding many of the negative consequences of premature expatriate departure.

[Referenced article:] Shaffer, M.A., and D.A. Harrison. 2001. "Forgotten Partners of International Assignments: Development and Test of a Model of Spouse Adjustment." *Journal of Applied Psychology* 86, no. 2: 238–254.

4.4 ADAPTING TO A BOUNDARYLESS WORLD: A DEVELOPMENTAL EXPATRIATE MODEL

Juan I. Sanchez, Paul E. Spector, and Cary L. Cooper

Adjusting to an international assignment can provoke feelings of helplessness in an unprepared executive, who may have difficulty sorting out appropriate from inappropriate behavior. In fact, learning to manage in and cope with a foreign environment involves such a profound personal transformation that it has an analog in the process of human development throughout the life-span. Expatriate executives are removed from the comfortable environment of their parental culture and placed in a less familiar culture. Indeed, a management style that works at home may fail to produce the desired response abroad, or it may be even counterproductive. The sudden loss of control in one's environment that results from cultural shock abruptly disrupts one's equilibrium. This uneven relationship between the executive and an environment that is perceived to exceed the executive's coping resources perfectly fits the definition of stress, which threatens well-being. A recent comparison of expatriate executives with a similar group that did not relocate revealed an alarming increase in the stress-sensitive hormone prolactin, reduced mental health, and an increase in cigarette and alcohol consumption in the expatriate group during the first year abroad.

Rivers of ink have been dedicated to the need to develop globally minded leaders. A better understanding of the stages involved in a successful adjustment to a foreign environment should help in the development of a global mindset. A profound personal transformation, involving the formation of a multicultural identity, is necessary to buffer the stress provoked by an international assignment.

Coping with stress can be seen as a process involving two steps—primary and secondary—in the evaluation of such adverse environmental conditions as having too much work and uncertain job responsibilities. Adverse environmental conditions function as work stressors when an individual recognizes them as stressful through the mental process known as primary evaluation. Secondary evaluation involves the selection of a coping response to deal with the stressor. The same two steps can be distinguished in coping with stress during an international assignment. First, coping requires an understanding of the new environmental conditions or stressors that demand adaptive responses from the executive. Second, leverage of the new stressors demands a revision of one's old repertoire of coping responses, which may no longer be effective in the new setting. Our goals in this article parallel these two steps and are to shed light on the nature of the primary stressors faced by the expatriate executive, and formulate recommendations regarding strategies that facilitate the adjustment of expatriate executives. Our recommendations are divided into two categories—those directed at expatriate executives and those directed at their employers. To provide a framework or roadmap, our review draws a parallel with the process of human development, proceeding along the developmental stages experienced by expatriate executives as they struggle to adapt to their new world. This progression is summarized in Table 1, which presents each stage, its primary stressors, and the recommended coping strategies for both executives and their employers.

Excerpted from *The Academy of Management Executive* 14, no. 2 (May 2000): 96–106. Copyright © 2000 Academy of Management Executive. Reprinted with permission.

Table 1

Stressors and Coping Responses in the Developmental Stages of Expatriate Executives

Stage	Primary stressors	Executive coping response	Employer coping response
Expatriate selection	Cross-cultural unreadiness	Engage in self-evaluation.	Encourage expatriate's self- and family evaluation. Perform an assessment of potential and interests.
Assignment acceptance	Unrealistic evaluation of stressors to come; hurried time frame	Think of assignment as a growth opportunity rather than an instrument to vertical promotion.	Do not make hard-to-keep promises. Clarify expectations.
Pre- and post-arrival training	Ignorance of cultural differences	Do not make unwarranted assumptions of cultural competence and cultural rules.	Provide pre-, during, and post-assignment training. Encourage support-seeking behavior.
Arrival	Cultural shock; stressor reevaluation; feelings of lack of fit and differential treatment	Do not construe identification with the host and parent cultures as mutually exclusive. Seek social support.	Provide post-arrival training. Facilitate integration in expatriate network.
Novice	Cultural blunders or inadequacy of coping responses; ambiguity due to inability to decipher meaning of situations	Observe and study functional value of coping responses among locals. Do not simply replicate responses that worked at home.	Provide follow-up training. Seek advice from locals and expatriate network.
Transitional	Rejection of host or parent culture	Form and maintain attachments with both cultures.	Promote culturally sensitive policies at host country. Provide Internet access to family and friends at home. Maintain constant communication and periodic visits to parent organization.
Mastery	Frustration with inability to perform boundary spanning role; bothered by living with a cultural paradox	Internalize and enjoy identification with both cultures and walking between two cultures.	Reinforce rather than punish dual identification by defining common goals.
Repatriation	Disappointment with unfulfilled expectations; sense of isolation; loss of autonomy	Realistically reevaluate assignment as a personal and professional growth opportunity.	Arrange pre-repatriation briefings and interviews. Schedule post-repatriation support meetings.

EXPATRIATE SELECTION STAGE

Technical skills, family situation, relational skills, and motivational state all play a crucial role in effective cross-cultural adjustment. However, 90 percent of all companies base their international selections on technical expertise while ignoring the other areas. Technically qualified candidates are not always capable of easily adjusting to critical cultural differences, such as those involving social status and group dependence.

Openness to the profound personal transformation that awaits the expatriate executive is perhaps the most fundamental sign of expatriate readiness. It is not surprising that courage and risk taking are among the core characteristics of successful expatriates who, knowing themselves, are willing to revisit their most deeply held assumptions. Authoritarianism, rigidity, and ethnocentrism are personality aspects that impede adaptation to a foreign culture. Because these are deeply ingrained personality traits that are not easily malleable, selection rather than training should be the strategy used to ensure that candidates possess these characteristics from the first day on the job. Although traditional personality inventories have not proven very effective at predicting expatriate success, available measures specifically designed to evaluate expatriate potential appear promising.

A frequently reported explanation for expatriate failure has been poor adjustment of spouses. Despite the key role of family-related variables in successful expatriate management, assessing the family situation without violating privacy rights is a real challenge. A practical and potentially useful strategy involves providing a realistic preview of the assignment, then instigating a self-evaluation of readiness among family members. By reflecting on the results of this evaluation, the executives can appraise their family situation and can voluntarily withdraw if the prospect is not altogether favorable.

ASSIGNMENT ACCEPTANCE STAGE

The excessive emphasis on technical skills also seems to dominate the decision-making process that the expatriate executive and family go through before the offer is accepted. Typically, the candidate selected has technical expertise and experience related to the assignment. Therefore, the candidate does not envision being incapable of performing an assignment abroad that he or she has already done at home. Why are some managers and employers prone to overlook the cross-cultural demands of the assignment? The answer lies in the psychological perspective of work stress, which is driven by subjective appraisals of the executive's environment. The objective reality of the situation does not directly provoke a stressful experience, but the subjective appraisal of the situation does. The subjective appraisal of stressors is, in essence, a judgment of person-environment fit. Therefore, when an offer to take an international assignment is extended, candidates are probably unable to anticipate stressors they have not experienced before, unless they have had a prior international assignment. Ignorant of the alien environment to which they are about to be transplanted, executives might also overestimate the effectiveness of coping responses that work at home but may not work abroad. For instance, being outgoing, as it is normally understood in the U.S., may be perceived as being rude in other cultures, thereby provoking rather than preventing social isolation.

Consider the case of an executive with a demonstrated competence in launching start-ups who was selected to head the Asian operations of a U.S. corporation. When considering the transfer to Asia, the executive dismissed the possibility of feeling socially isolated because he considered himself and his family outgoing and friendly, and thought they would have no problems making friends and adjusting. Six months after his arrival in Japan, the executive expressed frustration at his inability to communicate effectively with others and at his feelings of social isolation.

When weighing the pros and cons of an international assignment, the stressors to be encountered are thought to be alleviated by the prospect of career advancement once the executive returns home. Promises of immediate promotion upon return are often the main driver of an executive's decision to accept relocation.

The executive may use these promises to convince a spouse who hesitates to give up local friends, family, and perhaps a good job. However, once the executive starts the international assignment, the management representatives who were involved in selecting the executive may very well move on to other posts or other corporations. Witnessing these departures from afar, the expatriate may feel that the expectations that motivated the transfer are vanishing too. In the absence of a future payoff, the new stressors will be reappraised and may appear more unbearable than when the prospect of a red-carpet return was alive.

The offer to take an international assignment frequently comes from out of the blue. For instance, an executive previously uninterested in living abroad was motivated by a hefty relocation bonus to accept an unexpectedly sudden but nevertheless career-enhancing assignment. This kind of hurried decision may lead to an unrealistic appraisal of both the stressors awaiting abroad and one's cross-cultural skills.

How should executives and their employers cope with such unanticipated circumstances? One of the answers appears to lie in the clarification of expectancies beforehand. Executives who take on international assignments hoping that an immediate promotion will materialize upon return are oblivious to the pace of change in today's business environment, where vertical career paths are no longer the norm. Instead, executives should consider international transfers as an additional growth opportunity in their career development plans.

Rather than delivering hard-to-keep, long-term promises of promotion, employers should clarify expectations and highlight the developmental growth that will result from having completed the international assignment. For example, a U.S. executive who decided to take an assignment in Japan because it fit into his general career plan was not guaranteed a specific promotion upon repatriation. Instead, he was made aware of what his general opportunities would be if he met his goals in Japan.

PRE- AND POST-ARRIVAL TRAINING STAGE

Intercultural training can partly remedy cross-cultural insensitivity, but intercultural competence involves more than a series of country statistics and cultural gimmicks learned in a short, predeparture training session. Making executives aware that they will face different business and social customs is not sufficient, because awareness does not necessarily bring competence in the host culture.

The classic burnout symptoms of emotional exhaustion and a sense of reduced accomplishment of an American expatriate six months after he was put in charge of operations in Taiwan illustrate this point. Because he was unable to obtain collaboration from local executives, he followed the recommendations of his California team. The implementation of such recommendations, however, worsened the situation he had been called to improve. Even though this executive was made aware of such cultural differences as Asians being more deferential and less straightforward in their business dealings than Americans, he had neither the interest nor the patience to participate in extended discussions of family and non-business matters with his new business acquaintances. He decided to cut his losses and gladly accepted his CEO's invitation to repatriate him.

Many corporations are becoming aware of the need to provide continued hands-on training rather than just pre-departure awareness training. An executive's pre-departure evaluation of the stressors experienced abroad may be unrealistic. Without some on-site experience in the culture, executives may overestimate their future ability to cope. In contrast to pre-departure training, post-arrival training gives expatriates a chance to evaluate their stressors after they have encountered them. A good example of this kind of on-site training is provided by the British trade giant Jardin Matheson. The training format is project-based, with participants spending much of their time in their respective business areas. At regular intervals, they are brought together to discuss their experiences under the guidance of facilitators. Cultural differences are addressed when they surface in the context of working together, rather than as part of theoretical discussions regarding why Asians and Westerners behave differently.

Experiential training formats also provide an opportunity to react to cultural stressors and receive feedback about the adequacy of one's coping responses. One of these formats is the cultural assimilator, which employs descriptions of critical incidents involving stressful situations together with possible ways of coping with them. With the help of a facilitator, participants discuss the consequences of their individual responses. The exchange helps reduce feelings of stress, because it reinforces the perception that they hold a reservoir of potentially effective coping responses. Foreigners trained using a Greek assimilator, for instance, felt significantly better adjusted to Greece than untrained individuals.

From the employer's point of view, training is an opportunity to provide the social support that the expatriate executive needs. Social support, however, can either reduce or alleviate the effects of stressors. Pre-departure training sessions, for instance, can significantly reduce stressors by providing basic information about housing, schools, foods, and transportation that may help the executives get by in the first few weeks of their assignments. Pre-departure training, however, is not likely to buffer or alleviate the cultural stressors to be faced by the expatriate executive, because cultural differences are best understood in post-arrival training sessions once they have been experienced. Although identifying the potential sources of social support is a difficult task for executives who are still unfamiliar with their host environment, training can provide the encouragement and motivation to seek the social network and activities that will make the new stressors more bearable.

ARRIVAL STAGE

Understandably, the prospect of an international assignment provokes quite a bit of excitement. However, the executive's arrival in an unfamiliar environment may soon bring almost as much frustration. Many of these frustrating times can be explained by feelings of inadequacy. In fact, the executive's sense of control, which plays a significant role in healthy adjustment, may be dramatically affected by the transfer. Stressors like an excessive workload, which was not perceived as such because of the individual's sense of environmental control, suddenly turn worse because of what appears to be an uncontrollable new environment.

Feeling different, especially feeling that one is subject to differential treatment because of membership in a particular culture, can induce stress above and beyond that resulting from typical stressors such as conflict and ambiguity over perceived responsibilities. If the expatriate executives attribute differential treatment to their membership in a different culture or group, their rejection of the host culture is likely to intensify. Thinking of the environment as beyond one's control induces a sense of helplessness. For example, a U.S. expatriate executive in a Central American nation felt that his written requests for equipment maintenance were ignored because he was a foreigner. Later in his assignment, he learned that such written requests were routinely ignored, and that the way to get the work done was to drop by the maintenance shop or ask a maintenance employee for help at the beginning of the work day.

Social identity theory provides a vehicle to better understand and cope with feelings of cultural rejection. Individuals are likely to experience internal conflict when concurrent identification with two or more social entities is perceived as unacceptable. For instance, a U.S. expatriate in Mexico may feel that being an American and identifying with the Mexican culture are opposite poles of the same continuum and are therefore mutually exclusive. Feelings of frustration early in the international assignment may strengthen identification with the U.S. culture to the detriment of the host culture. When the executive construes his or her identification with the two cultures in this us vs. them manner, devastating psychological consequences may follow.

Expatriate executives who reject the host culture are destined to experience continuous frustration and negative feelings as they are forced to conduct business according to local usage. [In] the tortuous evolution of the internal struggle between executives' identification with the host versus the parent culture[,] [t]he two identifications compete for the same space. Whereas identification with the parent culture dominates in the early phases of the assignment, identification with the host culture will dominate later on. A successful adjustment implies a final identification midway between the host and parent cultures.

Understanding that identification with both cultures is possible is the safest way to prevent acculturative stress. The different degrees of identification with the host and the parent culture can be summarized in four quadrants (Figure [1]). The upper right quadrant represents dual identification, which is indeed possible and least stressful. A U.S. executive on assignment in Japan indicated that his high allegiance to both the parent and the Japanese operation led him to try to bring their interests together rather than choose one over the other whenever he perceived discrepancies in their expectations and goals. Reacculturation, as represented by the lower right quadrant, is significantly more stressful because one's parent culture is neglected rather than incorporated into the expatriate's new identity.

A better understanding of the host's ways should not necessarily be accompanied by a rejection of the parent culture. Executives run the risk of drifting in either direction by identifying too much with one of the cultures while rejecting the other. Rather than absorbing oneself in an internal battle for self-definition, the executive should learn to view identification with the host as compatible with identification with the parent culture.

NOVICE STAGE

At the beginning of their international assignments, expatriates may make the mistake of ignoring culturally critical aspects. Why is it so difficult to make sense of and cope with the new stressors? Executives who feel stressed are likely to search their repertoire of coping responses for adequate ways to confront situations. However, the choice of coping response would be determined by the effectiveness of responses used to cope with similar stressors in the past. Notions of response effectiveness are influenced by prior personal experience and culturally bound notions of response adequacy and likelihood of success. In other words, the choices of coping responses have been shaped throughout the executives' personal and cultural experience. The problem is that

85

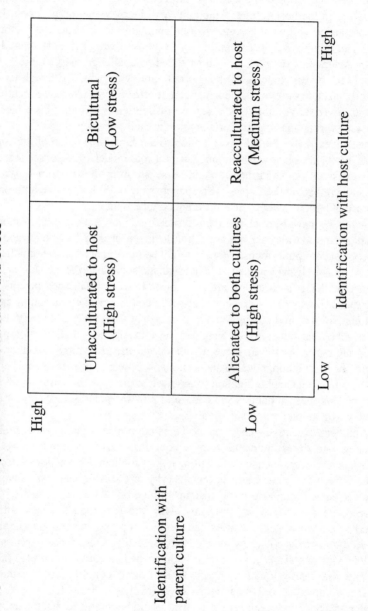

Figure 1 **A Model of Expatriate Cultural Identification and Stress**

Identification with parent culture

High

Unacculturated to host
(High stress)

Bicultural
(Low stress)

Low

Alienated to both cultures
(High stress)

Reacculturated to host
(Medium stress)

Low   Identification with host culture   High

such responses are no longer valid in a different culture characterized by different norms and values. Thus, the experience and knowledge of social norms that the expatriate executive used to select adequate coping responses at home have lost much of their informative value.

Expatriates need to become aware of the consequences that their old repertoire of coping responses has in the host culture. Ambiguity will be overwhelming at first. Uncertainty about what is demanded will be aggravated by one's inability to decipher the meaning of a situation. Blunders can be unwittingly committed by executives who misread culturally different situations. An American expatriate in Beijing dared to challenge his Chinese colleague's idea by saying, "That's a very good point, but I don't agree with you." Although this observation was respectfully made in the eyes of the American, it offended the Chinese executive, thereby straining the business deal. Another U.S. executive inadvertently offended his senior Mexican managers by asking for the junior manager's opinion in their presence.

Expatriate managers should pay attention to the functional value of the coping mechanisms employed by local executives, who make useful role models. Responses that imitate local uses can be successful, but expatriates should be sensitive to the true function of such responses, which can be rather subtle. Expatriate managers should think a bit like anthropologists trying to make sense of human behavior in a different cultural context.

Coping styles have been classified as problem-solving (taking direct action to solve a problem) versus emotion-focused (taking action to make oneself feel better about a situation one cannot control). Emotion-focused coping might be more characteristic of collectivistic societies, such as Asians or Hispanics, than of individualistic societies, like the U.S. or Australia, because members of collectivistic cultures are encouraged to subordinate their personal goals to those of stable groups. However, expatriate executives in collectivistic cultures may erroneously dismiss as mere emotion-focused coping some responses that are, in fact, culturally sensitive attempts to exert control over a situation. Showing deference to superiors, not questioning formal authority in public, aligning oneself with powerful others, and attending family functions provide not mere distraction or consolation, but also unquestionable power to influence one's environment in cultures where individual subordination to a powerful group is the norm to get ahead. Executives who understand these subtleties and choose to play the game stand the best chances of coping effectively with an unfamiliar situation.

An American executive who understood the importance of family and friendship in the Middle East made a point of reminding his business contacts there of his friendship by taking their picture together at every occasion and then mailing copies to them. This action may seem a bit manipulative to some, but we can attest to the sincerity of the American expatriate, who had already internalized some of the values and customs of his Middle Eastern partners.

More straightforward coping styles involving direct attempts to control situations of the kind expected in individualistic countries like the U.S. may be even counterproductive. A study of managerial stress in 24 countries revealed that exercising direct control over one's environment is associated with mental and physical well-being in the U.S., but not in many other countries. Thus, expatriates who insist on employing the kind of direct control responses that have made them successful at home may only add to their stress level abroad.

Expatriates from individualistic societies should be reminded that the lengthy social interactions observed in collectivistic cultures are not a waste of time, but a necessary conduit to doing business. Executives from collectivistic cultures transplanted to an individualistic one may make the opposite mistake. For example, a southern European executive assigned to a financial institution in a U.S. territory was used to having decisions backed by social consensus, which are the norm in the world of European labor relations. He insisted on creating task forces representing every constituent before a decision was made on nearly every human resource issue. The local executives were in turn frustrated by the slow pace of these task forces, which they considered unnecessary.

The employer should facilitate integration into a local or regional network of other expatriates, who can be an extremely valuable source of tangible and informational support in the beginning of the assignment regarding schools, shopping, obtaining a driver's license, and the like. Whereas physically distant friends and family provide simply emotional support and consolation, other expatriates provide the kind of tangible support that directly reduces stressors.

TRANSITIONAL STAGE

Executives' continued frustration may lead to identity crises when they choose to reject the parent culture by fully embracing the host culture, or vice versa.

The ability to form and maintain attachments plays a significant role in executive health in general. For example, keeping in touch with the expatriate community overseas allows executives to maintain their links with the parent culture. These links can be reinforced by Internet access to family, friends, and media from the parent culture. The employer's investment in such electronic communications should provide a significant return in the form of emotional support. Even though this support cannot reduce the stressors faced abroad, it should help alleviate the strain felt by the executive.

Going native by becoming too identified with the host culture may elicit a negative reaction at headquarters, because the executive's allegiance may be questioned. This reversed identification phenomenon may have the same kind of negative impact on the executive's well-being that the rejection of the host culture does, because a significant part of the self is being rejected.

Expatriate executives' conflicting feelings about identification with one culture to the exclusion of the other exacerbate the normally high levels of role conflict characteristic of executive positions. Successful expatriate executives cope with these conflicting roles through constant communication. Lags in communication provoke the kind of unhealthy us vs. them attribution mentioned earlier. An American expatriate in Holland negotiated for a trip to the U.S. every four months so he could bring the points of view of the Dutch operations to headquarters and also take headquarters' perceptions back to Holland. Physical separation and cultural differences made it difficult for the groups to understand each other's actions, and the tone of communications invariably deteriorated after three to four months. The executive's trips back and forth kept negative feelings from getting too far out of hand. In essence, expatriates are forced to cope with conflicting demands imposed by their dual identification with the host and parent organizations by functioning as boundary spanners that walk the line separating the two cultures. The need to maintain this delicate equilibrium among multiple stakeholders calls for skills similar to those possessed by political diplomats. The parent organization should not create additional role conflict for the expatriate with policies that are insensitive to cultural differences.

MASTERY STAGE

By the end of their assignments, successful expatriates have already developed the knowledge of cultural norms that allow them to understand their environment more fully. Over time, expats have also crafted a repertoire of coping responses adapted to their new stressors. Seasoned expatriates are capable of choosing among potential responses with a minimum of uncertainty because they have seen their choices succeed in the past. However, the developmental stages discussed here do not always follow a linear sequence, and making sense of a foreign culture will remain puzzling at times. This ambiguity should not bother effective expatriates, who have already learned to cope with feelings of divided loyalty. They understand that feelings of identification with the host and the parent culture are not mutually exclusive. Instead of being frustrated, they enjoy their boundary-spanning roles of bicultural interpreters who walk between two or more cultures.

Accepting the profound personal transformation that comes with an international assignment is not easy. Fearing identity loss and unable to cope with a myriad of new stressors, nearly 40 percent of American expatriates return early.

However, those who successfully complete their assignments become different people because they have experienced radically different events. Armed with the dual experience of having lived and worked both abroad and at home, expatriates are capable of seeing one culture through the eyes of the other. The ability to understand the cultural paradox that surrounds them and, most importantly, the fact that living with such a paradox does not bother them, represents the pinnacle of expatriate executive transformation. Not surprisingly, the healthiest expatriates are those who possess a strong sense of coherence and control. These individuals have learned to live with and enjoy membership in more than one culture—the essence of being a global executive. A U.S. executive working in Holland described how he had learned over the course of his assignment that being conspicuous was often frowned on in that country. He learned to be more reserved in what he said and to wear more formal clothes even when grocery shopping, so that he would not stand out as much. He and other expatriates explained that these changes did not interfere with their identification with the U.S., which they still genuinely felt.

REPATRIATION STAGE: THE MOST STRESSFUL PART OF THE ASSIGNMENT?

Executives' repatriation can turn into the most stressful time of the entire international assignment. A survey of repatriated executives found that 33 percent were still holding temporary assignments three months after repatriation, more than 75 percent felt that their permanent post upon repatriation was a demotion from their international assignment, and 61 percent felt that they did not have opportunities to put their experience abroad to work. Perhaps the most dramatic finding was that 25 percent of the executives had quit their jobs within three months of repatriation.

An expatriate banking executive working in Mexico returned to the U.S. to find an organization whose top management had radically changed and seemed unwilling to fulfill his previous bosses' promises of upward promotion. After lingering in support roles for about a year, the executive landed a job as vice president of international banking in another financial institution. Similarly, a Mexican executive was disappointed to learn that his employer planned to repatriate him to a relatively low-level management job back home. The executive had been known to share with his coworkers in the U.S. what he thought were his high chances of securing the general manager position in Mexico's operations. Dissatisfied with the repatriation offer, the executive quit his job and started an import-export partnership with one of the business acquaintances he had made during his assignment in the U.S.

Repatriation brings new stressors to executives. Feeling that others do not share their multicultural identification can create a sense of isolation. An expatriate who spent two years implementing a training program around the world characterized his repatriation as a much more traumatic event than going abroad. He complained about feelings of not belonging and about not having anyone to confide in. Repatriated executives may also find themselves making an effort not to stand out by hiding the new interests and behaviors they acquired abroad. An expatriate who headed the Dutch operations of a U.S. firm admitted that he was afraid that others might label his new manners as snobbish.

How can expatriate executives cope with these feelings of lack of fit? In a way, the repatriated executives had already coped with the feeling of not fitting in when abroad. The essence of being bicultural is being proficient in both cultures, and that includes dealing with members of one culture who, unlike the repatriated executive, are unfamiliar with the other. In short, learning to live with and not be bothered by these multiple cultural identities continues to be necessary even when executives return home.

Another dramatic change confronted by repatriated executives is the frequent loss of autonomy, augmented by possibly unrealistic expectations about being promoted upon return. The kind of bold management style that was accepted and even praised abroad may be unwelcome at headquarters. Insisting on this kind of bold style might provoke turf battles with executives from other functional areas. Employers can smooth this difficult transition by providing a sensible repatriation program that takes into account executives' interests and newly developed talents. In this sense, reentry training is at least as important as pre-departure training. Setting expectations about reentry well before it takes place is a fundamental component of this kind of training, which should begin when the expatriate is first selected and continue throughout the assignment prior to the return. Pre-repatriation briefings and interviews with parent organization representatives to inform executives of available opportunities should help clarify how such opportunities fit into executives' post-repatriation career plans. After reentry, follow-up meetings are critical because they provide information regarding how executives are adjusting, whether they need additional support to cope with new stressors, and whether their coping strategies should be revised. When suitable openings are not immediately available at the parent organization, Swedish employers place expatriate executives in a multi-employer pool. Executives from this pool are loaned out to other employers who need them as a short-term solution. . . .

A SURVIVAL GUIDE FOR EXPATRIATE EXECUTIVES AND THEIR EMPLOYERS

Employers need to actively support the adjustment process of their expatriate executives. Cross-cultural competence-oriented training should be provided before, during, and after the assignment. In addition, the parent firm should be sensitive to the delicate balance between the interest of the parent and the host firm that executives need to maintain, listening and working with them to define and achieve common goals.

Expatriation uproots executives from a familiar environment, thereby breaking the balance between the individual and his or her ability to cope with the environment. Feelings of internal conflict are likely to be aggravated by executives' inability to decipher the meaning of culturally different situations. Even though the strain associated with such negative feelings can be partly prevented by competence-oriented intercultural training, individual predisposition and courage to cross cultural boundaries of both a physical and a psychological nature are necessary for healthy expatriate adjustment. Perhaps the most challenging of all transformations is the ability to develop a dual identification.

Otherwise, the conflicting roles experienced by expatriate executives may be exacerbated by a divided sense of social identity that views identification with the host and the parent culture as mutually exclusive. In essence, an international assignment is not only a physical adventure in a more or less remote land, but also a psychological adventure that requires the willingness to revise deeply held beliefs concerning one's own identity.

PART II

VALUES AND ETHICS

SECTION 5. THE MEANING OF WORK AND PERSONAL VALUES

Work consumes a huge portion of most people's lives, yet it takes on varying importance in people's value systems. Work can be a vehicle for personal achievement, it can satisfy status or social needs, or it may be simply a way of making money. People often question the meaning of work and how it fits into their value system at crucial points in their lives. For the wealthy Czech businessman in "Rich Men Tend to Be Strange," that time comes when he falls ill. Until that time, he "loved money and subordinated everything else to it."

"The Retirement Party" records the pain of a woman for whom "that fateful hour strikes" after a forty-year career in which she had "healed herself with work." Now, alone and at a loss over what to do with her time, she wonders about the meaning of her life and where she belongs.

SECTION 6. ETHICS AND CORPORATE SOCIAL RESPONSIBILITY

Ethics and corporate social responsibility are the backbone of sound business practices. A number of fundamental principles are shared across cultures, such as the importance of keeping one's word. It is clear to virtually everyone when such universal principles are violated. The challenge arises for people working in cross-cultural settings when local customs and practices are at odds with those from one's own culture. Deciding what is an ethical practice and what constitutes good corporate social responsibility becomes more complicated.

The questionable business practices of an American-educated Japanese expatriate manager depicted in the story "In Los Angeles" are certainly not due to a lack of understanding of American culture: he is well aware that the United States is a country in which "survival depends on professionalism." His behavior is offensive to both his American business associates as well as his Japanese subordinate, on whom he tries to pin the blame for his wrongdoings.

Los Angeles is also the setting for an incident of unethical behavior by an exploitive and greedy American lawyer in "Payback (Dirty for Dirty)." After two years of the lawyer's inaction in helping him obtain legal immigration status, an angry Mexican construction worker storms into the lawyer's office and demands his $1,000 deposit back. Yet, "even though he himself felt angry and wronged by the crafty lawyer, a man had to behave according to courtesy."

"A Taste of Success" depicts corruption in a factory setting. A worker decides to steal perfume from his factory in Egypt, following the example of another worker who says, "There is plenty of loot for everyone. The little guys get some and the big ones don't care." Yet, all does not feel right to the worker, who feels "a bitterness he had never tasted before."

SECTION 7. MANAGERIAL INSIGHTS

"Navigating the Hostile Maze: A Framework for Russian Entrepreneurship" describes character-istics of entrepreneurs and discusses how the hostile economic and cultural environment are ob-stacles for instilling an entrepreneurial mindset and behavior. This reading can be useful for understanding the stories "Rich Men Tend to Be Strange" and "The Retirement Party," which depict Czechs and Russians working within the centrally planned economy under the communist regime. During that era, following rules and regulations and meeting plans set by central authori-ties were the hallmark of a good manager, while ambition and initiative were disparaged. To become successful in these emerging market-oriented economies now requires a vastly different set of traits.

"Settling Cross-Cultural Disagreements Begins with 'Where' Not 'How'" underscores the finding that people from different cultures can have different preferences for conflict-resolution strategies. While Japanese managers prefer to resolve conflict by deferring to status or power, German managers prefer following regulations, and Americans prefer integrating interests of all parties to maximize personal gain.

"Japanese and American Negotiators: Overcoming Cultural Barriers to Understanding" is a com-panion piece for "In Los Angeles." The article explores ways for managers in the American compa-nies and those in the Japanese trading company to come to mutually satisfactory agreements.

"Responsibility: The New Business Imperative" presents a model of the stakeholder, societal, and environmental pressures that shape the development of total responsibility management sys-tems in corporations. Adopting the principles of total responsibility management is viewed as a way for firms to be competitive and profitable. The reading can be used to analyze the business practices exhibited in the stories in the section on ethics and corporate social responsibility.

Section 5

—————— The Meaning of Work and Personal Values ——————

5.1   RICH MEN TEND TO BE STRANGE
Ivan Klíma

There are men who love women, there are men who love alcohol, nature or sport, there are men who love children or work, and there are men who love money. It is possible, of course, for a man to love more than one of these, but he will always give one priority over the rest. If he is sufficiently ambitious he can hope to achieve the thing he yearns for most.

Alois Burda loved money and subordinated everything else to it. Under the old regime he was the manager of a car mart, under the new one he opened one of his own. Under the old regime he had skillfully negotiated with the few cars he had for sale and soon found a way of maximizing bribes. After the revolution, his above-board commission gave him about the same income as he had enjoyed previously. Alois Burda was therefore a rich man and as early as the 1970s had built himself a family home with a living area (in accordance with the legislation then in force) of less than 120 square metres. In reality it was three times the size. The house contained a gymnasium, a covered swimming pool and three garages, and alongside it stood a tennis court, although he himself didn't play tennis. He had one secret bank account in Switzerland, and since the Swiss banks paid miserable interest rates, he had another in Germany. He had only been divorced once because he discovered that divorce could be a rather expensive business. With his first wife he had two sons, with his second, a daughter. He rarely saw his sons. Since they had grown up they didn't meet more than once a year. He soon grew tired of his second wife too, though she took fairly good care of the home and didn't bother him too much. Nor did she concern herself with how he spent his free time. She was fond of sports and went skiing and horse-riding, played tennis and golf and was a good swimmer, none of which interested him in the least. From time to time he would take a mistress, although he would seldom feel anything for her and expected nothing in return.

Occasionally he would ask his daughter for news from school, but he would forget her reply by the next morning and he was never entirely sure which class she was in. Then she too left school and got married. As a wedding present he gave her a new car that cost more than half a million crowns. The gift took her by surprise and she was almost ready to believe it was given with love, although it was more likely to salve his conscience or just a momentary whim. Besides, a sum like that meant nothing to Burda.

He knew a lot of people, since he had clients everywhere, but he had no real friends. At best he had a few cronies with whom he would go for a drink from time to time or dream up business deals.

As his sixtieth birthday approached, he suddenly started to suffer from exhaustion, lost his appetite and started losing weight. He put it down to his hectic lifestyle but his wife noticed the

From *Lovers for a Day* [Milenci na jeden den], trans. Gerald Turner (New York: Grove Press, 1999), 203–216. Translation copyright © 1999 by Gerald Turner. Reprinted with permission of Grove Atlantic.

transformation in him and told him to go to the doctor. He ignored his wife's advice on principle, and was afraid the doctor would discover that there was something seriously wrong. He decided he would take things more easily and even take a non-business trip abroad. He also visited a well-known healer who mixed him a special herbal tea and recommended that he eat pumpkin seeds every day. But none of it did any good. Burda started to suffer from stomach pains and would wake up in the night soaked in perspiration, thirsty and in the grip of a strange anxiety.

Finally, he decided to see a doctor who was one of his oldest clients and had treated his first wife. The doctor tried to give the impression that everything was in order and chatted for a while about the latest Honda.

"Is it serious?" the car dealer asked him.

"Do you want me to be totally frank?"

The car dealer hesitated, and then nodded.

"You need an operation without delay," the doctor said.

"And then?"

"And then we'll see."

"Aha," Burda realized, "it's life or death, then?"

"None of us is here for ever," the doctor said, "but we must never give up hope. When they open you up, we'll know more."

The car dealer knew, of course, that when his number came up that would be it, but he was shocked none the less. After all, he still had almost ten years to go before he attained the average life span for Czech men. He had always believed that death came most frequently in the form of a road accident. And he was an excellent driver.

"There are increasingly effective drugs around," the doctor added, "so don't give up hope."

"As far as drugs are concerned, I can afford anything, however much it costs."

"I know that," said the doctor, "but it's not a question of money."

"What is it a question of, then?"

The doctor shrugged. "Your resistance. The will of God, fate, or whatever you want to call it."

The operation was arranged for the following week. In the meantime he would have to undergo all the necessary tests.

When Burda came home and his wife asked what the doctor had discovered, he answered laconically, "I'm going to die. " Then he went to his room, sat down in an armchair and pondered on the strange fact that soon he might not be here any more. Human beings had always struck him as being like machines: machines and human beings wore out with use, but a machine could be kept going more or less indefinitely by replacing its parts. But how was it with a human being? It seemed so cruel and unjust that a dead machine could be virtually eternal, whereas human components were mostly non-renewable and people were therefore condemned to die before their time. Then he started to worry over what he would do about his property and with his secret bank accounts. When he died everything he owned would go to his wife and children. This seemed to him unjust because none of them had contributed towards the family income. And besides he had given his daughter a car not long ago—and his sons didn't want to know him. It was true that his wife took care of him, but he regularly gave her money for that and paid for her to go skiing in the Alps every winter and every spring. She was bound to have lovers all over the place, in fact he knew about one for sure. He had happened to come upon a letter from the man in his wife's handbag when he was looking for a bill or something. So why, in addition to all the property and money of his that she would inherit, should his wife get money that she didn't even know existed, just because he had married her?

Then he pondered on the doctor's words about hope and the will of God. To rely on the will of

God was as pointless as trusting in fate. The will of God was just something to pacify the weak and the poor, whereas fate did what it was bribed to do. So far he had successfully bribed it and now he shied from the thought of drawing a total blank.

That same afternoon, he climbed into his Mercedes, taking with him his passport and a suitcase, and set off for the border. There was only a hundred thousand francs in his Swiss account, but more in his German one. To the dismay of the teller he asked for it in cash. He returned with the money the next evening and hid the bank notes in a little safe to which he alone had the combination. The following day he went for his first test.

When he was about to go into hospital he was faced with the problem of what to do with the money. The doctor had warned him that he might be in for several weeks. That he might never leave was not mentioned, but the car dealer was all too aware that this possibility could not be ruled out. In fact he might never leave the operating theatre alive. He didn't feel like leaving the money at home, but he could hardly take it to the hospital. Where could he hide it? What would he do with it while he was lying unconscious on the operating table?

Eventually he made up his mind and divided up the hundred-thousand wads into smaller bundles which he stuffed into some old felt slippers and hid them with a pair of rolled socks. Then in his wife's presence he packed the slippers into a box and sealed it with sticking tape, asking her to bring it to the hospital along with a few other odds and ends, such as ordinary slippers, his toilet bag, two issues of a motoring magazine and his wallet with a few hundred crowns as soon as he asked for them.

He put aside a few thousand marks, sealing them in an envelope for the surgeon. However, the latter made some vague excuse about being superstitious and not wanting to hear about money before the operation, and refused to take the envelope from him.

When they opened Burda up on the operating table they discovered that the cancer had not only taken possession of his pancreas, it had also invaded other organs. A radical operation looked so hopeless that they simply sewed him back up again. After two days on the intensive care ward, he was transferred to ward eight which he shared with two other patients. The man to his left was an old blabbermouth from the country who spent most of his time telling trivial stories about his life back home and worrying over the fate of the smallholding that he had left his wife to look after on her own. In the bed to his right was an old man who said nothing and was most likely dying. Now and then, whether awake or asleep, he would produce strange, unintelligible animal-like screeches. These would disturb the car dealer even more than the smallholder's stories, which he simply ignored.

The doctors prescribed a great many drugs and once a day a nurse would bring a stand over to his bedside and hang a bottle from it. She would then insert a needle into one of his veins and he could watch the blood or some colorless liquid flow down the transparent tube and into his body. In spite of it, he felt more and more wretched with each passing day.

His wife brought him all the things he had asked for, adding a bunch of Gerbera and a jar of stewed fruit.

Flowers didn't interest him and he had lost all appetite for food. When his wife left, he opened the box with the slippers, took out the socks and checked that the wads of bank notes were there. He stuffed the socks back in, closed the box and hid it in his bedside table. He was still able to walk, but only to shuffle over to the window or into the corridor before returning to his metal bed. These days he didn't even like leaving the ward. His own death wasn't something he thought about as such, but he couldn't help noticing that his strength was steadily waning. Eventually he would have no strength left at all and he would close his eyes and be incapable of thinking or speaking, let alone making decisions. What was he going to do with that money?

His wife visited him twice a week and sometimes his married daughter would look in as well. Once his elder son came. They would each bring something he had no use for and he would put it away in his bedside table without interest, and it would either stay there or he would take it and throw it in the waste bin as soon as they had gone.

There were several nurses on the ward. Apart from one older woman, they were hardly more than schoolgirls. They all seemed alike to him and he could only tell them apart by the color of their hair. They treated him with professional kindness and sometimes would try to joke with him or cheer him up. Before sticking the needle into his vein they would apologize that it was going to hurt a little bit. But then a new nurse appeared—probably just back from leave. She seemed no older than the others, but he was immediately struck by her voice, which reminded him of the long-lost and almost forgotten voice of his mother. The nurse's name was Věra. He noticed that whenever she came over to him to do some routine job she would always find something to say. And to his surprise, it wasn't just the usual words of comfort, but something about the world outside; about the nice warm day, the jasmine in bloom or the strawberries already ripening on her balcony. He would listen to her, often unaware of what she was actually saying, conscious merely of the color of her voice and its soothing quality.

One day when he was feeling slightly better after a blood transfusion, he tentatively asked her if she would come and sit by him.

"But Mr. Burda,' she said in astonishment, "what would Matron say if she caught me slacking?' None the less she brought a chair and sat down beside him, taking his hand, punctured with so many injections, and stroking the back of it.

"What sort of a life do you have, nurse?' he asked.

"What sort of a life?' she laughed. "Average, I suppose.'

"Do you live with your parents?'

She nodded. She told him she had a little room in a block of flats. That the room contained just a bed, a chair, a bookshelf, and a bamboo stand with pots of flowers: a passion-flower, a fuchsia and a Crown of Thorns. She talked to him for a long time about flowers. Flowers had never interested him and their names evoked neither colors nor shapes, but he was conscious of the tenderness in the woman's voice and the gentle touch of her fingers on the back of his hand. He noticed that her eyes were dark brown even though she had naturally fair hair. She promised to bring him some of the flowers she grew on her balcony and then stood up and left.

The next day she really did bring him a lily and once again she came and sat by him.

He asked her if there was anything important that she lacked.

She didn't understand the meaning of his question.

So he asked her if she had a car.

"A car?' She laughed at the question.

"And would you like one? '

"You used to sell them, didn't you?" she recalled. Then she said she had never thought of having one. She lived with her mother and they scarcely had enough money to buy the occasional bag of tomatoes. Last year she had planted a few tomato plants on the balcony but they had been attacked by mould and there had been nothing to harvest. She asked him if he liked tomatoes. She asked him the way he used to ask people if they liked caviar or whether they preferred oysters. He replied that he liked them, although in fact he couldn't recall whether he had ever enjoyed them.

He was about to ask her if she found her life depressing, but at that moment he had a sudden spasm of pain and the nurse ran off to find a doctor who gave him an injection that left him groggy.

When he began to come round that night, he realized for the first time, with absolute urgency, that he was likely to die in the next few days. He switched on the light above his bed, leaned over and took the box of slippers out of his bedside table. Underneath the rolled socks lay a fortune that could buy whole wagonloads of tomatoes.

He tidied it all away again and returned the box to the bedside table; the wealth that usually imbued him with a sense of satisfaction was suddenly becoming a burden.

Should he give it to some charity? Or to the hospital? Give it to the doctors who weren't even capable of helping him? Or to his wife, so she could afford even more demanding lovers and go off skiing somewhere in the Rocky Mountains?

Then suddenly he could see the face of the nurse and hear the sound of her voice that so resembled his mother's. He wondered whether she would be on duty the next day and realized that he hoped she would.

She did come the next day and she brought him a tomato. It was large and firm and the color of fresh blood. He thanked her. He bit into it and chewed the mouthful for a long time, but was unable to swallow it for fear of vomiting.

The nurse brought a stand over to his bed, attached a bottle and announced: "We're going to have to feed you up a bit, Mr. Burda. You're getting too weak."

He nodded.

"Does your family visit you?" the nurse asked.

He ought to reply that he had no family, just a wife and three children, but instead he answered that it was a long time since anyone had visited him.

"They'll come soon," the nurse said. "That'll cheer you up."

He closed his eyes.

She touched his forehead with her fingers. "It's flowing now," she said. "God can work miracles and cure the sick as well as forgive the sinner. And He welcomes everyone with love."

"Why?" he asked, and meant why was she telling him this, but she replied, "Because God is love itself."

In spite of the strong tablets they were giving him, he could not get off to sleep that night. He was thinking about the strange fact that the world would continue, that the sun would still go on rising, that cars would go on running, that they would go on dreaming up new types of car, that they would continue selling them in the showrooms that his wife would no doubt get rid of, that new motorways and overpasses would be built, that the Petřín tunnel would be opened, but he would never hear about any of them. That realization was like an icy hand gripping him by the throat. He tried to fight it, to find someone to help him but he had no one to turn to. Then the face of the nurse who had sat by his bed appeared to him, saying that God can welcome anyone with love. God could do it, though he himself had never been able to. That was if God existed. If He did, then at least a little bit of love would reign on earth. He tried to remember those he had ever loved or who had ever loved him. But apart from his mother, who had been dead for thirty years, he couldn't think of anyone. Tomorrow he would ask the nurse where she had come by her belief in God, or in love, at least. Finally he fell asleep. When he woke up in the middle of the night, an absurd idea struck him: he would give the money to the nurse. For telling him those things about God and love. For stroking his forehead even though she knew he was going to die. She was aware of it just as all the others were, but they didn't stroke his forehead.

Then he tried to imagine how she would respond to unexpected wealth. Would she accept it? In his experience, people never refused money. Outwardly they hesitated, but eventually they succumbed. He couldn't just stuff several million into her pocket, though; he would have to ask her to call a notary. He would dictate his will and leave the money to her. What would she do with it?

The following day, instead of questioning her about her beliefs, he asked her whether she lived only with her mother, or if she was going out with someone.

She stared in surprise, but she answered him. Her boyfriend's name was Martin and he was a violinist. They had been at a concert together the previous evening. It had been a performance of Beethoven's D Minor concerto. Did he know it? Did he like it?

He wasn't familiar with Beethoven, even though he must have heard the name some time. He had never had any time for music. There was always music playing in the showrooms, but it was pop music.

She went on to tell him that she and Martin were getting married in the autumn. "Will you come to our wedding?" she asked.

"If you invite me."

The next day nurse Věra was off duty, so he had a chance to reflect on whether he had thought things through clearly, and whether his decision hadn't been over-hasty. What if he got better? What if God were to perform a miracle or one of the medicines they were injecting into him restored his strength? Why else would the nurse have invited him to her wedding? She would hardly have been joking with a dying man.

Besides, the sum was disproportionately large, and there was the risk that his gift might make them suspect her of malpractice. But he could make her a gift of some of the money—at least that bundle of 1000-franc notes.

The next day his condition deteriorated but he was fully conscious of nurse Věra coming to him and putting some fresh flowers into a bottle of water, and then bringing over the stand and inserting a needle into his left leg.

"I'll make it up to you," he said in an undertone.

"The way to make it up to me is by getting better," she said. Then she opened the window and said, "Can you smell it? The lime trees are in blossom already."

He could smell nothing. He just felt an enormous weariness. He ought to tell her to call the notary, but at that moment it occurred to him that the whole idea was ridiculous: he should simply put a few bank notes into the pocket of her overall. Even that would be a fortune as far as she was concerned.

The nurse stroked his forehead and went out of the room.

The next night Alois Burda died. Nurse Věra happened to be on duty and a few seconds before he took his last breath she came and sat near him and held his hand. By then it was unlikely that he even noticed.

Afterwards the nurse was given the job of removing the possessions from the dead man's bedside table and making a precise list of everything. She did so. The list had eighteen items; number eleven read: *One pair of felt slippers with one pair of socks inside.* The nurse was surprised at how heavy the slippers were and it occurred to her to take out the socks, list them separately and look inside the slippers, but she didn't as it would mean her adding another item to the list, and besides it seemed pointless to waste time on things that no one was likely to use any more.

When Burda's wife came to the hospital for the death certificate, they handed her a bag of the deceased's property and a list of its contents. His wife ran her eye down the list of things. In the last few years she had grown sick of her husband and the few pathetic items he had left behind sickened her even more. They handed her his wallet and the three hundred crowns. She took the bag and put it in the boot of her car. When she was driving away from the hospital she noticed an illegal rubbish tip. She pulled up in front of it and took a careful look around her. Then she opened the boot and tossed the bag onto the tip.

That evening nurse Věra had a date with her violinist. "That Burda on ward eight went to the mortuary the night before last," she announced. "He was supposed to be horribly rich—one of the richest men in Prague."

"And did he give you anything?"

"No," she said, "he only had three hundred crowns in his wallet."

"Rich men tend to be strange," he said. "Who do you think he'll leave it all to?"

"Goodness knows," she said. "I don't think he had anyone. He had no one to come and hold his hand, not even for those last few moments."

5.2   THE RETIREMENT PARTY*
Natalia Baranskaya

The ceremony was taking place in the auditorium. The narrow auditorium was almost empty. Some twenty people sat in the first rows, and three on stage. The stage was separated from the auditorium by an arch of three red calico curtains. White diamond patterns wound around them. Under the arch was a table with a plush tablecloth, a carafe and a pale pink hydrangea in a flowerpot. At the table sat a broad-shouldered man with an affable face—the director—and a heavy young woman in a bright green jumper—the union representative.

Nearby, in an old office armchair, sat a thin homely woman with deep-sunken eyes and a halo of permanent over her bulbous forehead. She sat erect, unmoving; only her thin hands twisted and untwisted a handkerchief.

They were celebrating Anna Vasilevna Kosova's retirement. The entire bookkeeping staff was assembled, as well as several of the oldest workers in the company—everyone who knew her. She was mild-mannered, taciturn, and had sat for almost twenty years hunched over the records, abacus and accounts on her desk. There weren't many who knew her.

The union representative spoke first. She said that comrade Kosova was one of the most senior workers in the company, always distinguished for her diligence, never late, never needed to be disciplined, in fact had received two commendations, and that it was from workers like her that one could learn a conscientious attitude towards work.

"You are leaving for a deserved rest, comrade Kosova," she concluded. "And we hope it goes well for you. The administration and the union extend their official gratitude for your long years of honest service, and your comrades tender you this precious gift." And she lifted a sheet of paper covering six teacups painted in yellow and violet.

There was scattered clapping. Anna Vasilevna raised her handkerchief to her lips and began to blink, suppressing the tears she had long been on the brink of.

The director raised a pudgy hand with a wedding ring on it. He asked for attention. He rose, and leaning on the table, spoke quietly, in a mild voice:

"Dear comrade Kosova, today we are sending you off to a deserved rest, as was rightly said. You have been spoken of as a good worker. I would like to add some words about you as a person." He paused a moment and continued: "You worked in the company twenty years—more precisely twenty-one years and eight months. I came here, as you know, two years ago. In the years that you have worked as an accountant, there have been four directors. What does that speak of, comrades? It speaks of the enviable human quality of Anna . . ." ("Vasilevna," the union representative prompted), "Yes, Anna Vasilevna, of her constancy."

He looked around the auditorium at the attentive faces and continued:

"Believe me, it's hard to part with such a person, comrades, but in each of our lives, as they say, that fateful hour strikes. We aren't saying farewell, Anna Vasilevna, we're saying 'till we meet again.' We hope to still work with you from time to time, at our mutual need."

From *Russia According to Women*, ed. Marina Ledkovsky (Tenafly, NJ: Hermitage Publishers, 1991), 67–77. Reprinted with permission. *Translated by Alan Shaw.

He concluded to loud, friendly applause. Anna Vasilevna's lips trembled, and for a long time she pressed the handkerchief to her mouth. "How well they speak, and how well they all think of me," she thought, flustered. "I wish they'd finish, I can't take any more."

But the chief accountant asked to say a few words. He mounted the stage with difficulty, drew a handkerchief from his pocket, wiped his glasses, started to put them in his pocket, then put them on again over his large nose and said in his sad, soft voice:

"My esteemed Anna Vasilevna, we worked many, many years together. You are a very good worker. And a very, very good comrade. . . ." He stopped, then added very softly: "excuse me, please," and returned to his seat.

Anna Vasilevna looked at him in alarm. But then a short-legged red-haired girl with a flushed, freckled face and carrot-colored curly hair jumped up on stage, shook her head, shot the director a quick look and shouted gaily to the auditorium:

"Our union committee invites you all to tea, on its own behalf . . . and Aunt Annie's, of course, so we ask you to come to the Accounting Office, all of you. . . ." She looked at the director again, giggled, jumped down wiggling her thighs, and finished on the run: "The samovar won't boil, the teapot's tee'd out—bring the new cups, we don't have enough!"

Everyone got up, started to talk all at once, crowded around Anna Vasilevna and in a decorous procession with flowered cups and saucers in hand filed out of the auditorium.

The director excused himself on the way—business, he said—and went home. "That redhead is hot," he thought, grinning.

Tea didn't last long. The women glanced at the clock and at their bags filled with things they'd bought during dinner break. Anna Vasilevna wanted to go home too. She was tired and hot in her woolen off-duty dress. They hurriedly rinsed out cups, packed the new ones in the cake box, took "Bologna" coats from the coatrack. They went outside together, then began to say goodbye. Some went left, others straight across to the streetcar stop. Anna Vasilevna went right.

Her friend Marya Petrovna went with her. They had known each other a long time. They worked in a sewing shop during the war, sewing quilted jackets for the army. They had both been soldiers. And in the same year they both lost their husbands. Panteleeva was left with two children, Kosova with one. The former had grandchildren now, the latter had nobody.

"Don't get upset, Nyura," said Marya Petrovna, looking into her friend's sunken eyes. "Think of your health."

"What good is it to anyone, my health," Anna Vasilevna replied.

"What can you do, it's all in God's hands."

Anna Vasilevna only sighed in reply. She didn't believe in God. In that terrible year when both had been felled by grief, Marya Petrovna found consolation in the church. Anna Vasilevna didn't. She healed herself with work.

She loved her uncomplicated profession. She never talked about it. What was there to talk about? It was funny. She simply never complained, never moaned like the others, never cursed her humble lot. She worked eagerly, adroitly, efficiently. No one could more quickly discover an error, find some damned kopeck that everyone was in a fever about at the end of the quarter. And everybody constantly came to her with requests—to check, to finish, to help. She never refused. She worked, and that was it.

She worked until that year, that month, when she was fifty-eight years old. And today they had given her a retirement party, and she was going home for the last time. How did all this happen?

This is how it was. First Masha Panteleeva said, as she had heard secretly from the typist, that they wanted to retire her, that is, Kosova. Masha didn't know if it was true. The typist didn't say where she got this information. They talked about it, and calmed down a bit: people would blather about anything. Still, from that day on, something came over Anna Vasilevna—she felt tight inside and couldn't breathe easily. When the union representative Antonina Rozhnova called her, she thought: "Well, so it's true," and her heart started to beat, and her throat was tight.

Rozhnova asked Anna Vasilevna how many years she had worked in the company, then inquired about her length of service as a whole. Anna Vasilevna began to count and counted almost forty years, maybe even forty-one. She was still a girl when she started working. The conversation proceeded in a casual way, as if Rozhnova was simply interested in Anna Vasilevna as a co-worker. Then all at once Antonina said:

"Comrade Kosova, the administration suggested that I clarify some questions concerning you, since there is a feeling that you ought to be recommended for retirement."

"What, Tonya, do I work any worse than the young ones? As far as I know no one's complained about me."

"No one's suggesting that you work any worse. You're just a lot older. They haven't reached retirement age, and you have."

"Then why do I have to leave, if I don't work any worse than they do, explain to me, Tonya?"

"Well what in the world do you want me to say?" Rozhnova flared up. "I didn't say you were worse. We aren't even comparing at all whether you work better or worse. We're talking about something else entirely. You've worked forty years, while the others, the younger ones, haven't yet. So give them a chance to work too."

In the face of this argument, as irresistible as a gravestone, Anna Vasilevna was silent. What could she say in reply to it? Antonina was probably right. Still, she expressed her desire to speak with the chief accountant—he understood her work.

"Don't make him go against regulations, Kosova. You can see the man can barely walk, he's clutching at his heart. Of course it's your right to talk to the administration. By the way, the director said: 'If she—meaning you—doesn't want to submit her request, bring her to me.' You may not agree with him, you may even have a grievance with him, but personally I wouldn't advise raising a ruckus."

Anna Vasilevna went back to her desk in accounting, wrote a request and took it right away to personnel. That was two weeks ago.

Three went to the left—the chief accountant Yakov Moiseevich Zuskin, the accountant Lyudmila Kharitonova and the bookkeeper Lelka Morkovkina. Lyudmila, calm and thorough, never hurried, while the redhead Lelka, or Carrot-top Lelka, was always in a rush, always late, always running. Now it was costing her a great effort to walk along with her companions. But today was a special day, and she felt sorry for Yakov Moiseevich: the old man was thoroughly out of sorts, that was a fact. Lelka listened out of one ear to his complaint and Kharitonova's sympathetic yeses, while she avidly thought over her own affairs.

"It'll be fine if Yurka has already run after Alka in the garden. But what if Yurka forgot about it playing? Which would be better—to look around the courtyards for Yurka or to run after Alka myself? I can make dinner in a jiffy: fry some chops, boil some noodles—it'll only take a minute. Benjamin isn't playing tonight, I think. Or maybe he is? Is he or isn't he? I forget . . . my memory's going! The fact is, I won't have time to iron him a white shirt. It's awful, the way he sweats at work! And they keep on saying: 'Some job—blowing a trumpet!' They ought to try blowing one themselves. . . . There'll be hell to pay if I don't have a shirt ready!"

Lelka's husband tormented her with two passions—clean shirts and jealousy. She cursed the first and welcomed the second. Jealousy wafted her an air of romance over the horror of everyday life. Lelka remembered the director. She would have to tell Benny about his syrupy glance . . . and how afterwards . . . when they were serving tea, the director put his hand on the back of her chair and whispered to her: "Pour me some tea—it's sweeter from your hands . . ." No, not that. "In your hands tea turns into wine. . . ." Or maybe: "Your tea makes me drunk when I look at you." Aha, that was it!

Finally, her corner! Still, on parting she tried to comfort Yakov Moiseevich:

"It won't help for you to carry on about Anna Vasilevna like someone who's died. It's not even good. A person has retired . . . why, that's happiness! If right now I was given fifty rubles and told: 'You're free, comrade Morkovkina,' why, I'd. . . ."

"Don't talk nonsense," Lyudmila interrupted her, "We'd do better to arrange with the whole accounting office to go visit her next week."

"Sure," Lelka said cheerfully. "See you later."

Soon Kharitonova turned off as well. Yakov Moiseevich went on. As soon as he was alone, his thoughts returned to that day in May.

Right after the May holidays the director of the company Shavrov called Yakov Moiseevich in.

"Good day, Yakov Moiseevich," the director greeted him, extending his hand and pushing a silver cigarette case towards him. "Have a smoke!"

"Thank you, Pavel Romanovich, I don't smoke," answered Yakov Moiseevich, touching two fingers to the left side of his chest, which meant, his heart wouldn't allow it.

"I wanted to ask you, Yakov Moiseevich, are there any employees of retirement age in the accounting office? Naturally I don't mean you." The director smiled; he was joking. The company couldn't do without Yakov Moiseevich; the director himself called him "the high-flying accountant."

"So what about the old ladies in your harem, eh?"

Yakov Moiseevich averted his eyes. He didn't want to talk about that. He tried to joke his way out of it.

"They're all young in my harem, the old ones are even younger than the young ones," he said despondently.

But the director was no longer disposed to joke. Glancing at some sheet of paper, he got down to business:

"You have a bookkeeper named Kosova, born in 1907. I think it's time she had a rest. What's her salary, seventy? Well, she'll lose a little, fifteen or eighteen rubles."

"She's a good worker," the chief accountant rejoined.

"We don't have any other kind, if I know you. And if we do, let's get rid of them. Is there someone in particular we could do without?"

Yakov Moiseevich was silent.

"Well, we'll just have to grin and bear it," the director said soothingly. "As far as I can see, Kosova is the most suitable candidate. It's time she had a rest! She can bake pies for her old man, look after her grandchildren."

"Her husband died in the war."

"And how long ago was that! The war has been over for twenty years. She must have found another one ages ago."

"She doesn't have anybody. Neither children nor grandchildren. And she's a good worker, an excellent worker."

"Please, Yakov Moiseevich, don't let's quarrel." Shavrov began to drum his fingers on the table. Everyone in the company knew this sign of oncoming irritation. "How does the song go? 'Our young will always have a way, our old are honored everywhere.' We have to break in new staff."

Yakov Moiseevich asked if the director had a specific candidate in mind.

"We'll see, we'll see," Shavrov answered distractedly, leafing through the papers in his folder. "So, are we agreed?"

"I don't want to hurt a good person," Yakov Moiseevich sighed.

"Don't hurt her, then; throw her the finest party, give her a nice gift. . . ." The director took out a zippered purse and rustled some bills. "Here," he said, taking a three-ruble note. "No wait, I have change." And he took a silver ruble out from under the bills. "And see that you don't skimp, either."

"Not now," Yakov Moiseevich objected. "Let the union representative take care of that."

"All right, all right," the director agreed. "Things are agreed with you, for the rest you aren't needed. We'll talk to Kosova without you as well." And he dialed the number of the union representative.

"Hello? Rozhnova? This is Shavrov. Listen Tonya, do you know Kosova from accounting? She was born in 1907. How do you find her? Slow? You hear, Yakov Moiseevich, your Kosova is slow. Okay, okay, stop by my office, Rozhnova, we're having a conference. In ten minutes or so. That's all."

Yakov Moiseevich rose. He wanted terribly to put his hand on his chest; his heart ached. But he restrained himself.

"Yes, Yakov Moiseevich, I've read your request. I'll talk it over with Rozhnova shortly. I want to accommodate you, but we can't forget about business either, of course."

This was a request for additional leave without pay. Yakov Moiseevich had long been waiting for a decision.

"Oh, how unpleasant, how bad," thought the chief accountant, descending the steps. "I've gotten old, really old."

And on his way he passed Rozhnova, smoothing her jumper, which was rising along her stout flanks.

Anna Vasilevna arrived home, sat down on a chair and sat for a long time without moving or thinking of anything. Afterwards she felt like having potatoes with green onion. She hadn't eaten since morning. She hadn't even been able to eat the cake—her stomach was too upset.

Anna Vasilevna took off her good dress, put on a robe and went into the kitchen. It was empty there. She was overjoyed: she didn't feel like talking. Anna Vasilevna ate, drank tea and washed the dishes. She thought about darning socks or reading a newspaper, but she was so sleepy that she barely had the energy to make the bed.

She lay down on her old bed with the sagging springs, put out the light, settled herself more comfortably on her right side and, sweetly sighing, closed her eyes. Through her head ran all sorts of trivialities, as always before sleep. Whether Carrot-top Lelka wouldn't forget to redo the account for payment of the trimmings . . . a burning smell was coming from the kitchen; that fat woman was always smoking up the apartment . . . where was her handkerchief? It wasn't in her bag—she must have lost it, too bad. . . . It would be interesting to know if Benjamin would be jealous tonight because Lelka was late. She'd tell about it tomorrow—a whole romance. . . .

But now it hit her like an electric shock—she wouldn't see Lelka tomorrow! She wouldn't be going to work tomorrow!

Anna Vasilevna tossed over on her back so that the springs nearly threw her on the floor. Anxieties—large and small—welled up in her. How would she live now? What would she do? How would she kill the time?

She hadn't mended her coat last year, she had gone on vacation. Now the coat was probably beyond her strength. If she set aside so much for food each day. . . and Anna Vasilevna began to think about her new budget. Then she was sorry that she hadn't saved money, she had spent it all. True, she never did have much to save. If earlier, when she had lived with her husband . . . but had they lived together long?

She had married late. She wouldn't have married at all, had she not met a man as modest, quiet and unsettled as herself. His first wife was disappointed in him because he didn't earn a good living, divorced him, sued him successfully for half a room, and afterwards drove him out altogether. He let a corner from the old woman in this very apartment. Anya lived then with her mother in the large room. At that time her room was only a piece out of the large one. The window was even somewhere in the corner.

She looked out the window—the sky was already getting light. She told herself sternly: "Better sleep, it's almost morning." But sleep didn't come.

In the predawn twilight Anna Vasilevna looked around at her room, as if she was seeing it for the first time. It was narrow and crooked. It was wider at the head, narrower at the feet. . . . "What is it, it's like a grave, really, it is." She was frightened. It seemed like the walls were pressing in, the ceiling was lowering onto her chest. It was hard to breathe. And there on a poplar under the window a crow woke up and cawed three times in a rusty voice.

"That's a bad omen, a very bad omen," she thought miserably. She felt on the brink of tears again. But her thoughts again kept her from crying. She remembered the last wearisome days.

In the accounting office they had talked a lot about Anna Vasilevna's leaving, made various speculations, pitied her, tacitly blamed Yakov Moiseevich and cursed Rozhnova. At first this made Anna Vasilevna feel better, as if the hurt were beginning to pass away. But these conversations quickly became unbearable to her—she was heartsick. There was still time left—let the days not pass, that was all.

Later everyone got tired of feeling sorry for Anna Vasilevna, and talked about the other one—whoever it was God would send them.

"The administration knows who God will send," Lelka giggled.

They began to think and guess what she would be like, the new co-worker. "Most likely some hoity-toity," said Kharitonova. Lelka began to picture her, this future hoity-toity. She made her lips into a trumpet, forcing her words through them, lisping, walking without bending her knees, on tiptoe, figured the account splaying her fingers out, and said, sadly rolling her eyes: "We have a total of a million kopeks and a hundred thousand rubles." Everyone laughed; things were never boring with Lelka around. But Anna Vasilevna's heart ached. They were already forgetting about her.

She fell asleep in the early morning. The top of the poplar was lit—the sun was up. The birds woke, and the yard was filled with twittering, singing, chirping. Loud sounds were heard, a child's crying, and somewhere the roar of a motorcycle. A woman shouted impatiently: "Vanya, are you coming?" People were going to work. Anna Vasilevna slept.

She was awakened by a loud ringing. The alarm clock had gone off—cheerfully, desperately, knocking its metal legs on the table and slowly turning its round body.

"Are you out of your mind?" She asked it tenderly, in a sleepy voice. She never set the alarm; she always woke up on time. But the hands already pointed to eight o'clock. "I'm late?!" she groaned and quickly sat up, immediately sliding her feet into her slippers.

And only then did she remember: she didn't have to go anywhere. There was no need to get up. There was no need to do anything.

She sat on the edge of the bed, with her hands hanging limp. The alarm clock rang and rang. It seemed as though that useless sound would never end.

Section 6
———— Ethics and Corporate Social Responsibility ————

6.1   IN LOS ANGELES
Saburō Shiroyama

I

Yukimura thought he had prepared himself for the worst, but the trip to the Los Angeles International Airport proved otherwise. Morito, the new branch manager, just in from Japan, berated Yukimura right there in the terminal. The Yukimura couple were quick to catch sight of the tall Morito stepping out of a customs gate in the JAL lobby and also very fast to duck their heads and bow. Morito, on his part, generously raised a hand and strode up to them. So far so good. But as soon as Morito had staged his formalistic handshake, he glanced all around the lobby and let the couple know of his dissatisfaction.

"Nobody here to meet me?"

"We . . ."

"I'm talking about others."

Because the tone of Morito's voice meant *You two don't count,* the Yukimuras were at a loss for words. They felt insulted, but even more, disheartened to find their new manager so unpleasant.

Most Americans, of course, do not have ceremonious greetings and farewells at airports as the Japanese do. It didn't seem possible that this "legend" who had studied in the United States shortly after World War II and who still spoke in English in his sleep was that ignorant about American ways. Besides, he should have known that the Los Angeles branch office of Yukimura's Q-Trading Company had only five staff members, including the local employees. Wasn't it good enough that the deputy manager and his wife had come to pick him up?

"Katō-kun is in Phoenix, and Nakano-kun is in San Diego at the moment," Yukimura spoke apologetically as he looked up at Morito's sparkling glasses.

"And our clients?"

Yukimura caught himself from saying *This isn't Japan, you know* only with some effort.

"Some asked for your arrival time, but I didn't give a definite answer."

"Why? Why didn't you have them come?"

"Because they are Aron Orchards, Halifax Limited, and other nettlesome companies." Yukimura listed the names of the companies that his former manager Ohkubo had tried to avoid and about which the new manager Morito was expected to do something. "They might have given you a hard time right at the first sight of you."

"You don't have to worry about me. I can take care of them. It's not your place to fix things for me," Morito chided unsparingly.

From *Made in Japan and Other Japanese "Business Novels,"* ed. and trans. Tamae K. Prindle (Armonk, NY: M.E. Sharpe, 1989). Translation copyright © 1989 M.E. Sharpe, Inc. Reprinted with permission.

Yukimura's wife, Sayoko, tensed up as she stood next to him.

"I'm not built as delicately as Ohkubo-kun. Nervous breakdowns and ulcers are foreign to me. I'm going to forge ahead without worrying about little things. Please keep that in mind," Morito went on.

Yukimura and Sayoko nodded together in a chain reaction. Actually, they felt that they had to.

This wasn't the end of Morito's carping. When Yukimura drove his Ford Capri from the parking lot to the terminal building exit, Morito looked down at it from where he stood.

"Are you driving it yourself?"

"Yes."

"Don't you have a driver?"

Yukimura's nerves seethed. In the United States, only corporate executives, millionaires, and the like could afford a private chauffeur. Morito should know that by now. What kind of nonsense was he spewing?

"If you don't have a driver, why don't you let your junior staff drive for you?"

This made no more sense than anything else Morito had said. All the Japanese staff were out of town, and no American employees would consider being treated like a chauffeur.

Morito finally settled into the back seat, plopping his gigantic rear onto it.

"You make me feel as if I'm here to depend on you." Morito's abusive talk was another way of scolding, *This isn't the way to receive your business manager. Don't take me for your friend visiting here for a vacation.*

Yukimura started the car wordlessly just as soon as Sayoko slid into the seat next to him. Silently, he retorted, *Coming to the airport with my wife was the best welcome a deputy manager of a small trading company could give to its new manager.*

"It would have worked better if you had brought me a car. I could have driven it back myself," added Morito with annoyance.

This was even more nonsensical. Even assuming that the company would buy a car for the manager, he would have wanted to select it for himself. Renting a car wouldn't have pleased him either.

Having run out of complaints, Morito cut the tip of a cigar and lit it. A powerful smell filled the car. Sayoko usually got a headache from cigar smoke but she was too frightened to roll down the window.

What a nuisance of a manager I've gotten, Yukimura commiserated with himself once again. He had heard of Morito's nickname and reputation, but this was the very first time he had to work directly under him. In a firm the size of his Q-Trading Company, a person with a degree from a top-notch national university and an American college as well was treasured as the company's "prince" from the beginning of his career. To Yukimura's knowledge, Morito was very demanding at work, yet he would also do a friendly thing like inviting his juniors to a house party. The "prince" used a whip and candy very generously, so to speak. He was thoroughly Draconian in business transactions but had been a big hit in his departments thus far. One could guess that Morito would join the board of directors just as soon as he turned forty if he straightened out the problems of the Los Angeles office during his tenure there. Morito was a big shot and he knew it—or rather, he was a bundle of self-importance. And he made sure that Yukimura felt it under his skin.

Yukimura drove on in silence. Off in the distance, the Santa Monica Bay glistened blue in the twilight. The wind seemed to have blown off the infamous smog. The sky of Los Angeles, with a hue of emerald green, was deep and high.

Suddenly, Morito started showering questions onto Sayoko's back.

"Mrs. Yukimura, how are your children? There's a girl in the sixth grade and a boy in the second grade, isn't there?"

"Yes!" Sayoko nodded in such amazement that her head almost knocked against the windshield.

"I hear that your daughter is good at drawing pictures." Morito had more surprises up his sleeve.

"Oh, no, not at all. . . ." Sayoko blushed like a girl whose hand had been asked for in marriage, and her body stiffened. Earlier, she had been frozen from trepidation; this time she sat in a rapturous trance.

It flashed across Yukimura's mind that this was Morito's trick. He must have checked up on the family situations of his subordinates at the personnel office or somewhere. But how did he uncover a detail like his daughter's drawings? This was the art of winning over people's hearts. It was something Yukimura begrudgingly had to take his hat off to.

"Art transcends nationalities. Things are more colorful, and sceneries have a larger scale over here. It will be good to take her for landscape painting and such," Morito continued as he blew out the cigar smoke. Sayoko nodded, drugged by the thick curtain of smoke.

The traffic on the freeway became more congested as Yukimura approached the downtown area. This time, Morito's voice took aim at Yukimura.

"Talking about pictures . . . isn't Fumihiko-kun,* President Hori's son, living with hippies and trying to paint somewhere near here?"

"I think he's taking it seriously these days."

"How hopeless! He has a degree in economics, and is supposed to be continuing his studies here in the United States. The president is very disappointed in him. How is it that a shiftless son like that comes from such an outstanding father?"

Yukimura knew that the question didn't ask for an answer, but he put forth his opinion just the same, "Maybe it's because his father is too outstanding."

"What do you mean?"

"He's compared to his successful father in whatever he does. It's hard for the son. In fact, I've heard Fumihiko-san* swear that he would give up his success so that his son wouldn't feel pressured. I think I can understand how he feels."

"Humph." Morito wheezed in a nasal tone. "No matter how you look at it, though, hippies and delinquents are human garbage. He has no right to lecture us as long as he is mixed up with that sort of gang."

"But Fumihiko-san doesn't use drugs; nor does he go for free love. He's just looking to be a free spirit. He just wants to indulge in art."

"If he's that serious, why doesn't he go to Paris or New York?"

"He says he'd be overwhelmed by too many recognized artists in Paris and New York. He feels that there's no spot left for him to sketch."

"Doesn't professionalism mean overcoming that sort of competition?"

Yukimura nodded lightly and continued, "But he's not sure if he really wants to be a professional artist."

"That's precisely where the problem lies. That's why he's a bungler. No wonder the president is disgusted with him."

Yukimura sidestepped Morito's comment and went on. "As you may be aware, the United States is a country of professionals. It's believed that survival depends on professionalism."

"It sure is."

---

*Note how Morito calls the president's son with the -kun suffix to show superiority to Yukimura. Yukimura refers to the same person with the -san suffix to show respect to both the president and Morito.

"But more and more laid back young people are choosing to do only what they believe in. You may call them anti-professionals. Success isn't part of their vocabulary."

"The Vietnam war has blighted their minds; that's it."

"Maybe so, but it seems to me that the United States has turned a corner in history. I feel that the whole country is drifting on a lake of lethargy, trying to survive on the borderline between professionalism and amateurism."

"Come on, you softboiled egg! This is why you can't make clear-cut decisions. If you had taken a firmer stance, you could have solved the problems with Aron and Halifax more forcefully."

Yukimura took it in stride. It was possible to insist on Q-Trading Company's way of doing business, but unfortunately the problems weren't the kind that could be solved in a hard-headed business manner. For example, Q-Trading Company was the only Japanese trading company that bought lemons, grapefruit, oranges, and other fruits from Aron Orchards in Riverside City. The original contract called for Q-Trading Company to purchase exclusively all the fruit products of Aron on the condition that Aron discontinue their business with large fruit retailers in the United States. But lately the Japanese market for lemons and grapefruit had become sluggish. And a chronic glut was projected for the future. As a result, Q-Trading Company decided to discontinue purchasing lemons and to begin selectively purchasing grapefruit and oranges. This change was advantageous to the Q-Trading Company only—and there was a ruthless calculation behind it: Aron Orchards wouldn't survive long; the bankruptcy would solve Q's problems.

Aron Orchards was outraged. Intimidated by Aron's violent reaction, Ohkubo, the former manager, stopped going to the Riverside region altogether. There was also a time when armed Aron-affiliated farmers barged in on Q-Trading Company. The branch office found it impossible to force the main office's decision onto the American producers and requested that the main office reconsider the new order.

A similar tension existed with the Halifax Distributor. Two years ago, Q-Trading Company nominated Halifax as a distributor of a Japanese spray system. Halifax Headquarters in Ontario City, some fifty kilometers east of Los Angeles, had a good reputation in the farming communities in southern California and the spray system sold better than expected. Q-Trading Company attributed its success to the high quality of the machinery, while Halifax assumed that it was due to its sales efforts. In either case, commissions bulged significantly along with the sales figures. The Q-Trading Company, now chary of the sales commission, decided to terminate the distributor contract at the time of its renewal. But the contract was supposed to be renewed every two years, unless a breach of confidence intervened. As a pretext, Q-Trading Company accused Halifax of negotiating with an American maker of spray systems. This was another source of headaches at the branch office.

Rather than lose its temper, Halifax went on pleading its case. Because Halifax had entrusted the sales to about twenty salesmen, the contract negotiations directly affected the employment of these people. Naturally, the salesmen came to the Q-office in relays. Some threatened to appeal to the court; others menaced the staff by showing their tattoos and guns. They implied, "If you go about it illegally, we will do the same." Ohkubo requested the contract be renewed once more, but the Tokyo office responded by replacing him with Morito.

Morito suddenly cried out, "Oh, the good old City Hall! It hasn't changed!"

The twenty-eight story, uniquely white City Hall loomed in front of the car.

"You must have lived in the Los Angeles area before." Sayoko turned around to keep Morito company.

"It was over fifteen years ago. I didn't actually live here. I used to live in San Bernardino. I came here from the country now and then. Every time I saw this building I was excited to be in Los Angeles. I felt much closer to Japan."

"It must have been difficult for you."

"Well, there still was a shortage of foreign exchange. I had to make my living at dishwashing lawn-mowing, orange-picking, and other odd jobs while going to school."

"San Bernardino is on the other side of Ontario and Riverside, isn't it?"

"Right."

Isn't this ironic? Yukimura was tempted to remark, *That's near Aron and Halifax!* But he said, "Do you have acquaintances around there?"

"There may still be some, but they were all my enemies. I was pushed into cheap labor everywhere. There was only one old man, the owner of an orchard, who was very nice to me. He was a 'half-breed' with American Indian blood. He told me to marry his granddaughter, get permanent residency, and manage his orchard with her."

"But you didn't."

"Of course not. Who wants to live an empty life at the end of the world? Also, how could I marry an Indian and have kids that holler 'wa wa' all the time?" Morito imitated the voice of American Indians in Western movies and made Sayoko laugh.

Yukimura drew a mental picture of Morito in a Native American village. Somewhere in a corner of that endless orchard, sunburned Morito would be working with his half-breed wife. Vigorous, coppertoned children of mixed blood would be circling around barefoot or on horseback. Not bad at all. Morito fit in the scene neatly. On the other hand, Morito now looked more like himself. One thing Yukimura knew for sure was that if Morito had taken the other path, he could have done without this nincompoop for now.

"The old man passed away last year. It seems that nobody was there with him. I think I will go to San Bernardino one day and build a grave for him."*

Sayoko nodded approvingly. Yukimura felt as if his wife's gaze had disparaged him in the light of Morito. He could almost hear her thinking, *My husband is so different. . . .* Yukimura was only one year younger than Morito, but there was nothing noteworthy in his schooling and degrees. A lack of business enthusiasm had already removed him from the success ladder. He had by now served as the deputy manager in Los Angeles for three years. If he didn't watch his step, he might very well be buried alive in this town.

Back in the apartment later that day, Sayoko let out a sigh, "He notices small things. Morito-san deserves his reputation." She looked at her husband with a fresh glance and continued, "Come to think of it, this is a rare opportunity. . . ."

"Opportunity for what?" Yukimura wanted to ask, *An opportunity to be flattened out?*

"You know, a chance to get on in the world," Sayoko smiled gently. "He is the future leader of our company. What if you followed him closely?"

"No way!"

"Not just to get ahead, but this may be a way to return to Japan a bit sooner."

Yukimura didn't bother to answer.

"Living like this, our children go funny. And you and me, too."

Again, Yukimura didn't reply.

"Or else, would you rather live with the Indians somewhere around San Bernardino, like mud dolls?"

"Why don't you shut up?"

---

*Building and attending the ancestral grave is highly regarded in Japan.

Sayoko became quiet for awhile; she checked Yukimura's face and repeated loudly, "It's a chance; believe me."

II

The Q-Trading Company was on the third floor of a small building on Flower Street near the University of Southern California. The first thing the new manager did was to remodel the small office. He enclosed a corner of the manager's section with a decorative glass partition, put in a new desk, and brought in a new set of waiting room furniture. He also put up an American flag and a Japanese flag beside his desk as some presidents of large American companies do. These modifications added dignity to his office, but made the rest of the floor space that much smaller. The sad thing was that, after all that renovation, Morito hardly ever stayed in his office.

He took off in his new Cougar XR7, always saying, "A trading company should be in motion." He visited customer companies, stopped by financial organizations, and met with banks and Japanese authorities. In between, he went to play golf for "socialization," as he put it. He was truly energetic. Yet, he left the negotiations with Aron and Halifax—the pending problems—to Yukimura. He didn't pay a single visit to these companies. If somebody from either company came charging in, he made Yukimura deal with them. The partitioned manager's room was a cozy den for Morito. One could even suspect that his frequent outings were a way of avoiding these unwanted visitors. The problem was that Morito, while taking no part himself, commanded Yukimura to bring the two contracts to complete closure exactly as dictated by the Tokyo office.

"There's nothing to negotiate about. Just spurn their requests. Don't give in to Americans. No, not an inch. Don't even give a hint of giving in," Morito tried to fire up Yukimura.

If Yukimura proposed, "But we need some kind of concession," Morito would raise his voice, "What the heck!" and yell, "We're not one of those large trading companies; we have to be grabby in order to survive; we must earn every penny we can."

"If you're that resolved, would you please talk to them directly?" Yukimura ran out of patience.

"My job is to march forward, to expand our business. This mess you are in is like a postwar cleanup job, a retrenchment, something your staff is entitled to." Morito pounded on the table, and repelled Yukimura with some insults.

Days went by. Yelled at by Morito and beleaguered by Aron and others, Yukimura was lonely. Local employees became standoffish towards him in deference to Morito and Aron. It was more like working in a one-man office rather than a branch office staffed by five. Before, the previous manager had been there to discuss problems and had tried to talk the Tokyo office into reconsidering the contract. But Morito was heartless and couldn't be caught off guard. He had trapped Yukimura behind an iron wall so there was no way out. Yukimura felt crucified. When he was threatened with murder, he felt like casually retorting, *Yeah, go right ahead!* He wasn't all that ready to die, but the apprehension that he might in fact be killed one of these days was always there. Q-Trading Company's business policies were so slipshod that such vengeance almost seemed fitting. But whenever Yukimura threw his life at his opponents, the aggressors backed down. In the end, Q-Trading Company scored a victory, and Morito as its manager got the credit. Yukimura vacantly brooded that the art of using subordinates to personal advantage was another of Morito's talents.

The only salvation for Yukimura was that both Aron and Halifax seemed to understand that their true enemy was not Yukimura but Morito. As their visits became more frequent, they gave up on Yukimura and became proportionately more inquisitive about Morito's whereabouts. The antagonistic clouds hovering over Morito became so thick that his enemies' hostility became palpable.

One day, the president's son Fumihiko showed up, dangling a large necklace of chained nuts and dragging a robe stained by oil paints. Morito abhorred hippies. He wanted to throw a bucket of water over the youngster, but had to politely receive the president's son into his office.

"I should have gone to inquire after you, but because Yukimura-kun told me that your residence changed constantly and it is rather difficult to find you . . . ," began Morito.

"My place isn't something you can call a residence. It's just a den, a temporal inn where a bunch of us sleep, so you'll never find me." After answering Morito, Fumihiko surreptitiously winked to Yukimura.

Actually, Yukimura knew where Fumihiko had his nest. Fumihiko had contacted him at home every time he moved. Not merely because Yukimura had been long in the area, but also because there was something about Yukimura that Fumihiko trusted. Yukimura knew he may have been thought of as easy to win over, but he didn't mind. It would have made him feel good to be depended upon by a young man, even if he weren't the president's son. Because Fumihiko had made it perfectly clear that he didn't want the new manager to know his address, Yukimura had kept it confidential as a token of his sincerity.

"The real purpose of my trip here is to borrow about three thousand dollars," said Fumihiko, brushing his long hair back with his fingers. He explained that his favorite avant-garde artist was holding a private exhibition in New York, he didn't want to miss it, and that, if possible, he wanted to purchase copies of his sketches and other works.

"Do you have your father's permission?"

"Of course not. My father is dead set against my getting into art."

"That's a problem." Morito put a hand on his forehead.

President Hori had a personal savings account with the Bank of America and his bank book was kept in the Los Angeles office. This was an emergency fund to be utilized at the manager's discretion. The exhibition had already started. Fumihiko said urgently, "I may miss the show if I don't get going soon."

Could this be called an emergency case? wondered Morito. If the president was against his son's art fad, drawing on the fund for this purpose would generate his resentment. Morito couldn't make up mind.

"Would you let me think about it? I'll get back to you. Please leave your address or telephone number."

"That's O.K. I'll come back tomorrow."

"In that case, how about dinner tomorrow?"

Fumihiko shook his head, "The kind of restaurants you go to don't like sloppy-looking people like me. I don't feel comfortable in those places, either."

Morito didn't reply.

"Do you know that some of us collect scrap cabbage and meat from the trash cans of those restaurants?"

"Like beggars."

"Not really. We do so for another reason. It's an effort to stay out of money-bound society. We don't spend money on luxury; we don't work for money. It's not the easiest thing in the world because we are living in a society where a bit of work can earn a meal, as you must know. It takes a good determination to go against the current."

Morito listened to Fumihiko open-mouthed. Fumihiko was talking about a world outside the imagination of a single-minded businessman like himself. The businessman didn't know how to respond other than saying, "It doesn't mean you have to follow their example. . . ."

"I'm not a thoroughbred. I still know the value of money. My visit here proves that."

"That sets my mind at ease a little."

"Also, I'm not about to deny the value of the older generation completely. It's awkward for a son to say this, but I think that my father is a fine man. At least he was good enough to build a company of this size in one generation." As Morito nodded deeply for the first time, Fumihiko added mischievously, "Although his contribution to the financial world may be cancelled out by me."

Having said all he wanted, Fumihiko left, the tail end of his long robe sailing in the air.

"What a scrap of human garbage that is!" Morito spit out. He was truly angry.

Yukimura felt like giving him a bit of a twit. "Isn't that an easy life, though? And, as Fumihiko-san always says, his son will have it made, won't he?"

"He has no qualification to be a father; no qualification even to live."

"But he is harmless."

Perhaps because this sarcasm was a bit too strong, Morito was offended. "What of it?"

Yukimura didn't confront Morito directly. He said, "There wouldn't be wars if the world were inhabited only by his type of people."

Morito lit his cigar and sighed deeply.

"So, what am I going to do about the three thousand dollars?" Yukimura didn't answer. This truly was none of his business, and it boosted his ego to watch Morito suffer. The easiest solution would be to telephone Tokyo, and ask the president. But the upshot would be at best a presidential scolding, "Can't you make up your mind about a small thing like that?" Morito probably would have to make his own decision and then report the result afterward. It was impossible to guess whether the president would be grateful or resentful for having spent the money. Morito appeared to be tearing his hair out over the problem. It was a very minor affair for the company, but it was a life-or-death problem to him.

Morito's cigar smoke rose higher and higher. In the end, he asked for Yukimura's help, "What do you think?"

"It's up to you."

"I know that, but what would you do in my place?"

"I would help him."

"Why? The president would rather get him out of art, you know."

"I just thought of Fumihiko-san. I didn't think of the president."

"Why not?"

"Well, the money isn't going to be spent for destructive purposes. On the contrary, it may serve as a springboard for Fumihiko-san's growth. Whatever profession he may eventually choose, there's no reason to deprive him of something that enriches his cultural background and spiritual life."

Morito remained silent.

"Furthermore, Fumihiko-san is not the type to ask for something so ardently. He is usually very nihilistic. He sounded unusually enthusiastic today. I could tell how earnest he was about the exhibition."

"Do you mean to say that a hippie may reform?"

"It's not a matter of reforming. I just think that we should give him the thing he truly craves, and beautiful things, too."

"All right, I get it. I'll handle the rest." Morito shut off Yukimura's advice with the whisk of a hand. His expression said that he had suddenly become exasperated at having consulted Yukimura.

"You seem to have lived here long enough to turn yourself into a hippie supporter. Just watch out for yourself so that you can still be useful in Japan," Morito snarled. "Are you ready to prove your worth with the Aron and Halifax cases? Go at it and teach them a lesson!"

In the end, Manager Morito handed Fumihiko the three thousand dollars. This pleased Fumihiko, but his father's response was different. When Morito reported to the Tokyo office with some fear and trepidation, the executive secretary conveyed the president's message that he was outraged by the manager's "putting his hand on uncalled-for business." Since the president was planning a trip to the United States in the near future, he would inquire about the details of the matter when he stopped in Los Angeles, so "Morito had better be prepared for the worst." The message was unexpectedly harsh.

Morito was out of sorts. He wreaked his frustration on Yukimura. "It wasn't my idea to give him the money. It's you who made the decision."

"But you said to leave the rest up to you."

"I just got here, and didn't know anything. That's why I respected your opinion."

"Even then . . ."

"I had nothing to base my judgment on. As a matter of fact, that was the first time I met Fumihiko-kun. How could a stranger to a place make the right decision? All I could do was to be guided by your information and suggestion." Morito got heated up by his own argument as he talked. "The original sin was that you let that hippie have the run of our office just because he's the president's son. You and Ohkubo-kun spoiled him. No, the general easy-handed way you go about managing welcomes this sort of disaster." Morito had completely forgotten how civilly he had welcomed Fumihiko into the manager's office. "Listen, this problem was handled by you, not by me. Let's make it clear that you took the responsibility; you made the decision. It's your job to vindicate everything to the president. Don't drag me into it because I have no idea what's going on." After this bout of excited proclamation, Morito swung his gaze behind his shiny glasses in another direction.

Yukimura couldn't believe it. He was dumbfounded. Not only was he irritated by Morito, but he had also become disgusted with the shallowness of his wife, who was infatuated by this man's personality. What did she know about big shots and great chances? Following this man would only make one rotten to the core.

How could a deputy manager venture to explain his position to the president? All Yukimura could do was to own up to the truth, to describe the situation plainly. After that, he would just have to sit through a flurry of presidential abuses and wait for the verdict, which would probably be a demotion.

"Enough. You may go back to your work." Morito was all authoritarian.

Yukimura was glad to leave; not seeing Morito was as much his wish as Morito's. He was beginning to fear that if he stayed there much longer he might throw Morito out the window.

III

Morito built a grave for the orchard owner who took care of him during his student days. He replaced the simple wooden marker, which had been put up by those who were not related to the orchard owner by blood, with an ostentatious black marble tombstone. The graveyard was in the suburbs of San Bernardino.

It was decided that the branch office staff would attend the renovation ceremony. Morito drove his Cougar XR7, and Yukimura and his junior staff member Nakano were instructed to follow in the Ford Capri. Morito assumed the role of an authoritarian leader, making them go in two separate cars when one would have done the job just as well.

Morito's tombstone renovation plan was picked up by a local paper, the *San Bernardino Times*, which didn't overlook even the smallest local event. Neighboring small-town newspapers like

The Ontario Chronicle and *The Riverside Evening* joined the chorus and printed flashy illustrated articles about the "beautiful Japanese spirit."

It was the "beautiful Japanese spirit" all right. Morito's feeling for the half-Indian orchard owner was genuine, the gravestone was of fine quality, and it was built with great care. Yukimura could appreciate this generosity. But Morito was embarrassed to have Yukimura and others see things in that light.

"I'm doing this out of sheer self-interest. No growing bud comes out of everyday business transactions. But this sort of publicity expands our business network. You people should quit digging small holes for yourselves and start looking for new ways," he said.

The newspaper articles struck some people quite differently. Many threatening letters and protesting telephone calls flew in from the Aron-related people around Riverside, and from Halifax salesmen based in Ontario. They threatened, "Don't try to make yourselves look noble at our cost," "Remember you're going to pay for this when you come this way," and many more male-dictions. The "beautiful spirit" grated on them. Their abuse was not in their words alone; a true threat of violence resonated between the lines. Any mention of this, however, only made Morito bellow with laughter.

"It's just the American way of doing things. The United States prides itself on toughness. Haven't you learned that yet?" After saying this, Morito suddenly frowned and added, "Business-men in trading companies are no different from the foot soldiers on the battlefront. Nobody says so, but we all came prepared to find a watery grave, and death in an open field. We don't get anywhere if we let these screwballs get on our nerves."

The sky was clear and there was no wind on the day of the renovation ceremony. This meant that a thin gray smog hung in the Los Angeles sky.

Morito, Yukimura, and Nakano left work early. The two cars, one following the other, sped straight east on Interstate 10. Up until halfway through the two-hour drive, the scenery was like an extension of Los Angeles, sprinkled with factories and clusters of houses. After that, farm-lands and orchards sprawled over the vista. Farmhouses played hide and seek every so often from behind avenues of palm trees and forests of eucalyptus. There were people driving tractors and spraying chemicals.

This part of the scenery was something Yukimura couldn't watch so innocently. The spray equipment might have been sold by the Halifax salesmen, and some of the orchard workers might be members of Aron-affiliated farms. He feared that his car as well as Morito's might be identi-fied by these people and ambushed. Maybe Morito shared the same anxiety. When they passed through the suburbs of Ontario City, where the Halifax headquarters was located, Yukimura sensed that Morito's car speeded up.

Before long, the San Bernardino National Forest and the Box Springs Mountains started to loom in the mist to the north and south of the highway respectively. San Bernardino was situated in the middle of a basin.

Morito had said that the orchard at which he previously worked was sold and the old man's house was torn down after his death. He had shown no interest in visiting the remainder of the orchard, but headed directly to the graveyard on a small hill slightly east of the town. It was surrounded by an ocean of orchards. In the orange orchard just before the graveyard, Mexican immigrants silently trimmed the lower branches. They wore rags and squirmed like mud dolls. Everyone had the gloomy face of a serf. Yukimura felt that calling them serfs was not too wide off the mark. Mexicans surge into the United States to escape poverty, but the immigration regula-tions are strict. The situation helps create a number of illegal immigrants who will put up with any adverse working conditions. Their "bosses," who use their influence to find employment for them, exploit them and may go so far as to cut their lives short. Only recently, for example, a "boss" who had murdered nearly ten Mexicans was arrested at an orchard in a border region.

Below their feet, ever so many oranges formed a carpet of golden yellow. Nature shakes off the bad oranges at an early stage; only the ripened, good quality fruit is harvested in the end. As a result of this highly expensive procedure, the oranges harvested in the end had the richness and luxury of having absorbed the life force of countless premature relatives.

Mulling these things over in his mind, Yukimura was suddenly wakened from his drifting thoughts. His Q-Trading Company had promised to buy all of these oranges but had suddenly switched to selective purchasing. They had reneged on the original contract and chosen a way that was much more costly to the producers. The angry oranges and the orange workers assaulted him in lifelike vividness.

The gigantic sun gradually reclined westward. A breeze had started to pick up. At the grave-yard, the priest gave a short prayer. Three men and women chosen from the church choir sang several hymns. Finally, Morito offered a bouquet of flowers and knelt in front of the tombstone. As directed, Nakano took some snapshots from different angles.

Morito remained motionless long after many pictures were taken. He would not get up. His large body froze into a statue, and a shadow drawn by the setting sun stretched along the ground. *Apricot flowers?* Petals of cherry-blossom-like flowers alighted on shoulders. Morito's glasses glistened in the twilight. Facing the sun, Yukimura couldn't tell for certain, but it seemed that Morito's tears made his glasses shine. The graveyard fell into total silence. The only sound was the movement of the Mexicans some distance away drifting up like waves. Morito did not raise his head. It looked as if he would stay there for many more hours.

The priest cleared his throat. Morito's large sunbeam-laden shoulders finally rose. Dark clay clung to his pants knees. Morito briefly thanked the priest and the choir, and took care of the business matters by himself, hardly looking at Yukimura or Nakano. He only said, "All right, let's go," and got into his Cougar XR7.

Yukimura and Nakano rushed to their Ford Capri and chased after him.

"The manager is acting strange today," said Nakano, who had joined the company only three years ago.

"He may have been crying."

"The old man must have taken really good care of him."

"I guess."

Their cars raced by the Mexican laborers. In the evening sun, the workers looked worn out. They turned vacant and apathetic eyes towards the cars.

"The manager must have been made to work like them."

"I doubt it." Yukimura answered dryly, but remembered that there were some places around there called "Chino," which was Spanish for "Chinese." There was a time when Chinese and Japanese were dirt-crawling laborers. It wouldn't be surprising if Morito had been included in the penurious labor force of Chinese and Japanese students during the postwar period. The shame and regret of having fallen slave to the pitiless drudgery . . . The difference in treatment must have made the old orchard owner seem like a saint. Was it an outburst of dammed up sentiment that had made Morito a praying clay statue?

Come to think of it, Morito had shown no interest in visiting the places of his memorable past other than this graveyard, after coming this close to them. Could it be that all the other places would only open old wounds with painful freshness? He had once said, "They all mistreated me." Stretching his imagination one step farther, Yukimura recalled that Morito had two false front teeth. Morito had casually explained that he fell and broke them while he was in the United States, but did they have a hidden connection with the hard labor? Yukimura also wondered if Morito's avoidance of Aron and Halifax might not have been rooted in his resentment of the white people of the region, and not a matter of business strategy.

The basin opened up toward the west as if beckoning to the open pasture. A huge red sun was about to set on the horizon. The Cougar XR7 sprinted past the vast scenery, like a white leopard, aiming at Los Angeles. Morito's silhouette looked much smaller than life-size. And every now and then, the gold of the setting sun bleached out the white Cougar and Morito's silhouette. They looked lonely and neglected.

"That car has been following us for a long time," said Nakano when they approached Ontario.

Yukimura looked in the rearview mirror. Two old cars were trailing behind them. Lanes were open on their right and left. The two cars had plenty of time and space to pass, but they stayed very close behind. Each had three or four passengers. Strange! Should he honk at Morito and let him know? What would Morito do about it? It was a straight highway in the middle of empty land. There was no service area; exits and junctions were some distance away. Oncoming cars floated up and down into their vision on the other side of the highway, but the lanes on this side had nothing other than the taillights that had just disappeared in the horizon. The highway was already darkened by the violet dusk.

"It's weird. What shall we do?" asked Nakano.

At that moment, the two cars suddenly sped up and pulled into the passing lane. They passed Yukimura's car. One of them raced its engine and flew in front of the Cougar. The other stayed right next to the Cougar to cage it in. The Cougar, now sandwiched between the two, reduced speed and stopped in the breakdown lane. Yukimura's Ford passed them before it came to an abrupt halt. Many shadows rolled out of the black cars and ran toward the Cougar. Then came the ring of swearing voices. The blasting of a bullet cut through the wind. With their doors open, Yukimura and Nakano hung back. Another bullet. The Cougar honked. It kept on honking. Morito's torso seemed to have fallen across the steering wheel. The men floored their accelerators, and the two cars that had swallowed those shadows sped off.

Yukimura and Nakano ran up to the Cougar. A front tire was shot out, tilting the car body. Morito's bloodless face hung over the steering wheel. It rose slowly and the honking stopped. Blood soaked his left thigh. Apparently the men didn't intend to kill him. But Morito's body was stuck to the steering wheel. When the two men tried to lift him, a horrible stench stung their noses.

"Oh, I . . . " Morito tried to say something with unfocused eyes. Yukimura and Nakano looked at each other. They detected the cause of the stench. Morito had excreted in terror. It wasn't anything to laugh about; it was pathetic.

IV

President Hori arrived in Los Angeles. Because Morito was hospitalized, Yukimura had to explain the three thousand dollar incident. The thought that he was saving Morito's skin rather than being incriminated by the manager made it easier to surrender himself to whatever fate awaited him. He prepared himself for the severest scolding, but the president started talking before Yukimura had finished, with a friendly smile on his face, "Fumihiko wrote to me from New York. He said that he gave up the idea of becoming an artist. He realized that he wasn't gifted enough. The show must have had some true masterpieces. He was crushed. He even hinted at coming back to Japan. He said that he couldn't keep on goofing off with the assumption that we are always there to wait on him."* The president then broke into a genuine smile and changed the subject, "I'm going to ask you to manage this office from now on. I don't mean temporarily; I mean officially."

"But Morito-san is . . ."

"I'll send him back to Japan as soon as he comes out of the hospital. I'll have him take it easy in our research division or somewhere. I misunderstood him. I used to think that his type made good businessmen, but I think perhaps not any more."

"His type?"

"You know what I mean. Those who have worked under him can explain better than I."

Does "his type" mean a practical and bluffing kind? Yukimura wanted to ask. Had the president seen Morito praying stone-still on a hill aglow with the setting sun? And what did the president know about Yukimura himself? Did he know that Yukimura wanted to go back to Japan? Rather than taking the managerial post, he wanted to go back now, even if he had to miss a promotion, and maybe catch another chance sometime later.

The president took Yukimura's silence as his expression of gratitude and carried on, "It's about time you made it to a manager's post. Besides, we need someone like you from now on who is familiar with the local circumstances. We are stepping into a world where many more conflicts, graver than those of Aron and Halifax, are likely to turn up."

The exhausted faces of the Mexican workers flashed in Yukimura's mind, and so did the golden carpet of oranges lying around their feet. He felt an unexplained load fall on his shoulders. Looking up with his inner eyes, he saw the white tower of the City Hall rise in the navy-blue sky of southern California, like an insensitive giant.

Amae, translated as "passive dependency" by psychiatrist Takeo Doi, is a strong component of the Japanese mentality, generated by the original mother-baby bond, developing into a master-disciple bond and other socio-psychological tendencies of Japanese life. It is an unspoken deep-seated trust and dependency on another.

6.2 PAYBACK (DIRTY FOR DIRTY)
Patricio F. Vargas

Wilshire Boulevard was bustling with people glad to be out during the lunch hour after a week of unusually heavy rain in Los Angeles. The wide, fancy street was crowded with people, mostly women, animated by the marvelous, pleasant change in weather: bees streaming out of dark, humid hives, into brilliant sunshine, coming alive.

Women seductively, attractively dressed, glad to expose their femininity in revealing clothing. Sexy shoes and alluring dresses with lively, inviting faces, their eyes darting, looking, addressing, flirting—just great to be out walking, letting men look at them. The two men, pretending nonchalance, using their peripheral vision, swiveling from side to side of the street, checking out all the possibilities for a flirtation or just an eyeful of female.

The blue pickup glided slowly down Wilshire towards the tallest of the buildings, on the 3400 block.

"You know what the son of a whore has done for me? For $1,000 I've gotten a receipt and a letter! ¡Hijo de su pinche, puta, perra madre! He made me so many promises. And to think I trusted that fucking lawyer!" the squat Mexican troglodyte said animatedly to the driver, another Mexican, who sat with an intense, preoccupied air as he drove and enjoyed the women on the busy boulevard.

"He said he could get all my family documented for only $2,300, and all I got in two years was a receipt!"

The driver, nodding in understanding and faint boredom at hearing the complaining repetition . . . rehearsing in his mind what his strategy was going to be once he sized up the lawyer. The simple peasant's litany and pleas for help were beginning to weary him.

They parked at the rear of the tall, ritzy, imposing building and headed for the 25th floor.

"You should have seen how well he treated me, had the two kiss-ass secretaries translate for me every minute . . . and once I handed him the $1,000 I never heard from him again!" The beefy man, grossly overweight at 5 feet 5 inches and 250 pounds, kept up his running commentary. An ambulatory washing machine of a man, his thick arms and thicker body thrashing through the air, trying to keep up with his rescuer; bull-like neck, powerful shoulders and trapezius bulging, years of plastering made visible in his bunched-up muscles as he trundled along.

Taking the elevator, they continued to speak in Spanish, disconcerting the other passengers, who outwardly pretended not to hear, but who inwardly strained their ears to catch the meaning of the alien sounds, recoiling slightly at the foreign look and sound of the two chattering Mexicans in the small space.

"Wanna see a guy named Phil, works here," said the younger man to the caged-in receptionist, and they were both admitted into the winding recesses of the plush law offices of twelve lawyers who had their full names inscribed in the tall wall of the wide, lush lobby, crowding each other out of the huge brass plate.

Philip Rombly III (as his business card read) was taller than the taller Mexican and wore a black suit. His thick, curly, dark hair surrounded a soft, unformed, tanned face that had a little

From *Best New Chicano Literature*, ed. Julian Palley (Tempe, AZ: Bilingual Press/Editorial Bilingüe, 1989), 100–104. Copyright © 1989 Bilingual Press/Editorial Bilingüe. Reprinted with permission of Arizona State University.

swarthy radish for a nose; small, blue, darting eyes that stood still and widened for emphasis completed his face.

"Manny Rodriguez! Glad to see you! What's up?" asked the lawyer in a silly, inappropriate way, of the peasant who stood in the doorway, unsure as to the strange etiquette of these white men who smiled and shook your hand warmly while you tried to look angry and offended.

"Came to get Manuel's $1,000," said the younger Mexican without preamble to the surprised lawyer.

"Now I told him that I needed a letter of employment from his employer before I could start the citizenship procedure. Tell him that."

The Mexican walked to the large easy chair opposite the lawyer's desk and sat down without invitation. Manuel followed suit.

"It's been two years and you never moved on the case. Now he wants his money back and we'll leave," he said, ignoring the lawyer's request.

"I can't move without that letter, you tell him that. It's all his doing. I've done a lotta work on his case. I've put in a lot of time." Putting his hand on the phone as he talked, he put on his professional voice and asked his secretary to bring in the "Rodríguez file."

They both ignored Manuel . . . he wasn't there. Manuel, the aggrieved party, sat silently, only half understanding the goings-on . . . a spectator in his own fight. He understood bricks, mortar and wood; they were honest, with straightforward natures, as long as you followed basic rules of nature and geometry.

Building materials had a noble simplicity; they were not out to trick or deceive you. Although some were easier to work with than others, you could always trust them to behave in a thoroughly predictable manner. Materials were so strong yet so vulnerable if only you knew their secrets. It was a matter of contradictions and opposite natures: his hands, though horny, were soft compared to wood, yet he could bend steel and order it around; concrete, in its liquid state, was a hapless gruel manipulated into any shape or container, but once hardened it became as immutable as any thousand-year-old rock. Wood and tile became plastic in his hands, yielding beauty and utility.

Soft hands enslaving hard wood and metal. Some materials were more slavish than others, but all surrendered their strength and might to the seductive cunning of manually applied physics, persuading, convincing them.

Materials he could understand, but men, who knew them? How could you tell? What was so right for one was nearly death to another. It was not possible to understand men.

His rescuer was a learned man, cultured; he could even speak English and write. And yet he seemed almost a hoodlum as he addressed the lawyer, so disrespectful! Even though he himself felt angry and wronged by the crafty lawyer, a man had to behave according to courtesy, even in anger, not like this, like a commoner! If only he could speak English, if only he could fight for himself, if only he knew what to do.

The secretary politely knocked, entered, and handed her boss the file.

"See, look here," he said, pointing to the bulging file the secretary brought in. "It's all there."

"We want the $1,000, not talk. I've already blown two hours on you; I can't wait anymore. We're going to lean on you if you don't deliver." The Mexican slouched, quietly menacing.

"I don't want trouble, but look at the work I've done. Can't we compromise, say $500? Tell him."

"Phil, you made a few calls, wrote a few notes maybe, that's about all. This guy's a working slob; he lives from hand to mouth, after busting his balls on any construction job he can find. He does real work; you're a lawyer." The Mexican took off his dark glasses with deliberate, slow movements as he sat up in the large chair, coming from his recumbent, leisurely slouch.

"This guy uses his body like a cheap tool every day. Parts of his body are older than the rest from overuse. He's 54 and all he has is a twenty-year-old truck and second-rate tools and you want to take him. He travels back and forth from Mexico without papers, doesn't speak English, and because you treated him nice after he put in doors for you, he thought he could trust you. I'm going to give you a hundred bucks for your work. Give him back $900 and we're even," said the Mexican, never looking at the apprehensive lawyer, speaking quietly into his lap.

The lawyer's mind raced, weighing the pros and cons; caught between his not wanting to "lose" $900 and the unknown fear that was overcoming his sense of economy.

He felt guilty and threatened. The work he had done on the case was minimal and he had never been so bluntly confronted. The Mexican's cold, indifferent manner had penetrated his social shell of self-confidence. It was eerie. The stocky, English-speaking Mexican reminded him of the mean neighborhood greaseballs he had grown up with in Pomona. That quiet, indirect, cold aggression that would suddenly explode in mindless fury. They didn't seem to care. If you were friends, they would slash their bellies open for you. But if you messed with their sisters, they would look up your entire family.

On the other hand, they were so dumb and fearful of authority. They would respectfully retreat before any show of authority or official sanction. They always seemed apologetic and smiley, especially the older ones. It was the younger ones that seemed to have a vague grasp of their rights. Still, you never knew. He might be able to talk sense into the spick, but he seemed so remote. These guys were primitive.

"Look, maybe we can talk about this," he said to the reclining menace. "I don't have any money right now."

"How much you got in your wallet? Take it out!"

Mechanically, realizing the Mexican was implacable, he took the wallet out and held out for all to see the $40.00 he had.

"See, I have no money!" he said, realizing his hopes for negotiations were evaporating.

"What about those rings? Take them off. How much are your teeth worth?"

The lawyer felt his composure fall from him; he was being robbed in his own office and he could not stop himself from cooperating. He felt ten years old again, being shaken down by neighborhood spicks. Oh, God.

"I can't take them off. I never do," he said, nearly whining, extending his large, soft hands, palms down, towards the Mexican, and then brandishing them like shields, waggling his large wooly head for emphasis, his eyes widening.

School had let out an hour ago and his mother would be searching the route to school. I got to get home.

"All right. Make out a check for $900."

"I haven't got it," squeaked out Phil, against the wall, his heart thundering.

"You don't seem to appreciate the gravity of your situation, Phil. I don't want to hassle with you; I now know what you look like, you know what I look like, and you'll never see me again. I don't ever want to see you again," the Mexican said, his droopy moustache making his face appear melancholy with his slow, soft, menacing voice contradicting his looks.

Phil scrambled in his mind for the checkbook, but in reality his ego moved slowly and calmly and wrote out the check in his large, tidy handwriting.

The Mexicans took the check and left.

The lawyer took the rest of the day off.

6.3 A TASTE OF SUCCESS
Mona Ragab

When he and all the other employees saw the beautiful woman parading across the television screen in living color with her heady perfume which he had created with his own hands, he felt certain he had mastered his craft. At least she had no fault to find with it—she was strutting like a peacock showing off his brilliant feathers. No one cared about what might be going on inside a person's head. In any case his fellow employees no longer shunned him like a mangy rat. He had at last learned not to talk about things that did not interest them. Only a few days before he had been thinking how impossible it would be to become one of them. Then one after the other they had started to befriend him—ever since he stopped counting the bottles of perfume, half of which they carried out the back door. He had cut down on his critical comments and no longer scowled or attempted to flaunt his moral idealism.

When they met the next morning inside the large factory, there was general rejoicing and delight everywhere. He found them, congratulating each other on what they had accomplished for the company and for themselves. But a bit of his conscience was still at large. It destroyed the chains he had tied around his tongue. It got up on its hind legs, challenging him, as if it wanted to speak for one last time, in spite of him. He went up to an older man who looked like someone who would have hoped for honest work to support him through his last years. He spoke to him of the sudden disappearance of conscience. It was buried, while everyone kept silent, deep underground reposing there with musty skulls. Shouldn't they dig it up and restore it to its rightful place? Then it could spread over the surface of the earth. Was it not fitting for the two of them to work together, waking those who slumbered, were heedless, deceived themselves? The man did not understand or pretended not to. He answered tersely. 'What's that you're saying? Don't get involved in something that would be fruitless. You come help me. We've got to put our minds to our work. In a few days we've got to deliver the new perfume."

So he proceeded with the work of producing the new perfume blend which was due to flood the markets shortly. A concentrated barrage of advertisements on television affirmed that the new perfume was the pride of Egyptian production for the export trade. Whenever he relapsed into absent-mindedness, the old man nagged at him to bring him back to his senses. "Why get involved? Come help me. Enough of this brooding. We've got to deliver the new batch on schedule."

The old man's lips parted in a lame, rubbery smile which added emphasis to his next words. "Did you see the blonde in the advertisements yesterday? I wish I were the young man who appeared with her to plant a kiss on her rosy cheek. If only she knew that I'm the one who prepared that magical formula for her which captivated his senses and made him chase after her, madly in love."

The young man moved closer to him, trembling. His steps became labored as his resistance faded. He noticed that the old man, who pretended not to see him, had once again deliberately not added the prescribed amount of jasmine essence to the new bottles, but had poured in some alcohol in its place. The old man paid no attention to him—as though he were a small, inquisitive bug prowling around the rooms without exciting anyone's attention. The old man completed his

From *Egyptian Tales and Short Stories of the 1970's and 1980's*, ed. W.M. Hutchins (New York: American University in Cairo Press, 1987). Copyright © 1987 American University in Cairo Press.

work with an astonishing assurance. Then he slipped the bottle with the remainder of the essence into his pocket to use as he saw fit afterwards. Perhaps he would sell it that way, or use it to mix up some additional bottles of the perfume blend which he could sell on his own. Before the older man started to leave, his pockets full, he gave the young man another sermon. "There's plenty of loot for everyone. The little guys get some and the big ones don't care. Let things go on as they are. It's to everyone's advantage."

Then he drew back and deliberately flexed his chest muscles to prove that at sixty he was more youthful and in better shape than the younger man. When he gave the young man a pat on the shoulder with his sinewy hand, the latter almost fell over backward as though he were a creature composed of a sorry stack of decaying bones. His struggle with himself had exhausted him. His muscles had started to sag. As his burdens increased, his power of resistance seeped away without his knowing how. It had seeped out until it was all gone, like a man's shadow which disappears gradually before his eyes until it is no longer visible as the sun rises directly overhead. After holding out for a long time, he finally had to give in. If he was to live among them and do as they did he must take a share in their booty.

How could he meet the cost of his recurring burdens? Living on ration-card rice had impaired the health of his family. It bloated their bellies without providing strength for their bodies.

He could not get out of his mind the long list the doctor had written out last week for his two-year-old son. "He needs proteins, fruit, regular doses of vitamins," the doctor had stressed after filling the white paper from top to bottom. His salary, which had not budged from its niche for years, would not suffice to buy half of what was required. His wife had become round and heavy. She had puffed out like a blimp. It was clear from looking at her that her diet consisted of rice and macaroni, the only things they could afford to buy on his salary. Her stomach had a wild craving for a piece of fresh meat. And there was no end to what the schools required. He would be obliged to buy the new school uniform for his middle son before the end of September, only one week away. In addition to that there were the annual fees, and the books, notebooks, and pens. His oldest daughter, who started middle school this year, had informed him importantly the day before that she needed extra lessons in math: the teacher did not explain enough in class. And now he brazenly holds out his hand for payment in advance: two pounds a lesson for a group, and four pounds a lesson if private. The teacher had told him bluntly, "She needs extra lessons like all the other students. Your daughter thinks she's a genius."

At midday he decided to take his share of the booty. When circumstances are compelling, it is not hard to be sneaky. All he had to do was to drop some bottles nonchalantly into a pocket of his trousers or shirt and excuse himself, alleging that something had come up. Then he would sell the loot for his own profit the way all the others did. The guard in his booth at the gate presented no obstacle: he was accustomed to overlooking the bulging pockets and their contents which slipped past. It was just a question of putting the price of a pack of cigarettes in his pocket. He was spurred on by the glowing headlines in the morning papers, describing the glorious success of their model company with its illustrious reputation. Everything around him confirmed the company's success and high productivity. Its figures demonstrated how hard they worked. The director general was well-liked. He was up to his neck in preparing the budget, setting up important meetings, putting out irrefutable propaganda, and endeavoring to select personally the dazzling models needed to display the merchandise, who were constantly being changed. The executive director was busy creating new products and seductive advertisements, releasing appropriate photographs to the newspapers to be tagged with particularly brilliant remarks, responding to telephone interviews, taking trips and buying clothes. It was the general supervisor who had until recently been his sole refuge. For a long time they had discussed all the shady goings-on. Then a couple of days ago he had seen the general supervisor turning a key suspended from a gold chain in the lock of a resplendent automobile. He learned that he had opened a private office where he worked after company hours. His experience in this successful firm had broadened his horizons. Now he directed his own firm which was an even more profitable enterprise for him.

When the new raises were announced, no one had time to be overjoyed or disappointed. They were preparing for a surprise visit by a high government official.

He asked his fellow workers, "How can it be a surprise visit when we are putting red carpets at the entrances, spreading clean sand by the gatehouse, and fixing broken-down equipment?"

No one bothered to answer such obstinate naïveté. In any case the answer was not long in coming. The exquisitely elegant government official soon made his appearance, arm in arm with the director general. He repeatedly expressed his admiration and his satisfaction with their modern managerial style, high rate of productivity, professionalism and morale. After the obligatory smiles and formal salutations, the workers gathered around to welcome them. The foreman delivered an overly long speech about working overtime, sincere toil, and sweat shed for the sake of the country. The executive director left his cubicle to make an official state visit throughout the premises. He presented the high-ranking government official with large parcels of innovative, new product samples, spreading before him palpable proof of progress and of an imminent export drive to European markets.

The last remaining sentient portion of his conscience almost left him. While he looked on in a stupor, everything proceeded in a way that strained his credulity. But proceed it did. Everyone was having a good time, relaxing either in the magnificent, glistening chairs or behind the silent metal instruments. On every floor people were being pleasant to each other. All he had to do was direct his mouth to emit vibrations of his voice, saying what would please them, now that he was finally able to keep his tongue from saying things that would alienate them.

The next day he took the plunge at work and emerged a champion. He fully grasped the concepts of graft and diligently acquired the methods of deceit. The old man gave him a pat on the shoulder to show his pleasure and approval when he observed the young man pop some bottles of perfume concentrate into his pocket. He sold them after work. He made good use of the money and returned home carrying packages stuffed with fruit and meat and colored tins. He entered his home like a warrior bringing back the spoils of victory. His wife greeted him with a deluge of kisses, of an intensity he had not experienced for years. She set to work untying and unwrapping the parcels.

When the advertisement came on featuring the beautiful model in the fiery dress who told about the new perfume, it found him seated, surrounded by his children. He felt convinced that as of that evening he had become a true partner in the glorious success of the company. His wife pointed to it with pride as her mouth sank into the food. When she invited him to join them at the dinner spread before them, however, he found he had no appetite.

She insisted and he agreed only grudgingly, although he had not eaten all day. She selected a gleaming apple from the large platter and presented it to him. When he bit into it, the drops of juice that trickled down his throat were of a bitterness he had never tasted before.

Section 7
———— Managerial Insights ————

7.1   NAVIGATING THE HOSTILE MAZE: A FRAMEWORK FOR RUSSIAN ENTREPRENEURSHIP
Sheila M. Puffer and Daniel J. McCarthy

A FRAMEWORK FOR UNDERSTANDING PROFESSIONALLY ORIENTED RUSSIAN ENTREPRENEURIAL VENTURES

In this article we develop a framework to help Western executives understand Russian entrepreneurs and their ventures. (See Figure 1.) We illustrate the framework with examples from five professionally oriented entrepreneurial service and production ventures we tracked throughout the decade of the 1990s. . . . Profiled in Table 1, these largely successful ventures were outnumbered by many others that failed. Vybor, one of the profiled firms, was profitable for many years, but went bankrupt in 1996. Drawing on the framework, the article concludes with actions for strengthening entrepreneurship in Russia.

MINDSET IS KEY IN RUSSIAN ENTREPRENEURSHIP

We view the entrepreneurial mindset as the key element in Russian entrepreneurship. This mindset, combined with the creative use of scarce resources and effective scanning of the hostile environment, can produce entrepreneurially oriented goals and decisions. These, in turn, lead to the relentless pursuit of outcomes, especially organizational survival, and, where possible, growth and profitability. The components of the framework can interact in various sequences. For instance, changes in resources, the environment, or the entrepreneurial mindset can affect one another. And once outcomes occur, they can influence resources, the entrepreneurial mindset, or even the firm's environment.

We developed our framework by analyzing professionally oriented entrepreneurial ventures. Thus it may not necessarily apply to less complex operations, such as retail kiosks, privatized state-owned enterprises, or underground-economy operations.

ECLECTIC RESEARCH FOUNDATION FOR THE FRAMEWORK

We have tied our framework to an eclectic body of research on entrepreneurship and strategic management. The definition of entrepreneurship we use is [by Ireland et al.]: "a context-dependent social process through which individuals and teams create wealth by bringing together unique packages of resources to exploit marketplace opportunities." . . .

Excerpted from *The Academy of Management Executive* 15, no. 4 (November 2001): 24–36. Copyright © 2001 Academy of Management Executive. Reprinted with permission.

Figure 1   **A Framework for Russian Entrepreneurship**

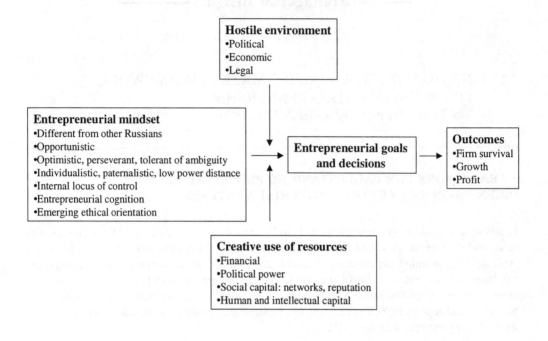

A general definition of an entrepreneur, which aptly applies in the Russian case, is: "an imaginative actor who seizes contingent opportunities and exploits any and all means at hand to fulfill a plurality of current and future aspirations, many of which are shaped and created through the very process of economic decision making and are not given a priori." . . .

Entrepreneurial Mindset Shaped by Adversity

. . . Like entrepreneurs elsewhere, Russian entrepreneurs see themselves as different from their countrymen, and have a strong sense of individualism and internal locus of control, and use entrepreneurial cognition to scan the environment. In contrast to their counterparts in other countries, because of a hostile environment and scarce resources, Russian entrepreneurs tend to be more opportunistic, optimistic, perseverant, and tolerant of ambiguity. Russian entrepreneurs also tend to be somewhat more hierarchical (higher power distance) and more paternalistic, and some may be less consistent in their ethical orientation than entrepreneurs elsewhere.

Different from Other Russians

. . . Research on Russian entrepreneurs has found that they see themselves as being different from other Russians, feel out of the mainstream of society, and are looked upon with suspicion for going against the collectivist and egalitarian culture. Entrepreneurs feel responsible for their own survival and success, whereas the former communist, centrally planned system fostered an

Table 1

Five Russian Entrepreneurial Ventures

Characteristics	Premier Bank	Aquarius Systems	BusinessLink	EpicRus	Vybor
Type of business	Commercial banking	Assembly and distribution of computers and cash register systems	Consulting, personnel search, advertising, real estate development	Software and systems for accounting and manufacturing	Trading company, distribution, and retailing of consumer goods
Year founded	1988	1992	1991	1993	1988
Locations	Moscow	Moscow and key Russian cities	St. Petersburg, Moscow, Novgorod, and Finland	Moscow, St. Petersburg	Moscow and 40 other Russian cities
Initial capital source	Founders, close associates	Equity raised as an open-stock company	Founders	Founder, close associates	Founders, credit from suppliers
Founders	Two professor/economists, male, 60s, succeeded in 1996 by a son with U.S. MBA	Computer scientist, lawyer/politician, male, 30s	Four university professors/senior administrators, male, early 40s	Big Five accounting firm manager with U.S. MBA, Russian Ph.D., female, 30	Two brothers, 30s, a musician and a mathematician, both won national awards in their fields
Highlights	First registered commercial bank; 25 full-time and 30 part-time employees and assets of $10 million by 1996, ranking in top 20 percent of banks; survived 1998 national financial crisis	One of top three Russian PC and server sales firms in 2001; 27 service centers and 76 regional service partners; sole Russian computer company with ISO 9002 certification	St. Petersburg's largest advertising agency by 1996; $14 million revenues and 200 employees in 1998; by 2001, main revenues from real estate company	Founder honored as one of Russia's top women executives; company named best accounting software firm in Russia in 2001; 150 employees; 200+ customers	One of top 50 trading firms by 1993, with 500 employees throughout Russia; bankrupt in 1996 with $2 million debt

entitlement mentality by guaranteeing jobs and social benefits. Russian entrepreneurs, like their counterparts in other countries, possess a risk-taking orientation. The general Russian population is much more risk averse because of a tradition of criticism and punishment for mistakes and initiative.

Nonetheless, it is inappropriate to categorize Russians: they often appear contradictory and incomprehensible to foreigners, as well as simultaneously dependent on, yet wary of, their leaders. Also, some older Russian managers endured many hardships during the communist period, causing them to be self-reliant to ensure personal survival and well-being, while also conforming to the collectivist system. Some older entrepreneurs have successfully made the transition. For instance, the 70-year-old founder of Premier Bank, after a successful academic career in finance and economics, decided to put his ideas about the market economy into practice and opened a commercial bank.

Opportunistic

Entrepreneurs have been characterized as opportunists rather than as risk lovers. The decision to become an entrepreneur in both Russia and the U.S. is due more to intelligent proactive thinking rather than a reaction to a negative job experience, and both groups optimistically seek opportunities. One reason that Russian entrepreneurs are likely to be more opportunistic than entrepreneurs elsewhere is that few other stakeholders, such as venture capitalists and bankers, were in place to restrain them in their decision making. As BusinessLink grew, for instance, the founders diversified into real-estate development, sparked by the rapidly increasing value of the building they occupied. Perhaps the most opportunistic of the entrepreneurs we studied were the two brothers who founded Vybor. As one explained at our first meeting: "I'll stay until it's not so profitable. Then, I'll make a change."

Optimistic, Perseverant, Tolerant of Ambiguity

Entrepreneurs are optimistic, believing that they have greater chances of success than others, are highly perseverant, and tolerant of ambiguity. In hostile transitional economies, they have also been called relentless. Russian entrepreneurs appear more optimistic than entrepreneurs elsewhere, perhaps due to a Russian cultural tendency to have unrealistic expectations, sometimes to the extent of believing in miracles. They also tend to be more perseverant, since alternatives for making a living are exceedingly limited. And their high tolerance of ambiguity arises from the need to function in a chronically hostile and unpredictable environment.

The entrepreneurs in all five firms we followed maintained an optimistic outlook even in dire circumstances. For instance, in 1996, after Vybor was $2 million in debt and went bankrupt, the co-founder started two new businesses. He stated:

> A few years ago, a lot of people practically wanted to steal what they could get from their companies and then leave. Now they want to work for what they get. So I'm optimistic. To live without optimism is impossible.

Perseverance paid off for Aquarius's founders. After selling their component-production plant because of adverse tax policies, they repurchased it and resumed production when those policies changed. Such bold actions helped them become Russia's leading computer producer.

An American executive described the perseverance of EpicRus's CEO:

She's very savvy and she'll survive no matter what. I can't think of another person who could have pulled off what she has pulled off.

Russian entrepreneurs typically show greater tolerance for ambiguity than managers from former state-owned enterprises, who often view plans as absolutes to be followed, rather than guidelines that can be changed. They also experience greater ambiguity than entrepreneurs in the West. As the CEO of EpicRus explained:

Americans are different because they were raised as part of a system that works for the consumer. It's too easy. The people are so much a product of their beautifully developed system. The system is much more complex here, and because of that, this country has not advanced as much as America.

Individualistic, Paternalistic, Low Power Distance

One study found that Russian respondents scored moderately on Hofstede's dimensions that could be considered supportive of entrepreneurship—individualism and low power distance—but higher on paternalism, which is not necessarily associated with entrepreneurship. These responses might result from traditional beliefs and values as well as the newness of entrepreneurship in Russia. Paternalism stems from strong collectivist traditions as well as vestiges of the communist system, which required enterprises to provide for employees' material and social needs. And higher power distance, with more hierarchical tendencies than entrepreneurs elsewhere, results from Russia's tradition of top-down organizational structures.

However, younger respondents exhibited more entrepreneurial inclinations, reporting the highest scores for masculinity and the lowest for paternalism. For instance, a young entrepreneur, who was in the process of setting up EpicRus's St. Petersburg office, stated:

The big attraction of this job was the excitement, the responsibility, and I said to myself, I'll go for it.

She felt very empowered in this team-oriented organization thanks to the founder's low-power-distance style. Similarly, BusinessLink organized itself as a holding company, allowing business-unit heads wide discretion. This is consistent with the finding that Russian middle managers generally prefer democratic, rather than authoritarian, leadership styles in their superiors.

Internal Locus of Control

Entrepreneurs generally have a high internal locus of control, perceiving that they can influence their own destiny. Although some Russian entrepreneurs have shown a lower internal locus of control than those in other countries, they see themselves as having a higher locus than other Russians. One study found that Russians generally viewed their physical and social environments as having a small zone of safety and a very large zone of danger, with the environment containing mostly hazards. In contrast, the founders and leaders of all the entrepreneurial firms we studied took control of their own destinies. For instance, the CEO of EpicRus demonstrated an extremely high locus of control:

I got into this role of general manager . . . and it just clicks all of a sudden. I'm in charge and I had this voice inside of me telling me what to do. It doesn't mean I don't make mistakes, but my judgment gets better, and I love it.

Entrepreneurial Cognition

The entrepreneurial mindset is also characterized by scanning and interpreting information through the process of entrepreneurial cognition. Entrepreneurs often interpret changes in their environments as opportunities, in contrast to others who might ignore them or interpret them as threats. For instance, BusinessLink's founder saw the government's privatization policies as an opportunity for diversification:

> Privatization is here, and to my mind it is foolish not to use the chance to buy real estate very cheap, or to buy industrial facilities or shares of companies which are also very cheap.

Entrepreneurs concentrate their scanning on areas in the environment they consider most important, and scan intensely when they perceive threats and opportunities. They use social cognitive interpretations in selecting, analyzing, and pursuing alternatives. Premier Bank's founder scanned constantly, utilizing personal information sources, and kept extremely well informed about potential government policies and economic events. For instance, he set a policy of making loans repayable in as few as 10 days because of the volatile and inflation-ridden ruble. The founder of EpicRus gained substantial intrapreneurship experience in software and systems development in her previous positions at Big Five consulting firms. With such a background, she needed to perform only moderate scanning when these activities became the focus of her new company.

Entrepreneurs prefer informal information sources to formal or official ones. They are seen as operating "at the edge of what they do not know," and develop metaphors and mental models to interpret situations. The Russian entrepreneurs we studied clearly preferred obtaining information from their own networks. They generally considered more formal sources, such as the government or the press, to be unreliable because of political objectives or inaccurate data. Russians also have a cultural tradition of using metaphors and stories with themes of overcoming hardships and obstacles to guide them during adversity.

Emerging Ethical Orientation

Russian entrepreneurs have had little consistent guidance on what constitutes ethical behavior. Many have difficulty fully understanding the ethics of their decisions because of cultural influences from the past. Many exhibit a dual ethical standard of adhering to universal ethical principles in close friendships, but not in impersonal business transactions. This leads at times to behaviors that cause distrust among business partners. Also, since many entrepreneurs came from the shadow economy, it is crucial that they learn about and adopt high ethical standards to gain credibility.

Russian entrepreneurs are also influenced by the new market-oriented economy, with its unfamiliar conditions and standards. This can result in confusion, sometimes making them seem to ignore ethics in their decisions, despite their intentions otherwise. In other cases, unethical actions result from blatant criminal intent, such as the illegal takeover, and physical threats against the owners, of the St. Petersburg franchise of Subway, a U.S. fast-food chain. Fortunately, in the past year or two the threat of the Russian mafia has become less pervasive.

Some Russian owner-managers have perceived themselves as less likely than Americans to engage in exploitive behavior, and as more rigid and less equivocal in their evaluations of ethical situations. All of the entrepreneurs in our study demonstrated high ethical standards. Such behavior was likely due to their own personal backgrounds and values, and reinforced by the professional requirements of their businesses. The CEO of EpicRus demonstrated her values:

> Everyone around me should see a positive impact. I am very lucky that I can make other people's lives better—customers, colleagues, employees, and family.

Hostile Political, Economic, and Legal Environment

. . . The environment in Russia and Central and Eastern European countries is often described as traditionally hostile to entrepreneurial activities; in Russia, it was aversive as far back as the tsarist era, when modest entrepreneurial activity was conducted primarily by minority ethnic groups. With some exceptions, entrepreneurship was illegal throughout most of the Soviet period, from 1920 through 1991. The 20th-century social experiment of central planning and egalitarianism had, in the early 1990s, given way to faltering attempts at developing a market-oriented economy.

In surveys throughout the 1990s, entrepreneurs reported that government regulations, taxes, the political situation, and financing were their most serious problems. Most entrepreneurs also reported counting on support from the state during their startup phase, but 40 percent also believed that the state was likely to create opposition and obstacles to their progress. In fact, it was less the absence of regulation and legal structure, and more the excessive proliferation of regulations and red tape, such as those required to start a business, that hindered development of entrepreneurial ventures. This was certainly the case for the founder of Premier Bank, who declared that his main headache was the Central Bank. It interfered in every aspect of his business, the most serious problem being that it kept 20 percent of each bank's assets as a reserve, severely limiting funds that could be invested. The Russian economic environment in the late 1990s was described by a number of Western joint-venture managers as alien, sometimes impossible, and absolutely unpredictable.

The country's financial crisis of August 1998 created serious problems, but eventually evolved into a relatively stable, though hostile, environment for entrepreneurs. Key developments were Vladimir Putin's election as president in 2000, the devaluation of the ruble, and the relative prosperity resulting from oil exports sold at high world energy prices. Business groups in transitioning economies were supported at times by policies of lower levels of inward investment, import substitution, and protection of domestic businesses. The dramatic devaluation of the ruble saw a marked decrease in competition from international firms whose imported products and services had become very expensive relative to those of Russian companies. By late 2001, promising developments occurred in tax legislation and corporate governance.

Hostile and complex environments can foster high levels of risk taking, innovation, and proactivity on the part of entrepreneurs. Volatility can bring with it greater opportunities, particularly if resource deployment is done in a way that controls the inherent risk. Aquarius, for instance, took advantage of the chaos affecting foreign companies like IBM, which stopped assembling computers in Russia due to the vacillating tax policy on imported components. Aquarius was able to fill the gap, since it produced parts in its own plant outside Moscow.

Creative Use of Scarce Resources

The ways in which Russian entrepreneurs obtained and allocated resources reflect the extraordinary scarcity of all types of resources after the fall of the Soviet Union in 1991. This scarcity was far more extreme than that experienced by entrepreneurs in more developed economies. With personal capital being the only source of financing for most Russian entrepreneurs, they were forced to be highly creative in developing other resources. They attempted to garner political power and influence, develop social capital through networks and building their reputations, and attract intellectual capital in the form of talented professionals. Marshalling such resources was extremely challenging in an environment hostile toward entrepreneurs and fraught with risks, including the omnipresent Russian mafia.

Financial Resources

Financial resources were exceedingly scarce for most Russian entrepreneurs, and the long tradition of bartering substituted at times for scarce capital. Still, access to adequate financial resources, primarily personal, was a key element for firm survival and growth. One source of help was the social safety net that some entrepreneurs retained by working in state-owned enterprises while simultaneously bootstrapping their new businesses. Startup funds drawn from personal sources were more common than in developed economies, and many outside investors were reluctant to work with entrepreneurs having questionable business practices, such as not registering their companies and operating in cash to avoid taxes.

The paucity of capital sources often led to professionally oriented service businesses, like BusinessLink and EpicRus, rather than physical-asset-based firms like Aquarius. The companies we studied were bootstrapped primarily by personal finances of the founders and their families. Premier Bank also obtained initial capital from close friends to meet government reserve-funds requirements. Aquarius and Vybor obtained supplier credit and bank loans to finance initial working capital, and Aquarius raised equity as an open-stock company. Vybor also engaged in barter, sold goods at reduced prices in exchange for shares of other companies, and accepted merchandise on consignment.

Political Power

Political power was found to be the most significant single resource in predicting survival and growth of small Russian companies in the 1990s. Access to power was important for obtaining permits to start companies, export, and conduct other activities. Such power could also bring favorable treatment regarding taxes, contracts, grants, real estate, and other assets.

Most new entrepreneurs did not have easy access to government officials, and tried many approaches, including making contacts in management training programs. Aquarius executives made political connections by joining the Moscow Information Technology Club, whose president was the director of information management in the Moscow city government. Aquarius's CEO noted that this political connection helped them gain the city as a client. In general, however, private spinoffs from state enterprises were better positioned than startups to gain access to officials.

Social Capital: Networks and Reputation

Social capital consists of the actual and potential resources entrepreneurs gain from knowing others, being part of a social network, or having a good reputation within a network. . . .

Russian entrepreneurs needed new networks because they usually lacked access to Soviet-era groups, as well as to new networks established among large companies and government officials. Commitment and trust among network members in Eastern European business networks are typically low, the ties extremely weak, the network knowledge poor, and participants few. Management and market institutions are so weak that individuals take care to sign agreements and contracts only with people they trust. However, networks have traditionally been a way of getting things done in Russia, and entrepreneurs well understood their value.

Some Russian entrepreneurs developed their reputations and networks from their employment in state-owned enterprises and state institutions. BusinessLink's founders continued working as high-ranking university administrators and professors, positions that allowed them to foster valuable relationships with colleagues abroad while growing their consulting, executive search, and advertising businesses. The CEO stated: "We saw Russia opening for business, and we had lots of Western friends. More and more clients came to us." . . .

Supportive networks also help combat hostile groups or hindrance networks that could disrupt the broader network through threats or sabotage. Thus entrepreneurs in hostile environments must be especially vigilant in selecting network members. For instance, Premier Bank utilized its network of influentials to retain its prime location near the Kremlin, in response to harassments from government groups that wanted its offices. Premier's founder explained: "Everything in this regard seems to work on who you know, not by the law."

Human and Intellectual Capital

We treat human and intellectual capital as an integrated resource base. Human capital is the source of innovation, which is "the means by which intellectual capital produces wealth," while intellectual capital is "the sum of everything everybody in a company knows that gives it a competitive edge." Intellectual capital can include knowledge, ideas, and inventions that are often protected by patents, trademarks, and copyrights. Because of an incomplete and inconsistent legal system, much of Russia's intellectual capital is not well protected. In a survey of 50 major foreign companies investing in Russia, half estimated their annual losses from intellectual property violations to be at least $1 million, with a third reporting $5 to $50 million in losses.

With patents and copyrights at risk, Russian entrepreneurs recognize that their intellectual capital resides primarily in their employees, and work hard to retain them. It has been difficult to attract Russians to entrepreneurial activities. Entrepreneurs have been envied, and even resented, for their success by more traditional individuals, partly because some of them, often called "New Russians," flaunted their new-found wealth. Still, attracting technical and professional talent, and individuals with international experience has been crucial. . . .

ENTREPRENEURIAL GOALS AND DECISIONS

The overall goals of entrepreneurship in transitional economies are said to stem from the lure of capitalism as a pull factor, and the failure of state-owned enterprises as a push factor. Many individuals in the public sector chose entrepreneurship to increase their wealth and exercise long-stifled leadership potential, and in the early years of the transition, Russian entrepreneurs reported their goals to be profits, wealth, independence, and economic security.

However, growth was often interrupted by external circumstances, requiring entrepreneurs to focus on survival and tighter internal controls. This happened to the profitable Premier Bank after the financial crisis of 1998, when the government defaulted on its loans. Like many entrepreneurial firms, the bank reverted to goals and strategies of the survival or startup stage. At Aquarius, the original founders regained control and refocused on computers, retrenching from the overdiversification pursued by other owners. After their trading company failed, Vybor's founders started new companies since their primary goal was to run profitable businesses. The CEO of EpicRus, after the country's 1998 financial crisis, replaced her growth strategy with a near-term goal:

> To become one of the few survivors in the industry thanks to the quality of [our] products, services, people, and reputation.

. . . In the mid-1990s, many Russian entrepreneurs shifted their goals from making profits to utilizing skills, being their own boss, and feeling a sense of accomplishment. The early emphasis on profitability and wealth could well have been due to the Russian tradition of seeing things as being achievable without sufficient effort or resources. Additionally, profit was likely misunderstood at the outset, since the concept had a different meaning under communism.

Entrepreneurs rely more than managers on vivid incidents as decision criteria rather than systematic data. Russian entrepreneurs do so because they view more formal sources of information as unreliable. Other heuristics common to entrepreneurs include relying on their own ideas rather than seeking the advice of experts. For instance, Aquarius's executives needed to decide what types of activities to pursue when they regained control of the company. The CEO stated:

> We had a lot of discussions about what was missing in Aquarius. We didn't have a marketing service. We had a pretty good idea what it was but, as we say, we know everything but we don't do it. That, unfortunately, is our weakness.

OUTCOMES: SURVIVAL, GROWTH, AND PROFIT

The extremely hostile environment and scarce resources, coupled with a distinctive mindset, help explain why the goals, decisions, and outcomes of Russian entrepreneurs differ in various ways from those of entrepreneurs in other countries. The entrepreneurs in the five ventures we followed focused on firm survival, growth, and profit, with varying degrees of emphasis, and their decisions reflected constantly changing circumstances.

Premier Bank had to focus on survival rather than growth, primarily because the government defaulted on bonds the bank held in 1998. The new CEO, a son of one of the founders, stated that the country had been thrown into an economic morass, and that banks and businesses could expect little help from the government. Yet he did not see the situation as hopeless. Premier continued to serve its clients, and cut salaries by 40 percent rather than laying off employees.

Aquarius emerged as the leading Russian computer company, having expanded its product line, distribution channels, and service-center network. It partnered with other Russian distribution firms, and with Newbridge Networks of Canada, to land major contracts, including one with the Russian social insurance fund. The company also focused in 2001 on expanding its trademarked Aquarius brand throughout Russia.

BusinessLink also grew throughout the decade and weathered the 1998 financial crisis. It cut personnel, rationalized its businesses, and lost some key international clients, but forged ahead optimistically because of its solid financial condition and business base. All business units continued to operate in 2001, with an emphasis on advertising and real-estate development. The advertising unit included a new Web-based business, Media International, and the personnel search unit's Web site advertised many managerial positions with leading international and Russian clients.

EpicRus, known as Platinum Russia until late 2000, was ranked that year as the best Russian software company in a Moscow International Accounting Forum survey. The company continued to grow profitably by following its strategy of providing localized versions of its licensed enterprise-resource-planning systems. By 2001, EpicRus offered software and systems development, technical support, training, and customization services for more than 200 international and domestic customers. Among its many partners were Microsoft, the Big Five U.S. accounting firms, and many well-known Russian systems integrators and consulting companies.

Vybor went bankrupt in 1996. Remaining true to their objectives of running businesses as long as they remained economically viable, they immediately started an imported shoe-distribution business, and one brother also became the head of a plastic-pipe plant.

STRENGTHENING RUSSIAN ENTREPRENEURSHIP

Strengthening Russian entrepreneurship is an obligation for some, and an opportunity for many. Drawing upon the framework in this article, we suggest actions for Russian entrepreneurs and Westerners who might do business with them.

Russian Entrepreneurs

Work with the Russian government and other groups to build a positive image of entrepreneurs. Russian entrepreneurs must emphasize that their reputation can be a critical resource to counteract the traditional Russian disdain for and suspicion of entrepreneurs. Working with the government and other Russian organizations, as well as respected entrepreneurs from other countries, entrepreneurs should publicize positive messages and incidents of legitimate entrepreneurial activities.

Demonstrate an ethical approach to doing business. Russian entrepreneurs can demonstrate the positive aspects of their entrepreneurial mindsets by doing business according to guidelines for ethical business behavior. They can utilize guidelines developed by the U.S.-Russia Business Development Committee and the Russian Chamber of Commerce and Industry, as well as publications by other Russian and international experts in business ethics.

Attend seminars and programs at home and abroad. Such activities can confirm for Russian entrepreneurs the effectiveness of their mindsets and provide opportunities to compare themselves to other entrepreneurs. They can also develop personal relationships with other Russian and international entrepreneurs to expand their networks and skill sets, and possibly connect with potential investors in such arenas as Harvard's annual Russian Investment Symposium.

Become involved in far-sighted organizations like Club 2015. Building a positive reputation for entrepreneurship can enhance the resource base for individuals and their ventures. A prominent group of progressive Russian business people founded Club 2015, based on a new social-contract scenario, with the goal of building trust among the Russian government, citizens, and the business community. Membership in such groups is a signal of reliability to potential partners and other sources of resources and support.

Western Business Partners

Develop relationships with Russian entrepreneurs built on trust and action with those who warrant that commitment. Becoming involved in partnerships can provide participants with additional resources such as networks that may produce mutual benefits. However, they must have reasonable assurance that the risk-return proposition makes it attractive to do so. A fundamental way of building trust is by treating partners with respect and following through on commitments.

Provide valid sources of information to supplement Russian entrepreneurs' more typical reliance on single incidents for information. Doing so can help strengthen relationships and build trust. Because trust is a two-way street, Western partners might approach members of respected organizations like Club 2015, and select entrepreneurs who do business according to ethical guidelines.

Look beyond short-term results achieved, which may be temporary. It is helpful to understand decision-making processes and their associated goals and outcomes from the Russian entrepreneurial perspective. Entrepreneurs who appear to be inconsistent in following their goals may, in fact, be guided by a vision, but must adapt quickly to their ever-changing and hostile environment. . . .

NAVIGATING THE HOSTILE MAZE

The framework developed in this article can be utilized as a tool for assessing entrepreneurship in Russia. For instance, the environment is beginning to show signs of becoming less hostile, with judicial and tax reforms underway, as well as progress in corporate governance and transparency. The objective for all stakeholders should be to help create the positive scenario articulated by Dmitry Kozak, the deputy head of the Russian presidential administration:

> I hope there comes a time—and on our part we will do everything for it to come as soon as possible—when there will be no obstacles to cooperation in conducting business within the USA or Russia—neither for Russian nor American entrepreneurs.

REFERENCES

Ireland, R.D., M.A. Hitt, S.M. Camp, and D. Sexton. 2001. "Integrating Entrepreneurship with Stategic Management Actions to Create Firm Wealth." *The Academy of Management Executive* 15, no. 1: 49–63.
Tepitskaia, H. 2001. "Interview with Dmitry N. Kozak." American–Russian Chamber of Commerce *Business Report* 9, no. 3: 13.

7.2 SETTLING CROSS-CULTURAL DISAGREEMENTS BEGINS WITH "WHERE" NOT "HOW"
Susan M. Adams

Disagreements and conflict are inevitable aspects of organizational life. Even when employees agree on desired outcomes, differing interpretations of a problem or its potential solutions can create conflict. As if the original problem isn't enough to handle, disagreements over how to solve it can create secondary problems. And as we all know, the consequences of mishandling disagreements are often messy and can lead to further discord.

For multinational organizations, however, conflict may be particularly problematic. Researcher Catherine Tinsley, of Georgetown University, believes that cultural biases may exacerbate the potential for mishandling disagreements. Her research suggests that organizational members from different cultures hold distinct preferences for how conflict should be resolved. Understanding cultural preferences for conflict resolution can help managers avoid the secondary problems that arise from mishandling disagreements.

Tinsley identified three culturally determined strategies for resolving conflict. First, individuals in disagreement can defer to status or power. Under this approach, those involved in a dispute look to high-ranking individuals for advice, for justification of their positions, or for personal status enhancement. Second, conflicting individuals can turn to rules as the way to settle conflict. They may focus on identifying the appropriate rule or regulation that would apply to the matter in dispute, or they may rely on an interpretation of existing rules in order to resolve a specific disagreement. Third, conflict participants may seek a solution that satisfies the underlying concerns of those involved by integrating their various self-interests. Individuals using this approach may look for ways to maximize their own interests and at the same time satisfy the concerns of others. Conflict resolution strategies such as prioritizing or sharing information, making concessions, or brainstorming may lead to innovative solutions that incorporate diverse interests.

Tinsley's research examined the extent to which cultural differences influenced managers' preferences for one of these three conflict resolution strategies. She chose to survey managers from Japan, Germany, and the United States, since these cultures differ in a number of ways that closely match the three methods for resolving disagreements. Tinsley expected Japanese managers would prefer to resolve conflict by deferring to status or power, since the Japanese culture honors status and authority and is characterized by a stronger degree of hierarchical differentiation than German and American cultures. In contrast, the German culture values formal, explicit agreements as means for regulating social interactions to a greater extent than Japanese or American cultures. Therefore, Tinsley expected German managers to prefer to resolve conflict through a reliance on regulations. Since Americans are considered to be polychronic, or able to handle several issues at once, particularly in order to maximize personal gain, Tinsley expected American managers to prefer an integrating interests strategy to resolve conflict.

Tinsley presented a hypothetical conflict scenario to Japanese, German and American managers similar in age, education and socioeconomic status. She asked the managers to then rate the importance of various conflict resolution methods for solving the hypothetical conflict. She

From *The Academy of Management Executive* 13, no. 1 (February 1999): 109–110. Copyright © 1999 Academy of Management Executive. Reprinted with permission.

also asked the managers several questions designed to measure their perceptions of relevant cultural dimensions.

As expected, Japanese managers preferred deferring to status power more than German and American managers. German managers preferred applying regulations more than American and Japanese managers. However, Germans were not solely bound to their preference for applying regulations, but indicated an almost equal preference for integrating interests. American managers preferred integrating interests more than German and Japanese managers.

It is no wonder that managers working in new cultures become frustrated and confused. What seems like a perfectly reasonable approach in one culture may seem ridiculous, disrespectful, inefficient, or unfair to managers from other cultures. Tinsley warns that American managers may be surprised to find that others do not share their preference for integrating the various interests of all parties to a disagreement. When their German colleagues insist upon following bureaucratic regulations, and their Japanese colleagues wish to solicit the advice of superiors, American managers may grow frustrated by the lack of attention given to negotiating a settlement that satisfies all parties' concerns. Similarly, Japanese and German managers may be uneasy with conflict resolution preferences that differ from their own.

Although this study did not specifically look at preferences of managers working in multicultural environments, at least one prediction is possible. If managers insist on their cultural preferences as the way to resolve disagreements, more disagreements will emerge because of misunderstood processes for resolving disagreements. The results of this study suggest that effective conflict resolution may need to begin with the recognition of different cultural preferences for resolution strategies. Only then can further attempts at resolution proceed effectively. In other words, focus on the "where" before jumping into the "how."

[Referenced article:] Tinsley, C. 1998. "Models of Conflict Resolution in Japanese, German, and American Cultures." *Journal of Applied Psychology* 83: 316–323.

7.3 JAPANESE AND AMERICAN NEGOTIATORS: OVERCOMING CULTURAL BARRIERS TO UNDERSTANDING
Richard Menger

Do cultural differences significantly impede the success of intercultural negotiations? Certainly, in today's global landscape, managers of international firms must be able to negotiate successfully with buyers, sellers, and suppliers from other cultures. Unfortunately, some evidence suggests that cultural differences may stand in the way of open communication between negotiators from different cultural backgrounds. Recent research now suggests that a lack of appreciation for the implications of cultural differences may mean that cross-cultural negotiations may be less successful than either party desires.

Researchers Jeanne Brett, of Northwestern University, and Tetsushi Okumura, of Shiga University, examined the influence of cultural differences on negotiations in a study of negotiators from the United States and Japan. They wanted to learn the extent to which the negotiators differed in a few basic cultural values and, in turn, whether those differences would interfere with achieving joint gains in intercultural negotiations.

Brett and Okumura argue that differences in cultural values and norms between U.S. and Japanese negotiators are likely to influence their strategies and processes as well as the negotiation outcomes. For instance, differences in the cultural values of individualism versus collectivism are likely to be expressed as differences in negotiators' levels of self-interest in a negotiation. In collectivist cultures such as Japan, the definition of self and personal goals are highly interdependent with group membership. There is also an emphasis on social obligations. In individualistic cultures such as the U.S., where the definition of self is independent of group membership, goals may be independent of the group, and emphasis is given to satisfying personal needs over social obligations. Therefore, individualistic negotiators may be more likely to emphasize self-interest when entering into negotiations.

Brett and Okumura also suggest the cultural values of hierarchy versus egalitarianism should influence the way in which power might enter into intercultural negotiations. In a hierarchical culture such as Japan, power is associated with a party's status in the social structure and generally may be viewed as fixed across negotiations. However, in an egalitarian culture such as the U.S., power differences are less likely to be tied to social status, but may instead be associated with bargaining position. For instance, the party with the strongest BATNA ("Best Alternative to a Negotiated Agreement") may actually hold the more powerful negotiating position.

Brett and Okumura further argue that these culturally based differences may lead to different information-sharing perspectives that are adopted by parties engaged in intercultural negotiations. Earlier researchers found that U.S. negotiators tend to communicate directly, and disclose information as a negotiating strategy to gain information. In contrast, Japanese negotiators are more likely to communicate indirectly, and hide information. As a result, information may be lost when U.S. negotiators do not fully understand information that is communicated indirectly by Japanese negotiators. Moreover, if Japanese negotiators do not share information as directly as the U.S. negotiators, the U.S. negotiators may be less likely to continue sharing information.

From *The Academy of Management Executive* 13, no. 4 (November 1999): 100–101. Copyright © 1999 Academy of Management Executive. Reprinted with permission.

The central assumption of Brett and Okumura's research was that cultural differences would interfere with the negotiation of joint gains in intercultural negotiations, but not in intracultural negotiations. In other words, the gains in negotiations between culturally matched sets of negotiators, either U.S. or Japanese, would be greater than those of cross-cultural sets of U.S. and Japanese negotiators.

To test the validity of their proposed outcomes, Brett and Okumura developed a negotiation exercise that was completed by samples of U.S. managers and Japanese managers. Intercultural negotiations were conducted between teams made up of Japanese managers who represented Japanese firms in the U.S. on one side and U.S. managers on the other. Intracultural negotiations took place between teams of U.S. managers in the roles of both buyer and seller and similar teams of Japanese managers who were working in Japan in buyer and seller roles.

As they expected, the researchers found significant differences between their U.S. and Japanese negotiators. Consistent with earlier research findings, the U.S. negotiators were significantly more individualistic and egalitarian than the Japanese negotiators. They also were far more likely to link negotiating power to a strong BATNA. Although the Japanese negotiators, more than the U.S. negotiators, focused on power during their preparations for the negotiation, there were no differences in the way in which both groups considered the status of the roles of buyer and seller.

Brett and Okumura found that cultural differences do indeed affect negotiation processes and outcomes. Overall, the intercultural negotiations between Japanese and U.S. managers realized significantly lower joint gains than the intracultural negotiations between Japanese managers or the intracultural negotiations between U.S. managers.

One explanation for these results is their finding that U.S. managers and Japanese managers appear to adopt different information-sharing scripts during the negotiation process. In intercultural negotiations, there was an asymmetry in understanding of the other party's priorities. The Japanese negotiators understood the U.S. negotiators' priorities, but the U.S. negotiators did not understand the Japanese negotiators' priorities. In intracultural negotiations, information-sharing strategies resulted in no information asymmetries or gaps.

These results do not necessarily mean that the Japanese negotiators were not sharing information. It is possible that they were more apt to convey information indirectly, and the information was either misinterpreted or misunderstood by their U.S. counterparts. However, this kind of miscommunication in intercultural negotiations is important since the value of issues that may be critical to a successful negotiation needs to be fully understood by both parties. One potential outcome associated with differences in information-sharing strategies is that negotiations may be terminated prematurely or the focus of the negotiation may be too narrow.

Power also played an important role in intercultural negotiations. Consistent with a cultural emphasis on hierarchical values, the Japanese negotiators indicated that they paid much more attention to power relationships than the U.S. negotiators. Moreover, the Japanese negotiators were less likely than the U.S. negotiators to view a strong BATNA as a source of power, which may have contributed to the low level of joint gains in intercultural negotiations.

The researchers' findings also indicate that self-interest mismatches may have led to premature closure in intercultural negotiations. Early closure may result when self-interested negotiators are willing to cease negotiating after their personal goals have been met, rather than continue to negotiate for terms that may be of more value to their group or organization.

The findings from this study clearly indicate the importance of understanding cultural differences during intercultural negotiations. One implication is that members of negotiating teams should study the other team's culture to gain a better understanding and appreciation of the perspectives from which they are negotiating. Achieving cross-cultural understanding may be especially critical in terms of each culture's perspectives on information sharing, individualism versus collectivism, and hierarchy versus egalitarianism. In this way, it may be possible for inter-cultural negotiators to achieve outcomes that are mutually advantageous, much as intracultural negotiators are able to achieve.

[Referenced article:] Brett, J.M., and T. Okumura. 1998. "Inter- and Intracultural Negotiations: U.S. and Japanese Negotiators." *Academy of Management Journal* 41: 495–510.

7.4   RESPONSIBILITY: THE NEW BUSINESS IMPERATIVE
Sandra A. Waddock, Charles Bodwell, and Samuel B. Graves

A wide range of stakeholders is pushing companies to respond in a more responsible way to the numerous pressures that today's organizations face. . . . This article argues that companies are responding to the pressures for accepting greater corporate responsibility by developing systemic approaches to managing the balancing of all these responsibilities. We term the recognition and integration of these triple-bottom-line performance expectations total responsibility management or TRM. . . .

PRESSURES ON COMPANIES FOR RESPONSIBLE PRACTICE

The stakeholder pressures framework (see Figure 1) highlights the key demands facing companies today to be more responsible. . . .

Pressures from Primary Stakeholders

. . .

Pressures from Investors (Owners)

Investors naturally desire a reasonable return on their investments through profits, increases in share value, company growth, and market potential. Performance pressures are a normal part of corporate life; however, there are some growing investor pressures that are expanding the definition of corporate responsibility.

Social Investing. The social investment movement represents a significant source of pressures by investors and potential investors on companies to manage all of the corporation's responsibilities. By 2001, the amount of money invested in socially screened equities of one sort or another had passed the $2.03 trillion mark with one out of every eight professionally managed investment dollars being part of a socially responsible portfolio. The long-held assumptions in the financial community regarding a trade-off between returns and responsible investment practices do not appear to hold up under examination. . . .

The Link Between Financial Performance and Responsibility. Significant evidence from a large and growing body of academic research suggests at minimum a neutral, and quite likely a positive, relationship between responsible corporate practices and corporate financial performance. . . .

Shareholder Activism. Another owner/investor group exerting pressure for corporate responsibility is shareholder activists. In the U.S., activist groups such as the Investor Responsibility Research Center (IRRC) provide interested investors with impartial information about corporate practices. . . . Among the focuses of ICCR's [Interfaith Center on Corporate Responsibilities] activism are sweat-

Excerpted from *The Academy of Management Executive* 16, no. 2 (May 2002): 132–148. Copyright © 2002 Academy of Management Executive. Reprinted with permission.

Figure 1   **Stakeholder and Societal Pressures on the Development of Total Responsibility Management Systems in Corporations**

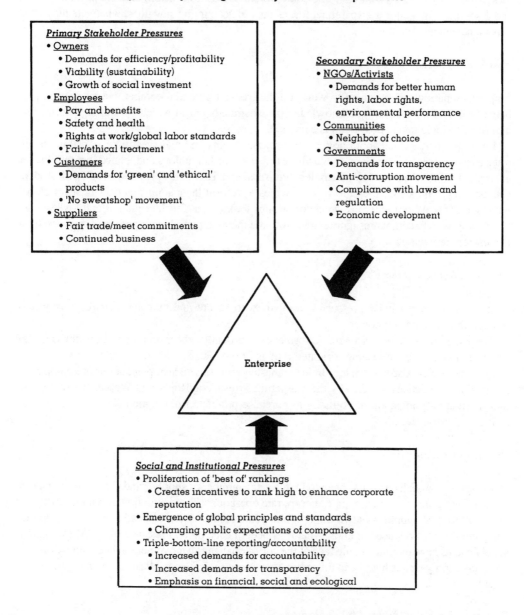

Primary Stakeholder Pressures
- Owners
  - Demands for efficiency/profitability
  - Viability (sustainability)
  - Growth of social investment
- Employees
  - Pay and benefits
  - Safety and health
  - Rights at work/global labor standards
  - Fair/ethical treatment
- Customers
  - Demands for 'green' and 'ethical' products
  - 'No sweatshop' movement
- Suppliers
  - Fair trade/meet commitments
  - Continued business

Secondary Stakeholder Pressures
- NGOs/Activists
  - Demands for better human rights, labor rights, environmental performance
- Communities
  - Neighbor of choice
- Governments
  - Demands for transparency
  - Anti-corruption movement
  - Compliance with laws and regulation
  - Economic development

Enterprise

Social and Institutional Pressures
- Proliferation of 'best of' rankings
  - Creates incentives to rank high to enhance corporate reputation
- Emergence of global principles and standards
  - Changing public expectations of companies
- Triple-bottom-line reporting/accountability
  - Increased demands for accountability
  - Increased demands for transparency
  - Emphasis on financial, social and ecological

shops and human rights abuses, ecological issues such as global warming, equal opportunity, safety of genetically modified food, decreasing military actions, and similar social issues. . . .

Transparency of Corporate Responsibility Data. The growing availability of data on corporate practices makes it easier to assess how companies respond to the many pressures to accept the need to manage responsibility as what they do is more visible. Among the factors currently assessed are labor issues, ecological issues, community issues, and public controversies. That these internal practices are regularly evaluated by outside agencies creates incentives for companies to monitor their own behaviors and controversial issues from within to avoid problems. Data and assessment make for transparency, for, as the old accounting saw goes, what gets measured gets management attention. . . .

Pressures from Employees

Employee opinions about where to work are the basis of potential competitive advantage, particularly in an information- and knowledge-based strategy era in which continuing shortage of highly skilled and talented workers is expected.

Employee perceptions about how a corporation accepts and manages its responsibilities are often part of employee decisions about where to work. Further, unions and related institutions, for example, UNITE (Union of Needletrades, Industrial and Textile Employees), work with student activists to put increased pressure on companies to reform their labor practices to meet global labor standards. With numerous watchdog groups looking out for the rights of employees, e.g., Sweatshop Watch, companies ignore their own and their suppliers' labor and employee practices at their reputational peril.

Pressures from Customers

Customers are increasingly pressuring companies to accept and manage their responsibilities through their purchasing power.

Consumer pressure on corporate performance is brought to bear on corporations through, for example, J.D. Power's consumer-oriented ratings of products.

Some customers also say that they base purchasing decisions on their perceptions of a company's responsibility practices. Studies by the marketing firms Cone/Roper and Walker Research both indicate that customers are more likely to purchase products from companies they perceive as acting responsibly. . . .

Pressures from Suppliers

One impact of globalization has been to increase the number of supplier and distributor alliances, making the supplier an integral part of corporate operations. The devolution of responsibility for manufacturing to suppliers has resulted in new relationships between headquarters and supplier companies, since both need to know what to expect of each other. Pressures for TRM throughout supply chains have mounted in the face of the anti-globalization movement. Indeed, abuses within company supply chains have been the target of numerous negative media and watchdog reports in recent years. . . .

Pressures from Secondary Stakeholders

. . .

NGOs and Activists

Non-governmental organizations (NGOs) and activists, aided by the global ease and transparency of electronic communication, are sources of pressure for total responsibility management.

Global activists and NGOs have emerged demanding that companies adhere to high expectations regarding labor standards, human rights standards, and national sovereignty. . . .

Environmentalists consistently pressure companies for better environmental management and more sustainable practices. Information about toxic releases and other ecological problems created by corporate activities is increasingly available. . . .

Communities and Governments

Communities and even nations, many of which have been in a competitive battle with other communities, provinces, or states for businesses, are beginning to become aware of the negative consequences of eroding tax bases and lack of company commitment to a locale. Companies may increasingly find it necessary to act as—and become—"neighbors of choice," living up to high standards of excellence with respect to their communities. . . .

Social and Institutional Pressures and Trends

A number of institutional developments have led to pressures for responsibility management, creating a need for greater transparency of and accountability for corporate impacts. These pressures have become even more urgent in the face of Enron's collapse, in part because despite Enron's active assertion of environmental, human rights, climate-change policies, their actual practices anal financial condition were impenetrable.

Current institutional pressures for total responsibility management derive from: 1) the visibility and attention given to the proliferation of "best of" rankings, 2) a growing array of principles and global standards promulgated by major international bodies, and 3) related reporting and accountability initiatives that expand corporate responsibility from only an economic focus to the triple bottom line. These institutional pressures create growing demands for transparency and accountability.

Ratings, Rankings, Research, Awards

A major source of pressure on companies' stakeholder-related performance (or corporate responsibility) is the numerous ratings and ranking schemes that have emerged in recent years, as well as highly visible awards for best practice. In contrast to traditional corporate rankings that have largely evaluated companies on financial criteria, size, and growth rate (e.g., the Fortune 500), ratings and rankings now regularly evaluate companies' performance with respect to their treatment of a whole variety of different stakeholders and issues. For example, *Business Ethics* magazine's annual 100 Best Corporate Citizens ranking, which uses the KLD data discussed above, gains considerable attention. . . .

Emerging Global Standards

Global standards and principles are another source of institutional pressures. The UN's Global Compact represents one prominent example. Drawn from internationally agreed to principles focusing on human rights, labor, and the environment, the Global Compact is an effort to promote values-based practices in global corporations.

The Global Compact principles are only one set of what has become a virtual flood of new standards which business is expected to meet. . . . For example, the Business and Social Initiatives (BASI) database put together by the International Labour Office lists over 400 different initiatives related to codes of conduct, principles, and standards, most of which were developed since public attention began to focus on this issue during the 1990s. . . .

Reporting and Accountability Initiatives

Demands for improved triple-bottom-line performance represent the last societal or institutional source of pressure to be discussed. The triple bottom line, pioneered by the Institute of Social and Ethical Accountability, emphasizes that companies are responsible for multiple impacts on society, with associated bottom lines. Standards, principles, and codes are only useful if they are implemented and to the extent that companies can assure stakeholders that they are living up to them. To establish credibility with stakeholders, particularly with activists and critics, some companies are beginning to engage in more transparent reporting practices, many of which are now emerging from international multi-stakeholder coalitions. . . .

THE TRM APPROACH

Demands that companies adopt a set of values-based operating principles, a code of conduct, or a set of standards are likely to increase in the future. As primary and secondary stakeholders gain ever greater ability to mobilize their own resources against corporate practices they find objectionable, a company's willingness to monitor and report out verifiable information on the triple bottom line to external stakeholders is likely to become, as quality has already done, the *sine qua non* of competitive advantage.

Although no company is immune to the forces highlighted above, ironically it is the companies whose reputations have been most sullied that have perhaps moved the farthest to implement responsibility management systems and make them marginally transparent. Approaching responsibility through integrated management systems is in the early stages of development in most companies, but the outlines of this emerging approach can be delineated in what we have called total responsibility management (TRM). . . .

The TRM approach is derived from a study of emerging responsibility practices in international brand companies. The research points to the importance of integrating responsibility into vision and values, strategies and practices, and improvement and learning systems. In implementing their codes of conduct, many brand multinationals are working increasingly closely with suppliers to ensure that suppliers meet the standards embedded in codes. Further, these multinationals are joining or helping to form organizations and initiatives like the Fair Labor Association (FLA), GRI, or the Global Compact, to assure the credibility of their report on these activities.

The research, qualitative in nature, has involved over a hundred interviews with managers of multinational brand companies (MNCs) and their suppliers. Research teams traveled to MNC headquarters in the United States and Europe, as well as sourcing offices of MNCs in Asia. Senior managers, line supervisors, and others were interviewed in Cambodia, China, Costa Rica, Poland, Russia, Sri Lanka, Thailand, Turkey and Vietnam. The field research involved observation of factory-level activities, with factory walk-throughs in about three dozen factories in the Asia region.

This research indicates that companies respond in a variety of ways to the pressures and forces identified earlier but that their responses bear commonalities in the development of responsibility management systems. Responsibility management as it is evolving in these companies is a systemic approach to managing the complete set of a company's responsibilities to its stakeholders and the natural environment, similar in many respects to quality management. TRM approaches involve three major processes: *inspiration* or institutionalizing a vision of responsible practice throughout the enterprise, *integration* of responsibility into corporate strategies, building human resource capacity, and management systems, and *improvement and innovation* through indicators that measure responsibility and learning from experiences (see Figure 2).

Inspiration: The Responsibility Vision

A key element of a total responsibility management (TRM) approach is ensuring that responsibility is built into the corporate vision and associated values. Top management not only needs to make a serious commitment to responsible practice and articulated values, but also to ensure that everyone in the organization and its supply chain is aware of that commitment and seeks to meet it. The research indicates that the support of top management can strengthen responsibility initiatives and, conversely, that the lack of support can cripple any progress on integrating responsibility issues into corporate practices. . . .

To cope with the need for a responsibility vision, many companies have developed and are implementing codes of conduct that explicitly set out their expectations for both internal units and suppliers. . . . Successful institutionalization of a code of conduct depends on a long-term commitment to systemic change, rather than a "once and done" memo from management. . . .

> *Example A. Manager of Corporate Social Responsibility, Multinational Corporation (MNC), China*
> With the code, you need to have buy-in from top management. Knowing that the president was behind it got it into our performance objectives and made us roll it out with our leadership partners [supplier managers]. We started with the leadership partners; we had several people who traveled country to country explaining the code and its impact.

The multinational corporation in the example has been actively pushing its code of conduct through its supply chain for several years. . . .

The institutionalization of responsibility is not downwardly unidirectional and internal to the firm; rather, it is a two-way street, down *and* up within the firm and its suppliers. Institutionalization involves input from key stakeholders in a process of mutual learning and engagement. . . .

One key primary stakeholder whose voice is critical, albeit not frequently enough heard until problems develop, is the employee. . . . Leading firms, however, have learned that there are significant benefits to be gained by empowering the workforce, as Example B suggests.

> *Example B. MNC Manufacturing Managers, China*
> If I was going to introduce CSR [corporate social responsibility] to a company, I think first of all you would need to communicate to workers information on the company they are working at [the supplier] and information on the company they are supplying to [the MNC], information on what we stand for and also what rights are, and what the obligations of the company are. I would also have a suggestion box.

The manager went on to provide an example—admittedly based on the use of suggestion boxes, a tool of often limited effectiveness—of how dialogue can work to improve working conditions:

Figure 2   **An Integrated Model of Total Responsibility Management**

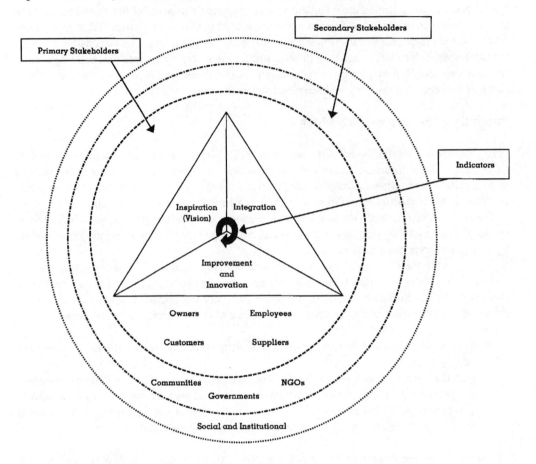

This factory has a monthly newsletter, and we put some of the responses to the letters [placed in the suggestion box] there. Also, using a randomly selected group of workers, we went on a tour of the dorms. And the workers mentioned that the lighting during the day does not come on, and that some of them might not be working during the day and that they need lights. So now the electricity is available at all times.

Other stakeholders' points of views, particularly critical external stakeholders, also need to be heard if the company's responsibility commitments are to be met. Among relevant external stakeholders are non-governmental organizations (NGOs), particularly activists who raise critiques of corporate behaviors, governments, and consumers. . . . Listening to external voices and increasing dialogue with a variety of stakeholders can support a healthy reassessment of an organization's vision of itself or its markets, as Example C illustrates, with the example of one manager who had to consider the meaning of campus protests targeted at his company's sector.

Example C. MNC Headquarters Managers
With the student protests, we had a real challenge figuring out "if the students are anti-sweatshop, then what are we?" It took me months until I realized that we are too. There is

no way that policies that abuse workers or abrogate rights benefit companies in any way, shape, or form.

Among the first steps in implementing total responsibility management systems is articulating clear corporate vision and values and engaging stakeholders to ensure that appropriate inputs into the company's policies and practices have been heard and, where appropriate, incorporated into the company's values. Further, as the last quote suggests, meeting a fundamental level of foundational values (based on the global standards discussed above) is important for the company to avoid being criticized in the first place. Top management, having made the explicit commitment to responsible practice, needs to clearly and repeatedly communicate the vision to the rest of the enterprise so that total responsibility management can be integrated into corporate systems and practices. . . .

Integration: Putting TRM into Practice

The next element in developing a TRM approach is integrating the responsibility vision into strategies, practices, and measurement systems, thereby translating vision into reality. Example D from an MNC manufacturing manager in Vietnam illustrates the complexity of this integration process. The manager highlights only the communication and training aspects of the new corporate code, without even getting into what this process entailed for actual processes outside of training.

> *Example D. MNC Manager, Vietnam*
> Manufacturing managers in the factories are really businessmen. Before, they worried about prices and quality. They rolled out the code to us and put us through extensive training, two to three days, and then a pretty hard test. At the same time, we rolled it out to the factories, starting at the top with the general managers, and again training, tests even, then we had them move it down. They also had to put labor-practice managers in place together with their whole supporting organization. It was a huge job.

Many firms have found it beneficial to designate a local group for ensuring implementation of the code through training and skill development. Implementation of responsibility management today typically involves a "responsibility assurance" manager of some sort (analogous to the early days of quality management, when quality was checked at the end of the line). Today's responsibility officer is like a quality assurance officer was, typically someone external to day-to-day operations responsible for assuring responsible practice. Many companies today establish a "department" responsible for assuring responsibility rather than integrating responsibility into the jobs of all managers and workers. The duties of this corporate responsibility (CR) department might include coordinating responsibility policy and the implementation of the code, communicating policies and practices to stakeholders, and maintaining and adjusting the code as necessary over time. . . .

Taking a TRM approach requires reviewing problems faced in reaching all responsibility objectives and the systems that cause them to persist. In the sectors researched, some companies' CR managers work closely with compliance officers, as well as manufacturing and audit personnel, beginning the long-term process of integrating responsibility into day-to-day operating practice. Example E illustrates the evolution of responsibility management in one company in its China operations, which is well along in the integration process.

Example E. MNC Manufacturing Manager, China
We have a new structure here. Before [a manufacturing manager] was in charge of production for all operations in the country. It was too much. So since then he handles production at [supplier], and I handle things here. Before, development, commercialization, and production were separate organizations, with him in charge of production in this country, someone else in charge of other functions in another. Implementing code was under production. Now it is much cleaner, with me in charge here of both development/commercialization/production and code.

Reasons given for keeping responsibility management less integrated in some companies resemble reasons initially given for keeping quality separate from manufacturing: need for independence, conflict avoidance, and the need for different skills. Further, implementation of responsible practices throughout factories and even into the supply chain (where, perhaps, it is even more important because that is where many of the issues have arisen), even when the integration process is in its early stages, is an enormous task, as Example F indicates.

Example F. MNC Manufacturing Manager, Vietnam
The first step for a new factory, just starting with code, you have to organize a team. You need a group dedicated to this. Second, you have to make sure that everybody understands what the code means. Third, you give seminars on the code to all the workers. All the new employees have to attend a briefing on the requirements of the code. Next, we used the code guidelines and developed an action plan to meet the code. The factory develops the action plan then we [MNC factory level staff] review and discuss it. Then [the national level CR team members] review it, and if they have points, then we adjust it accordingly.

Again, similar to the adoption of the quality management principles over the last 20 years, the implementation of corporate responsibility objectives across an organization and through its supply chain will be dependent on a systems approach to the processes and practices. As pointed out in the example below, the use of ad hoc or fire-fighting approaches to responsibility management is simply unworkable. The infrastructure specifically dedicated to responsibility issues is usually too thin to deal with dynamic environments where suppliers are numerous.

Example G. MNC CSR Manufacturing Manager, Headquarters
There are hundreds of factories and hundreds of thousands of employees [in our supplier firms], and we are the minority buyer in each of these. If we don't have a calendar, standards, and practices for when these standards are not met, then we would have a disaster on our hands. To make the management of this whole thing effective over time, you need a system.

TRM goes well beyond labor practices to other systems within the company. The reward, information, measurement, and reporting systems are particularly important in assuring the integration of responsibility into the company's operations.

Linking measurement systems to those providing workers and management feedback to guide decision-making is central both to quality and responsibility management, particularly if the linkage is tied to some form of incentive. . . .

Improvement, Innovation, and Learning

Total responsibility management works only when companies learn from what has been done in the past and use that learning to make improvements. Learning requires new forms of measurement and assessment that not only transparently provide feedback to external stakeholders, who are increasingly seeking information about corporate activities, but also provide important internal information about performance to managers and employees. And credibility, reliability, and validity of these data are enhanced when the systems are externally monitored, audited, and reported, along lines suggested by the Global Reporting Initiative (GRI). . . .

Indicators: TRM Measurement

Indicators are the ways in which a company measures performance and progress toward meeting its responsibility goals. Although indicators are critically important to the improvement and innovation process, they are also needed to assess the inspiration and integration processes, as Figure 2 illustrates. A necessary condition of these communications, particularly for the many critical external stakeholders who seek to redress problems with MNCs, is that the information communicated be credible and reliable. Those requirements mean that companies implementing responsibility management systems need measurement systems that can accommodate, at minimum, the triple bottom lines of economic, social, and environmental reporting. Indeed, many companies in the reputational spotlight are creating TRM reporting systems internally and then asking their suppliers to provide evidence that they too are meeting their responsibilities.

As with quality, indicators are needed at a variety of levels, in particular wherever decisions need to be made. In our research, we found examples of responsibility indicators and potential, yet under-utilized, indicators at all points in supply chains and up and down corporate hierarchies. In factories, measurements linked to health and safety provided workers and management with information on toxic vapors; in sourcing departments, purchasers sometimes had access to information on compliance audits of suppliers; and with regard to external reporting, some firms have developed annual social reports and/or actually allowed third-party auditing of various sorts.

Although many multiple-bottom-line reporting systems today are still internally audited and verified, there is intense pressure on companies to use external auditors and publish the results of responsibility audits. The power of transparency is, in fact, practiced quite extensively in some of the firms studied, both in their own reporting and with their suppliers. Indeed, some managers suggest, as the comment in Example H illustrates, that a degree of competition among suppliers can enhance not only responsible practices but also performance.

> #### Example H. MNC Country Manager
> We are starting a rating system and we do let the companies [suppliers] know that this could impact their getting business in the future. There is a competition between the suppliers. OK, this factory now has a supermarket. Then the others feel pressure. And there is close communication between factories. There has to be an open spirit and a balance of competition and sharing. On EHS [environmental, health, and safety] we don't want any secrets. We just brought all the EHS managers [from suppliers] together for that reason.

Information, measurement, and reward systems need to be integrated into reporting systems and fed back to decision makers so that the data can help improve practice. . . .

. . . Additionally, many companies are moving toward external auditing, verification, and monitoring systems, such as those emerging from the Global Reporting Initiative, because they need to establish credibility and trust with the critical external actors discussed earlier, as the following quotation from a MNC headquarters CR manager in Example I suggests.

Example I. MNC Headquarters CR Manager
People don't trust us. We need to explain to people, we need to get external monitoring going, the [NGO initiative] we just joined. The most important for us [internally] is self-study and monitoring. But for outside, they want confirmation.

RESPONSIBILITY: THE NEW IMPERATIVE

. . . We can distill out from the pressures described earlier the actual demands to which the companies in this study are responding. These demands seem to come down to a few concepts, simple to articulate though perhaps more complex to enact in practice:

> *Integrity:* Stakeholders demand that companies be honest, firmly adhere to their stated codes and values, be healthy, whole, and sound financially and in other ways relevant to specific stakeholders, and essentially that the reality of company actions and impacts matches company rhetoric.
> *Respect:* Stakeholders demand that companies' relationships with different stakeholders are interactive, engaged, and take into account different points of view in decisions.
> *Standards:* Stakeholders demand that articulated values be met in practice and, at minimum, that a baseline of internationally agreed values (e.g., around core issues like labor/working conditions, human rights, environmental health, and integrity) are achieved.
> *Transparency:* Stakeholders demand company openness about company performance on the triple bottom line of economic, social, and environmental impacts.
> *Accountability:* Stakeholders demand that the company acknowledge its impacts and take responsibility for them.

What all these demands require can be summed up in one word: integrity. Corporate integrity is what the TRM approaches described above attempt to ensure.

We have derived several ideas from our research that can be used by managers interested in creating a TRM systems approach for their company:

1. Create a vision and related set of values that articulate the company's core responsibilities and relate those responsibilities to corporate strategies. Values should be aligned with baseline global standards. Communicate the vision regularly and often so that it becomes a shared vision throughout the company and its supply chain. For example, BP Amoco was the first oil company to take seriously the threat of global warming, creating a vision for itself of becoming a "green" energy company.
2. Engage all stakeholders in continuing dialogue to ensure that the company's values and actions are in accord with society's and stakeholders' expectations. Get feedback and inputs on possible problem areas, and develop responsive internal systems to nip problems in the bud, avoid them altogether, or take advantage of new opportunities that emerge from the stakeholder engagement process. As an illustration, in an effort to avoid the negative effects on its reputation that Royal Dutch/Shell suffered in the mid-1990s when it tried to dispose of the Brent Spar oil rig and raised the ire of Greenpeace, the company has developed extensive stakeholder engagement policies. By getting feedback from stakeholders before problems arise, the company hopes to better position itself for the future.

3. Integrate the TRM vision into corporate strategies and management systems in ways that build employee capacity to understand and take responsibility for corporate impacts. For example, Timberland Corporation has a long-standing corporate responsibility vision of "Pull on your boots and make a difference." When the company experienced a liquidity crisis in the mid-1990s, the integration of this vision into the daily life of the company as part of its operating practices made it possible for CEO Jeffrey Swartz to state, "We got together and figured out how to deal with our problems."

4. Become a learning organization by creating a TRM system based on key performance indicators that measure improvements or highlight problems that can be fed back to relevant stakeholders to generate new learning, improvements, and remediation. One company that attempts to do this is the energy company AES, which is "based on values from the start," decentralizes decision making, and pays strict attention to key performance indicators.

Although managing responsibility through TRM might seem complex and new, most managers are already familiar with the basic processes on which TRM approaches rest through their experiences in managing quality. Managing for quality and managing for responsibility both require systemic approaches to a long-term process of continual organizational improvement based on a vision that is shared among relevant stakeholders. The real difference between the economic-results-only model and the modern TRM approach is that TRM includes the perspectives, needs, interests, and concerns of the multiple stakeholders interested in today's corporate integrity and responsibility. TRM provides a basis for meeting corporate responsibility in a world where corporate integrity matters more than ever.

PART III

POWER AND GROUP DYNAMICS

SECTION 8. POWER AND AUTHORITY

Power and authority are distributed unevenly in most organizations, and national cultures vary greatly in power distance between people at different hierarchical levels. The power of corporate board members is evident in the Austrian story, "Welcoming the Board of Directors." A nervous, unidentified person tries to assure the board members that "the structure of the company is not creaking," and that "the executive board is unimpeachable." Yet these exhortations sound suspect under the extreme conditions in which the meeting is held. The board's power seems, in fact, to be abruptly cut short.

An unconventional way of gaining power, at least to Western eyes, is described in "Government by Magic Spell." A young girl in Somalia is possessed by a spirit that gives her a "feeling of power, as though she could do things beyond the reach of ordinary human beings." Her family and clan put their faith in her ability to do good, and summon her to the capital. However, her people control the government and use her special powers to enrich themselves at the expense of the general population.

The authority vested in religious figures is depicted in the Iranian story, "The Mullah with No Legs." Neighbors have mullahs with different personae and various powers to fulfill specific needs of the people they serve. A carpenter's mullah delivers sermons over a loud speaker to confirm the craftsman's religious devotion. The mullah with no legs helps a family pray for their dying husband. "Unlike the neighbor's mullah, he did not glitter like a freshly opened present, but he was a decent man with close ties to God."

Occasionally, people with little power have an opportunity to retaliate against their exploiters. In "One of These Days," an impoverished, uncertified Latin American dentist devises a way to make the corrupt and powerful mayor "pay for twenty dead men." Revenge against social injustice is in the dentist's hands.

Saving face is a crucial mechanism for respecting status differences and maintaining harmonious relationships in many cultures, particularly in Asia. The Chinese story, "The Explosion in the Parlor," highlights the importance to both host and guest of saving face for each other. Although the nature of the relationship and the social status of the two individuals are unspecified, both parties rush to smooth over an accident involving a broken dish.

SECTION 9. INDIVIDUALS AND GROUPS

"In the Footsteps of a Water Buffalo" depicts human beings as having lower status and value than water buffalo in communist-controlled Vietnam. Collective farm workers toil "like beasts of burden, yet nobody dared emit one peep in their defense." Since the all-powerful party secretary controls everyone's fate, "the best thing is to sit still, and the next best thing is to say yes." A conscientious elderly couple suffer great hardship and indignity to gain favor with the party secretary.

"Action Will Be Taken: An Action-Packed Story" describes the frenetic atmosphere in a German company in which the owner goes from department to department exorting, "Let's have some action!" And everyone answers in return, "Action will be taken!" A new employee, who is "inclined more to pensiveness and inactivity than to work," nonetheless throws himself into his job and takes action by handling thirteen phones on his desk at a time. When the owner dies suddenly, the worker finds a new profession that fits his natural preference for inaction.

In "Ode to Joy," while buttoning his coat for work, an office worker in the former Czechoslovakia was astonished to find that his right hand had fallen off cleanly at the wrist. His major concern was wondering what his coworkers would think: "I would hate to make it seem as if by complaining about my wrist I were trying to avoid the work I carry out most zealously and, in a sense, even enjoy." As other body parts fell away, the man kept his positive attitude, feeling joyful and smiling constantly. Such was his "ode to joy."

SECTION 10. MANAGERIAL INSIGHTS

The readings in this section focus on characteristics of specific cultures. "Leadership Made in Germany: Low on Compassion, High on Performance" is useful for analyzing "Welcoming the Board of Directors" and "Action Will Be Taken," which take place in Austria and Germany, respectively. The reading presents findings for German managers from the GLOBE leadership study and compares them with results from sixty other countries. To meet today's globalization challenges, the traditional German leadership style of "tough on the issue, tough on the person" is seen as needing to change to "tough on the issue, soft on the person."

"Working in a Vietnamese Voice" describes the Vietnamese cultural dimensions of "right relationship" underlying social and work dynamics, as well as respect, community, and indirectness. Cultural foundations of work relationships are then presented along with practical considerations for doing business in the country. The reading helps shed light on the behaviors of the farmers in "In the Footsteps of a Water Buffalo" by explaining such cultural mainstays as the indirect Vietnamese way of saying "no" and the seriousness of the expression, "Better to die than to lose face."

"Building Competitive Advantage from *Ubuntu:* Management Lessons from South Africa" explains the concept of *ubuntu,* or humaneness. The article discusses various work situations in which compassion and communality inherent in *ubuntu* can be found. It then discusses how companies can gain competitive advantage by incorporating the principles and practices of *ubuntu* in African workplaces. The reading is useful for understanding the importance of ceremonies and rituals and the special powers of religious healers depicted in "Government by Magic Spell."

The last reading in this section, "Matching Management Practices to National Culture in India, Mexico, Poland, and the U.S.," presents research evidence on how two management practices—empowerment and continuous improvement—fit in four different cultures. Empowerment reflects the amount of discretion or autonomy over one's work, and continuous improvement refers to encouraging employees to take the initiative to improve themselves and their skills. The relationship between these two management practices and worker satisfaction is examined for cultures having different levels of power distance and individualism/collectivism. The research findings help explain the various power relationships as well as the decisions and attitudes of the characters depicted in all the stories of Part III. For instance, "One of These Days," "Ode to Joy," and "In the Footsteps of a Water Buffalo" take place in relatively high power-distance and high collectivism cultures in which empowerment of workers and continuous improvement are typically very low.

Section 8
———— Power and Authority ————

8.1 WELCOMING THE BOARD OF DIRECTORS
Peter Handke

Gentlemen, it's rather cold in here. Let me explain the situation. An hour ago, I called from the city to ask if everything had been prepared for the meeting, but no one answered. I immediately drove here and looked for the porter; he was neither to be found in his booth, in the basement near the furnace, nor in the auditorium. But I did find his wife there; she was sitting in the darkness on a stool near the door, her head bent, her face in her palms, her elbows resting on her knees. I asked her what had happened. Without moving, she said that her husband had left; one of their children had been run over while sledding. That is the reason that the rooms were unheated; I hope you will take this into account; what I have to say won't take long. Perhaps you could move your chairs a bit closer so I won't have to shout; I don't want to make a political speech; I merely want to report on the financial situation of the company. I'm sorry that the windowpanes have been broken by the storm; before your arrival the porter's wife and I covered the spaces with plastic bags to keep the snow from coming in; but as you can see, we weren't entirely successful. Don't let the creaking distract you as I read a statement on the net-balance of this business year; there is no reason for concern; I can assure you that the executive board is unimpeachable. Please move closer if you have difficulty understanding me. I regret having to welcome you here under such circumstances; they are due to the child having sledded in front of the oncoming car; the porter's wife, as she was fastening a plastic bag to the window with string, told me that her husband, who had gone down to the basement for coal, howled; she was arranging chairs in the auditorium for the meeting; suddenly she heard her husband howl from below; she stood riveted to the spot where she heard the scream, she told me, for a long time; she listened. Then her husband appeared at the door, still holding a bucket of coal in his hand; in a low voice, his eyes averted, he told her what had happened; their second child had brought him the news. Since the absent porter has the list of names, I will welcome you as a group and not individually. I said, as a group and not individually. That's the wind. I thank you for coming in the cold through the snow to this meeting; it's quite a walk from the valley. Perhaps you thought you would enter a room where the ice on the windows would have melted and where you could sit by the stove and warm yourselves; but you are now sitting at the table in your overcoats, and the snow which fell from your shoes as you came in and took your seats hasn't even melted; there is no stove in the room, only a black hole in the wall where the stove pipe had been when this room and this empty house were still inhabited. I thank you for coming in spite of all the difficulties: I thank you and welcome you. I welcome you. I welcome you. Let me first welcome the gentleman sitting near the door where the farmer's wife had sat in the darkness; I welcome the gentleman and thank him. Perhaps when he received the registered letter a few days ago informing him of this meeting at which the accounts of the

From *Bergrüssung des Aufsichtsrats,* trans. Hebert Kubner (Salzburg: Residenz Verlag, 1967), 111–116. Reprinted with permission..

executive board are to be reviewed, he didn't think it imperative to attend since it was below freezing and snow had been falling for days; but then he thought that perhaps everything wasn't as it should be in the company; there was a suspicious creaking in its structure. I said that perhaps he thought that its structure was creaking. No, the structure of the company is not creaking. Pardon me, but what a storm this is. Then he got into his car and drove from the city in the cold through the snow to this meeting. He had to park the car in the village below; a narrow path is the only way up to the house. He sat in the tavern reading the financial section of the paper until it was time to leave for the meeting. In the woods he met another gentleman who was also on his way to the meeting; the latter was leaning on a wayside crucifix holding his hat in one hand and a frozen apple in the other; as he ate the frozen apple snow fell on his forehead and hair. I said that snow fell on his forehead and hair as he ate the frozen apple. As the first gentleman approached him, they greeted each other; then the second gentleman put his hand in his overcoat pocket and brought out a second frozen apple which he gave to the first gentleman; at that the storm blew his hat off and they both laughed. They both laughed. Please move a little closer, otherwise you won't be able to understand me. The structure is creaking. It's not the structure of the company that's creaking; you will all receive the dividends that are due to you in this business year; I want to inform you of that in this unusual meeting. As the two men trudged through the snow in the storm, the limousine with the others arrived. They stood in their heavy black overcoats next to the car, using it as protection against the wind, and tried to make up their minds whether or not to climb up to the dilapidated farmhouse. I said: farmhouse. Although they had their doubts about making the climb, one of them persuaded the others to overcome their fears and reminded them of the grave situation that the company was in; after reading the financial news in the tavern, they left and trudged through the snow to this meeting; they were sincerely concerned about the company. First their feet made clean holes in the snow; but eventually they dragged their feet, making a path in the snow. They stopped once and looked back at the valley: flakes floated down on them from the black heavens; they saw two sets of tracks leading down, one set was faint and almost covered with snow; they had been made by the farmer when he had run down after hearing of the child's accident; he often fell on his face without trying to break his fall with his hands. He often found himself buried in the icy snow; he often dug himself in with his trembling fingers; when he fell, he often licked the bitter flakes with his tongue; he often howled under the stormy skies. I repeat: the farmer often howled under the stormy skies. They also saw the tracks that led to the dilapidated farmhouse, the tracks of the two gentlemen who discussed the situation of the company and suggested that the capital should be increased by distributing new stocks and ate glassy pieces of the green apples as they trudged through the storm. Finally, after night had fallen, the rest of you arrived and entered this room; the first two gentlemen were sitting here, just as they are now, with their notebooks on their knees holding pencils in their hands; they were waiting for me to deliver my welcoming address so that they could take notes. I welcome all of you and thank you for coming; I welcome the gentlemen who eat the frozen apples as they write my words down; I welcome the other four gentlemen who ran over the farmer's son with their limousine as they sped over the icy street to the village: the farmer's son, the porter's son. The structure is creaking again; the roof is creaking, the creaking being caused by the heavy weight of snow; it isn't the structure of the company that's creaking. The balance is active; there are no irregularities in the business management. The beams are bending from the pressure on the roof, the structure is creaking. I would like to thank the farmer for all that he has done for this meeting: for the last number of days he climbed up to the house from the farmstead, carrying a ladder so that he could paint this room; he carried the ladder on his shoulder, holding it in the crook of his arm; in his left hand he carried a pail with whitewash with a broken broom in it. With this he painted the walls after his children had removed the wood that lay piled up to the window sills and had carted it to the farmyard on their sleds. Carrying the pail in one hand and holding the ladder with the other, the farmer walked up to the house to prepare this room for the meeting; the children ran shouting in front of him carrying their sleds, their scarves fluttering in the wind. We can still see the over-lapping white rings on the floor where the farmer placed the pail when he climbed the ladder to paint the walls; the black rings near the door where the powdery snow is now coming in are from the pot with the boiling soup which the farmer's wife brought at mealtimes: the three of them sat or squatted on the ground and dipped their spoons in; the farmer's wife stood at the door, her arms crossed over her apron and sang folk songs about snow; the children slurped the soup and rhyth-mically swayed their heads. Please don't worry: there is no reason for concern about the com-pany; the creaking you hear is in the structure of the roof and is being caused by the weight of the snow which is causing the structure to creak. I thank the farmer for everything he has done; I would address him personally if he weren't down in the village with the child that has been run over. I would also address the farmer's wife and I would thank her, and I would address the children and give them my heart-felt thanks for everything that they have done for this meeting. I thank all of you and welcome you. I beg you to remain seated so that your movement doesn't cause the structure to collapse. What a storm! I said: What a storm. Please remain seated. I thank you for coming and welcome you. It is only the structure that is creaking; I said that you should remain seated so that the roof doesn't cave in. I said that I said that I said that you should remain seated. I said that I said that I said that you should remain seated! I welcome you! I said that I said that I welcome you. I welcome all of you who have come here to be made an end of! I welcome you. I welcome you.

8.2   GOVERNMENT BY MAGIC SPELL
Saida Hagi-Dierie Herzi

AT THE VILLAGE

When she was ten, Halima learned that she was possessed by a jinni. The diagnosis came from the religious healer of the village, the Wadaad. Halima had been ill for several months. The Wadaad had tried all his healing arts on her till he had understood that there could be no cure: Halima was not ill in the ordinary sense of the word; she was possessed—possessed by the spirit of an infant, which she had stepped on by accident, one night in front of the bathroom. Fortunately for Halima, the sage expounded, the jinni was of the benevolent sort, one that was more likely to help than to harm her. But it would never leave her—not leave her voluntarily, not even yield to exorcism. And it would forever be an infant jinni.

With that Halima became famous. The story of her jinni was known from one end of the village to the other within hours after the Wadaad had told her mother. Everyone talked about Halima and her jinni—what it might do and what it might be made to do, for her and for the village. In no time at all, the villagers had convinced themselves and each other that Halima had the power to foretell the future and to heal the sick. And it was not long before Halima herself was convinced.

Before long, Halima began to act the part. At times she would sit staring off into space. People assumed that she was listening to her jinni. Or she would actually go into a trance—she would talk, though no one was there to talk to; she would shout at the top of her voice and sometimes she would even cry. Those who witnessed these scenes were filled with holy dread. All were careful not to disturb Halima, during those moments or at any other time, for fear that they might offend the jinni. If people talked about Halima they did so in whispers, behind her back.

Halima made believe that the spirits of the infant's parents visited her during those moments of trance. They came to enquire of the infant, she told people, came to teach her how she could make the jinni happy. At the same time, Halima affirmed, they told her all manner of things about life in general, about the people of the village, things past, things present and things yet to come.

A question that was on the minds of many people in the village was who was to marry Halima when she reached the marriageable age. No one doubted that she would marry. It was what women were for—marriage and childbearing. But there was the problem of the jinni. Wouldn't it be dangerous to be married to a woman possessed? Would there be men brave enough to want to marry Halima?

When Halima did reach the marriageable age, a problem presented itself which no one had anticipated. Halima did not *want* to get married. There were indeed men brave enough to want to marry her, but Halima turned them all down. The Wadaad himself proposed to her. He, people thought, would have been the ideal husband for Halima: he, if anyone, should have been able to cope with a woman possessed. But Halima turned him down too.

Not that possession by a jinni spirit was something unusual in Halima's village. Stories of jinnis abounded—of people who were possessed by jinnis, of people who had jinni spirits that

From *The Heineman Book of Contemporary African Short Stories,* ed. Chinua Achebe and Lynn Innes (Jeddah, Saudi Arabia: King Abdulaziz University, 1992), 94–99.

were like invisible twin brothers, or people who had jinni spirits as servants. It was common knowledge that one of Halima's own forefathers had had a jinni twin brother called Gess Ade, and one of her mother's grandfathers had had, in addition to a jinni twin brother, three devoted jinni servants called Toore, Gaadale, and Toor-Ourmone respectively. When Halima's mother had problems, she called on those three for help and protection. The ancestors of several clans were believed to have been born twins, a jinni being the twin partner of each of them. The tribe of Halima's brother-in-law had a twin jinni by the name of Sarhaan.

When animals were sacrificed, the jinni twins had to get their share. In return, the jinnis were expected to give support and protection to the clan. First the animals would be butchered. Then, the ritual songs having been sung, the carcasses would be cut open and the inner organs removed. These were to be given to the jinnis. Admonitions would be mumbled such as "Let's not forget Gess Ade's share; or Toore's, Gaadale's, Ourmone's . . ."

The parts set aside for the jinnis would be taken to a remote place up in the hills, and, because they invariably and mysteriously disappeared, the villagers were sure that the jinnis devoured them. No one, therefore, would dream of cheating the jinnis of their share. This had been so for generations and would continue to be so. Children were made to memorize the ritual songs so as to keep the ancestral rites intact from generation to generation.

When Halima was under the spell of her spirits, all her emotions seemed intensified. She experienced a feeling of power, as though she could do things beyond the reach of ordinary human beings. She felt good then. Moreover, whatever she undertook, her spirits seemed to lend a helping hand. Because the fortunes of her family, indeed those of the whole clan, prospered at the time, Halima as well as other people assumed that it was the spirits' doing. In time, Halima came to be regarded as a blessing to her family, an asset to the whole clan. And she gloried in the special status her spirits gave her.

TO THE CAPITAL

It was because of her special powers that Halima was summoned to the capital. A big part of her clan was there. The most important and the most powerful positions in the government were held by people of her clan. It had all started with one of their men, who had become very powerful in the government. He had called his relatives and found big government jobs for them. They in turn had called relatives of theirs till the government had virtually been taken over by Halima's people. And that had meant quick riches for everyone concerned. Nor had they been very scrupulous about getting what they wanted: anything that had stood in their way had been pushed aside or eliminated. At the time when Halima was summoned, her clan controlled the government and with that the wealth of the country so completely that no one dared to challenge them any more and they could get away with murder. Still they wanted to secure for themselves the extra protection of Halima's supernatural powers.

They had tried to get Halima's father to come to the capital as well. He was a man of stature, whose presence would have done honor to the clan. But he did not want to go. Old and resentful of change, he did not want to leave the peace and security of his village for the madness of the big city. But he was also afraid for his reputation. It was solid in his village but joining this gang might tarnish it, something he did not want to risk so near the end of his life. However, though he did not want to go himself, he had no reservations about sending his son and his daughter there. On one hand he hoped that they might get a slice of the big pie for themselves and so for the family. On the other hand he thought it would do no harm to have Halima there to protect the clan and to ensure its continued domination. Perhaps she could come to a deal with her spirits—she to continue looking after their infant and they to look after the welfare of the clan.

Halima did let herself be persuaded to go, but, before she went, she consulted her spirits. They asked her to perform two rituals. One was to prepare "Tahleel," a special type of water, over which certain rituals were performed. People drank it or bathed in it to benefit from its powers. The second was to perform daily annual sacrifices to Gess Ade, the clan's twin spirit. Select parts of the innards of thousands of animals—hearts, kidneys, intestines and others—were to be offered to him every day on the eastern shore.

When Halima and her brother were ready to go, a cousin of theirs came from the big city to fetch them. From this cousin, who was an important government official, the two learned many things. They learned about the great privileges their people enjoyed in the city. They got an idea what wealth they had amassed since the clan had come "to power." They found out how completely the clan was in control of the government. They were awed, the more so when their informant told them that the clan had "achieved" all this greatness in ten short years and that most of the people who now held important government positions were illiterate.

IN THE BIG CITY

In the city, the two were given a beautiful villa complete with lots of servants and security guards. Within days, Halima's brother obtained an important government position of his own. He was made the head of the department that handled the sale of all incense, both inside and outside the country. Its official name was Government Incense Agency.

And Halima wasted no time carrying out the two requests of her spirits. She asked two things from the leaders of the clan. She asked them to bring all the water resources of the city together in one central pool to facilitate the performing of the "Tahleel" and she requested the building of a huge slaughterhouse at the eastern shore. The leaders readily granted her requests since they were convinced that Halima's ministrations were of crucial importance for the continued success of the clan.

To centralize the city's water system, two huge water reservoirs were created, one in the eastern half and one in the western half of the city. Eventually all the wells of the city were destroyed, even the ones in private houses, and all water systems were connected to the two reservoirs. This way all the water consumed in the city came from the same source, and when Halima put the spell of her "Tahieel" on the two reservoirs, it reached everyone.

One of the effects of the "Tahleel" was to cure people of curiosity. Those who drank it stopped asking questions. Above all they stopped wondering about the actions of the clan's leading men. They became model subjects doing without questions, without objection, what they were told to do. And Halima kept putting ever new spells on the water, faster than the old ones wore off. Though no one but she herself knew what kind of magic she put on the water, rumors abounded. One rumor had it that she performed certain incantations over the bath water of the leader and then released it into the reservoirs. There was no doubt in her mind and in the minds of the leaders that as long as everyone drank the water that carried her "Tahleel" everything would go according to their plans.

When the new slaughterhouse went into operation, all other slaughterhouses were closed down. Unfortunately the new slaughterhouse was close to the Lido, the most popular of the city's beaches. In no time at all, the waters off the Lido swarmed with man-eating sharks, drawn there by the waste of blood and offals discharged by the slaughterhouse. After a number of people had been killed by the predators people stopped going to the Lido. There was no comment from the government. Quite obviously the slaughterhouse, where the sacrifices to Gess Ade were performed, was more important to the rulers of the country than the beach.

Every so often Halima would come to the slaughterhouse to check on the performance of the animal sacrifices. Here too she modified the rituals periodically to strengthen their effect.

As things kept going well for the tribe and her, Halima became more and more sure that she was the cause of it all. The clan's leaders too were convinced that they owed their continued success to Halima and her spirits. They heaped honors on her. They consulted her on all important issues and her counsel often proved invaluable. It was Halima, for instance, who thought up the idea of the shortages to keep the common people subdued. Shortages of all basic commodities were deliberately created and they kept people busy struggling for bare survival. They did not have time or energy to spare worrying about the goings-on in the government. The leaders of the clan felt more secure than ever.

Nearly twenty years have passed since Halima first went to the city. She is still performing her rituals, and the affairs of the clan are still prospering. Its men still hold all the important posts in the government and they still control the wealth of the country. As for the rest of the nation—they are mostly struggling to make ends meet, something that's becoming more and more difficult. And if there should be a few that might have time and energy left to start asking questions, Halima's Tahleel and her various other forms of magic take care of them. The men of the clan continue to govern with the help of Halima's magic spell.

8.3 THE MULLAH WITH NO LEGS
Ari Siletz

The mullah with legs always came in a shiny taxi. Framed by the richly tasselled, tinted windows of the bright orange car, he arrived in a rumbling rainbow of flashing chrome. The apparition briefly scintillated in front of the house next door while the mullah got out and Aunt Tooran's neighbor, the carpenter, rushed out to pay the driver. Soon the powerful P.A. system, courtesy of the carpenter, would blast the neighborhood with the mullah's mournful Arabic.

The mullah with no legs always came mounted on the back of a man wearing faded plaid. The two appeared on Aunt Tooran's doorstep, a large hump of brown on top of a pale tangle of rectangles. A subtle movement of the mullah's elbow directed his mount to clop up the stairs into the hall. There the plaid young man would remove his shoes and bring the mullah into the guest room. A few more elbow signals and the mullah would be propped up ready to perform. The young man would leave the room and sit on the mosaic steps of the hall entrance.

I always volunteered to take the mount his dish of *halvah* and glass of tea. (Halvah is a caramel-colored confection of flour, sugar, rosewater and saffron with the texture of modeling clay.) While the mullah talked, the mount and I played the Iranian game of learn everything, reveal nothing. He was curious about who was who in our family; I mainly wished to know how the mullah lost his legs. Tooran had told me that she thought the mullah was born without his legs.

The mount's curiosity was not idle: one needs to know who can pull what strings. My curiosity was teenage fascination with dismemberment. I was no match for him, which is just as well. He used the knowledge he captured from me to make things easier for himself and his clan. I longed to be able to tell the neighbor's children that while their mullah was sleek, our mullah had lost his legs to a crocodile while he was studying at the seminary in Egypt.

I envied the neighbors for their mullah. Our mullah did not wear a bright green shawl; he, unlike the neighbor's mullah, did not consider himself to be a direct descendant of the Prophet. He did not come and go in flashy taxis. I had seen him in the streets, always riding the plaid, never on anything with wheels. He did not have the neighbor mullah's elegance and youth. He wore such an old *abba* (mantle) that passersby, thinking he was a crippled beggar, stopped to give him money. He gratefully accepted and sent loud prayers after the alms-giver. Unlike the neighbor's mullah, he did not glitter like a freshly opened present, but he was a decent man with close ties to God. The first real beggar that crossed his path would receive the misdirected alms with instructions to pray after the kindly passerby who had made the mistake.

Looking back, I am not so envious, as it seems each mullah filled a particular need. The carpenter was a businessman. It was important to his livelihood that the neighbors be aware that he was a devout Moslem. Being fully regulated by the agencies of heaven, devout businessmen do not overcharge or misrepresent their product. So he had set aside an advertising budget that paid for a flashy mullah and a P.A. system that spared no one within miles. With God's help, his business was doing well enough that he was even thinking of investing in the new and risky business of raising American chickens.

Aunt Tooran needed a different kind of intercession. Her husband, Farabi, was very ill. The logo mullah would have been useless to her. She needed a mullah who could bring cures, console

---

From Ari Barkshei Siletz, *The Mullah with No Legs and Other Stories* (Yarmouth, ME: Intercultural Press, 1992). Copyright © 1992 Ari Barkeshei Siletz. Reprinted with permission.

the grieving, and give the strength of faith to the dying. Also, it is believed that God lends a kinder ear to the handicapped, so a mullah with no legs appeared heaven-sent.

Because the mullahs addressed different markets, their visits need not have caused a rivalry, but Aunt Tooran and the neighbor's wife, neither of whom could withstand much tranquility, had fashioned a conflict out of this seemingly unpromising material. Their previous battle had been mercilessly resolved by the fruit and vegetableseller who had started to stagger the opening of new crates of grapes throughout the morning. This way, early risers like Tooran did not ravage the best grapes, leaving only mushed ones to sleepers-in like the carpenter's wife.

The rivalry had started when, one day at the marketplace, Tooran informed the fruit and vegetableseller that she was accompanying her husband to a pilgrimage to Mashad. The shrine of Imam Reza in Mashad is the source of many miraculous healings. Men who visit the shrine come back bearing the once-prestigious title of *Mashadi*. Tooran also let it be known that in these godforsaken days not enough pilgrimages were being made, the pilgrimage funds being wasted on P.A. systems.

The news and commentary were intended for the ears of the carpenter's wife, who told the fruit and vegetableseller that her husband was saving for a trip to Mecca. This, the most prestigious pilgrimage of all, would earn him the title *Haji*. Many businessmen in the bazaar bear this title; it is so important to business that some people use the title even before making the pilgrimage. If his business is obviously doing well and if a man is obviously rich, it is a disgrace for him not to have made the pilgrimage, which is required of all who can afford it.

The carpenter's wife also added, for the enlightenment of the fruit and vegetableseller, that chadors with little flower designs were undignified as they defeated the very purpose of the chador, which is to keep visual attention away from the wearer. Tooran was a handsome woman with no incentive for deflecting attention away from herself. Except on solemn occasions, her chadors were extremely short and botanical.

From then on, a rivalry ensued as to who was more Moslem than whom. I doubt that the mullahs ever became fully aware that they were being used as pawns in a contest of piety, but the broadcasting mullah may have suspected something from the number of times he was requested to mention the undesirability of flower patterns on chadors. Because of the spiritual depth of our mullah, morale was better on our side, but the neighbor clearly had the upper hand in hardware. As the neighborhood was entirely Moslem to begin with, the P.A. system would not make any converts, but it was overwhelming in its ability to convert electricity to loud Arabic. Many nights we lay awake to the lullaby of amplified Koran, dreaming of ways to reconcile Tooran and the carpenter's wife.

A good way for neighbors to forgive each other is provided by the *nazr* custom. Plates of food and pieces of sacrificial lamb are distributed among the neighbors so that they might add their prayers to those of the benefactor. One can hardly continue to bear a grudge against a person who sends a plate of food, requesting in return a prayer for the recovery of a loved one. When the foe brings back the empty plate and the plate owner says, "You did not have to return it so clean, I would have washed it myself," good will is rekindled. The neighbor made frequent nazrs because only the youngest of her seven children could get passing grades without divine intervention. Aunt Tooran also made nazrs because of her ailing husband, but now the plate of *nazri* appeared to be hypocritical piety and intensified the rivalry even further. With the olive branch interpreted as yet another weapon, the neighbor's children continued to fail and Aunt Tooran's husband continued to die.

Farabi's illness had started soon after the evening known to Tooran as "The Night the Owl Came." It was a few months before the mullah with no legs entered our lives. Aunt Tooran's girl servant, on her way back from putting out the trash, brought home a curious clump of very pretty feathers. "Look what I found!" she hollered, rushing into the kitchen. In her childish excitement she had forgotten that animals are not welcome in the house, particularly in the kitchen. The children all ran to see what the girl had captured. "It was hobbling on its wings, so easy to catch, . . ." she began.

Aunt Tooran was squatting on the kitchen floor, salting eggplants for tomorrow's lunch (they would soak up less oil that way). She started up to see what the girl was so eagerly extending toward her. There was a small movement of feathers as the bird turned its head to reveal the face of an owl. Tooran froze halfway up from her squat. Her face paled, her eyes bulged in throbbing terror. She began to scream, "Throw it out, throw it out, get it out of here!"

The terrified servant, not realizing what an awful thing she had been holding, threw the owl on the kitchen floor in a panic. Tooran's screamings became unintelligible. The frightened children scattered out of the kitchen to get help. Tooran screamed and shook as though a demon inside her were being exorcised. Her husband came leaping down the stairs ready for the worst.

When he saw his wife cornered by the bird, he exhaled his alarm and slumped in relief. Then he became angry. "Tooran, I thought someone was strangling you. Who is going to explain to the neighbors tomorrow what the screaming was about? Do you want the children to have nightmares?" He took the bird out, mumbling something about when he was a boy in the village, he used to play with owls all the time. When he came back from throwing the owl in the trash, he berated Tooran for being superstitious, irrational, and hysterical. "An owl is just another bird," he explained, "nothing unlucky about it." Tooran, still shaky and pale, appeared genuinely ashamed and repentant.

The next day, the entire house was scrubbed, starting with the kitchen. All present at last night's scene were sent to the bathhouse where their outer skins were scraped away with pumice. All clothes were boiled and a new trash can was appointed. Nevertheless, a month later Tooran's husband began to feel unusual muscle fatigue. He was quickly diagnosed as having myasthenia gravis and told there was no cure.

Farabi was sure that an old car accident had something to do with it. The doctors could not speculate. Tooran was sure it was the owl. She was even bold enough to suggest it to a doctor, who ridiculed her. But the doctor had not seen the dying owl keep its face hidden until it was time to show it to Tooran. He had not seen the demon inside Tooran throw a fit. He had not seen the owl's face looking devilishly amused by the joke. So what did the doctor know? Did he have a cure?

Aunt Tooran was not paranoid; she had reason to fear a curse. She had been bad. I had heard people say, "Tooran has worms" (Iranian for "she enjoys tormenting people") or "She is full of broken glass" ("she cannot be trusted"). All of this was true. Tooran's soul profited from trouble. She had a genius for quoting one's most harmless statement in situations where great damage would be done. Like a demolitions expert, she knew exactly where to put the charge to bring the whole structure down. Once, noticing that my mother was getting along too cordially with Aunt Effat, she invited Effat to her house to tell her that my mother was two-faced about her affections. To prove it, she called my mother on the phone and complained bitterly about Effat, bringing up cleverly catalogued and cross-referenced old issues. My mother fell for the trap and sympathized by voicing some of her own complaints—only Tooran was no longer on the phone, she had passed the receiver to Effat. The ensuing hostilities refreshed Tooran greatly.

But her wickedness had a practical side: if ever a conspiracy was needed, Tooran would be called to mastermind it. My mother went to seek her counsel on how to deal with the new servant who refused to go shopping. He was a little boy, Mahmood, whose mother had taught him to pretend ignorance as to the whereabouts of the marketplace. It did no good to show him time after time; his mother had taught him well and my mother was no match for her. The mother worried that her little boy would be lost or run over by a car, but it was exhausting not to be able to send the boy on errands outside the house.

Tooran told my mother to send the boy to the grocery store, telling him that he could also buy himself an ice cream. A decent enough solution except that Tooran called Agha Ali, the grocer, and told him that if Mahmood showed up to buy ice cream, to tell him that they were out of it. Why would Agha Ali agree to such a thing? For someone of Tooran's skills, a coconspirator was as easy to find as a bridge partner.

Tooran had another use for us. She spared nothing in the defense of her relatives against outsiders. Once she gave such a tongue-lashing to one of my teachers, who had been overzealous with the whip, that he stopped whipping his students altogether. But she was just as vicious in defending her immediate family against the rest of the clan. To her, humanity was a structured priority of loyalties. Her allegiances were hard-wired such that it was impossible to override this circuitry of instinct with truth, friendship, beauty, logic, justice, religion, or even magic.

But though she continued to defy the powers that cursed her, it was obvious that the owl incident had somewhat humbled her. For when the mullah with no legs visited her home, that evil, troublemaking spark in her eyes vanished. It was as though the demon inside her had hopped fearfully out of sight of the mullah.

Holding a thick black chador tightly around her face, Tooran had brought up her owl theory with our mullah. He did not profess ignorance of the occult, nor did he wish to encourage inquiry into these matters, but his evasion was satisfying. "The owl is God's creature," he said. "Fear only God and you have nothing to fear."

The mullah with no legs knew how to conquer fear. Farabi often questioned the mullah about the moment of death and the first night in the grave. He suspected the mullah had come very close to dying himself. After their talks, the mullah recited the Koran with a deeply meditative lilt that left behind a cleansed feeling, like a good night's sleep.

The other mullah barked the revealed verses with an enthusiasm and vigor the likes of which I would not encounter until years later in America. He always ended his sessions with this syco-phantic reminder of the truce between the clergy and the Shah: "May the Almighty preserve the monarchy and bestow upon our Shah the long life of Noah." This last statement also served to keep the neighbors from complaining about the noise. Although there was a city ordinance for-bidding such broadcasts on the pain of the offender's electricity being shut off, no one would dare bring a complaint against a loudspeaker that spoke favorably of the Shah. It was quite possible, they thought, that this was a trap set by the secret police to flush out the malcontents.

The carpenter delighted in all of this. With God and the Shah in his corner, how could he lose? Against all odds, the American chicken business was not doing badly. The Iranian palate com-plained that the birds did not taste gamey enough and that their eggs were sallow and runny. But despite their unpopularity, these chickens were making slow but stubborn headway into the Ira-nian chicken market. Iranians often repeated this conversation someone had overheard between a resentful Iranian chicken and an American chicken:

American chicken (boastfully): "My eggs are so much bigger than yours and they sell for so much more. Just look at the size of that egg."

Iranian chicken (snobbishly): "Shoo, shoo, you big white lump. We Iranians don't be-lieve in busting our anuses for money."

Years later, I would write home to explain that it was wrong to malign the American chicken as a class. In county fairs in America I had met an astonishing variety of chickens and realized that "American chicken" as known to Iranians is just a single subvariety of leghorn with a sorrowful history of genetic manipulation and mass imprisonment.

Given the magnitude of anti-American chicken sentiments, I cannot explain why the bird persisted. Clearly a miracle was at work. The logo mullah was gaining the advantage over the mullah with no legs: while the neighbor was slowly getting richer, Farabi was slowly getting sicker. The neighbors were winning the piety war. But Tooran was not an easy opponent. She would demonstrate a tactical versatility I did not think she possessed.

She knew that at the hotel where Farabi was employed, there worked a talented electrician by the name of Torab. Tooran was sure that Torab would be able to build a jamming device that could turn the tables in her war. Torab was in charge of setting up sound and electricals for the hotel's nightly entertainment. It was a luxury hotel that catered to foreigners. Unlike the modern cement hotels that were being poured by the dozens on the chic northern slopes, this old brick hotel lived in the shade of mature sycamores and cypresses in the no-longer-fancy part of town. Because of its humble location, the hotel was never booked solid, but those foreigners who still benefited from the presence of vegetation and suffered from the sight of concrete and whose skins could sense the difference between a cool breeze and mechanically chilled air stayed nowhere else.

These foreigners had inadvertently helped Farabi keep his accounting job long after the disease had made him useless to his employers. We had found a relative in the Ministry of Labor who was in charge of issuing work permits to foreign workers. Since the hotel's international clientele required international entertainment, the hotel needed work permits for foreign talent. The relative had made it clear that business-is-business notwithstanding, no work permits would be issued unless Farabi kept his job. The inequity in the disability insurance regulations had, at least locally, been remedied. Farabi became accountant emeritus with some cut in pay, and an assistant was hired to do the accounting. As part of the settlement, the hotel management had insisted that he show up for work every day.

Very early each morning, Tooran would dress Farabi in suit and tie. Daryoosh, their son, would slowly walk him to the bus station. There the conductor helped him into the crowded bus and cleared a place for him. A special stop was made near the hotel, where Farabi's brother, who also worked at the hotel, took over his care. In the afternoon, Daryoosh waited for him at the bus station to bring him home. Farabi leaned on Daryoosh's arm and took slow shuffling steps. The two had become the other symbiotic pair in the neighborhood. But while the mullah and the plaid seemed to communicate with elbow signals, Daryoosh and his father were always telling stories and laughing. It was hard to imagine what a dying man and his son had to say to each other that was so entertaining. Day after day they could be seen in the streets, one animated, the other limp, and both thoroughly amused.

One day father and son returned bearing Torab's electronic jamming device. The inventor had warned them that the device might not work. It could render useless all the radios and televisions in the neighborhood, but a closed circuit P.A. system would be harder to affect.

For a week before the neighbor's next broadcast Daryoosh had fun jamming Radio Iran. He was ignoring another one of Torab's warnings: for security reasons any unauthorized use of the airwaves was highly illegal. Even owning a walkie-talkie or a remote-control toy could win the offender a tour of SAVAK (the Shah's secret police) facilities. A monstrous hybrid of CIA training and domestic brutality, SAVAK made the KGB look like a petting zoo. But what was worse, if the neighbors found out that it was Daryoosh who had jammed the final episode of a popular mystery, he would have longed for the relative comfort of the SAVAK torture chambers.

That Friday we all sat around Torab's box waiting for the broadcast to start. Daryoosh was not wearing a lab coat and his hair was combed down, but otherwise he was behaving quite like a mad scientist. Sitting at the controls of Torab's box (a single on-off switch), his eyes glowed with Faustian passion. His fingers quivered hesitantly over the switch which, once thrown, would irreversibly transform Life As We Knew It in the neighborhood. Would God permit this? We all wondered.

The broadcast began. The mullah started with a few clever salutations. He was beginning to sound like a disc jockey. Let him warm up, we thought. As long as he spoke Farsi, we listened, giggled, and waited. As soon as he plunged into his imitation Arabic, Tooran nodded meaningfully to Daryoosh who, with historical emphasis, threw the switch.

The crashing sound of hopes being dashed drowned out whatever meager effect Torab's gadget had on the loudspeaker. There was a faint raspberry loud enough perhaps to annoy an audiophile but certainly far too soft to thwart the mullah's sonic rampage. Tooran, disappointed in electronic warfare, left the room heavyhearted. The rest of the household, also in a somber mood, abandoned Daryoosh and went back to mundane existence. Daryoosh, like a believer whose UFO was late, refused to abandon the sham. He sat pawing the gadget mournfully.

About a half hour later, we were all busy doing unmemorable things when we noticed that something was different. The continuous Arabic had subsided and was replaced by a curious sequence: the mullah said "birthday" loudly and waited. The faint raspberry loud enough to annoy the audiophile followed. The mullah repeated "birthday" and waited. Again the faint raspberry sound. We all rushed to Daryoosh's room. He was on the floor having a seizure of laughter. The mullah's sermon had to do with an imam's birthday, so Daryoosh activated the gadget only after the word "birthday." Religious sermons characteristically feature repeated words, and it was not long before the mullah realized that the word "birthday" caused a funny buzzing in the system. His scientific curiosity aroused, he had temporarily abandoned God and was seeking his own answers to the ways of nature. Tooran was trying to rebuke Daryoosh for his irreverence. It was one thing to jam a loudspeaker, quite another to make light of an imam's birth. Did he want Farabi to get worse? But she could not contain the chuckles that kept bursting through her frowning face. The demon inside her was excitedly peering through her eyeballs, happily waving to get the attention of an offspring it had not known about—the demon inside Daryoosh. This tearful reunion of mother and child demons was touching to see.

Chuckles still percolating through her scowls, Tooran made Daryoosh stop the heresy. She reminded him that this sort of thing could backfire. Not only would it not stop the mullah's broadcasts, it might intensify them. Also, if anyone found out about the mockery, who could stop the angry mob? Certainly the neighbors would put two and two together and realize it was Daryoosh who was jamming their radios and televisions.

Torab's box was returned. He was told that his invention did not work. No mention was made of the use that was made of it. It is probably now forgotten in the dank hotel tool shop, covered by dust and grease. Maybe it is still smarting from the dent inflicted by its disappointed creator, who was never told how marvelously his brainchild had performed. Such is the fate of boxes that mock the Unseen Powers.

Next time the mullah with no legs showed up, Tooran mentioned the broadcasts. Could he persuade his colleague to give up the microphone? The mullah said he had more pull with Allah than with the theological establishment. He would pray for a solution. Why did we not think of this before? It would have saved us many nights of sleepless agony. Miraculously, within a few months after the mullah with no legs started his prayers against the P.A. system, the neighbors moved out. There was much ecstatic revelry. The victorious Tooran set the fruit and vegetableseller to the task of researching the carpenter's downfall so she could gloat over the details.

Though the mullah's prayers quickly rid us of the P.A. system, they were helpless against myasthenia gravis. The disease began to affect Farabi's respiration and he asphyxiated slowly. I remember Farabi fighting for breath in a hospital bed. As a last effort to save him, the doctors had removed his thymus gland. It did not work. He lay in the bed rasping and exchanging jokes with his son. "Mohammad, Jesus and Moses were stranded on an island with Sophia Loren. . . . "

The night before his father's death, Daryoosh pulled out a tiny box from his desk and showed me its contents.

"What is it?" I asked.

"*Kafoor* (camphor)."

"What is it good for?"

"It was secretly taken from the mummies of Egypt. If my father were to eat even a pinhead of this, he would be completely cured."

I was about to ask the obvious question, but his teary eyes pleaded with me to humor him.

"Where did you get it?" I finally asked.

I saw the mullah with no legs seven nights after Farabi's death. He had a larger audience than usual. The clan, numbering perhaps a hundred, had been staying at Tooran's since the death. I knew I would not see the mullah again. I would be leaving to study in the U.S., so I was desperate to find out how the mullah had lost his legs. He never talked about it, and the plaid sitting on the stairs in the hall had resisted my subtle probing for years. I had told him everything, he had told me nothing. He told me he was the mullah's uncle's son on the mother's side; later he told me he was the mullah's aunt's son on the father's side. When I asked him how the mullah had lost his legs, he would say, "I don't know."

When an Iranian says, "I don't know," most of the time he means, "I don't trust you." He made me do most of the talking. I had told him I had been to England and he seemed most interested. But all he told me about himself could be placed in a joke jigsaw puzzle—none of the pieces seemed to fit. He was consistent in one thing, however. When I first met him, he said he had been carrying the mullah for five years to the month. As the years went by, he never contradicted himself as to the date he entered the mullah's service. The plaid had trusted me in a way by giving me a strong clue. When I was smart enough to piece his clues together, I would be smart enough to be entrusted with the secret.

When I told the plaid I was leaving Iran for the U.S., he decided to take a risk with me and asked if I had ridden in any Rolls Royces in England. I told him that I had.

"Really, did you ride in Rolls Royces a lot over there?" he said as though he would accept anything I said. He was testing me.

"No. Just once."

"When was that?"

Was he fantasizing that someday he would be carrying the mullah in a plaid Rolls? I told him the story over a plate of halvah. Afterwards he asked me if all Rolls Royces had bulletproof windows. Why would he want bulletproof windows on the mullah's Rolls? I said I did not think so.

"The Shah's Rolls Royce has bulletproof windows. Why do you think that is?" he asked. I was jolted. No sane Iranian brought up the Shah in the context of assassination. What was his fantasy leading to? But a jolt was what I needed to put everything together.

I was completely off the mark: this was no fantasy of grandeur. He was leading the horse to water and he had to jolt me into taking a drink. He could not remind me outright of the violent clash between the followers of Khomeini and the forces of the Shah on the fifth of June 1963. On that day, the fifteenth of Khordad 1342 by the Iranian calendar, hundreds of members of the Iranian clergy were rounded up by the secret police. The plaid could not directly tell me that when the mullah was dragged to the SAVAK chambers, he still had his legs. He could not say that, because how did he know I was not one of thousands of SAVAK informers still on the lookout for any remnants of resistance to the Shah? For that matter, how did I know *he* was not a SAVAK informer feeling out how *I* stood on the issues? This dangerous conversation had to be broken off. A little confirmation is not worth risking so much.

That afternoon I went upstairs to tell Tooran why I thought the mullah had lost his legs and why the mullah never sent blessings after the Shah.

With all the relatives around, it had been a hectic seven days. There had been much cooking, many children, plenty of fights, and much weeping. Tonight Farabi's soul would ascend to heaven. After tonight, Tooran would be left alone to grieve. But now, in the afternoon heat, the guests were all napping.

I found Tooran sobbing in Farabi's empty closet. The clothes had been given away to charity, but the closet still smelled like him. I thought I would wait for a better time to talk to her about the mullah. For a few minutes, I watched her mourn in a rocking huddle, then left quietly without being seen. By the time a better opportunity arose to talk to Tooran, I had decided to keep the secret. It would not have been good for the mullah's business if people feared they were associating with a dissident. I almost betrayed the plaid; I certainly would have if Whatever Protects Us had not kept my mouth shut long enough for me to become a little bit more Iranian.

With Farabi gone and the logo mullah no longer keeping our ears busy, the neighborhood felt lonely. I missed the logo mullah; he pumped energy into the community. I have since wondered if it was not his energy that kept Farabi alive. I am sure the carpenter's wife would not resent our benefiting from the spillover from her mullah, especially if she knew what a great debt she owed Tooran.

The fruit and vegetableseller filled in the details. A few months after the mullah with no legs agreed to pray for a solution to the P.A. problem, the carpenter had a windfall and bought a luxurious house on the cooler foothills of north Tehran. While the logo mullah's prayers had helped only to keep the chickens alive, the mullah with no legs made the business take off overnight. The carpenter imported a technique for making chickens lay eggs with two yolks inside. The double-yolk egg is considered a sign of luck among Iranians, so the carpenter became a very successful egg merchant. I had a hunch our mullah was better than their mullah, but the way this superiority was confirmed left us feeling cheated. Was it Allah's infinite wisdom or just a devilish prank? I have it on my list of things to ask when *I* meet the Almighty.

8.4   ONE OF THESE DAYS
Gabriel García Márquez

Monday dawned warm and rainless. Aurelio Escovar, a dentist without a degree, and a very early riser, opened his office at six. He took some false teeth, still mounted in their plaster mold, out of the glass case and put on the table a fistful of instruments which he arranged in size order, as if they were on display. He wore a collarless striped shirt, closed at the neck with a golden stud, and pants held up by suspenders. He was erect and skinny, with a look that rarely corresponded to the situation, the way deaf people have of looking.

When he had things arranged on the table, he pulled the drill toward the dental chair and sat down to polish the false teeth. He seemed not to be thinking about what he was doing, but worked steadily, pumping the drill with his feet, even when he didn't need it.

After eight he stopped for a while to look at the sky through the window, and he saw two pensive buzzards who were drying themselves in the sun on the ridgepole of the house next door. He went on working with the idea that before lunch it would rain again. The shrill voice of his eleven-year-old son interrupted his concentration.

"Papá."

"What?"

"The Mayor wants to know if you'll pull his tooth."

"Tell him I'm not here."

He was polishing a gold tooth. He held it at arm's length, and examined it with his eyes half closed. His son shouted again from the little waiting room.

"He says you are, too, because he can hear you."

The dentist kept examining the tooth. Only when he had put it on the table with the finished work did he say:

"So much the better."

He operated the drill again. He took several pieces of a bridge out of a cardboard box where he kept the things he still had to do and began to polish the gold.

"Papá."

"What?"

He still hadn't changed his expression.

"He says if you don't take out his tooth, he'll shoot you."

Without hurrying, with an extremely tranquil movement, he stopped pedaling the drill, pushed it away from the chair, and pulled the lower drawer of the table all the way out. There was a revolver. "O.K.," he said. "Tell him to come and shoot me."

He rolled the chair over opposite the door, his hand resting on the edge of the drawer. The Mayor appeared at the door. He had shaved the left side of his face, but the other side, swollen and in pain, had a five-day-old beard. The dentist saw many nights of desperation in his dull eyes. He closed the drawer with his fingertips and said softly:

"Sit down."

"Good morning," said the Mayor.

"Morning," said the dentist.

From *No One Writes to the Colonel and Other Stories* [Coronel no tiene quien le escriba], trans. J.S. Bernstein (New York: Harper & Row, 1968), 107–110. English translation copyright © 1968 Harper & Row Publishers, Inc. Reprinted with permission.

While the instruments were boiling, the Mayor leaned his skull on the headrest of the chair and felt better. His breath was icy. It was a poor office: an old wooden chair, the pedal drill, a glass case with ceramic bottles. Opposite the chair was a window with a shoulder-high cloth curtain. When he felt the dentist approach, the Mayor braced his heels and opened his mouth.

Aurelio Escovar turned his head toward the light. After inspecting the infected tooth, he closed the Mayor's jaw with a cautious pressure of his fingers.

"It has to be without anesthesia," he said.

"Why?"

"Because you have an abscess."

The Mayor looked him in the eye. "All right," he said, and tried to smile. The dentist did not return the smile. He brought the basin of sterilized instruments to the worktable and took them out of the water with a pair of cold tweezers, still without hurrying. Then he pushed the spittoon with the tip of his shoe, and went to wash his hands in the washbasin. He did all this without looking at the Mayor. But the Mayor didn't take his eyes off him.

It was a lower wisdom tooth. The dentist spread his feet and grasped the tooth with the hot forceps. The Mayor seized the arms of the chair, braced his feet with all his strength, and felt an icy void in his kidneys, but didn't make a sound. The dentist moved only his wrist. Without rancor, rather with a bitter tenderness, he said:

"Now you'll pay for our twenty dead men."

The Mayor felt the crunch of bones in his jaw, and his eyes filled with tears. But he didn't breathe until he felt the tooth come out. Then he saw it through his tears. It seemed so foreign to his pain that he failed to understand his torture of the five previous nights.

Bent over the spittoon, sweating, panting, he unbuttoned his tunic and reached for the handkerchief in his pants pocket. The dentist gave him a clean cloth.

"Dry your tears," he said.

The Mayor did. He was trembling. While the dentist washed his hands, he saw the crumbling ceiling and a dusty spider web with spider's eggs and dead insects. The dentist returned, drying his hands. "Go to bed," he said, "and gargle with salt water." The Mayor stood up, said goodbye with a casual military salute, and walked toward the door, stretching his legs, without buttoning up his tunic.

"Send the bill," he said.

"To you or the town?"

The Mayor didn't look at him. He closed the door and said through the screen:

"It's the same damn thing."

8.5   THE EXPLOSION IN THE PARLOR*
Bai Xiao-Yi

The host poured tea into the cup and placed it on the small table in front of his guests, who were a father and daughter, and put the lid on the cup with a clink. Apparently thinking of something, he hurried into the inner room, leaving the thermos on the table. His two guests heard a chest of drawers opening and a rustling.

They remained sitting in the parlor, the ten-year-old daughter looking at the flowers outside the window, the father just about to take his cup, when the crash came, right there in the parlor. Something was hopelessly broken.

It was the thermos, which had fallen to the floor. The girl looked over her shoulder abruptly, startled, staring. It was mysterious. Neither of them had touched it, not even a little bit. True, it hadn't stood steadily when their host placed it on the table, but it hadn't fallen then.

The crash of the thermos caused the host, with a box of sugar cubes in his hand, to rush back from the inner room. He gawked at the steaming floor and blurted out, "It doesn't matter! It doesn't matter!"

The father started to say something. Then he muttered, "Sorry, I touched it and it fell."

"It doesn't matter," the host said.

Later, when they left the house, the daughter said, "Daddy, *did* you touch it?"

"No. But it stood so close to me."

"But you *didn't* touch it. I saw your reflection in the windowpane. You were sitting perfectly still."

The father laughed. "What then would you give as the cause of its fall?"

"The thermos fell by itself. The floor is uneven. It wasn't steady when Mr. Li put it there. Daddy, *why* did you say that you . . ."

"That won't do, girl. It sounds more acceptable when I say I knocked it down. There are things which people accept less the more you defend them. The truer the story you tell, the less true it sounds."

The daughter was lost in silence for a while. Then she said, "Can you explain it only this way?"

"Only this way," her father said.

From *Sudden Fiction International: Sixty Short-Short Stories*, ed. Robert Shapard and James Thomas (New York: Norton, 1989). *Translated by Ding Zuxin.

Section 9

———— Individuals and Groups ————

9.1   IN THE FOOTSTEPS OF A WATER BUFFALO
Nhat Tien

When the production unit assigned him the task of harrowing the little patch of rice field along the creek flowing past Cong Quan, Vinh was beside himself with joy. At least that was a less punishing job than carrying baskets of clay from the ends of a shoulder pole for the local brick-making cooperative.

But Vinh had not reckoned with the abnormal sluggishness of the water buffalo. Admittedly, it was an old, old beast—a scrawny thing, weaker than the other fourteen buffalo belonging to their February 3 agricultural cooperative, but a water buffalo balking at the plow or harrow—that was unacceptable behavior. So Vinh made maximum use of the bamboo whip, lashing at the beast's ash gray skin while blustering and shouting himself hoarse. The torrid sun had him sweating profusely, and his eyes were blurry. Under his feet, the paddy slosh that had been baking since daybreak was scorching hot. And the water buffalo kept plodding on his way ever so slowly and wearily. Vinh could hear its labored breathing through the gaping mouth dribbling saliva and froth. Its entire skeleton jutted against wrinkled skin, and he could count every rib.

Apparently, Old Man Thuoc had once warned everyone against overworking the water buffalo. The creatures were always being called upon to do this or that. Plowing. Harrowing. Hauling lumber. Transporting goods. Carrying tons of brick. Old Man Thuoc had spoken up at a general meeting: "You comrades should go easy on the buffalo if you want them to work for many years. Overtax their bodies and they'll give out on you in no time."

Thuoc had spoken without malice or innuendo. He only worried about the draft animals, and far from his mind were all those aged humans on whose wizened backs were saddled sundry chores in the cooperative. To his simple way of thinking, water buffalo represented the most precious capital: when one fell sick it was cause for grave concern. If a man was ill, well, that was different: he could get back to work in a few days.

The secretary of the Party branch, however, chose to interpret Thuoc's guileless words in a completely different manner. At a restricted session of the village council, which included leaders of various groups—workers, women, youth, and the supervisory board of cooperatives—he pronounced his verdict: "Old Man Thuoc holds the most reactionary views possible. All of you, comrades, must maintain your vigilance and keep to a minimum his remarks in public on any subject."

All present understood. While innocent enough, Thuoc's words unwittingly reflected the truth of their lives. Old men and women had to bend their shrunken backs hauling bricks, pushing carts, and lugging baskets of dirt with shoulder poles like beasts of burden, yet nobody dared emit one peep in their defense. Why contradict the most powerful voice in the village and court trouble? "The best thing is to sit still, and the next best thing is to say yes." So went proverbial wisdom at meetings under the socialist regime.

From *To Be Made Over: Tales of Socialist Reeducation*, ed. and trans. Huynh Sanh Thong (New Haven, CT: Yale University Press, 1988).

Thuoc's incident eventually blew over, and he avoided pursuing the issue any further. On the contrary, both he and his wife eagerly took on any task entrusted to them. So later, when their son signed up for military service, no matter how vigilant the village council wished to appear, it was obliged to offer one of its "progressive family" certificates of merit to Thuoc and his wife. Thuoc was promoted to foreman of the production unit at the brick kiln, and his wife was admitted to the Association of Elderly Women and put on the advisory committee, even though she never opened her mouth or ventured a single opinion at any meeting. From start to finish, she could be seen lifting her apron to her rheumy eyes and dabbing at them all the time.

Then one day, from out of the blue, a warrant from the district came for the arrest of Thuoc's son for desertion. Now, if a young man fell for the "artificial prosperity" of Saigon, or flinched from his international proletarian duty in fraternal socialist Kampuchea, he would hardly be so foolish as to return to his native village. In all probability, the boy had disappeared into the corrupt society of the South, but the comrades of the security police intended to carry out the directives of the district Party committee to the letter and in earnest. Flourishing their weapons, they stormed Thuoc's house as if they were hunting enemy troops. The hut was virtually bare of furniture, and there was not much worth rummaging through, but, all the same, the gang went through the motions of searching, strutting back and forth and turning the place upside down for a whole hour. During all that time Thuoc's wife sobbed and blubbered, crying again and again, "O my son! Where have you gone? Why have you left your ma?"

As for Thuoc himself, he simply squatted at the foot of a post and hugged his knees in stony silence. He was very angry with his boy. The brat might have found a refuge somewhere for himself, but he had brought disaster down on both his father and his mother. In a twinkling their so-called revolutionary contribution to the cooperative, what they had achieved over many years, went up in smoke. Thuoc and his wife would lose their positions in the community and their jobs. They would be ostracized and punished not only in reprisal but as a pointed warning to any other youngsters who might feel tempted to follow their son down the reactionary road to decadence and hooliganism.

All of a heap, man and wife became outlaws and pariahs, doomed to live apart from society. When they met someone out on the road and ventured a hello, that person would look the other way, feigning nonrecognition. A few friends or acquaintances in whom persisted some shreds of decency might bestow on them a commiserative glance, but they would at once look around nervously, as if they had committed a crime and were afraid of being observed.

What they had dreaded, and what hurt most, was that from now on Thuoc and his wife would be cut off the ration-coupon system. With ration coupons they had found it possible to buy staples at official prices. Without the coupons, they would consider themselves evicted for good from the community dining table, even if what was spread upon the board was nothing more than potato and cassava.

Thuoc now had to journey all the way to the next village and beg better-off families for work on mutual-help teams. His wife was forced to search through the mire of flooded fields and creeks for crabs and snails to help eke out their meager fare. Both came to look like woebegone souls risen out of the mud. Their plight gave the Party branch secretary much occasion for gleeful gloating. He kept repeating, as if to drill a lesson into the village folks, "This is what will befall all those who go against the Party line and state policy! It's historical necessity—there's no getting around it."

At the very moment when Vinh was struggling with his old water buffalo in the slush of the rice field, Thuoc's wife was floundering in the creek with a basket for collecting snails hung on her back. She clearly heard Vinh curse the beast. She clearly saw his hand wave the bamboo whip and lash repeatedly at its wizened skeleton. But instead of hastening its pace, the buffalo slowed down little by little until it came to a standstill, trembling all over. Utterly exhausted, it seemed unable to pull its foot out of the mire for even one more step. The harrow stuck fast. The steaming paddy slosh beneath burned at Vinh's feet and drove him close to frenzy. He flogged the beast so hard he drew blood from its flank, yet still the buffalo would not budge. Its body was bathed in sweat when, stretching out its neck and rearing its head, it exhaled something like a soft moan. Then the whole mass slumped down. The decrepit animal collapsed in the paddy like some old soldier fallen on the battleground.

This unexpected turn of events stunned Vinh. At first, he stood there staring dumbfounded at the beast asprawl in the field, his every limb numb with fear. Then he flung the bamboo whip down beside the buffalo and rushed off screaming, "Comrades! Comrades! Come out, take a look—the buffalo is dead!"

As he reached the road running and screaming, Vinh bumped into Thuoc's wife, whose eyes were wide with astonishment. The wretched buffalo had been not unlike a close acquaintance to her and her husband. They knew all about it, when and where it had been born, to whom it had belonged. They knew how many cowlicks there were on its head, how many rings there were around its horns, even what made it tick. And now it was dead!

Forsaken by kith and kin, Thuoc's wife suddenly realized what the buffalo had meant to her. Never had it glowered at her with contempt or hatred since the day her wretched boy had bolted from the army. Never had it averted its gaze when she came up to it and patted it on the back. Thuoc's wife dissolved into tears, mourning a good friend.

Vinh's news struck the cooperative like a thunderbolt. They all dropped whatever they were doing and hurried toward Cong Quan. Water buffalo were more valuable than people. During the war, many people had perished, but no death had ever caused as much consternation as that of this animal.

The person most shocked and astounded was the cooperative chief, a fat, heavy man who never walked quickly, let alone run. Today he broke into a gallop, and younger folks had trouble keeping up with him. His crimson face and eyes glared fury, and in his hand he held a bamboo cane, which he flourished to make his point as he talked to the crowd clustered around him by the paddy: "Which boys are in charge of gathering hay on Team Four? Damn you all, little rascals! You were too busy with your fun and games to feed the buffalo—no wonder it's dropped dead. I'll strip those red scarves off your necks and teach you to love games and sports less!"

In principle, what the cooperative chief had said was a grave offense to the whole Ho Chi Minh Vanguard Youth Corps, an attack on its honor. Had anyone else made the same statement it would have provoked an uproar, but the Party branch secretary shared in his comrade's anger completely. Indeed, the two men differed only in the way they expressed their displeasure. While one burst into shouts and curses, the other clamped his lips tightly with a livid look on his face. Children young enough to be the cooperative chief's sons and daughters were too intimidated to make an issue of their corporate pride.

Some boys standing on the fringe of the crowd whispered among themselves:

"Whose turn is it this week to tend the buffalo of Team Four? Is it Nang's group?"

"No. It's Quy's group. And I've seen Quy and his teammates catching crabs up there around the Ong Sung fields!"

A young tattletale, overhearing the conversation, spoke out loud enough to be heard by the cooperative chief: "It's the turn of Quy's team to cut grass for the buffalo!"

The chief swung sharply toward the boy, pouncing on him as if he were a piece of irrefutable proof. On the tip of his tongue was a string of epithets unflattering to Quy's ancestors, which he was just about to rattle off before discovering in time that the culprit was a son of the village security commissioner. As the proverb says: "Before you stroke the face, beware the nose." You don't touch relatives of an acquaintance, let alone one who wields much clout. And so the cooperative chief twirled his cane once more and said, addressing no one in particular, "I don't care whose shift it is! This time I'm going to punish them all. No letters of commendation from me, not even those I've already signed!"

Then he turned to the boys and asked them to carry the beast onto the roadside. Here they found out that the buffalo, while far from well, was not dead: it had simply collapsed from exhaustion.

Relieved, the cooperative chief looked less grim. Somewhat ashamed of his outburst, he now spoke in a more conciliatory tone. "The buffalo is hungry—that's all. Give it a good day's rest and plenty of straw to eat and it'll be back on its feet in a jiffy."

So the water buffalo enjoyed a vacation without benefit of a national holiday to thank. However, the cooperative chief's veterinary assessment fit his own hopes better than it did the facts, soon to transpire, for, on being hauled back to the barn, the buffalo simply lay there like an inert hulk. It was not hungry. A trough full of tender, mouth-watering grass was placed right next to its chops, but it would not even bother to open them. A top whose spinning force runs out will drop to the ground, and the buffalo was like that. There was no way it could pick itself up and go again. It lay there lifeless in the barn, staring stupidly with the glazed vacancy of its eyes, dribbling froth and saliva out of both corners of its mouth.

The deputy chief of the cooperative made a flat statement, mincing no words: "Let's butcher the buffalo."

People who all year round had been dreaming of meat rejoiced, hollering, "That's right! Let's slaughter it now while it's still alive. In a few days we'll have to eat carrion from a dead animal!"

The idea received collective approval. Here was a rare opportunity to forget their starvation diet and feast on meat. Surely, not much more service could be squeezed out of that old water buffalo anyhow, even if it could be cured of whatever ailed it. But, with the buffalo out of commission, the cooperative had to confront and solve another problem, and to talk of butchering the beast at this moment seemed out of place; it smacked of irresponsible gluttony. So the cooperative chief refrained from giving his consent immediately.

That night he convoked an emergency session of the village council to discuss how to replace the sick buffalo. Somebody suggested, "Without the buffalo, a number of our tasks will be crippled. And our cooperative also happens to be in the period of most intense activity. Let's lay out funds and purchase another buffalo."

The cooperative chief dismissed that idea out of hand for this reason: "If the solution were so simple, why hold a special session of the village council at all?"

The truth of the matter was that, deep in his heart, he did not want to spend one damn penny from the budget on anything whatsoever. It had to be further replenished until his cooperative could afford a small automobile. He had always put forward the view that an automobile would be of critical importance to the growth of the cooperative. It would give its chief mobility, allowing him to travel one day to the district seat and the next to the provincial capital. He could keep in touch with various commissions and agencies and arrange trade or exchange for all sorts of products and commodities: seed, fertilizer, gasoline, kerosene, and whatnot. A car would be the magic key to unlock and open wide the door to the world of abundance.

The women had their say too. One comrade recommended that a set of water pumps be purchased to replace the old-fashioned system of irrigation scoops and buckets, all those gua-dais and *gau-songs,* which not only did a slow job but also involved a large labor force—made up primarily of women.

She said, "We are living in the age of science and technology. Let's bring science and technology to bear on production!"

But one brother countered the sister's proposal with this heroic argument: "I agree with our sister that it would be better if we could use science and technology. However, let's not forget the words of our communist poet: 'Our hands turn even pebbles and rocks to rice!'"

The sister huffily retorted, "If so, then why don't you take the place of the buffalo and pull the plow yourself, brother? We'll have rice to eat just like when we still had the buffalo!"

That was it! What the sister said in pique struck the cooperative chief as a brilliant idea, a stroke of genius. He slapped his thigh and exclaimed, "Sister Tai is right on target! With determination we can overcome any and all difficulties. Like this problem of the buffalo. I propose that you brothers and sisters discuss the substitution of human strength for animal motive power as a stopgap measure."

In amazement, the sister asked, "You mean somebody will have to pull the plow?"

"What's wrong with that? Years ago, during the war, many agricultural cooperatives took that measure to make up for shortages and to push production."

No one quarreled with the idea that the problem could be solved in that fashion. But the meeting was deadlocked on who was to fill in for the buffalo pulling a plow or harrow. The women, who had always defended equal rights, preferred to forgo this privilege and pass it on to the male members of the Ho Chi Minh Vanguard Youth Corps. But the boys had minds of their own. They would and could do anything only if they cared to. One couldn't lean too hard on them or they might sabotage the cooperative, put it out of business. The cooperative chief knew that. Nevertheless, he made a perfunctory attempt to enlist them, virtually pleading for their help. "Well, let me suggest that the comrades in the Youth Corps hold a separate session and agree among themselves to take turns substituting for the buffalo. I hope that you all will carry out in practice the spirit of your proud motto: 'Where they are needed, Youth Corpsmen will be there; where the job is tough, there will be Youth Corpsmen!'"

The comrade who represented the Youth Corps realized at once that he'd been given a tough nut to crack. He suspected, and rightly, that none of the boys would take the place of the buffalo and pull a plow. Not that any of them lacked the physical strength and stamina to do it. But once you've played buffalo, how on earth can you face a girl and talk to her seriously? That would be the overriding reason for the boys' inevitable lack of enthusiasm. It was on everybody's mind but went unspoken.

Sure enough, after the local branch of the Youth Corps held two meetings and all means of persuasion were applied, no one volunteered with socialist "joy and zeal" to be cast as a buffalo. A daylong palaver failed to force the impasse.

Meanwhile, Vinh kept a close eye on the buffalo's deteriorating health and reported it hour by hour, minute by minute. The beast could no longer raise its head. It had begun to gasp for breath. Its hind legs had gone into spasms. And he would conclude each account with the refrain "Butcher it now or we'll end up picking the bones of a rotten dead buffalo!"

The next day, Thuoc could be seen cringing and fawning in the cooperative chief's office. The Party branch secretary was also present. It seemed a unique opportunity had arisen for the old man to atone for his son's sins and to earn his way back into the Party's favor. After living as an outcast for almost a year, Thuoc had learned with terror what it meant to lose ration coupons and to suffer social quarantine: the State had cut out all roots, both material and psychic, from under him. Now he begged for mercy and a second chance. "May I submit a request to the two comrades? Though advanced in years, I'm still strong enough to pull a plow. And I have my wife to lend me a hand. She may not look it, but she's as tough and resilient as a leech!''

As he said that, Thuoc glanced outside. Through the wide open window, both the Party branch secretary and the cooperative chief could see Thuoc's wife in the courtyard, squatting under a tree with her arms clasped around her knees. Beside her there was a basket for crab collecting. She sat there huddled up like a sick cat, gazing fixedly beyond the hedgerow toward a vast field where shadowy figures scurried back and forth lugging stacks of blood-red bricks.

Despite the distance, she could spot friends and acquaintances, even the teenagers as they moved bricks from the kiln to the dirt floor, piling them up in long rows. They looked like ants busily gathering materials for a nest, and they formed a community—a famished and tattered society in which the last ounce of energy was being squeezed out of each of them. But from Thuoc and his wife that society still withheld its ultimate blessing, and hope seemed far beyond their reach.

Over the past year, Thuoc's wife had never had a chance to touch and fondle sheets of ration coupons: this one good for rice, that one for potatoes, another for oil or firewood, for some thread or a needle, and, once in a long while, for a kilo of sugar or a square of cloth. And she had been denied the privilege of standing in line and jostling, of squabbling and fighting outside the state-run store, sometimes in the rain, sometimes under broiling sun, while all around the air was thick with the composite odor, sour and pungent, of many types of sweat.

When Thuoc's wife slogged through the mud for crabs in flooded fields, she often prayed to both Heaven and the Buddha that her prodigal son would come back home after he'd had his lark. At worst he might go to jail, but she would at least still have her boy. Time served, he'd be set free, and the state might then relent and restore the family to the ration-coupon system. She thought longingly of the ration-coupon sheet—her pipe dream.

Now she waited for her husband under the tree with all the anxiety and dread of a convict on whom the judge is about to pronounce sentence. As soon as he appeared in the doorway to the cooperative chief's office, she sprang to her feet. She saw him toothlessly grinning from ear to ear. Both Heaven and the Buddha had heard and granted her prayer! Indeed, her husband came running toward her, waving both his hands and shouting jubilantly, "Those gentlemen said yes! We'll take the place of the buffalo!"

9.2   ACTION WILL BE TAKEN: AN ACTION-PACKED STORY
Heinrich Böll

Probably one of the strangest interludes in my life was the time I spent as an employee in Alfred Wunsiedel's factory. By nature I am inclined more to pensiveness and inactivity than to work, but now and again prolonged financial difficulties compel me—for pensiveness is no more profitable than inactivity—to take on a so-called job. Finding myself once again at a low ebb of this kind, I put myself in the hands of the employment office and was sent with seven other fellow-sufferers to Wunsiedel's factory, where we were to undergo an aptitude test.

The exterior of the factory was enough to arouse my suspicions: the factory was built entirely of glass brick, and my aversion to well-lit buildings and well-lit rooms is as strong as my aversion to work. I became even more suspicious when we were immediately served breakfast in the well-lit, cheerful coffee shop: pretty waitresses brought us eggs, coffee and toast, orange juice was served in tastefully designed jugs, goldfish pressed their bored faces against the sides of pale-green aquariums. The waitresses were so cheerful that they appeared to be bursting with good cheer. Only a strong effort of will—so it seemed to me—restrained them from singing away all day long. They were as crammed with unsung songs as chickens with unlaid eggs.

Right away I realized something that my fellow-sufferers evidently failed to realize: that this breakfast was already part of the test; so I chewed away reverently, with the full appreciation of a person who knows he is supplying his body with valuable elements. I did something which normally no power on earth can make me do: I drank orange juice on an empty stomach, left the coffee and egg untouched, as well as most of the toast, got up, and paced up and down in the coffee shop, pregnant with action.

As a result I was the first to be ushered into the room where the questionnaires were spread out on attractive tables. The walls were done in a shade of green that would have summoned the word "delightful" to the lips of interior decoration enthusiasts. The room appeared to be empty, and yet I was so sure of being observed that I behaved as someone pregnant with action behaves when he believes himself unobserved: I ripped my pen impatiently from my pocket, unscrewed the top, sat down at the nearest table and pulled the questionnaire toward me, the way irritable customers snatch at the bill in a restaurant.

Question No. 1: Do you consider it right for a human being to possess only two arms, two legs, eyes, and ears?

Here for the first time I reaped the harvest of my pensive nature and wrote without hesitation: "Even four arms, legs and ears would not be adequate for my driving energy. Human beings are very poorly equipped."

Question No. 2: How many telephones can you handle at one time?

Here again the answer was as easy as simple arithmetic: "When there are only seven telephones," I wrote, "I get impatient; there have to be nine before I feel I am working to capacity."

Question No. 3: How do you spend your free time?

My answer: "I no longer acknowledge the term free time—on my fifteenth birthday I eliminated it from my vocabulary, for in the beginning was the act."

From Heinrich Böll, *Eighteen Stories,* trans. Leila Vennewitz (New York: McGraw-Hill, 1966). Copyright © 1994 Verlag Kiepenheuer & Witsch Köln. Reprinted with permission.

I got the job. Even with nine telephones I really didn't feel I was working to capacity. I shouted into the mouthpieces: "Take immediate action!" or: "Do something!—We must have some action—Action will be taken—Action has been taken—Action should be taken." But as a rule—for I felt this was in keeping with the tone of the place—I used the imperative.

Of considerable interest were the noon-hour breaks, when we consumed nutritious foods in an atmosphere of silent good cheer. Wunsiedel's factory was swarming with people who were obsessed with telling you the story of their lives, as indeed vigorous personalities are fond of doing. The story of their lives is more important to them than their lives, you have only to press a button, and immediately it is covered with spewed-out exploits.

Wunsiedel had a right-hand man called Broschek, who had in turn made a name for himself by supporting seven children and a paralyzed wife by working night-shifts in his student days, and successfully carrying on four business agencies, besides which he had passed two examinations with honors in two years. When asked by reporters: "When do you sleep, Mr. Broschek?" he had replied:

"It's a crime to sleep!"

Wunsiedel's secretary had supported a paralyzed husband and four children by knitting, at the same time graduating in psychology and German history as well as breeding shepherd dogs, and she had become famous as a night-club singer where she was known as *Vamp Number Seven.*

Wunsiedel himself was one of those people who every morning, as they open their eyes, make up their minds to act. "I must act," they think as they briskly tie their bathrobe belts around them. "I must act," they think as they shave, triumphantly watching their beard hairs being washed away with the lather: these hirsute vestiges are the first daily sacrifices to their driving energy. The more intimate functions also give these people a sense of satisfaction: water swishes, paper is used. Action has been taken. Bread gets eaten, eggs are decapitated.

With Wunsiedel, the most trivial activity looked like action: the way he put on his hat, the way—quivering with energy—he buttoned up his overcoat, the kiss he gave his wife, everything was action.

When he arrived at his office he greeted his secretary with a cry of "Let's have some action!" And in ringing tones she would call back: "Action will be taken!" Wunsiedel then went from department to department, calling out his cheerful: "Let's have some action!" Everyone would answer: "Action will be taken!" And I would call back to him too, with a radiant smile, when he looked into my office: "Action will be taken!"

Within a week I had increased the number of telephones on my desk to eleven, within two weeks to thirteen, and every morning on the streetcar I enjoyed thinking up new imperatives, or chasing the words *take action* through various tenses and modulations: for two whole days I kept saying the same sentence over and over again because I thought it sounded so marvelous: "Action ought to have been taken;" for another two days it was: "Such action ought not to have been taken."

So I was really beginning to feel I was working to capacity when there actually was some action. One Tuesday morning—I had hardly settled down at my desk—Wunsiedel rushed into my office crying his "Let's have some action!" But an inexplicable something in his face made me hesitate to reply, in a cheerful gay voice as the rules dictated: "Action will be taken!" I must have paused too long, for Wunsiedel, who seldom raised his voice, shouted at me: "Answer! Answer, you know the rules!" And I answered, under my breath, reluctantly, like a child who is forced to say: I am a naughty child. It was only by a great effort that I managed to bring out the sentence:

"Action will be taken," and hardly had I uttered it when there really was some action: Wunsiedel dropped to the floor. As he fell he rolled over onto his side and lay right across the open doorway.

I knew at once, and I confirmed it when I went slowly around my desk and approached the body on the floor: he was dead.

Shaking my head I stepped over Wunsiedel, walked slowly along the corridor to Broschek's office, and entered without knocking. Broschek was sitting at his desk, a telephone receiver in each hand, between his teeth a ballpoint pen with which he was making notes on a writing pad, while with his bare feet he was operating a knitting machine under the desk. In this way he helps to clothe his family. "We've had some action," I said in a low voice.

Broschek spat out the ballpoint pen, put down the two receivers, reluctantly detached his toes from the knitting machine.

"What action?" he asked.

"Wunsiedel is dead," I said.

"No," said Broschek.

"Yes," I said, "come and have a look!"

"No," said Broschek, "that's impossible," but he put on his slippers and followed me along the corridor.

"No," he said, when we stood beside Wunsiedel's corpse, "no, no!" I did not contradict him. I carefully turned Wunsiedel over onto his back, closed his eyes and looked at him pensively.

I felt something like tenderness for him, and realized for the first time that I had never hated him. On his face was that expression which one sees on children who obstinately refuse to give up their faith in Santa Claus, even though the arguments of their playmates sound so convincing.

"No," said Broschek, "no."

"We must take action," I said quietly to Broschek.

"Yes," said Broschek, "we must take action."

Action was taken: Wunsiedel was buried, and I was delegated to carry a wreath of artificial roses behind his coffin, for I am equipped with not only a penchant for pensiveness and inactivity but also a face and figure that go extremely well with dark suits. Apparently as I walked along behind Wunsiedel's coffin carrying the wreath of artificial roses I looked superb. I received an offer from a fashionable firm of funeral directors to join their staff as a professional mourner. "You are a born mourner," said the manager, "your outfit would be provided by the firm. Your face—simply superb!"

I handed in my notice to Broschek, explaining that I had never really felt I was working to capacity there; that, in spite of the thirteen telephones, some of my talents were going to waste. As soon as my first professional appearance as a mourner was over I knew: This is where I belong, this is what I am cut out for.

Pensively I stand behind the coffin in the funeral chapel, holding a simple bouquet, while the organ plays Handel's *Largo,* a piece that does not receive nearly the respect it deserves. The cemetery café is my regular haunt; there I spend the intervals between my professional engagements, although sometimes I walk behind coffins which I have not been engaged to follow, I pay for flowers out of my own pocket and join the welfare worker who walks behind the coffin of some homeless person. From time to time I also visit Wunsiedel's grave, for after all I owe it to him that I discovered my true vocation, a vocation in which pensiveness is essential and inactivity my duty.

It was not till much later that I realized I had never bothered to find out what was being produced in Wunsiedel's factory. I expect it was soap.

9.3   ODE TO JOY
Marta Kadlečíková

When I think about it sometimes, it seems that it has always been this way. I cannot visualize the past. It is as if it were separated from the present—which already has its memories, too—by a hard and impervious shell. My only vivid recollections are of the period of the change that brought me to where I am now.

Back then, we were beginning to get lovely late winter mornings. The days were awakening early and they were filled with bright sunshine. Precisely the way they are now. Perhaps this is why I am recalling it now. But that year we had much more snow; the winter had been long and spring was anticipated more anxiously. The gutters were incessantly spouting water, bits of dirty, icy snow were falling off the roofs, and during the nights beautiful icicles formed on everything, only to melt again, helpless, in the morning sun. Birds started chirping eagerly, the pavement glistened wet from all the melting, and the music of brass bands, deployed all around town, sounded even more festive and cheerful than usual. It strikes me that those town musicians have it pretty hard during the winter months. Maybe they are rotated more frequently then. I don't know. But I suppose that they are aware of their joyous mission to remind people that life is beautiful and cheerful and that they ought to smile all the time.

During those late winter days I occasionally noticed strange weakening of my right wrist. I remember it very clearly. It somehow felt too loose. This may sound strange, but if individual parts of the human body were bolted together, I would have said that my right wrist needed adjustment with a screwdriver. A little tightening or something. Of course I did not permit this to ruin my spirits. Only once or twice did I mention it to my cleaning lady.

Old Felicie shook her head with concern, and then she illogically but soothingly proclaimed that spring was coming. She had a point, even if the tree branches were still all bare and black, and the grass, lurking underneath the melting snow, was gray. However, as soon as the sun came up, people would rush outside in the thin light coats they had kept ready in their closets so long, just to prove to themselves that spring was at the gates. And in some windows—despite the dampness—featherbeds appeared in the mornings.

When I was buttoning my coat before leaving for the office on one such delightful morning, the forementioned right hand suddenly refused to obey me. It bent limply at the wrist, then swayed like a broken flower stalk and fell to the ground. Mechanically, I finished buttoning my coat and gazed numbly at my hand lying on the carpet, its fingers helplessly extended. At first I only felt astonishment so powerful it did not leave the least bit of room for shock or any other stirring of the mind. I assume that such an unexpected incident, defying reason, would disconcert anyone, but on top of everything I am a man who detests any kind of change. I bent down and, baffled, inspected the hand for a moment. It had broken off precisely at the wrist joint, which was clean, smoothly sliced. I looked at the stump protruding from my coat. Not a drop of blood was anywhere to be found, nothing. I was reminded of my dear mother, who on Sunday mornings would stand at the kitchen table and, using thread, cut neat slices from freshly cooked loaves of bread dumplings. The hand rested heavily on my palm. It was warm, alive. What to do with it. Such an

From *Daylight in Nightclub Inferno: Czech Fiction from the Post-Kundera Generation,* trans. Dana Loewy with Robert Wechsler, ed. Elena Lappin (North Haven, CT: Catbird Press, 1997), 264–276. English translation copyright © 1997 Catbird Press. Reprinted with permission.

unexpected, unpleasant complication. The striking of the kitchen clock roused me from my reverie. It was high time I left. I dread arriving late at the office. Not because of the fines that are imposed. It is simply my nature always to appreciate order and the following of rules. I placed the hand in my left pocket and walked out of the house.

The sun was shining splendidly, as if the sky were never to darken again; the birds were jubilant in their song; the melting snow was flowing off the roofs in dirty streams; and like every other day, marches blared out cheerfully. I patted my left pocket and shrugged, annoyed. What to do with it, to be sure. I had planned to take a little carefree walk before work and instead I was unpleasantly forced to take some kind of a stand.

The faces of the passersby were lit up with smiles. Everyone was rushing eagerly to work or to school, everyone was looking forward to his duties, everyone had a jubilant gleam in his eyes; I was the only one shuffling along the street like a sourpuss. I felt a pang of shame for allowing such an unpleasant yet purely private matter to run away with me. I straightened my back, lifted my eyebrows, and extended—not without a certain amount of effort, I must admit—the corners of my mouth. Such a beautiful morning, I reminded myself. I was lucky that no one took any notice of me. If a patrol of the public order squad had seen me, I would have been issued quite a fine for my gloom. And rightly so. Only children up to the age of eight were allowed to cry or lament in public. They do not understand. What does my hand matter to anyone. On top of it all, I had been observing the loosening of my wrist for some time, and it was no one's fault but my own that I had failed to consult a physician. The more I silently reproached myself like this, the harder it was for me to keep a brisk pace and a joyful expression. I began to look for excuses. Although a person like me must be well beyond suspicion, I would hate to make it seem as if by complaining about my wrist I were trying to avoid the work I carry out most zealously and, in a sense, even enjoy. Well, yes, in a sense. By the way, I presume that I'm not an exception. Otherwise we would not be able to live in such a perfect solidarity and rejoice in our existence from morning till night.

Deep in thought, I came to the main thoroughfare and, as usual, stopped at the newsstand. When it came time to hand the fellow some change, which I carried in my right pocket, I had to reach across for it with my left hand. Very inconvenient. But just a cursory glance at the newspaper headlines helped to improve my mood significantly. Nothing but pleasant items and useful information. As usual. Sometimes it occurs to me that we are being pretty spoiled. We cannot imagine that there were times when many unpleasant things were being published. That must have been awful.

I slipped the paper under my right arm and again harkened to the vigorous, uplifting tune that was floating above the busy morning avenue. My thoughts again wandered to the contents of my left pocket. I had to arrive at some decision before I reached the office. Ah, what a pleasant little walk this might have been. I had only two alternatives. To keep secret the fact that I had lost my right hand would most likely not prove successful, but perhaps I could gloss over the whole matter, say, by adopting a light-hearted, jocular tone and then managing to do my work left-handedly, as it were. Had my left hand fallen off instead, it would have been easy, I muttered irritably to myself. Then again, learning to stamp and sign with one's left hand cannot pose such an insurmountable problem, I immediately consoled myself. The second alternative was to go and confide in a doctor. Perhaps a doctor could help me. Given my hitherto impeccable record, suspicions would be minimal. Besides, I intend to assert right from the start, most emphatically, that I will continue working. However, it is conceivable that a visit to a doctor would be pointless. It's rather likely, in fact. Suspicion would be the only consequence of such a visit. So what should I do? I must admit that I was considerably uneasy when I entered the office building.

And rightly so. I don't even want to think about that morning. I was wounded in my softest spot. I found out how little trust I enjoyed in the eyes of my colleagues. At first I attributed their furtive glances to amazement and perhaps even sympathy. After all, pieces of extremities do not simply fall off of people like overripe pears from trees. But no, soon I realized the painful truth. In short, they assumed I wanted to help myself to disability payments. By no means do I want to diminish the respect which we customarily accord, which by law we must accord the disabled, but if it were not for my savings and a small inheritance which I had prudently left untouched, I don't know how I would have resolved my current predicament. And yet my coworkers were such splendid citizens. Surely they rejoice just as I do. I am not talking about sorrow, for which there are no reasons. Of course not. Not even that hand—one can live easily without a hand, I said to myself. After this disappointment, I concluded that, amidst an atmosphere of general mistrust, I am not taking any risks if I consult a doctor. Quite the contrary.

Yet the visit did not cheer me up a great deal. I myself was partly to blame. I should have conceived a plausible accident. I should not have been surprised that the physician mistrustfully shook his head. He put one hand into the pocket of his black overcoat, while his other hand played with a golden watch chain. Only when I repeated for the third time that I would not request any support and intended to continue my work at the office, did he put on a long white lab coat and examine both my wrist and the hand that had been sitting on his desk throughout our conversation. He shrugged and called a colleague. They debated for a while before sending me out in the hall to wait. After a long wait, I was led to a small examining room, where another physician sewed the hand back onto my wrist, supporting it with a small plank and binding it all up with stiff calico. This small operation cheered me up at last. You see, a simple procedure is all it takes for everything to be all right again. At the office I proudly showed off my splint to my colleagues; I think they were impressed. Suspicious looks turned into astonished ones and even those gradually vanished, because I came to the office regularly and promptly as ever before.

Every morning I left the house at the usual hour, feeling joy at the sight of the trickling eaves and at the sound of the birds' songs and the lively music. But I was not at ease. My hand was in a strange state. Again my colleagues began to turn away from me but this time I could not blame them. My fingertips were turning blue, and the splint was beginning to give off an unbearable odor. Not even the eau de cologne with which I liberally doused my splint relieved its effects on my environment. I would even have to say that it made the odor still worse. At my next visit to the doctor, they removed the bandage; the hand fell off when they removed the plank. Now it looked like a dead extremity. Perplexed, the doctor stared at it and then used large pincers to throw the hand into the wastebasket. Then he questioned whether I still intended to keep up my work at the office. "Yes!" I exclaimed joyfully, and with that we parted.

Slowly, things were getting back to normal again. I learned to sign, stamp, greet, eat, and dress—in short, to do everything—with nothing but my left hand. I got used to it so much that slowly I began to forget that I ever had a right hand. My colleagues were also getting used to it, because the odor was a thing of the past and along with it, thank God, perhaps also the suspicion that I wanted to shirk my duties. In the mornings I rose gaily once again, whistled a tune, fed my canary, watered the flowers, and left the house with a joyful smile on my face. Most of the time, the sun was shining brightly, and on the trees the first tiny greenish-yellow leaves were appearing. If it were not inappropriate, one would have liked to jump for joy. However, I know my limits. A grown man, even more so a clerk with a claim to a pension, must painstakingly avoid disgracing his position. The only thing that somewhat marred my splendid mood was Felicie, the cleaning lady, who could not conceal her sorrow at my loss and from time to time would uninhibitedly lament. I felt ashamed for her, repeatedly admonished her, and was glad that no one heard her. And so life went on in an orderly fashion: working days were punctuated by Sundays and holidays, the weather was warming up, joy all around. Until, unfortunately, one literally fine day, things turned complicated again. Thoroughly. That morning I left the house a little earlier than usual in order to have breakfast at a small dairy bar on the corner, something I like to do every once in a while. Refreshed by the meal and elated after conversing with the genial waitress, I contentedly went on my way again.

The town, glistening in the morning sun with all the shades of gray, was thrusting its many spires into the translucent haze; from wetly shimmering roofs chimneys were sending encouragingly ample puffs of smoke into the sky.

I turned into a short, quiet street, no pedestrians anywhere, and I think I was even whistling softly to myself. Suddenly, in my wrist—the other one, my last—I felt that strange loosening, that limpness, which I would have liked to have forgotten forever. Alarmed, I quickened my pace, as if it were possible to elude one's unpleasant sensations. After a few steps, my hand limply swung and fell to the pavement with an embarrassing slap. My first thought was, what will people say! I looked around. Fortunately, the street was completely deserted. I bent down and tried to pick up the hand. However, for an untrained man that is a very difficult task to accomplish, especially if he is upset. To make matters worse, I heard someone approaching. With lightning speed I stood up, stuck my stumps in my pockets and gazed at a faded poster advertising an old theater program. The passerby was a little boy carrying a school bag on his back and, thank goodness, he walked quickly and inattentively. I stared at the worn letters in front of me and gradually it began to dawn on me how nonsensical my undertaking was. Why scramble to pick up the hand if the first one ended up in the trash? As soon as the boy disappeared around the corner, I pushed the ill-fated limb to the gutter with the tip of my shoe. A hand barely measures eight inches from the wrist to the tip of the middle finger. But alas, it was too thick and would not squeeze through the bars of the grate. For a while I used force to try and stuff it between the narrow openings. It did not work. Infuriated, I kicked it hard. The hand filled me with fearsome hatred. More than anything, I would have liked to trample it to bits. Monstrously nonsensical, it was lying contemptibly in the middle of the street where I had propelled it with a vehement kick. At that moment I completely forgot that I was in public, that I was a decent, even-tempered man, and that my behavior was utterly improper. My stumps in my pockets, I ran over to the hand rather clumsily and glared at it for a moment; then I spat on it and, with another kick, dispatched it onto the opposite sidewalk.

Unspeakable dejection overpowered me. This was the end. I would not be able to stamp anything anymore. Theoretically the possibility remained that I could learn to do it with my foot, but in practical terms this was probably not realizable. Could one deal with people barefooted, leg up on the desk, without causing the reputation of the office to suffer? That moment I became a parasite, a loafer, an applicant for assistance. Against my will. But who will believe me? That day, while passing through the gate, I had to exert a great deal of effort to put on a suitably merry smile. In the office I silently held up both my stumps for my colleagues to see. Their joyful work expressions suddenly vanished from their faces. I recognized my impertinence and hid the stumps in my pockets again. My nearest coworker turned to me and inconspicuously sent me out into the hallway. After a moment, he came out after me and, in a whisper, told me to meet him in the men's room. I was starved for any word of encouragement, for a sign of trust, so I waited for him, resigned and patient. But it would have been better had that conversation never taken place. Even today, the memory of it brings me sadness. And that is something I desire least of all. When my colleague finally appeared, he locked himself into a stall with me and in the gurgling of flushing water he confessed to me how much he admired my determination. I looked at him with amazement, and he added with unexpected bitterness that he understood me, that anything was better than this, and his hand circumscribed a sweeping half-circle. At last he wished me good luck and told me to be careful and not to show myself at the office from now on. Man's envy is dangerous, he said. He slapped me on the back and slipped out.

I stood above the toilet bowl comfortably aghast. The gurgling of the water mournfully subsided. No, this man did not belong in the joyful world, filled with smiles and the enjoyment of work well done, in which I had been living until now. I was incapable of admitting that someone would not be proud to be part of our mighty institution, which determined the fate of so many people. I regained control of my emotions. Heaven knows what that man was thinking. Still, I stumbled out of the bathroom as if drugged. The words I had just heard troubled me more perhaps than the loss of my second hand.

This time the doctor examined the stump with a great deal of suspicion, and he demanded to see the lost appendage. After I explained, he hesitated for a moment, then reluctantly scribbled something on a piece of paper and dismissed me with the words, "Submit this with your application."

Never had I walked the street with such an unbecoming expression on my face. My painful feelings were only aggravated by the blaring sound of a jolly march and the happy faces of people rushing past me.

I reached my building, I wanted to go inside. It occurred to me that with those wretched stumps I would not be able to unlock the door to my apartment. Fortunately, a little boy was playing in front of the building. It was very awkward, but finally he understood, reached into my pocket, took out my key, walked upstairs with me, unlocked my door, and left. I was sorry I could not reward him for this favor, but he would have had to reach into the pocket of my coat himself to extract the money, and I did not have anything else on hand—God, what an empty expression. I slammed the door shut and wanted to unbutton my coat. Again I had to come up against the stumps. For the first time in my life I regretted not being married. Then I remembered that Felicie was supposed to come, and I calmed down somewhat. With one stump I lifted my hat and tossed it to the ground. Just as I bent down to try and pick it up—I had to learn to do it, I told myself— my right foot fell off. Including the shoe, naturally. It happened so suddenly, I lost my balance. My left leg, unsupported by its right counterpart, buckled under. It wouldn't have taken much to twist my ankle. I let the hat be and hobbled to the kitchen on my left leg, with the intention of eating a little something. Again, those stumps. The only accessible food was a forgotten piece of bread lying on the table. I took hold of it very clumsily and bit off a piece. But it was too difficult. I dropped the bread and hopped to the bedroom. My bed was still unmade, just as it had been when I rushed out in the morning. With my coat buttoned up—as there was no other option—I rolled onto the bed and lay there exhausted.

Streaks of golden sunlight were falling across my featherbed and my winter coat. From the street came cheerful music, the din of traffic, and the cries of children playing. In my overcoat I was hot, and muddled thoughts were spinning through my head, out of which the same one kept emerging—it would be best if I never rose again. And yet I did not want to think this thought and I refused to accede to it. It kept intruding between memories of a happy life, filled with industrious work and joy, between memories of my quiet pleasures, my childhood, my mother, whom I could see bending over me, taking me to church—I could discern her shape very clearly but, strangely enough, I could not picture her face. I recalled scenes from my school days, images of vacations complete with yellow fields and ponds; my Sunday bachelor outings filed past. All this was interfused with water flushing and a toilet bowl, everything was whirling through my head in extremely rapid succession, incoherent fragments, one image after the next, full of colors, suffused with radiant sunshine. Only the one persistent sentence, out of all the things reeling through my head, had neither color nor shape: it was black, composed of flat, distinct letters, as if someone were relentlessly etching it painfully onto my forehead with a thin, bony finger.

At last, I fell asleep despite the heat. I must have slept for a very long time, because I did not wake up until Felicie's arrival. She reacted as usual when something astounded her. She threw up her hands and shook her head. Then, without having to ask me many questions, she grasped the situation, approached the bed, and proceeded to pull off pieces of my clothing. My left shoe, including my other foot, was lying limply on the featherbed. The rest Felicie shook out of my pant legs and my sleeves, and then she lowered her eyes. "Oh my goodness," she said after a moment of silence, but she uttered it very quietly, knowing I cannot stand whining, and left the room.

Astonished, I surveyed my substantially diminished body. No reason to give in to panic. The essentials, namely my torso, neck, and head, remained, I said to myself, and then I wearily closed my eyelids once more. When I opened my eyes again, I saw Felicie stowing what had fallen from my clothes into her battered, red canvas bag. She glanced at me and, with a self-conscious, apologetic smile, she remarked that anything might come in handy. As she was putting the foot into the bag, she said she'd like to remove the shoe. I observed to her that, from this day on, I would not need shoes any longer. "True," Felicie said as if she were amazed she hadn't thought of it herself. Then she inquired where the other one was. I was so benumbed after my long nap that it took a moment for me to remember that it was lying in the hall. Poor Felicie, how joyful she was about the shoes. And even more so when I told her she could take the other clothes in my closet.

She clapped her gaunt hands joyfully, carried the red bag outside, and returned with a huge laundry basin. It was evident that she had quickly thought things over. My dear Felicie, I would have never guessed that she would become such a great support to me. She lifted me off my bed and set me into the basin. It was as if it had been molded for me. There was—actually there still is—enough room around my ribcage, and the brim of the basin reached up to my neck, so that the view was sufficient. What am I saying, sufficient—it was downright magnificent. Then Felicie covered me and the basin with a checkered cloth, carefully tucked it in under my chin so that I would not be cold, opened the window, and lifted me onto the sill.

Below, in the tiny park, two little girls were playing with hoops. One of them had pretty blond hair flowing down her back. It was softly waving in the azure air of spring. The birds' songs quivered beneath a translucent sky, and in the corner of the building's small garden forsythias were blooming.

After Felicie made the bed and covered it with a spread embroidered with violets, I dictated to her my application for assistance. She handwrote it in an awkward script, and I had to point out several errors to her, but in the end the result was passable.

That sunny morning my present life began. The days are once again well structured and orderly. In good weather I spend my days in the basin on the window sill. In the morning Felicie brings me the newspaper; before she goes home, she carries me to the bathroom, cleans out the basin, and turns down the bed for me. She feeds me three times a day; she had the rest of the day to attend to her own business. Over time we have come up with some minor improvements: a small reading stand, a board across the brim of the basin with a little bell I can easily hold between my teeth and ring by shaking my head when I need to summon her. The only problem is that, lately, the poor woman is a little hard of hearing, so that the bell may be becoming a mere formality. But this is a minor issue, since I do not need anything anyway most of the time. Of course, she must come every day now, and I have to pay her much more than I did before. However, if I factor in how much money I save on shoes, tailors, cabs, and myriads of other expenditures which now I no longer incur, it is not so bad at all.

Felicie bought me a used baby carriage for my birthday, and she takes me out for a walk on occasion. We undertake such outings at dusk in order to avoid attracting attention. The face of a grown man in a baby carriage looks somewhat bizarre, if not downright comical. But despite the twilight, I derive great pleasure from our excursions. I always display the most joyous expression with utmost spontaneity. I don't have to strive for it, it is always there. In the basin, in the bathroom, in my bed, perhaps even while I'm sleeping. The alarm that I experienced standing over that toilet bowl has been mercifully shrouded by time. Life is joyful, so joyful I sometimes feel sorry I am unable to snap my fingers with good cheer. It doesn't matter. As I said on that first morning after awakening into the present situation—the essential part of me remains. Especially my face, which is unwaveringly able to fulfill its duty, smiling constantly. Cheerfully, by all means cheerfully, I tell Felicie when sometimes she shakes her head at me with concern. Poor old woman, I don't hold it against her. She hasn't learned anything. She is up to her neck in her old ways. Almost as much as I am in my basin.

Section 10
———— Managerial Insights ————

10.1   LEADERSHIP MADE IN GERMANY: LOW ON COMPASSION, HIGH ON PERFORMANCE
Felix C. Brodbeck, Michael Frese, and Mansour Javidan

. . . The stereotypical German business leader of post-war Germany has been described as a person with a formal interpersonal style and straightforward behavior, technically skilled, a specialist rather than a generalist, neither bureaucratic nor authoritarian, who emphasizes "Technik" as both means and ends. This leader believes in the motto that "well-made products will be eagerly bought." Since the mid-70s, concepts like interpersonal skills, delegation, participation, inspiration, and empowerment have become popular among German managers to reflect the broader changes in German attitudes from materialistic to post-materialistic values. Despite these value changes, German-style management is still often characterized by the "competence first" principle.

What are the current hallmarks of leadership "made in Germany" in comparison to other cultures across the world? Given the increasingly global world of business and Germany's powerful position in Europe . . . and globally, it is important to answer this question.

This article describes the hallmarks of culture and leadership in Germany based on a large-scale study conducted as part of the GLOBE (Global Leadership and Organisational Behaviour Effectiveness) program. . . . The German data is directly compared to data obtained from about 17,000 middle managers in over 800 organizations in 61 countries representing all major cultural regions in the world. Our purpose is to help executives in the U.S. and other countries to better understand German cultural practices and values, and their implications for effective leadership. Such an understanding will be helpful in such activities as managing German operations, negotiating with German counterparts, and in managing cross-border mergers, acquisitions, and alliances with German corporations.

We first present the findings on Germany's societal culture using the multi-nation GLOBE data as a frame of reference. We then describe German leadership prototypes. Finally, the necessities and opportunities for change in the German leadership culture are explored, and practical implications for managers—in Germany and world wide—are discussed.

THE GERMAN GLOBE STUDY

We contacted the top 50 organizations in the telecommunications, food processing, and finance industries. Four hundred fifty-seven middle managers from eighteen organizations participated in the survey (average age 43 years; 21% women; 88% West Germans; 12% East Germans). The German translation of the GLOBE standardized questionnaire was used to measure the managers' perceptions of societal culture, organizational culture, and leadership prototypes. Managers were

Excerpted from *The Academy of Management Executive* 16, no. 1 (February 2002): 16–29. Copyright © 2002 Academy of Management Executive. Reprinted with permission.

asked about their perceptions of current practices ("as is") and ideal values ("should be") pertaining to the nine societal and organizational culture dimensions defined within GLOBE. . . . Respondents also identified those characteristics and attributes that contribute to or inhibit outstanding leadership. . . . Since organizational cultures were found to be very similar to the national culture, we only present the national culture results to save space. Individual ratings on all societal culture and leadership dimensions were aggregated onto the country level for each of the two subcultures in Germany, West (FRG) and East (former GDR).

SOCIETAL CULTURAL PRACTICES AND VALUES IN GERMANY

. . .

Individualism with a Collectivistic Element

Germany's comparatively low ranking on *group/family collectivism* and low-to-moderate ranking on *institutionalized collectivism* speak to a mainly individualistic society. Differences between cultural practices and values on these dimensions are not particularly pronounced. The *institutionalized collectivism* "should be" score for West Germany, which is slightly above the median, relates well to the ideal of a social welfare state in Germany. Low scores on collectivism scales are typical for highly developed western societies, such as the U.S. and the U.K. Individualism means that resources and rewards tend to be distributed on the basis of individual rather than collective achievements. Individuals express pride in their individual achievements rather than in group achievements, and they value individual self-esteem higher than group loyalty, cohesiveness, or viability.

Advancement of the Female Work Force

Germany's score on *gender egalitarianism* "should be" ranks very high within the GLOBE sample. . . . Gender egalitarianism is more highly valued than actually practiced in just about all societies studied. . . . For Germany, the "should be" gender egalitarianism ranks in the highest 25% of all countries . . . whereas the "as is" cultural *practice* ranks in the low 25%. . . . The difference between "ideal" and "real" for gender egalitarianism in Germany significantly exceeds the magnitude of the global trend. . . . Thus, in the decades to come, women will probably experience a steeper social advance in Germany than in most of the other GLOBE countries.

Zeitgeist of Consolidation

Traditionally, high *performance orientation* has been seen as an "ideal" in German society. This view is still reflected in the highest score for performance orientation compared to the scores of all other cultural dimensions in Germany. . . . However, compared to all other countries studied, Germany ranks just above the median, as it also does for its cultural practices in performance orientation. It no longer seems to be a leading country in that respect. Middle managers in Germany perceive the current "real" society to be lower in performance orientation than it "should be."

In contrast, West Germany's *future orientation* "as is" ranks among the highest 25%, whereas the "should be" score ranks within the lowest 25% of all GLOBE countries. This difference is the reverse of the global trend of a higher "ideal" than "real" future orientation. . . . It seems that middle managers in West Germany anticipate only moderate engagement in future-oriented behaviors such as delayed gratification, planning, and investing in the future. German society in the

1990s was considerably skeptical of technological innovation. Furthermore, the findings may be symptomatic of a current Zeitgeist of consolidation as a response to the straining experience of German reunification. . . .

Uncertainty Avoidance and Assertiveness

Germany's scores for societal-culture practices ("as is") on the dimensions *uncertainty avoidance* and *assertiveness* . . . are among the highest 25% of all GLOBE countries. These findings correspond to Hofstede's findings about Germany's work values several decades ago and suggest stability in those dimensions over a considerable time span.

High *uncertainty avoidance* means that Germans prefer their lives to be structured, well organized, and secure. They rely on rules and institutionalized procedures to reduce stress and anxiety when facing ambiguity and uncertainty. Germany ranks among the highest 25% on uncertainty avoidance "as is" and among the lowest 25% on uncertainty avoidance "should be." . . . In other words, compared to the GLOBE country sample as a whole, German managers see far too many rules, regulations, and constraints in people's lives and seem to be interested in reducing them. . . .

High *assertiveness* means that Germans are more confrontational in their relationships with others than members of most other societies are. Interpersonal interactions at work tend to be aggressive and assertive. The language that people use tends to be straightforward and stern. This characteristic also means that conflict and confrontational debate are acceptable approaches at work. On the "should be" assertiveness dimension, Germany ranks very low, considerably lower than the "as is" score for cultural practices. This low "should be" ranking may reflect the desire for a less confrontational and more humane approach to interpersonal relations.

Low on Compassion

Germany ranks very low on *humane orientation* "as is" (lowest 25%). . . . Because Germany also ranks low on the "should be" dimension, a more detailed inspection of what humane orientation actually means seems appropriate. The GLOBE concept of humane orientation measures the degree to which a society is perceived ("as is") and expected ("should be") to encourage and reward individuals for being fair, altruistic, generous, caring, and kind to others. The items in the GLOBE scale address mainly pro-social behavior in interpersonal situations (e.g., concern about others, tolerance of errors, being generous, being friendly, and being sensitive towards others). Expatriates with experience in Germany may have felt a lack of such behaviors in German companies. Social interaction in German companies tends to be more task-oriented, straightforward, and less "kind" than in many other countries. This form of interaction is in line with the high assertiveness cultural practices reported above. There is a story of Siemens CEO Dr. Heinrich Von Pierer who yelled at his teammate in a tennis match: "You have to hate your opponent!" Open verbal aggression and confrontational behavior seem to be tolerated in German society more than in many others. Getting the task done, minimizing errors, and achieving high quality standards seem to be more important than compassion and interpersonal consideration.

The Paradox of Low Compassion and the Ideal of Social Welfare

Some findings seem to present a paradox. On the one hand, Germany scores low on humane orientation and compassion at work. On the other hand, Germany enjoys many humane-oriented institutions and legal practices. The highly valued principles of social justice, which pertain to social fairness, altruism, generosity, and caring, are institutionalized and enshrined in German law, for example, by measures of the social market economy, co-determination, and workers' councils. These principles are also reflected in the typical German insurance systems (health, unemployment, and pension schemes) with obligatory membership, redistribution of wealth between high- and low-income classes, and substantial contributions from the employers' side. The country ranks second in terms of total expenditures on health as a percentage of GDP.

In Germany, the free-market capitalist system is constrained by the principle of social responsibility, which is anchored in the German constitution. The relationship between "labor" and "capital" is cooperative in nature, shaped by the fundamental assumption that economic prosperity and growth can be best attained through cooperation. The doctrine of social market economy (*"soziale Marktwirtschaft"*) defines the obligations of government, trade unions, and companies to maintain public welfare, social justice, and cooperative industrial relations which give employees not only a relatively strong voice but also a comparatively high level of job security.

Thus, the German approach to humane orientation seems to be manifested in institutionalized societal caring for people, especially the disadvantaged, rather than in interpersonal relations at work. The strong tendency to avoid uncertainty in people's lives may have prompted the development of very elaborate institutionalized social systems to take care of people and to reduce risks to individuals and institutions.

Moderate Power Distance Appears to Decline

The GLOBE results on *power distance* point to an interesting finding. . . . Quite understandably, middle managers in all countries seem to prefer lower levels of power distance than they actually experience. Germany's moderate ranking on power distance "as is" versus a low ranking on power distance "should be" seems to indicate a preference for a more egalitarian approach to status in the society. The desire for less privilege for people in positions of power is reflected in a report in the February 22, 2001 issue of *BusinessWeek* which discussed the sudden departure of BMW's CEO and number-two executive:

> Unceremoniously axing a top exec just wasn't done—till now. In the old days, a CEO practically had to steal money from the company to lose his job," says Frank F. Beelitz, head of Lehman Brothers Inc.'s German unit. "Now, the life expectancy of an underperformer is getting shorter.

East Meets West

Overall, East and West German middle managers' perceptions of Germany's societal culture are remarkably consistent. Only a few noteworthy differences were found. . . . When interpreting these differences, we should keep in mind that the process of German reunification in 1990 created an asymmetric situation which is still not resolved today. . . . The reunification was not a cultural merger of equals. Instead, the West German system was substituted for the old system in East Germany virtually overnight. Thus, the East German respondents' perceptions about the dominating West German societal culture are likely to be influenced by the "modernization shock" and its repercussions. . . . The West German style of capitalism with its emphasis on individual achievements and high flexibility made East Germans more aware of their collectivistic cultural inheritance, for instance the merits of close bonds with friends and family in overcoming everyday difficulties at work and in private life. . . .

The Paradox of Germany's Twin Accomplishments

The paradox of Germany's twin accomplishments in the second half of the 20th century, high economic success and high standards in social welfare, may be related to the above-described paradox of low interpersonal compassion at work and high social welfare. From a cultural-values-and-practices point of view, Germany's past economic success may have resulted from high performance orientation and assertiveness paired with low interpersonal compassion at work. This combination allows for higher levels of conflict and controversy at work. If constructively handled, task conflict does not turn into relationship conflict, and if a minimum of mutual trust is given (granted in Germany by the institutionalized cooperative capital-labor relationships), conflict is likely to result in high quality and efficiency at work. Anxiety and stress usually resulting from interpersonal conflict and controversy may not surface to the expected extent because they are counteracted by the institutionalized social welfare and strong labor representation systems, which satisfy personal needs for security and job safety in Germany's uncertainty-avoidance culture.

Do Germany's Historic Twin Accomplishments Have a Future?

. . . Underpinning the high taxes, excessive regulations, high labor costs, and extensive social safety net is a set of cultural values and practices—high uncertainty avoidance, high assertiveness, low interpersonal humane orientation, high institutionalized humane orientation, i.e., social welfare and strong labor representation—that have evolved over many decades. As has been reasoned above, this system of cultural practices and values may have contributed to Germany's economic success in the past, in close interaction with factors such as high performance orientation and high tolerance for conflict and controversy. However, many of the cultural practices described above fit better in stable times dominated by large industrial companies and labor unions. How will German firms compete in a faster-changing global environment? Even more importantly, is the German leadership culture prepared for the changes to come? These questions remain to be answered.

EFFECTIVE BUSINESS LEADERSHIP IN GERMANY

. . . In all [61] countries *charismatic/transformational* and *team-oriented* leadership are perceived as clearly outstanding. Accordingly, these dimensions are rated highest in Germany as well. However, Germany ranks just below the median on charismatic/transformational leadership (low 25%) and even lower on team-oriented leadership (lowest 25%). The latter finding corresponds with the comparatively high individualistic societal cultural values in Germany. The relatively high ranking on *participative* leadership sets German leadership culture apart from most other countries. It can be seen as a leadership style that responds to high individualism, on the one hand, and to the institutionalized systems of social justice and labor representation giving employees a voice, on the other. In an interview with the *Wall Street Journal,* in response to the question "What aspects of the American business model would you say are not worth adopting?" Dr. von Pierer, the CEO of Siemens, responded:

> The way one deals with people. One example is the German co-determination. Today I met with 30 representatives of works councils from all the operations in Berlin. In the

Anglo-Saxon world that always sounds so nice. But today the discussion focused on large drives, which we are restructuring. . . . The works council representative came and said, "We've taken a look at the master plan and we have suggestions from our plant, which is where our know-how lies, about where we could develop new business." That's great. That's part of co-determination, that the people come with their own suggestions. . . . You have to understand, you come into a German board meeting and there you have 10 capitalists and 10 labour representatives. That demands different behavior.

On *humane-oriented* leadership, Germany ranks comparatively low (lowest 25%) while on *autonomy* it ranks particularly high (highest 25%). This pattern corresponds very well with the high levels on assertiveness and the low levels on humane orientation reported for Germany's societal and organizational cultures. *Self-protective* leadership is clearly perceived to inhibit effective leadership in Germany. High self-protective behavior of a leader would inhibit open conflict and controversy in favor of saving face. Interestingly, East German managers seem to be more lenient towards self-protective leadership attributes than West German managers.

The German Ideal-Leadership Profile

Altogether, the German profile of attributes and behaviors associated with ideal leadership matches closely the profiles of societal and organizational culture in Germany. What sets the German business leadership culture apart from the leadership cultures in most of the other GLOBE countries is the combination of low-to-moderate team orientation, high participation, and low self-protection, with high autonomy and relatively low interpersonal humane orientation. In line with the global trend, ideal leadership in Germany is perceived to be charismatic/transformational, which includes high performance orientation and decisiveness.

PROTOTYPES OF BUSINESS LEADERSHIP IN GERMANY

To better understand the leadership culture in Germany, a three-step analysis was conducted to identify and visualize more clearly the different leadership prototypes. Each bubble identified by our analysis in Figure 1 represents a leadership cluster or prototype. As can be seen, five leadership prototypes are distinguishable: *transformational/charismatic, humble collaborator, individualist, bureaucrat,* and *oppressive.*

The Transformational/Charismatic Leader

The most positive leadership prototype in Germany comprises the attributes of integrity, inspiration, performance orientation, vision, administrative competence, and team integration. We termed this prototype *transformational/charismatic* because three of the attributes listed are described in theories of transformational leadership (inspirational, visionary, performance orientation). However, the other two attributes, administrative competence and team integration, are not reported in the leadership literature to be related to transformational leadership. Nor are they part of the GLOBE charismatic dimension. . . . The cluster shown in Figure 1 seems to represent a German version of transformational leadership, which incorporates administrative competence and team-integrative behaviors.

198

Figure 1   Semantic Network of West German Leadership Concepts

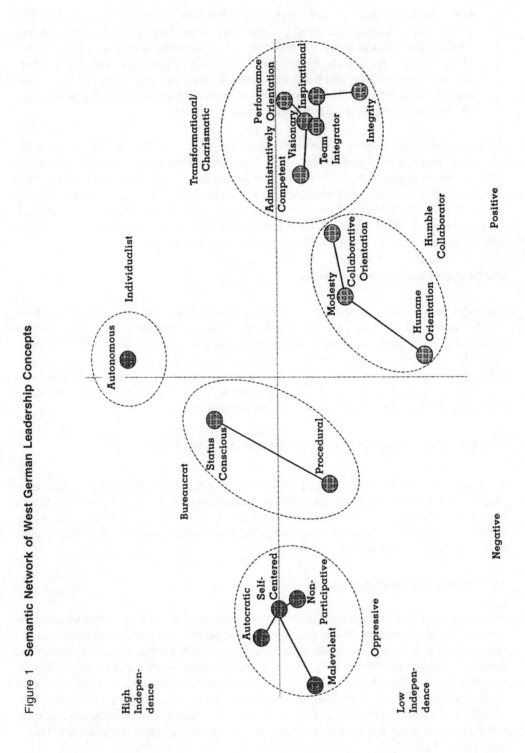

The Humble Collaborator

The second positive leadership prototype comprises collaborative orientation, modesty, and humane orientation as its central attributes. We termed this prototype *humble collaborator* because the attributes emphasize leadership on an equal basis with followers, be it in team collaborative work (e.g., group-oriented, loyalty, fraternal, consultative, mediator), in personal temperament (modesty, self-effacing, patient), or in interpersonal humane orientation (concerned about others, tolerant, generous, sensitive towards others). Although the humble collaborator leader is not perceived as positively as the transforming leader, this prototype is clearly desirable. The perceived importance of humility and collaboration reflects the German value of participation. A humble collaborator leader reduces status differentials in organizations and encourages participation and collaboration. It is noteworthy that the attribute of humane orientation is the least positive in this prototype (nearest to the midpoint of the scale), reflecting the low scores on humane orientation for Germany's societal culture.

The Individualist

Not surprisingly, the *individualist* prototype (autonomous, individualistic, independent, unique) ranks highest on the independence scale. Despite the fact that the individualist prototype is opposite to the previous prototype of the humble collaborator, it is still viewed somewhat positively by German managers. It represents the unique, independent, and individualistic manager who stays apart from the crowd. A typical representative of an individualist leader can be seen in Alfred Herrhausen, former president of the Deutsche Bank, who was murdered in 1989 by terrorists. His impressive career began in 1970 when he became a member of the board of directors. In biographies and the public press reports of his time, he was described as a courageous risk taker, rational in thinking and straightforward, energetic, enforcing, and purposive in temperament, with high performance and power orientation. Most prominently he was described as an individualist, an outsider, often reserved and distanced with a high need for recognition.

The Bureaucrat

The *bureaucratic* leader's attributes of status consciousness and procedural orientation (ritualistic, formal, habitual, and cautious) are perceived to inhibit outstanding leadership. This leadership type scores neither high nor low on the independence scale. Leaders who are visibly attracted to status and privilege, and are very focused on rules and procedures, are not seen as outstanding or effective. This negative opinion seems to be rooted in the strong German desire for performance orientation and the desire for reduced prevalence and intrusion of rules and procedures.

The Oppressive Leader

Finally, the *oppressive* leader embodies the attributes of a German leader who is neither trusted nor loved by the followers. An oppressive leader tends to be non-participative, a micro manager, autocratic, elitist, vindictive, cynical, and hostile, among other characteristics. The oppressive leader does not recognize the followers' views or contributions, partly because of complete self-absorption and partly because of cynical and malevolent views towards others. This leader is disliked by followers partly because of a negative impact on their emotional well-being and partly because the leader is the ultimate representation of low participation.

The GLOBE data cannot give direct evidence for actual prevalence rates of these leadership styles in Germany (or any other country) because the managers' ratings in the GLOBE questionnaire focused not on actual leadership but on prototypes of what makes for outstanding leadership. Actual leadership perceived by followers to be outstanding fits the leadership prototypes held by followers most strongly. When the fit is good, followers are more motivated, committed, and willing to be led. The transformational/charismatic leader (who is also administratively competent and team integrative) and the humble collaborator (who also reduces status differentials and encourages participation) seem best to fit the leadership prototypes held by German middle managers. However, as we all know, not very many real leaders have all of the attributes that ideal leadership types comprise.

Furthermore, leadership prototypes are seldom found in purity. Their overlap with each other and their relationships to societal cultural values are of particular relevance to predicting which leadership style will be successful even if not fully positively valued. For example, some of the oppressive leader's attributes resemble those of the individualist leader (e.g., loner, asocial) who is perceived as contributing to outstanding leadership and who can thus gain at least some emotional and motivational commitment from followers. The overlap between the autocratic and individualistic leader types suggests that German middle managers are more tolerant towards autocratic leadership styles. As another example, a person with high assertiveness and low humane orientation may still be perceived as a transformational/charismatic leader in Germany (and get away with poor interpersonal behavior) because interpersonal humane orientation is less highly valued in German society and organizations than performance orientation and decisiveness.

PRACTICAL IMPLICATIONS

Considering Cross-Cultural Differences

Our empirical findings support the notion that, in line with the overall findings from GLOBE, the elements of Germany's societal and organizational cultures and leadership style overlap strongly. A theoretical line of reasoning that connects the three can be outlined as follows. Societal and organizational culture define a set of acceptable and unacceptable behaviors. Individuals learn to conform to these norms through acculturation and socialization. Over time, individuals become particularly skilled at acceptable behaviors. Successful managers are well socialized and acculturated. They tend to be good at acceptable behaviors. This ability can also be dysfunctional, e.g., when managers are placed in an environment with different cultural values and when change is forced upon organizations or societies. Furthermore, successes (and failures) in the past generate experiences; formerly successful behaviors will be repeated elsewhere and also when change is actually required.

The previous findings and discussion support two general conclusions. *First, when cultures are relatively similar in content—that is, their dimensional profiles have considerable similarities—transacting business is easier with not much change in behaviors.*

GLOBE has produced a database that can help us identify the cultural similarities and differences among countries and organizations. However, we have learned that it is useful to develop a better understanding of a foreign culture even when it seems to closely match our own. The GLOBE data shows the cultural profiles of Austria, German-speaking Switzerland, and Germany to be highly similar to each other and dissimilar to those of 19 other Pan-European countries. A manager from Japan or any other culture distant from Germanic cultures may view representatives from these three countries as highly similar in behavior and value systems.

However, subtle but disturbing differences may surface when representatives from highly similar cultures are working together. For example, closer inspection of the GLOBE database revealed that German-speaking Swiss managers differ in some subtle ways from their German counterparts. They rank slightly lower on autonomy and somewhat higher on modesty, diplomacy, and team orientation than their German counterparts. . . .

A second general conclusion: When cultures are different in content—that is, their dimensional profiles are significantly different—adjustment is generally necessary in proportion to the cultural distance.

Knowledge about specific cultural characteristics (e.g., the type of conflict and controversy at work endorsed in Germany) can help expatriate managers to anticipate potential benefits (constructive controversy leads to high quality) and potential problems (interpersonal conflict leads to stress and emotional strain) in cross-cultural interactions. Furthermore, the knowledge derived from GLOBE about the particular leadership profiles that most strongly differentiate two target countries (e.g., Germany: lower on compassion and higher on autonomy than the UK) is a useful tool to supplement cross-cultural management training with a set of tailor-made training situations that are likely to generate typical cross-cultural disturbances between representatives from the target countries. . . .

An important implication here is that a manager successful in one culture may not be able to adjust sufficiently to another culture. In contrast, a manager who is maladjusted at home might actually be a better fit in an overseas position. For example, as was described above, assertiveness in Germany is associated with straightforwardness, tolerance for conflict, and controversy. Paired with low interpersonal humane orientation, these characteristics can be humiliating in cross-cultural situations involving people with a cultural background of high interpersonal humane orientation. In contrast, paired with high performance orientation, the characteristics can be creative, efficient, and productive, especially in cross-cultural situations involving others with a cultural background of high performance orientation. If a UK manager is to be assigned to Germany, a person with high tolerance for conflict and controversy paired with high performance orientation, who is not too easily disturbed when facing low compassion in interpersonal behavior, may be a better fit than a typical representative of the UK culture, which endorses interpersonal humane orientation to a great extent.

Considering Change: Managers Becoming Leaders

For Germany to compete successfully in the global markets of the 21st century, a change in its societal and organizational cultures and leadership style seems unavoidable. However, not all changes are possible. Therefore, let us take a closer look at the cultural content of each cultural level analyzed above and its potential for adaptive change.

Societal cultural values are difficult to change, especially when evolutionary rather than revolutionary change is envisaged. And some cultural dimensions are so deeply rooted in history and society that they are unlikely to be changed at all. On the one hand, Germany's moderate to high individualism, high uncertainty avoidance, and high assertiveness seem to be deeply rooted in its history; it ranks similarly in various studies from the early 1960s to the late 1990s. On the other hand, prompted by the demands of the free-market economy and globalization in the 1990s, Germany has witnessed a questioning of the ideal of the welfare state in favor of the neo-liberal concepts of self-reliance and individual commitment to smaller, organically grown units such as family and work groups. The country has entered a post-modern type of democracy, in retreat from state intervention and disenchanted with the welfare state. The first concrete steps are visible; Germany now focuses on providing fewer resources to its social programs (e.g., encouraging private contributions to health care, "Pflegeversicherung," and additional private pension schemes, "Private Zusatzrente").

Our own data supports the view that some cultural aspects are already differently valued in Germany than they were some decades ago. German society and its organizations in particular seem to be ripe for more advancement of the female work force. Actually, female managers could be the ones who bring more interpersonal compassion to work and who can stimulate their male colleagues to do the same. The dislike for overly low compassion, also shown in German societal culture, should work to the same end. What is missing, though, is a level of future-orientation "should be" among German middle managers that compares better to its very high levels in many other GLOBE countries. A management-education system that is more in line with international programs and that allows for more and longer assignments abroad may work wonders here.

The German Zeitgeist of consolidation, possibly still a consequence of the tremendous costs of the reunification process (today visible in high unemployment rates, high public spending, and debt), seems to be a major obstacle. A critical challenge is how to restructure the traditionally institutionalized mechanisms for maintaining social welfare, cooperative capital-labor relationships, and personal safety while at the same time cutting down on high taxes, high labor costs, and a cumbersome bureaucracy.

Last but not least are the consequences of having managers who are insensitive to the feelings of employees and so task focused that learning and development are not on their agenda. Especially in these times of globalization and multicultural work forces, the so-called soft skills (e.g., cosmopolitanism, consideration of people, compassion in interpersonal conduct, team leadership) become critical attributes for success. While conflict and controversy have their merits in a highly task-focused and performance-oriented society, German managers need to be aware of the pitfalls of their "tough on the issue, tough on the person" approach. This is particularly true when institutionalized humane orientation via publicly sponsored social welfare—which appears to cushion the anxiety and emotional stress resulting from ruthlessness—is on the decline. The benefits to be gained by Germany from a leadership style that might be called "tough on the issue, *soft* on the person!" need to be intensively explored.

Effective leadership is about dealing with people (compassion) as much as it is about dealing with change (future orientation). We think it is time for German managers to become more effective leaders in that respect.

[Referenced article:] "Boss Talk: Goal Is Game, Set, and Match—Siemens' CEO Allies Tactics of Tennis to Management: Rules of Winning, Losing." *Wall Street Journal*, February 2, 2001.

10.2 WORKING IN A VIETNAMESE VOICE
Lady Borton

> To be sure,
> Build a house of brick;
> To be clean,
> Sweep with a worn broom.
> —*Vietnamese proverb*

For Vietnamese, the autumn of 2000 was one of celebrations: the 55th anniversary of independence from France; Hanoi's 990th birthday; and Vietnam's first 11 years of peace in modern memory. Foreigners visiting Vietnam find a country bursting with exuberance. At peace, Vietnam is on the move.

War damage, two post-1975 wars, the U.S. embargo, and Vietnam's command economy created desperate poverty. In December 1986, the Communist Party's VIth Congress affirmed a policy of Renovation, which instituted transition to a market economy, openness to the West and to ethnic Vietnamese overseas (*Viet Kieu*), and greater personal freedom. The resultant changes have been stunning. Government, banks, businesses, laws, rules, and the culture itself are in flux, creating a challenge for Vietnamese and expatriates alike.

With a few exceptions, foreigners' perspectives on post-war Vietnam span only a few years. Foreigners tend to compare Vietnam with their own countries or with other developing nations, with their most common mistakes arising from not accurately perceiving Vietnam's dizzying change when compared with itself. A common fallacy is to assume Vietnam is like other ASEAN nations or other former colonies; even more imprudent is to assume Vietnam is like Cuba, North Korea, or China. However, perhaps the most complications arise from thinking Vietnam today is like former South Vietnam. U.S. citizens are particularly likely to assume they will bring development to Vietnam, forgetting that huge changes have already taken place, despite U.S. Government obstacles.

In contrast, Vietnamese colleagues remember 10, 20, or 30 years ago. A National Assembly delegate recently described Vietnamese institutional changes for business leaders visiting from the U.S.: "Vietnam has passed more laws in the last 10 years than in the previous 200." A former southern revolutionary meeting a delegation from the U.S. remarked, "My country has developed more in the last 10 years than in the previous thousand." These rapid changes have challenged Vietnam's institutions, both old and new.

VIETNAMESE CULTURAL DIMENSIONS

Vietnamese are quick to adapt, yet take a considered approach to fundamental change. Work styles successful elsewhere will not transfer completely to Vietnam and may not transfer at all. Vietnamese are, as former North Vietnamese military commander General Vo Nguyen Giap recently noted, "very Vietnamese, and very international."

From *The Academy of Management Executive* 14, no. 4 (November 2000): 20–29. Copyright © 2000 Academy of Management Executive. Reprinted with permission.

Right Relationship

In Vietnam, right relationship underlies social and work dynamics. Right relationship dates from ancient ancestor cults overlaid with Confucianism from a thousand years of Chinese occupation. Nationalist socialism as described by the late North Vietnamese President Ho Chi Minh tempered this heritage into a uniquely Vietnamese form.

In Vietnamese thinking, every person has his or her place within the family, the village, and the wider society. One's place determines duties, responsibilities, and privileges. Relationships are not rigorously formalized as in some Asian cultures. In fact, some Vietnamese abandon right relationship in settings such as traffic and queues. Nevertheless, in the work setting, right relationship is omnipresent.

The Vietnamese language reflects right relationship through its many pronouns. Most name family relationships resting on a paternal-maternal branched hierarchy that, for instance, differentiates "uncle" into a half dozen words and identical twins into "older" and "younger." Pronouns change according to speakers' ages, sex, social status, and level of intimacy, with every pronoun establishing and reinforcing right relationship.

Pronouns also challenge Vietnamese who have trouble guessing Westerners' ages. Vietnamese often ask new acquaintances' ages in a way Westerners may find intrusive; they are simply trying to determine whether their guest is an "older brother" or a "junior uncle," so they can then think in their own language and feel comfortable in future interactions.

Respect

Although Vietnamese pronouns change, the underlying premise is always respect. One enlarges the respect given the addressee and diminishes the respect applied to oneself. By giving respect, one gains respect. The essential principle is: Show other people more respect than they apparently deserve; simultaneously expect and assert less respect than you deserve.

Vietnamese convey respect by increasing the status choice for "you" and decreasing the choice for "I." Since the English language has no structural equivalent, Westerners can best compensate with gracious phrases. Flowery language ("If it's all right with you, I'd like to suggest an idea. . . ." or "Allow me to suggest. . . .") is about right.

Gestures help. The primary gesture of respect is a gentle bow. On first meeting, Vietnamese shake hands and usually look down or to the side, indicating respect for the other person. The handshake is gentle, also indicating respect. Westerners often misinterpret these gestures as weakness. Similarly, Vietnamese can easily misconstrue the Westerner's firm handshake and eye-to-eye gaze as arrogance.

Informal greetings may also cause confusion. Initial questions Vietnamese ask ("Where have you been?" and "Have you eaten yet?") are simply greetings and not serious queries. The former is similar to "What've you been up to?" and the latter to "How are you?" Neither requires a direct answer, any more than "How are you?" invites a full description of one's health.

Vietnamese consider guests precious and will drop everything to tend to a guest's needs. Punctuality signals a respectful visitor; lateness implies disrespect.

Community

Western cultures place high value on the individual, whereas Vietnamese culture emphasizes the community. Vietnamese may view individual assertiveness as arrogance. Conversely, Westerners often view Vietnamese consensus-building as bureaucratic red tape. Recognizing and discussing cultural differences with Vietnamese colleagues and partners can facilitate adjustment on both sides.

Indirectness

Vietnamese tend to be indirect, Westerners direct. In Western communication, the main point comes first and details follow. Vietnamese often use proverbs and parables that tell seemingly irrelevant anecdotes, describing context while spiraling so subtly toward the issue at hand, that Westerners may miss the point. This indirectness is a question of tact, not of sincerity.

A Vietnamese writer jokingly illustrates this dynamic with a story of a mandarin's sumptuous feast. A servant waiting on guests compliments the mandarin on his robe, describing how mulberry trees were planted and grew and how their leaves were gathered, how silk worms were fed and how the silk worms grew and how they spun their cocoons, how (speaking a bit faster) the cocoons were boiled and how silken thread was gathered from the worms' cocoons and spun, how (speaking even faster) the brocade was woven with gold and silver threads and then embroidered, too, and then how (speaking faster still) the robe was perfectly tailored to fit the mandarin's august and magnificent frame. Finally, the breathless servant blurts: "Sire, your robe is on fire!"

Westerners in Vietnam may feel it takes forever to reach the flame. Indirectness is particularly frustrating for project managers driven by a time-is-money orientation. Like many Asians, Vietnamese engage their counterparts through casual conversation to build a relationship. Then and only then can the discussion successfully approach business. Entering too soon violates trust-building; pushing too fast risks everything.

The Vietnamese have a proverb, "When entering a family, follow its practices," which is akin to the Western saying, "When in Rome, do as the Romans do." An indirect style to create a context first is more apt to create acceptance than making a point in 30 seconds. A useful beginning is: "I don't know how it is in Vietnam, but in my country (or company or organization), . . ." Describing how the issue plays out elsewhere enables one to build toward the main point one would normally say first to a Westerner.

Vietnamese will be direct once they know you. When discussing a complicated project, a Vietnamese colleague laughed, saying: "In Vietnam, the shortest distance between two points is not a straight line!" He wriggled his hand, suggesting steps to take.

FOUNDATIONS OF WORK RELATIONSHIPS

Equal Partnership

Cultural differences that can produce misjudgments in minor matters signal the need for alertness to possible misinterpretation in many areas. Expatriates who project themselves as high-energy, assertive experts with resources, capital, and all the answers unintentionally create a self-destructive differential by placing Vietnamese in a lesser role. Those who lecture usually have trouble securing cooperation. Shouting and temper tantrums are even less effective. Foreigners' expectations of meeting senior leaders on a level they would not see at home are unrealistic.

Poverty and Vietnamese cultural modesty often cause foreigners to misgauge Vietnamese educational level and capacity. Vietnamese have had higher education for senior national leaders since the founding of Hanoi's Temple of Literature, Vietnam's first university, in 1076. The emphasis on education has extended to modern times, with successive generations of Vietnamese studying in France, China, the former Soviet Union and its allies, and, recently, all over the world.

Expatriates who work effectively in Vietnam think of themselves as equal partners, replacing assertiveness with graciousness. This is a question of style and attitude, not of content. They learn about the Vietnamese system. They replace paternalism with mutual respect and friendship. They listen and try to imagine the Vietnamese point of view.

Introduction and Sponsorship

Project relationships in Vietnam, as in many places, begin through introduction, but introduction in Vietnam is more like sponsorship. During the French and U.S. wars, small secret groups within a huge citizens' resistance web depended on linked sponsorships. A mistake in introduction could bring arrest, torture, captured information, and a major setback. Introduction was critical, with the introducer responsible for the introduced person's behavior, both for benefits and mistakes.

This thinking still holds. The sponsor guides the newcomer and maintains tangential involvement and ultimate responsibility. Everything must be clear and open in order to build trust. Careful and appropriate introductions can prevent mistakes and save years of trust-building. Usually, sponsorship includes preliminary conversations without the newcomer. Thus, the sponsor needs to understand the introduced individual and organization's values and objectives. Keep your sponsor informed of plans, outcomes, and extracurricular activities.

Belonging

The Vietnamese concept of belonging originates in ancient Vietnamese culture and its Confucian overlay but has changed through years of socialism. Belonging embodies right relationship within families, the village, an institution, and the nation; it also assigns official responsibility.

Every expatriate organization and individual belongs somewhere in the Vietnamese system. A government office where one belongs is similar to a Vietnamese older sibling, who cares for and protects the younger. The office obtains expatriate visas, signs off on permissions, and takes responsibility for the project. In difficult times, this office can be the project's best advocate. Thus, frequent communication pays future dividends.

Foreign businesses belong to the Ministry of Planning and Investment (MPI); INGOs to the People's Aid Coordinating Committee (PACCOM); academic institutions to the Ministry of Education and Training (MOET) or Ministry of Science, Technology and Environment (MOSTE).

Foreigners usually implement projects in collaboration with a Vietnamese partnering business or organization, sometimes called the focal point. These Vietnamese partners also belong somewhere in the Vietnamese system. Vietnamese colleagues and experienced expatriates agree it is best to have only one focal point for a given project. That focal point will draw in other appropriate partners. Foreigners who create several focal points for the same project usually find themselves beset by overlap, inaction while one focal point waits for the other, and confusion when two focal points act in conflict.

Step-by-Step Path

Vietnam has about one-third the population of the U.S., with most Vietnamese living in a space about the size of Indiana. Years of war and the needs of so many people crowded on land prone to typhoons, floods, and droughts have taught Vietnamese to see the big picture and the small steps leading to larger goals.

Relationships in Vietnam move through layers. First-time visitors are graciously welcomed acquaintances, second-time visitors return as friends, third-time visitors as old friends. Foreigners should consider managing layers of intimacy by making multiple visits that move both the relationship and project plans forward step-by-step.

Comprehensive Consultation

In Vietnamese *xin phep* means "Allow me," "Permit me," or "Be kind enough to listen to me." The phrase invites what can be described as comprehensive consultation. For Westerners, comprehensive consultation implies relinquishing power, yet *xin phep* has little to do with the "yes" and "no" of power and control. For a Vietnamese, *xin phep* shows respect and right relationship; it invites community input, elicits advice, builds consensus, and develops support to help a project run more smoothly.

A useful phrase is, "If you agree, we thought we might. . . ." The speaker then describes the idea and rationale, giving much more detail than is usual in the West. No one takes the proposed steps until everyone is comfortable. *Xin phep* with Vietnamese colleagues about anything and everything that affects them. Trust built through consultation about little details makes quick decisions possible for later, larger concerns.

Some activities (such as press conferences, publications, conferences, workshops, and some meetings) require formal permission. Vietnam must still deal with a marginalized but vocal community of overseas ethnic Vietnamese who would like to overthrow the state. The Vietnamese government would likely open faster and require fewer permissions were there not this challenge. A project's character and monetary investment determine the permission level. Since requirements change constantly, comprehensive consultation is both common courtesy and essential behavior.

A consensus culture often seems cumbersome to Westerners. Discussion requires time and effort, but, as in Western organizations, failure to engage in comprehensive consultation may result in lost productivity. Watch Vietnamese life: everyone discusses details to exhaustion. As one Vietnamese editor says: "We have too much 'democracy.'"

Understanding "Yes, Yes"

Expatriates all too often incorrectly assume that "yes, yes" means agreement, but the phrase only means "I'm listening." Some businesses and INGOs have planned events, printed programs, invited international consultants, and even met these guests at the airport, only to discover that their Vietnamese partners had never agreed to host the events. A U.S. citizen traveled to Vietnam for an event limited to Vietnamese; although she had heard "yes, yes" to her request to attend, she had never received even a verbal invitation.

The words for affirmation during negotiations and incidental personal arrangements are "agree" or "consent," whether in Vietnamese or another language. To be sure, when Vietnamese colleagues say "yes, yes," I ask whether they mean "agree." "Oh! 'Agree,'" they usually answer, but if they have reservations, I'm apt to hear them.

Listening for "No"

Vietnamese rarely say "no" because a refusal causes a loss of face. Loss of face is painful in any society, but unbearable in Vietnam. The Vietnamese have an expression: "Better to die than to lose face." Of course, Vietnamese have ways of relaying negative decisions, but Westerners often misunderstand and misinterpret these messages.

Vietnamese usually say "no" indirectly, such as: "It's complicated," "It's a little difficult," "It's not the right time," or "There's a problem. . . ." Most Westerners hearing such phrases shift into problem-solving mode. They roll up their sleeves, lean forward, and charge ahead: "There's a problem? Let's solve it!" However, the Vietnamese think they've communicated a firm but gracious "no."

Prevention is the best solution. Mention the foreigner's difficulty understanding Vietnamese complexities of "yes" and "no." This will likely bring the laughter of recognition. Try something like: "If anything is complicated or difficult, if this isn't the right time, or if there's a problem, just let me know. We'll stop, or change directions, or wait." Respond to Vietnamese negatives by asking the counterpart to suggest a first small step toward solution.

This approach may seem perplexing to those beset by deadlines and a bottom line. However, in the yin and yang of Vietnamese culture, yielding control creates trust and access. Again and again, particularly with breakthrough projects, a Vietnamese partner has said: "This is so complicated." I've answered, "Maybe we should wait." "Oh no," the Vietnamese partner has said, "I just wanted you to know it's difficult! We're not stopping."

PRACTICAL CONSIDERATIONS

In Vietnam, I work almost entirely on the informal level because I have relationships that span decades, a history of project work, and few financial program resources to tempt the unscrupulous. Start-ups—whether business or development projects—need to build their relationships. The greater the capital involved, the more complicated that process becomes, and the more prone to slippage.

Building a Local Staff

The manager's most important decision will be hiring the first Vietnamese staff member. Although this point may seem obvious, many foreigners overlook it and learn painfully from that mistake. The first Vietnamese colleague is an essential buffer and guide through Vietnam's intricacies. She or he can help find other honest, motivated staff.

You can find this important first staff member by talking with Vietnamese whose values and work you admire. Ask them for introductions. If you have no Vietnamese contacts, ask expatriate friends and colleagues for suggestions. The trick is to find the right word-of-mouth contacts. Key qualities needed are honesty, appropriate attitude, and motivation. Skills can always be learned. Provide sufficient training so staff can succeed.

Foreign organizations are alien cultures to Vietnamese staff, just as the Vietnamese culture is strange to the newly arrived expatriate. The result is often confusion on both sides. As a senior UN agency Vietnamese staff person said: "We Vietnamese look to expatriate managers to set standards. Micromanagers soon lose our respect. When faced with them, we stop offering advice. We stop taking initiative."

A seemingly obvious answer to cultural differences is to hire *Viet Kieu*, expatriates of Vietnamese ethnic background. This fits with the expatriate organization's needs, with Vietnam's openness to ethnic Vietnamese in other countries, and with the wish of returning ethnic Vietnamese to serve their homeland. Nevertheless, managers may do well to consider extra guidance and careful supervision for these staff.

Ethnic Vietnamese from abroad have gained their Western expertise after great effort and at great personal cost. However, once in Vietnam, they may become over-confident experts, unintentionally displaying arrogance toward Vietnamese nationals. As strange as this may seem, similar arrogance displayed by ethnic Westerners is easier for Vietnamese nationals to endure.

Misunderstandings and discrimination exist on both sides. Ethnic Vietnamese from abroad often do not know modern, post-war Vietnam's culture and may bring a hidden or subconscious agenda, yet they may also be held to higher standards than visitors who are completely foreign. Managers can avoid confusion, pain, and lost productivity through careful applicant interviews, thorough orientation including emphasis on right relationship and comprehensive consultation, and rigorous supervision.

Administrative Bureaucracy

Vietnamese bureaucracy is a challenge for foreigners and Vietnamese alike. When the party secretary, Vietnam's top leader, was asked about the country's greatest challenges, his answer was direct: "Corruption and bureaucracy." Nevertheless, foreigners who complain publicly cause the Vietnamese present to lose face; this in turn causes the complainer to lose effectiveness. Foreigners seeking visas from their own embassies for Vietnamese colleagues traveling overseas soon learn that their home bureaucracies are also onerous.

Generally speaking, a president or director in Vietnam is similar to a Western board chair. This person is consulted on major decisions, connects the organization to the next higher level, and attends formal occasions. The vice president or vice director is responsible for daily management and is similar to a Western CEO. Thus, a person with a vice-head title is often the one to see.

The Vietnamese bureaucracy is struggling to redefine itself amid colossal change. Many bureaucratic layers ("doors" or "gates") still remain. Foreigners tend to forget that the behaviors essential to working productively at home still apply. In any bureaucracy—whether business, government, INGO, or academic—the worst blunders occur when supervisors find out from someone else something they should have learned directly. The supervisor loses face. The negligent staff person involved, in turn, loses out.

In Vietnam, "the emperor's rule stops at the village gate." Westerners sometimes try to pull rank by meeting a senior-level official and then presenting the desired decision as a fait accompli to their lower-level partners. Pulling rank is perceived as manipulation, not oversight; it causes the Vietnamese partner and others in the bureaucracy to lose face, creating an unintended result—"worse than death." A quick apology will not easily remove the resulting strain.

Typical Vietnamese praise for a foreigner is "She's clever (at working the system)," or "He's smart. . . ." The most negative criticism a Vietnamese will offer of a foreigner to a foreigner is "She doesn't yet understand Vietnam." To work effectively, keep your sponsor and focal point informed. During each visit to Vietnam, check in with all appropriate and active bureaucratic layers (national, provincial, district, commune) where your organization belongs. This builds right relationship and creates an opportunity to clarify your needs as parameters change. As your working relationship strengthens, the check-in process becomes quicker and more informal.

Seasons of Opening and Closing

The stunning opening during the past decade has not been a continuum, but rather a variation of Newton's third law of motion: For every opening, there has been a nearly comparable apparent closing, a pause, a chance to catch a breath and absorb the change.

The Vietnam-U.S. Trade Agreement is yet one more example of a major opening, which will likely be followed by smaller closings. "The overall vector is up," the Vietnamese head of a major government office handling Vietnam-U.S. relations said. He laughed, his hand fluctuating like a rising roller coaster.

Vietnamese often use the image of gates. If a large irrigation sluice gate opens, but the small gates behind it swing shut, little water flows out until the small gates open one by one. These seasons become predictable if we remember that Western institutions exhibit similar patterns. Managers will not make a startling decision when a new CEO is taking office; high-level U.S. civil servants will not take controversial positions during a closely contested presidential election; university faculty harbor pet research projects until they can gauge a new dean's disposition.

Vietnamese instinctively hunker down and wait during seasons of huge change and comparable caution; they pay more attention to both formal and informal relationships; they keep required permissions in order and insure that informal comprehensive consultation is more detailed; and they delay new projects or phrase them as continuations. Expatriates working in Vietnam would do well to follow their Vietnamese colleagues' lead.

Corruption

Corruption is another favorite topic within both the Vietnamese and expatriate communities. Vietnamese media report regularly on smuggling and on embezzlement from businesses, development projects, and government offices. Although corruption exists in every country, it is more pervasive and apparent in Vietnam than in the West.

During the French colonial period, the Vietnamese had a saying: "Stealing from the French is not stealing." A similar version existed in South Vietnam during the war. Expatriates who take a neocolonialist attitude unintentionally set themselves up as unwary participants in a tradition of "legitimate stealing."

Even those sensitive expatriates who do listen face a quagmire. The command economic system encouraged reports based on preestablished quotas rather than on strictly gathered data. Poverty then added a fertile environment for corruption during the sudden influx of foreign capital in the mid-1990s. Indeed, Transparency International's 2000 Corruption Perception Index ranked Vietnam 76th–78th (shared with Armenia and Tanzania) among 90 countries according to the degree of corruption perceived to exist among public officials and politicians.

Comments from the party secretary and other key leaders provide a suitable basis for requiring transparent management practices. Transparency means keeping all files, budgets, ledgers, financial reports, minutes, correspondence, e-mail, and personnel records as accessible as possible. Secrecy and gray areas surrounding expatriate compensation encourage comparable gray areas in Vietnamese reporting.

Commissions

Vietnam has yet to implement a comprehensive tax structure to replace the one from the command economy. In 1988, the Vietnamese government began to cut its subsidies to government offices. Although salaries were low under the command economy, income included subsidized housing, water, and electricity. As these benefits ceased, government employees could not realistically cover their needs through salaries alone. So-called commissions became common.

Upon mutual agreement with a foreign partner, a Vietnamese office may take a management fee; this is an auditable, above-board expense. However, each bureaucratic level handling funds may also take a silent fee; these are nonauditable, below-board costs. For some despairing novices, the first indication of silent fees comes when all money has been spent, yet the factory (or school, etc.) is roofless. One expatriate INGO colleague describes this potential slippage as being similar to moving a 50-kilo block of ice from Hanoi to Ho Chi Minh City in July: you're lucky to arrive with a damp spot.

Less obvious commissions may include a monthly percentage of rent for having introduced the site (similar to a Western real estate agent's fee); a monthly percentage of a newly introduced staff member's salary (similar to a head-hunter's fee); fees for steering orders to vendors (similar to contractors' fees); or percentage return of purchase price (similar to a discount). Unless your organization has an explicit policy to the contrary, a staff member's taking or giving a commission is not necessarily a betrayal of trust.

The foreign side has its own version of slippage. Only 50 to 70 percent (and sometimes as little as 30 percent) of INGO, UN, and overseas development assistance and business capital reaches intended beneficiaries. Sometimes as much as 40 percent of foreign assistance budgets leaves Vietnam in salaries deposited, untaxed, into overseas banks for expatriates who live off in-country allowances. Vietnamese are well aware of these double standards, in which expatriate colleagues doing similar work made 10 to 15 times as much income. Many Vietnamese see these high salaries as personal profit similar to Vietnamese commissions.

Vietnamese also become cynical when expatriate managers hire personal friends as consultants. These friends visit Vietnam for a month or two at great cost and then present a report; however, the Vietnamese consultants working with them were often more knowledgeable, did much if not most of the research, analysis, and report-writing yet received a fraction of the pay. Vietnamese also know expatriates sometimes set up nonprofit legal structures that are actually highly profitable businesses paying huge expatriate salaries. However, although similarities exist between these expatriate and Vietnamese benefit systems, one is above the line and auditable; the other is hidden and perhaps—but not necessarily—more subject to abuse.

Gifts and Envelopes

Vietnamese hosts customarily present visitors with a small gift. In return, gifts from your home town—such as local crafts, calendars, books, or picture puzzles featuring local landmarks—are appropriate and appreciated. Kept to a small scale, presenting and receiving gifts is important in right relationship. However, as in any society, large gifts can easily imply accompanying obligations. Special perks, such as scholarships for Vietnamese partners' children or expensive gifts, are potential sources of trouble.

Vietnamese customarily present envelopes with cash inside to friends and employees for the Tet new year celebration and for weddings; to teachers on Teachers' Day; and to attendees at seminars, conferences, workshops, political training sessions, and even office meetings. Envelopes may be given publicly or privately and are similar to personal gifts, perks, and bonuses in the Western corporate world. They are given with sincerity; not accepting an envelope can make presenters feel they have lost face.

In recent years, envelopes have become fees-for-services supplementing low government wages. As one Vietnamese working in government said: "In the past, getting things done depended on knowing the right person. Nowadays, we have to pay too." You may be asked to pay for an envelope as a cost of doing business. Your Vietnamese staff will likely be offered envelopes in return for bringing business to Vietnamese vendors. These costs will be built into suppliers' estimates.

In 1997, the prime minister publicly admonished government employees for giving and receiving envelopes and requested that this practice stop. Establishing an organizational policy that forbids giving and receiving envelopes requires a willingness to enforce it. Younger staff are particularly vulnerable and have indicated their relief when clear policies are in place. Unless there is a policy to the contrary, exchanging envelopes does not imply a betrayal of trust.

Getting to Agreement

While a Western CEO may delegate decision making, Vietnamese culture does not to the same extent. The slower Vietnamese decision process is a cultural tradition likely to remain in the near future. Vietnamese know they lack tools for analyzing investment proposals and are understandably cautious. A first-time visitor with a great idea should not expect to sign a contract. Relationships count, listening is more important than talking, and nothing replaces having reliable Vietnamese staff in Vietnam to move the relationship along. As in the West, unofficial levels also affect the agreement process and are often stronger. Patience, endurance, and a sense of humor are key.

TEN PRINCIPLES FOR WORKING WITH VIETNAM

These 10 principles reflect hard lessons from projects the Quaker Service staff wishes it had done differently. The principles are listed starkly, but when negotiating with local partners, the staff works in a Vietnamese way, circling in on a point by developing a context for each principle.

- *Listen, and communicate in a Vietnamese voice:* To keep your project moving successfully, you must learn to listen. Vietnamese dislike confrontation and will try to compromise. A strong Vietnamese reaction against a proposal signals a real obstacle. Control anger and avoid cutting ties. If the agreement gap is too large, consider letting a project go by saying something like: "It seems like this just isn't the right time," "Maybe if we waited," "Maybe if we take a break and meet for supper." This leaves the topic gently but firmly on the table. A recess creates time for new ideas and allows consultation with those absent. Vietnamese rarely do direct business while eating. Nevertheless, a meal and shared stories can lighten the atmosphere; a solution may appear with the last sips of tea.
- *Hire the best possible Vietnamese staff:* Check references carefully and seek additional references from résumé data. Many Vietnamese job candidates have attended workshops on interviewing skills, will likely be charming, and say what they know employers want to hear. Structured interviewing using specific examples presenting a difficult choice with no apparent right answer helps illuminate underlying values and traits.
- *Gather and share all relevant project planning materials:* Insist on access to relevant Vietnamese project planning materials, including the partner's mission statement, long-range plans, comprehensive surveys, designs, maps, proposals, and plans under consideration by other partners. Learn how each project fits into the partner's strategy. Ignoring these steps invites overlap. Share comparable information. The clearer the information, the clearer the expectations, and the greater the chance of success. Plans change. Update this process.
- *Require transparency in accounting and program records:* Be sure all financial expectations and responsibilities are clear, transparent, and written to avoid later claims that promises were made. Government registration documents may require a proposed budget, which in Vietnam signals assured funds. Note budget items subject to change. Set up transparent accounting systems with clear outside financial controls. Insist all fees be overt.

- *Try a pilot project:* Start with only one project, and start small. Several projects started simultaneously tend to meld; money disappears, leaving half-finished, low-quality results. Insist one project be finished before releasing funds for another. Move to a larger format only after sharing lessons learned.
- *Employ step-by-step stages:* Advance funds for the first step. Release funds for the next step only after the previous stage has been completed, monitored, all advances accounted for, and all receipts checked against current prices. Build in a final payment to be made only after the entire project has been satisfactorily completed; this retains control and helps guarantee results according to specifications.
- *Supervise staff and monitor projects closely:* Vietnamese colleagues' friends and relatives may put intense pressure on local counterparts for a slipped share of project resources. Rigorous monitoring protects honest Vietnamese colleagues, giving them an easy answer: "I can't. The boss checks." Transparent accounting also protects honest staff members, allowing them to say: "I can't. An auditor examines every receipt." Build monitoring into each step to prevent stucco results that are stellar only on the surface. Use spot checks.
- *Make and enforce a clear policy about commissions, kickbacks, envelopes, and gifts:* Avoid commissions by advancing funds directly to those implementing the project. Help staff understand that accepting commissions and envelopes compromises their ability to monitor. Graciously communicate a clear policy about commissions, kickbacks, envelopes, and gifts to staff and partners. Consider providing training, supplies, or equipment to collegial government offices to increase capacity while lessening the need for silent fees. Avoid providing vehicles; often they are not used as intended. Ask that all gifts be public, small, and locally produced.
- *Build in a local contribution:* Require a local contribution from project partners to insure local ownership and sustainability. Depending on the project, local contributions may be land, locally available materials (sand, gravel, stone), unskilled labor, on-going maintenance, training, administration, or record-keeping. Construct development projects so that beneficiaries make a contribution to the wider community.
- *Evaluate projects:* Include midterm and final evaluations, with the project's second half dependent upon the midterm evaluation results, and subsequent projects dependent upon the final evaluation.

Bright Prospects

Effective managers recognize Vietnamese customs and practices and communicate through careful listening. They honor the core cultural assumptions: belonging, comprehensive consultation, right relationship, and respect.

As Vietnam implements regional and global agreements, foreign managers might assume they can work with Vietnamese partners purely on their own terms. Quite the contrary. The Vietnamese fought hard for national independence; they are not likely to surrender their country's economic management to others.

The new lens of normalizing U.S. trade may well bring administrative tightening. However, once mutual trust is established, just about everything is possible. Future prospects are great. That is why Vietnam is such an exciting place to work.

10.3 BUILDING COMPETITIVE ADVANTAGE FROM *UBUNTU*: MANAGEMENT LESSONS FROM SOUTH AFRICA
Mzamo P. Mangaliso

. . .

UBUNTU AND COMPETITIVENESS

The dismantling of apartheid in the 1990s was a watershed of historic development for South Africa. The world watched as the country charted its course toward the establishment of a democratic, nonracial, nonsexist system of government. With democratic processes now firmly in place, the spotlight has shifted to economic revitalization. South Africa has shown steady economic progress since the days of apartheid, and stands 42nd in the 2001 IMD world competitiveness rankings. This recovery is a welcome sign that South Africa has turned the corner. Now it can focus on those practices that will allow it to excel domestically and globally. An important step will be to understand the culture, values, norms, and beliefs held by the largest segment of the population, the Africans. The premise of this article is that observable workplace behavior is strongly influenced by latent, unobservable social attitudes. Such social attitudes manifest the philosophical thought system of the group from which the individual comes. The philosophical thought system itself is a product of various factors including history, folklore, mythology, culture, norms, values, and religious beliefs. . . .

COMPETITIVE ADVANTAGES FROM *UBUNTU*

Ubuntu can be defined as humaneness—a pervasive spirit of caring and community, harmony and hospitality, respect and responsiveness—that individuals and groups display for one another. *Ubuntu* is the foundation for the basic values that manifest themselves in the ways African people think and behave toward each other and everyone else they encounter. One of the most important attributes of *ubuntu* is the high degree of harmony and continuity throughout the system. Unfortunately, with all the talk about *ubuntu,* the philosophy has not been fully embraced in the workplace since its strategic advantages are not fully appreciated by managers. Traditional management systems are guided by misapplied economic assumptions about human nature: that self-interest is the ultimate determinant of behavior, and it is maximized when employees earn as much as possible from contributing as little as possible. The focus in this article will be on the various aspects of *ubuntu* as they relate to relationships with others, language, decision making, attitudes toward time, productivity and efficiency, leadership and age, and belief systems. These will each be discussed in turn, with implications for competitive advantage. (See Table 1.)

RELATIONSHIPS WITH OTHERS

An organizing concept of *ubuntu* is human interdependence. The driving norms are reciprocity, suppression of self-interest, and the virtue of symbiosis. Hence it is often repeated that *umntu ngumntu ngabanye* [a person is a person through others]. This statement conveys the notion that

---

Excerpted from *The Academy of Management Executive* 15, no. 3 (August 2001): 23–33. Copyright © 2001 Academy of Management Executive. Reprinted with permission.

Table 1

Competitive Advantages from *Ubuntu*

Assumptions about	*Ubuntu*	Competitive advantages
Relationships with others	Relationships are reciprocal vs. instrumental. Treat other as your brother/sister. Individual predicated upon belonging to collective. "I belong, therefore I am."* Extended family is important.	People are intrinsically motivated to contribute more when they are valued members. Mutual respect and empathy are *ubuntu* advantages.
Language and communication	Oral tradition. To name is to create. Meaning of words strongly related to context. Poetic expression and ability to play with words are signs of wisdom.	Shared understanding of deeper meanings supports complex consensus. *Ubuntu* communication means concerted action that is adaptable.
Decisionmaking	Decisions by consensus. Dissenters compensated for. Process is circular. Polyocular vision. Dispute resolution to restore harmony.	*Ubuntu* might be slow to action, but greater commitment to goals means more long-run effectiveness and efficiency.
Time	Not a finite commodity, it is the healer, allow enough of it for important issues before arriving at a decision.	Punctuality is a virtue, but time's healing dimension is a hidden competitive advantage for *ubuntu.*
Productivity	Must be optimized. Solidarity, social harmony important. Rewards are shared, so is suffering.	Sustainable competitive advantage comes from strong loyalty to group goals in *ubuntu.*
Age and leadership	Age is an ongoing process of maturing and acquiring wisdom. Older people are respected. Gray hair is a sign of wisdom.	Older workers bring experience, wisdom, connections, informal networks. Competitive advantage from *ubuntu.*
Belief systems	Belief in the Creator, *uNkulunkulu,* and the existence of the *mesocosmos.* The mediating role of the *isangoma.* Christianity is now prevalent.	Spirituality brings out the best qualities in humans. *Ubuntu* has the edge.

Source: Hampden-Turner, C., and Trompenaars, A. 1993. *The Seven Cultures of Capitalism.* New York: Currency/Doubleday.

a person becomes a person only through his/her relationship with and recognition by others. This recognition has far-reaching implications for day-to-day interactions among people and for an individual's status in society.

The preeminence of the collective can be observed more closely in the extended family as a unit of organization. Here the emphasis is on the unity of the whole rather than the distinction of the parts. This holistic approach is supported by an ideology that reveres the concentric linkages of individual to family, to extended family, to clan, to village, and ultimately to the entire community. The individual is a member not just of the nuclear family, but also of the extended family or clan. This has often presented problems to companies that offer paid leave of absence for the death of immediate family members. A white manager of a large multinational corporation once alleged that an employee was being dishonest when he requested a few days off for the death of his father. Company records indicated that, two years before, the same employee had already taken three days' paid leave for the death of his father. In the Western understanding, an uncle is not considered to be a father. However, under *ubuntu,* he is. If your mother has an older and a younger sister, then you have three mothers: a mother, an older mother, and a younger mother. Kinship ties also play an important part in hiring. Modern organizations usually frown on the hiring of relatives because of the negative stereotypes associated with nepotism. However, the opposite is true under *ubuntu,* which considers kinship ties within the organization to be a plus. After all, who can be trusted more than one's own relatives? Kinship is also formed with people who graduated from the same school, and with people whose origins can be traced to the same home town or village, commonly known as the "homeys." The presence of these kinship ties in the workplace provides a layer of emotional and psychological support to workers.

An equally important aspect of relationships with others is teamwork. The solidarity spirit of *ubuntu* simultaneously supports cooperation and competitiveness by allowing individuals to contribute their best efforts for the betterment of the entire team. Everyone understands that together the team can accomplish more than if each individual worked alone. The notion of synergy, i.e., the creation of a whole that is larger than the sum of the individual parts, is an integral part of *ubuntu.* Organizations can ensure that individuals continue to uphold this spirit, by linking their reward systems to team performance.

The similarities between *ubuntu* and its related social traditions and some of the recent writings on management theory are striking. For example, recent research in leadership uses the word "fusion" to characterize a style of management that achieves a sense of unity. Fusion offers a view of others as part of the same whole, recognition of similarities rather than differences, and an identification of common ground and a sense of community with shared vision, norms, and outcomes. This may sound revolutionary to classically trained managers who emphasize individuality, competition, and control. In the context of *ubuntu,* fusion is merely the recognition of social reality and traditional relationship patterns.

Two imperatives can be delineated from the foregoing. First, it is important to treat others as members of one's own family, i.e., with kindness, compassion, and humility. Such a cordial regard will likely engender respect, deference, and compliance from those with whom a manager works. This is strikingly similar to Chester Barnard's notion that authority resides with those to whom it is directed. If people sense that they are being treated with respect and dignity, they will respond by showing greater commitment to organizational goals. Second, it is important to recognize and acknowledge the significance of kinship ties in the workplace. If kinship ties result in harmony and commitment to the workplace, then companies ought to consider it positively in their hiring decisions. Whenever practical, these relationships should be taken into account in formulating company policies such as recruitment, placement, promotion, transfer, reward, discipline, and even retirement. In the new millennium, it is those organizations that can match their corporate strategies, policies, and procedures with the values and beliefs of local communities that will enjoy sustainable competitive advantage.

LANGUAGE AND COMMUNICATION

Communication is to the organization as blood is to the body. However, major ontological differences exist in communication between the linguistic world of the African and that of the Westerner. In the African milieu, children are socialized from birth to listen to the context and nuances of language in conversation. The importance of language in establishing a sense of community, belonging, shared heritage, and common welfare is emphasized. Words are woven in dense fabrics of association that may be unwittingly activated by mere mention. The pervasive axiom is that to talk and to name is to create experience, to construct reality. Until the middle of the 19th century, it was through oral tradition that African folk proverbs, ballads, legends, and mythology were sustained and kept alive, rather than through written history. These intergenerationally transmitted stories formed the bedrock of reason, wisdom, and morality. A mastery of the art and skill of oratory is still a prerequisite for leadership. This becomes even more so during celebrations when skillful orators take center stage with their poetry and praise singing.

Traditional management training places greater emphasis on the efficiency of information transfer. Ideas must be translated quickly and accurately into words, the medium of the exchange must be appropriate, and the receiver must accurately understand the message. In the *ubuntu* context, however, the social effect of conversation is emphasized, with primacy given to establishing and reinforcing relationships. Unity and understanding among affected group members are valued above efficiency and accuracy of language. A premium is placed on personal rapport, i.e., the general sense of what is being said, which can easily get lost in translation. That is why it is encouraging to see that many white South Africans are learning to speak African languages as an important means of understanding the indigenous culture and patterns of interaction.

In many organizations, work is divided into individually structured jobs and tasks, with performance evaluation and accountability being directed at the individual. This is consistent with the ideas of Frederick Taylor at the beginning of the last century, and Adam Smith before him. Concerned more with efficiency than with healthy relationships, supervisors may discourage conversation and other forms of socializing in the workplace. What they fail to recognize is that this creates tension among employees and produces social distance between them. Needless to say, this contradicts the core values of *ubuntu*. Isolation results in a psychic conflict in the worker's mind, which eventually manifests itself in lowered morale, reduced productivity, and an environment that impedes the realization of the worker's full potential.

One way to break this psychological impasse is to periodically hold company-sponsored events and ceremonies. Ceremonies are commonplace in many cultures for punctuating major accomplishments. *Ubuntu* boasts an extremely rich repertoire of rituals and attending forms of music and singing, dance, and the eloquent verbal expressions of praise singers. Western-style year-end socials, and celebrations of important anniversaries of service with the company conveniently satisfy the need for ceremony. Many companies hold ceremonies to celebrate people with 10, 15, 20, and 25 years of service with the company. *Ubuntu*-style ceremonies can also be witnessed in trailblazing American companies such as Southwest Airlines. These practices are fun while at the same time promoting a sense of trust and belonging, which supports the basic human values in *ubuntu*. It is not surprising, therefore, that employees of companies like Southwest Airlines exhibit a great degree of loyalty to their company.

Even at work, people enjoy interacting with each other. Work environments where appropriate interaction is discouraged may lead to dysfunctional behaviors and ultimately to an alienated workforce. Allowing workers to establish relationships, even when not required by the task structure, improves effectiveness and decreases antagonistic feelings toward the organization. Above all, a periodic celebration of the milestones accomplished goes a long way in building a sense of belonging and commitment to organizational goals and objectives. Here again, the culture of *ubuntu* can provide sustenance. *Ubuntu* is about what people value and what they aspire to be. Peter Drucker notes that organizational effectiveness results when both individual and organizational needs are harmonized. Organizations that provide an opportunity for their employees to give expression to their values and beliefs in the course of carrying out their corporate responsibilities are likely to gain competitive advantage over those that do not. The lesson here: Provide opportunities for self-expression, achievement, and self-fulfillment, consistent with employee values.

DECISION MAKING

Decision-making processes followed under *ubuntu* differ markedly from those found in classical management textbooks where decision making is defined as the conscious choice of a course of action from available alternatives. The textbook process is linear: problem definition, determination of causes of the problem, generation of alternate solutions, choice of the best solution, implementation of the decision. Speed to closure is taken to be meritorious. Vision is usually monocular because unity of vision is idealized. Under *ubuntu* the decision-making process is a circular, inclusive one, proceeding at a deliberate speed, and often given to deviations in order to delve into other matters, however remotely related to the issue at hand. Vision tends to be polyocular. In other words, those who look at issues from different angles are seen as interesting and as providing valuable insights. Diversity of vision is not only permitted but also protected and encouraged. Before closure, considerable time is allowed to assure that all voices have been heard, and that a consensus has been reached. The goal of decision making in this context is to preserve harmony and achieve consensus. A decision that is supported is considered superior to the "right" decision that is resented or resisted by many. Unity is more valued than the utility of the decision reached.

Nowhere are these differences better demonstrated than in the way negotiations were conducted between the white South African government and the various black political movements during the CODESA (Convention for a Democratic South Africa) talks held near Johannesburg in the early 1990s. Although they outnumbered the government representatives by far, not once did the ANC-led national liberation organizations call for a vote on any of the critical decisions. Major decisions were made by consensus, often after a lot of behind-the-scenes discussions to bring other parties into agreement. These talks resulted in the formation of a Government of National Unity, which went on to govern the country peacefully for the next five years.

The success of the CODESA experience is not to suggest that decision making by majority has no place. However, because of the large base of support it enjoys, a solution based on African *ubuntu*-style consensus decision making will usually be more successful at the implementation stage. Equally important is that the new spirit of democracy that is prevailing around the world today requires that management be willing to negotiate with workers. Prior to the recognition of labor unions during the years of apartheid, management had been reluctant to enter into collective bargaining with employee representatives for fear of eroding their power. The reality that they found once they entered into negotiation with workers surprised them. They found employees not only willing to find the middle ground, but, as an executive of a large corporation in KwaZulu-Natal once noted, "Blacks have taken to negotiation as ducks take to water." He had just discovered something he should have known long ago, that negotiation is an intrinsic component of *ubuntu*.

The distinctions between the classical management and *ubuntu* decision approaches suggest that paying heed to the latter will result in more effective implementation. By imposing control over employees and limiting their involvement, the classical management approach often leads to ineffective organizational outcomes and dysfunctional behaviors in the workplace. Consensus-based decision making, although initially costly in terms of time and effort, is more likely to result in improved commitment to organizational goals. The results will be seen in reduced supervisory requirements, decreased turnover and absenteeism, and increased efficiency.

TIME

Differences in attitudes toward time often present a problem when people conduct business across cultures. For instance, researchers in sociolinguistics have demonstrated that there is a level of discomfort in the different ways that Western and African cultures interpret pauses and silences during conversations. The discussion here refers mostly to how the available time is allocated. Westerners are inclined to fill the pauses with words; Africans appreciate periodic gaps of silence within a conversation.

A case in point involves a sales representative who had secured an hour-long appointment with a Zulu customer at her home near Stanger in Kwa Zulu-Natal. When the salesperson arrived punctually, he was upset that his host was not ready. It took a while before the host finally came out to meet him and begin the scheduled discussion. The salesman found out later that, in the Zulu culture, when you have an appointment at someone's home, it means he/she has control over what happens in that time period. By agreeing to meet at the home of the client, the salesperson was tacitly agreeing that it was up to his host how she would prioritize her time between family activities and business discussion.

Unlike the classical management context in which time is a strategic commodity to be prudently used, in the *ubuntu* context it is treated as a healer. Time is not a commodity to be frugally consumed, a tool to be carefully utilized, or a regulator to be dutifully observed. Instead, it is a reference that locates communities with respect to their collective past and shared future; it assigns significance to patterns of events; and it orders relationships and affairs. Time is not an independent quantity that can be divided into ever-smaller units; it is a continuum that has meaning only as it is experienced. In the context of *ubuntu,* time is reflected as a unifying and integrating construct that emphasizes interdependence, shared heritage, regularity, and congruity. Furthermore, time is not experienced only in the present; it also heals past experiences and allows for reflection. The world saw this healing aspect in action in the truth and reconciliation hearings that were chaired by Archbishop Tutu, when the victims' relatives were told to "take your time" while giving testimony, often during prime-time TV. There is a saying: "God gave the African time, and the Westerner a watch."

Misunderstandings over time are often a source of friction in cross-cultural interactions. They arise not because of different priorities assigned to time commitments, but because of fundamentally different meanings attached to time. This is a difficult gulf to span because it requires adopting a different worldview, or at a minimum, accepting the validity and reasonableness of a different worldview. Modern people understand the merits of punctuality and deadlines, when it comes to the corporate context. But when Western timing conflicts with African timing (e.g., in task completion, healing, reconciliation), where expectations regarding speed to closure differ, traditional management may have something to learn. The Western concept of time management will be ineffective at best, and dysfunctional at worst, if it is carelessly pitted against the African conception of time.

PRODUCTIVITY AND EFFICIENCY

Efficiency—the ratio of output value to input cost—is assumed to be a critical determinant of organizational viability. Maximizing efficiency is the *sine qua non* of traditional management theory. In the *ubuntu* context, on the other hand, the emphasis is on social well-being rather than on technical rationality. The objective is to optimize efficiency rather than to maximize it, and that allows higher priority for peaceful and harmonious relationships. In this context, an optimized solution is one that leads to the most favored outcome by a much wider group of stakeholders in the long run. In the short run, this will yield lower efficiencies than the maximized solution. Attempts to maximize efficiency often incur the cost of fractured relationships, and social disruption can have unintended consequences.

Traditional training often emphasizes "denominator management." A cutback in the number of employees is a means to increased productivity. Under *ubuntu,* the numerator and denominator in the productivity equation cannot be seen as independent variables. Employee layoffs (denominator reduction) would have a significant negative impact on output, likely resulting in reduced, not increased, productivity. This is especially so when a highly valued "output" is employee well-being and community. Multinational corporations often resort to between-country productivity comparisons and overlook the national contexts of the countries being compared. In most multinational corporations, it is commonplace to hear comparisons between headquarters operations and those of overseas subsidiaries. In those comparisons the subsidiary's production lines often come across as overmanned, implying that some of the "extra" workers should be removed from the line (eventually to be laid off). Workers in the West might accept the rationale behind the decision to downsize, even though many would struggle to understand its logic when the top management of the same companies receive hefty pay raises. Under *ubuntu,* such an action would constitute a direct affront to the norm of fairness. Believers in *ubuntu* trust that humans take care of each other, and violating that trust runs the risk of alienating the entire workforce and might result in a decrease in productivity as well as other disruptions. In a culture that is high on collectivism, *ubuntu* dictates the sharing of burdens during hard times because, in so doing, the suffering is diminished. In that sense, across-the-board pay reductions would be much preferred to targeted layoffs. A good example comes from a recently reported case. A company had initiated a program for building immaculate three-bedroom, carpeted houses for its black workers in one of the South African black townships. But the CEO was surprised when he learned that the employees would have preferred the money be used instead to upgrade a greater number of existing dwellings, so that more of the company's employees could benefit.

The unfortunate legacy of apartheid is that it systematically discriminated against blacks to the point that they are now grossly underrepresented in the key decision-making positions in many organizations. A recent report on employment equity in South Africa indicated that, although African males constituted 39 percent of the workforce, they made up 10 percent of management. By contrast, white males, who constituted 13 percent of the workforce, made up 52 percent of management. Corresponding figures for females would probably indicate even wider disparities. Thus there is an urgent need to identify, attract, recruit, and promote capable blacks into management positions.

This case demonstrates the dilemma facing managers of Western-based firms in developing countries such as South Africa. The performance criteria of the organization—productivity, efficiency, increased output—may be in direct conflict with the indigenous values of the country's people—solidarity, group well-being, social harmony. The two are not necessarily incompatible, and, if some consideration is given to protocols and proprieties, change can be introduced with minimal disruption. In fact, as with decision making, when properly communicated and deliberated, even the most difficult changes can be implemented effectively. The lesson can be summed up in the following way: blind application of traditional management notions of productivity and efficiency in the African context might unleash a number of complex problems. Attempts to increase efficiency without consideration of concomitant social impacts might end up actually reducing organizational productivity and efficiency at the same time. If important changes are to be introduced, this must be done using consultation and inclusive decision processes. Otherwise, implementation will be fraught with disruptions.

AGE AND SENIORITY IN LEADERSHIP

The context within which leadership choice and style operate is equally important to understand. In Africa, leadership is easier to accept from a more experienced (read, older) individual. This means that rarely would a younger person be comfortable leading a group of people he/she regards as his/her seniors. Equally, it would be awkward for older employees to take instructions from a supervisor whom they perceived to be their junior. This would be particularly difficult in an environment with highly structured tasks, where compliance is expected without question and the leader is required to be more directive. Such a requirement goes against the grain of African culture, particularly if carried out by a junior (younger) member of the community. The following example illustrates the point.

One senior manager at a major industrial firm in South Africa reported that, when the company initiated a black advancement program, the first blacks promoted to supervisory positions were young men (20–24 years old) who had performed very well. The workers of the group these men were assigned to supervise refused to work for them. When senior managers probed, they found that, within the culture of workers, older men do not work for those "youngsters." Management then revised their promotion criteria to include age as well as capability.

Sometimes the "professionalism" displayed by young, Western-trained managers is misinterpreted and resented by other employees, as in the case of an African manager who was summoned before his family elders because he did not treat the workers as brothers and sisters but as employees. An older person might not necessarily possess all the expertise for the task at hand, but through wisdom, vision, and ability to maintain harmonious working relations, he/she can get others to perform well.

The role of the leader is to show by example, yet the best operatives often do not become the best managers. The manager's job is to get things done through others, to integrate the various factors that contribute to organizational effectiveness. The manager in an African work environment must have the appropriate balance between the demand for technical competence and social savvy. This approach to managing is gaining acceptance in more contemporary management thinking. More successful managers are seen to act as coaches, cheerleaders, and "nurturers of champions," rather than as cops, experts, and naysayers. The lesson is that, in the African thought system, age is regarded as an ongoing process of maturing and acquiring wisdom. Gray hairs are respected. Organizations that understand this difference in their selection and promotion of people into leadership positions are bound to have competitive advantage over organizations that do not.

All things being equal, in choosing someone for a leadership position from among equally qualified employees, the *ubuntu* ethos would tip the scales in favor of the candidate with more seniority in terms of either chronological age, service to the company, or experience in the position. The corollary is that the more junior employee will get his/her turn in the future. The Nguni idiom, "*Zisina zidedelana*," signifies that in a dance everyone will eventually get his/her turn on center stage. Criteria for selecting employees into leadership positions must not be limited to demonstrated mastery of technical skills. Age must be taken into account as an asset, not as a liability associated with senility. After all, older workers do have wisdom, experience, and strong informal networks. They can use these characteristics to the company's competitive advantage. Often *ubuntu* has it right, and the West misses the point.

BELIEF SYSTEMS

Christianity is the dominant faith for most South Africans, including over 90 percent of the African population. But prior to the arrival of Christian missionaries, indigenous people believed in the existence of the omnipotent, the creator, whom they called *uQamata, uNkulunkulu,* or *Modimo.* But not everyone could communicate with the creator, only those with special qualities. It is also believed that people who die join the ancestors in the *mesocosmos* to become mediators to the Creator on behalf of the living. Among the living are those who are anointed with special gifts of being able to communicate with the *mesocosmos.* It is from this ability that the *isangoma* or the traditional healer derives his/her power of healing and seeing things that other humans cannot. Hence when there is a medical problem, it is not uncommon, especially for rural Africans, to consult an *isangoma.* Although over 80 percent of the black labor force consult the *isangoma,* company managers have tended to downplay their centrality, or ridicule their involvement in their employees' health maintenance. Other companies have taken full advantage of the power of the *isangoma* as the following real-life case illustrates.

Faced with large-scale pilfering, one company tried everything—including peer monitors, fingerprinting, and police investigations—to stop it. After all efforts to stop the pilfering had failed, the CEO finally called in an *isangoma.* The *isangoma* told the employees that the person who had stolen the goods would die from a spell cast on all employees if he/she did not confess within 24 hours. Within eight hours, an employee confessed.

In this case, foreign-evolved management tactics, such as peer control, police investigations, and fingerprinting, did not work. Here we see that management and the workers came from entirely different worldviews. The successful strategy engaged employees in their own worldview. In general, if a large proportion of the workforce believes in the existence of *mesocosmic* spirits, why not formally retain the services of a company *isangoma?* This would result in mutually beneficial outcomes for both the company and its employees (and the *isangoma*). Of course, it would be necessary to orient the *isangoma* in the company's vision and mission for him/her to have sufficient appreciation of the symbiotic relationship between community values and the continued viability and competitiveness of the company. He/she would not just finger-point wrongdoers, but could also suggest appropriate remedial action that would accommodate both worldviews. After all, companies do hire company lawyers, company public relations officers, and consultants to solve ad hoc problems as they arise. The concurrent belief in the *mesocosmos* and the role of the *isangoma* makes him/her a key player in the process of mediation and arbitration.

The importance of *ubuntu* is clear. South Africa—and the world—consists of an array of peoples with diverse cultures and traditions, woven together in a colorful fabric of folklore. Until recently, Western norms were accepted as the *modus operandi* in business. But other traditions are increasingly gaining commonplace acceptance, for example the *isangoma* in the above case. The best strategic posture for companies is flexibility and willingness to learn from local cultures. Successful companies will treat each cultural exigency with caution, care, and understanding. Flexibility and accommodation will go a long way toward creating an atmosphere of mutual respect and an increased sense of company identity among employees. Companies that stick rigidly to the traditional Western management value system should be prepared to face major disruptions like the work stoppage discussed above.

IMPLICATIONS FOR MANAGEMENT

Before discussing the implications of *ubuntu* in South Africa, it is important to offer some disclaimers. The first is a caution against wholesale acceptance of all African customs and practices.

Several customs and practices carried out in the name of *ubuntu* are based on erroneous superstitions. Such practices can be oppressive and sexist, and often stifle individual aspirations and progress. In the contemporary African milieu, the conventional wisdom is that customs will only be endorsed to the extent that they serve the common good. Otherwise, they will be challenged and changed.

Another caution is against the assumption that culture is static and that there is a one-way causal relationship between culture and behavior. Changing behaviors also causes changes in culture through feedback and reinforcement over time. Differences between the behaviors of younger and older generations contribute to the generation gap. Also, through years of contact with non-African cultures, the majority population has adapted the principles of *ubuntu*. There are differences between the cultural practices of urban and rural people, between college-educated and semiliterate people, and between migrant workers and middle-class people. In general, *ubuntu* helps in affirming universal human values, like humaneness, dignity, empathy, and compassion for others.

What are the management implications of *ubuntu* in the transformation process now taking place in South Africa? To start off, foreign and local white-controlled companies must be willing to work in partnership with indigenous people, with the understanding that they will listen to and learn from them. There have been several cases of successful collaborations. One example is the partnership between the giant American advertising company, McCann-Erickson, and the South African black company, HerdBuoys, to form HerdBuoys McCann-Erickson. McCann-Erickson contributes to the partnership its years of experience in advertising around the world, and HerdBuoys contributes its intimate knowledge of the South African market, and the marketing savvy of its founder, Peter Vundla. The result is a dynamic company that has risen from 14th to the top five in South Africa. Another example is the joint venture formed by American Express and the black company, PulaNala, in the travel and tourism industry. As a result of this partnership, American Express has become highly responsive to shifts in the travel industry. According to CEO Mike Mohohlo, the relationship benefits PulaNala through the transfer of business skills and the accelerated development of personnel into areas of executive responsibility. To sum up, *ubuntu* is an important legacy from South Africa that can be parlayed into the practice of management for competitive advantage.

GUIDELINES FOR IMPLEMENTING *UBUNTU*

Several South African companies have begun to embrace the guidelines of *ubuntu* and to introduce them in their corporate practice with notable success. Also, more writings are coming forth from authors giving advice ranging from corporate governance to marketing. Some guidelines for helping managers in the process of incorporating the philosophy of *ubuntu* in their organizations are discussed next. Though not exhaustive, the guidelines are meant to provide a good starting point for managers wishing to incorporate the principles of *ubuntu* in their organizations.

- *Treat others with dignity and respect.* This is a cardinal point of *ubuntu*. Everything hinges on this canon, including an emphasis on humility, harmony, and valuing diversity. Helpfulness toward others creates an environment of collegiality based on caring and sharing. After all, who would not like to be appreciated, valued, and respected for their contributions for what they bring to the workplace?
- *Be willing to negotiate in good faith.* Take time to listen with empathy, especially in conflict resolution. Being listened to is tantamount to being acknowledged. In *ubuntu*, being

acknowledged is a very important first step toward agreement and cooperation. Transparency and trust replace suspicion and hostility.

- *Provide opportunities for self-expression.* Honoring achievement, self-fulfillment, and affirmation of values are all important aspects of creating goodwill among employees. Periodic celebrations to punctuate achievement are one way to fulfill this need.
- *Understand the beliefs and practices of indigenous people.* Carefully incorporate into standard corporate policies the indigenous practices and beliefs discussed above. If employing people who are relatives has been successful, use it. Learn more about the belief systems that employees subscribe to. Engaging them in their own belief system will go a long way toward ensuring employee self-fulfillment and thus smooth-running operations.
- *Honor seniority, especially in leadership choices.* All things being equal, seniority adds value through experience, connections, and the wisdom that older employees have from their record of past experiences.
- *Promote equity in the workplace.* Fairness is a value that is upheld in most cultures. But it takes a special significance in countries such as South Africa, where there has been a history of sociopolitical inequities. Recruiting and promoting into senior management ranks qualified individuals from previously disadvantaged groups, i.e., blacks and women, is essential. This is not reverse discrimination. There is no room for discriminatory practices in the *ubuntu* philosophy.
- *Be flexible and accommodative.* Applying the recommendations above will require a careful balancing act by management between the imperatives of *ubuntu* and other tried and tested management principles. A carefully balanced blending, with flexibility and accommodation, holds the promise of greater value added to corporate performance. . . .

10.4 MATCHING MANAGEMENT PRACTICES TO NATIONAL CULTURE IN INDIA, MEXICO, POLAND, AND THE U.S.
Marc C. Marchese

Should multinational corporations opt for consistent management practices across national borders, or should they employ culturally specific management techniques? If a management approach works well in the United States, is it safe to assume it will work in other countries?

In a study of management practices in India, Mexico, Poland, and the United States, researchers Christopher Robert, of the University of Missouri at Columbia; Tahira Probst, of Washington State University at Vancouver; and Joseph Martocchio, Fritz Drasgow, and John Lawler, of the University of Illinois at Urbana-Champaign, examined important aspects of the relationship between culture and management practices. Their underlying question was whether management practices should be considered in the context of a particular cultural environment, an approach they refer to as practice-culture fit.

The researchers believe that two management practices, empowerment and continuous improvement, may be particularly sensitive to practice-culture fit. Empowerment is the process by which employees are given significant amounts of autonomy regarding their work. Empowered employees have discretion in how they handle work assignments. They also have considerable authority to make decisions concerning their jobs.

Since empowerment implies the sharing of authority, the researchers expected that this management practice would be better received in cultures that embrace equality between individuals. Power distance, or the degree to which people accept and expect differences in authority, is a distinct cultural dimension. In high-power-distance cultures, inequalities in authority are common and well accepted. In contrast, low-power-distance cultures are defined by a belief that power should be shared or at least attainable by all. In low-power-distance cultures, anyone who works hard, works well, and has the right experiences should be able to increase his or her power. Thus the researchers expected to find the fit between empowerment and power distance to be best in low-power-distance cultures.

Robert and his colleagues also examined practice-culture fit between continuous improvement and the cultural dimension of individualism/collectivism. In organizations that practice continuous improvement, employees are regularly engaged in training and development activities to increase their work competencies. Continuous improvement practices encourage employees to take the initiative to improve their skills.

Since continuous improvement is centered on employees' improving themselves, it was expected that this management practice would be a better fit in individualistic, rather than collectivist, cultures. In individualistic cultures, people value individual accomplishments. Personal goals are typically placed ahead of group goals. In contrast, in collectivist cultures, people's identities tend to be based on social-group membership rather than personal achievements. The group's goals have higher priority than individual goals.

To examine the influence of practice-culture fit, outcomes associated with management practices were included in the study. Those outcomes included satisfaction with coworkers, supervisors,

---

From *The Academy of Management Executive* 15, no. 2 (May 2001): 130–132. Copyright © 2001 Academy of Management Executive. Reprinted with permission.

and the work itself, commitment to the organization, work withdrawal (e.g., being late often, taking long lunches, taking frequent breaks), and intention to leave the company.

The data for the study were collected from employees of a U.S.-based multinational company specializing in light manufacturing. Of the company's 40 plants worldwide, four comparable plants were chosen: one in the midwestern U.S., one in central Mexico, one in west-central India, and one in southern Poland. Prior research has generally established that the U.S. is highly individualistic and scores low in power distance. India, a hierarchical society, is considered to be high in power distance and collectivism. Mexico also is considered to be a collectivist, high-power-distance country, and Poland is considered to be moderately individualistic and somewhat higher in power distance.

In terms of overall findings, the management practices of empowerment and continuous improvement were shown to have numerous desirable consequences for organizations. Empowerment was positively related to employees' satisfaction with their supervisors. Supervisors who gave employees freedom to do their work were viewed very favorably. Continuous improvement showed strong positive associations to satisfaction with coworkers as well as satisfaction with the work itself. In general, allowing employees opportunities for self-improvement was often related to positive opinions of both their work and coworkers.

The outcomes associated with empowerment were quite different across the countries. Employees in the U.S., Mexico, and Poland had favorable views of their supervisors when empowerment was high, whereas Indian employees rated their supervisors low when empowerment was high. Satisfaction with coworkers was positively related to empowerment practices in Poland, but in India, empowerment was shown to have a negative impact on coworker satisfaction. In the U.S. and Mexico, empowerment was unrelated to coworker satisfaction.

A very different picture emerged with continuous improvement, which was related to high levels of satisfaction with coworkers and with the work itself for all four countries. No negative findings were associated with continuous improvement in any of the countries.

Taken as a whole, the results suggest that multinational firms may wish to consider the cultural context of the management practices they employ. The very negative reaction of the Indian employees to empowerment practices underscores the potential for U.S. management practices to cause more harm than good when they are exported to other cultures. Yet the study also suggests that assumptions regarding practice-culture fit may not yield accurate assessments of appropriate management practices. Theoretically, differences in individualism/collectivism should have influenced outcomes associated with continuous improvement. The researchers expected to find low levels of satisfaction with continuous improvement practices in Mexico, India, and Poland, which are collectivist cultures, and high levels of satisfaction in the U.S., a strongly individualistic culture. However, they found no differences at all among the four countries, suggesting that continuous improvement may not be as sensitive to cultural differences as other management practices, such as empowerment.

Moreover, defining cultures through the use of broad behavioral dimensions may not adequately capture national differences. For instance, Robert and his colleagues point to the inadequacy of the individualism/collectivism dimension to accurately predict employee attitudes toward continuous improvement practices. They suggest that continuous improvement practices may be popular in both individualistic and collectivist cultures, but for quite different reasons. It may be that individuals in collectivist cultures do not identify with their organizations as relevant social groups. Alternatively, in some national contexts, such as India, self-improvement through training or other continuous improvement activities may provide opportunities for individuals to better support their families or social groups.

Therefore, organizations may be better off considering the local organizational culture of each location rather than the larger societal culture when deciding how to manage employees. It is possible that the organization's staffing process may produce a workforce whose values, beliefs, and expectations differ from those of the surrounding community. In addition, political upheaval in various countries (e.g., Poland, Russia) may make it difficult to get an accurate or stable assessment of a given national culture. A facility-by-facility cultural audit may be the most effective course to determine practice-culture fit.

[Referenced article:] C. Robert, T.M. Probst, J.J. Martocchio, F. Drasgow, and J.J. Lawler. 2000. "Empowerment and Continuous Improvement in the United States, Mexico, Poland, and India: Predicting Fit on the Basis of the Dimensions of Power Distance and Individualism." *Journal of Applied Psychology* 85: 643–658.

PART IV

DOING BUSINESS TOGETHER

SECTION 11. THE MULTICULTURAL WORKPLACE

Citizens of many countries need not leave their homelands to interact with people from other cultures. The U.S. and Canada are particularly rich in a diversity of cultures. These cultures can add a richness of different ways of thinking and interacting, but they also pose challenges for meeting the needs of every individual in the workplace and bringing out the best in him or her. Immigrants show resilience and resourcefulness in establishing themselves in their new countries. "Immigration Blues" depicts marriages of convenience among Filipinos wanting to remain in the U.S. This story could well apply to people of many nationalities who go to great lengths to have a chance at the American Dream.

"Señor Payroll" is an amusing look at Mexican workers who give their American bosses a run for their money by cleverly getting around various policies intended to curb their habit of requesting cash advances.

"No One to Yell At" brings more of the old world to the new. A Turkish immigrant to Canada, frustrated that women employees would rather quit than fetch him coffee, fondly recalls that his employees back in Turkey "knew how to be errand boy and clerk" and that he "knew how to be boss." He finds a way to get the type of respect he needs.

SECTION 12. CUSTOMER SERVICE

Providing good customer service is essential in today's highly competitive business environment. However, in some parts of the globe, such as in countries transitioning from centrally planned to market-based economies, the concept of customer service has been virtually nonexistent. "A New Customer" is a satirical look at the abysmal way that customers were typically treated in Russia under the old system. A diner, not wanting to disturb the waiter who preferred not to serve him, makes a meal for himself: "The people who were at this table before me left some bread, there is mustard. What else does one need?"

"A Brief History of Capitalism" is a sobering look at a tense interaction between an auto mechanic and an abusive wealthy customer in Brazil. While the mechanic feverishly tries to repair his expensive car, the angry customer curses at him and criticizes his skills and work ethic: "In this country that's the way it is. Nobody wants to do any work, nobody wants to get his act together."

229

SECTION 13. TEAMS AND ALLIANCES

Much of the work in organizations is done in teams rather than individually, and organizations themselves form alliances with others to cut costs, share resources, penetrate new markets, and the like. Many of these teams have international members, and organizations form alliances with others from different countries. The stories in this section depict teams and alliances in various parts of the world.

In the satire "Mister Taylor," Bostonian Percy Taylor arrives penniless in the Amazon in 1944. By chance he stumbles on the macabre opportunity to export shrunken heads to America at a great profit. To keep up with demand and continue making profits, he and his South American Indian suppliers resort to extreme measures, including starting a war with other tribes. "This was progress," yet it couldn't last. "And everyone felt as if they had awakened from a pleasant dream . . . and . . . when you wake up, you look for it and find emptiness."

"The Zulu and the Zeide" is a touching description of an unlikely alliance between a young Zulu man and the zeide, or grandfather, whom he was assigned to care for. "Paulus knew only Zulu, the old man knew only Yiddish, so there was no language in which they could talk to one another. But they talked all the same: they both explained, commented and complained to each other of the things they saw around them, and often they agreed with one another, smiling and nodding their heads and explaining again with their hands what each happened to be talking about." The old man's son was filled with wonder and envy at the bond the two formed with each other.

Competition among teams can be heated in both business and sports. In "Only Approved Indians Can Play: Made in USA," the eligibility of players in an All-Indian basketball tournament was questioned when their team was coming on strong: "The Tucson players were mostly very dark young men with long black hair. A few had little goatee beards or mustaches though, and one of the Great Lakes fans had started a rumor that they were really Chicanos." Various rationales and criteria are offered for deciding whether players met the criteria of one-quarter or more Indian blood to be eligible to play.

SECTION 14. MANAGERIAL INSIGHTS

"Foreign Knowledge Workers as a Strategic Staffing Option" addresses the controversial policy of granting temporary employment visas in the United States to foreign professional workers. The article examines the various types of visas that are offered, discusses how hiring foreign workers can fit into a firm's strategy, and offers advice to managers at various levels in helping foreign workers adapt effectively and perform their assignments well. The article can be read with the stories "Immigration Blues," "Señor Payroll," and "No One to Yell At" to discuss the multifaceted aspects of hiring workers from abroad.

"Four Seasons Goes to Paris" is an inspiring account of how the Canadian-owned Four Seasons hotel chain inculcated a first-rate customer-service culture in its new hotel in Paris. In what could have been a contentious and resistant confrontation with employees and unions, the management successfully instilled the company's values and standards in the new location while being flexible in adapting to French culture and work practices. The lessons could well be applied to the woeful customer service depicted in "A New Customer" and "A Brief History of Capitalism." With thousands of small businesses in the service sector in the former Soviet Union and Eastern Europe having been privatized in the past decade, improving customer service should be a high priority for owners who now must find ways to survive in a competitive environment.

"Keys to Effective Virtual Global Teams" offers advice on how to manage team members who are physically dispersed around the world and have limited face-to-face interactions. Such advice might have altered the long-distance relationship in "Mister Taylor" between Percy Taylor and his uncle, who were based on different continents while conducting their shrunken head business.

"Cultivating a Global Mindset" presents a framework for assessing the global mindset of individuals as well as organizations and differentiates a global mindset from parochial and diffused mindsets. The reading then outlines steps that companies and individuals can take to cultivate a global mindset, one that reflects awareness of diversity across cultures and markets as well as an ability to synthesize across that diversity. The mindsets of the characters in "Mister Taylor," "The Zulu and the Zeide," and "Only Approved Indians Can Play: Made in USA" can be analyzed using this framework and ways of developing global mindsets in such varied situations can be explored.

Section 11
————— The Multicultural Workplace —————

11.1 IMMIGRATION BLUES
Bienvenido Santos

Through the window curtain, Alipio saw two women, one seemed twice as large as the other. In their summer dresses, they looked like the country girls he knew back home in the Philippines, who went around peddling rice cakes. The slim one could have passed for his late wife Seniang's sister whom he remembered only in pictures because she never made it to the United States. Before Seniang's death, the couple had arranged for her coming to San Francisco, filling all the required petition papers to facilitate the approval of her visa. The sister was always "almost ready, all the papers have been signed," but she never showed up. His wife had been ailing and when she died, he thought that hearing of her death would hasten her coming, but the wire he had sent her was neither returned nor acknowledged.

The knocking on the door was gentle. A little hard of hearing, Alipio was not sure it was indeed a knocking on the door, but it sounded different from the little noises that sometimes hummed in his ears in the daytime. It was not yet noon, but it must be warm outside in all that sunshine, otherwise those two women would be wearing spring dresses at the least. There were summer days in San Francisco that were cold like winter in the Midwest.

He limped painfully to the door. Until last month, he wore crutches. The entire year before that, he was bed-ridden, but he had to force himself to walk about in the house after coming from the hospital. After Seniang's death, everything had gone to pieces. It was one bust after another, he complained to the few friends who came to visit him.

"Seniang was my good luck. When God decided to take her, I had nothing but bad luck," he said.

Not long after Seniang's death, he was in a car accident. For almost a year he was in the hospital. The doctors were not sure he was going to walk again. He told them it was God's wish. As it was he was thankful he was still alive. It had been a horrible accident.

The case dragged on in court. His lawyer didn't seem too good about car accidents. He was an expert immigration lawyer, but he was a friend. As it turned out, Alipio lost the full privileges and benefits coming to him in another two years if he had not been hospitalized and had continued working until his official retirement.

However, he was well provided. He didn't spend a cent for doctor and medicine and hospital bills. Now there was the prospect of a few thousand dollars compensation. After deducting his lawyer's fees it would still be something to live on. He had social security benefits and a partial retirement pension. Not too bad, really. Besides, now he could walk a little although he still limped and had to move about with extreme care.

When he opened the door, the fat woman said, "Mr. Palma? Alipio Palma?" Her intonation sounded like the beginning of a familiar song.

From *Scent of Apples: A Collection of Stories* (Seattle: University of Washington Press, 1979). Copyright © 1979 University of Washington Press. Reprinted with permission.

"Yes," he said. "Come in, come on in." He had not talked to anyone the whole week. His telephone had not rung all that time, not even a wrong number, and there was nobody he wanted to talk to. The little noises in his ears had somehow kept him company. Radio and television sounds lulled him to sleep.

The thin one was completely out of sight as she stood behind the big one who was doing the talking. "I'm sorry, I should have phoned you first, but we were in a hurry."

"The house is a mess," Alipio said truthfully. Had he been imagining things? He remembered seeing two women on the porch. There was another one, who looked like Seniang's sister. The woman said "we," and just then the other one materialized, close behind the big one, who walked in with the assurance of a social worker, about to do him a favor.

"Sit down. Sit down. Anywhere," Alipio said as he led the two women through the dining room, past a huge rectangular table in the center. It was bare except for a vase of plastic flowers as a centerpiece. He passed his hand over his face, a mannerism which Seniang hated. Like you have a hangover, she chided him, and you can't see straight.

A TV set stood close to a wall in the small living room crowded with an assortment of chairs and tables. An aquarium crowded the mantelpiece of a fake fireplace. A lighted bulb inside the tank showed many colored fish swimming about in a haze of fish food. Some of it lay scattered on the edge of the shelf. The carpet underneath was sodden black. Old magazines and tabloids lay just about everywhere.

"Sorry to bother you like this," the fat one said as she plunked herself down on the nearest chair, which sagged to the floor under her weight. The thin one chose the end of the sofa away from the TV set.

"I was just preparing my lunch. I know it's quite early, but I had nothing to do," Alipio said, pushing down with both hands the seat of the cushioned chair near a moveable partition, which separated the living room from the dining room. "It's painful just trying to sit down. I'm not too well yet," he added as he finally made it.

"I hope we're not really bothering you," the fat one said. The other had not said a word. She looked pale and sick. Maybe she was hungry or cold.

"How's it outside?" Alipio asked. "I've not been out all day." Whenever he felt like it, he dragged a chair to the porch and sat there, watching the construction going on across the street and smiling at the people passing by who happened to look his way. Some smiled back and mumbled something like a greeting or a comment on the beauty of the day. He stayed on until he got bored or it became colder than he could stand.

"It's fine. It's fine outside. Just like Baguio," the fat one said. "You know Baguio? I was born near there."

"We're sisters."

Alipio was thinking, won't the other one speak at all?

"I'm Mrs. Antonieta Zafra, the wife of Carlito. I believe you know him. He says you're friends. In Salinas back in the thirties. He used to be a cook at the Marina."

"Carlito, yes, yes, Carlito Zafra. We bummed together. We come from Ilocos. Where you from?"

"Aklan. My sister and I speak Cebuano."

"Oh, she speak? You, you don't speak Ilocano?"

"Not much. Carlito and I talk in English. Except when he's real mad, like when his cock don't fight or when he lose, then he speaks Ilocano. Cuss words. I've learned them myself. Some, anyway."

"Yes. Carlito. He love cockfighting. How's he?"

"Retired like you. We're now in Fresno. On a farm. He raises chickens and hogs. I do some sewing in town when I can. My sister here is Monica. She's older than me. Never been married."

Monica smiled at the old man, her face in anguish, as if near to tears.

"Carlito. He got some fighting cocks, I bet."

"Not anymore. But he talks a lot about cockfighting. But nobody, not even the pinoys and the Chicanos are interested in it." Mrs. Zafra appeared pleased at the state of things on her home front.

"I remember. Carlito once promoted a cockfight. Everything was ready, but the roosters won't fight. Poor man, he did everything to make them fight like having them peck on each other's necks and so forth. They were so tame, so friendly with each other. Only thing they didn't do is embrace." Alipio laughed, showing a set of perfectly white and even teeth, obviously dentures.

"He hasn't told me about that, I'll remind him."

"Do that. Where's he? Why isn't he with you?"

"We didn't know we'd find you. While visiting some friends this morning, we learned you live here." Mrs. Zafra was beaming on him.

"I've always lived here, but I got few friends now. So you're Mrs. Carlito. I thought he's dead already. I never hear from him. We're old now. We're old already when we got our citizenship papers right after Japanese surrender. So you and him. Good for Carlito."

"I heard about your accident."

"After Seniang died. She was not yet sixty, but she had this heart trouble. I took care of her." Alipio seemed to have forgotten his visitors. He sat there staring at the fish in the aquarium, his ears perked as though waiting for some sound, like the breaking of the surf not far away, or the TV set suddenly turned on.

The sisters looked at each other. Monica was fidgeting, her eyes seemed to say, let's go, let's get out of here.

"Did you hear that?" the old man said.

Monica turned to her sister, her eyes wild with panic. Mrs. Zafra leaned forward, her hand touching the edge of the chair where Alipio sat, and asked gently, "Hear what?"

"The waves. Listen. They're just outside, you know. The breakers have a nice sound like at home in the Philippines. We lived in a coastal town. Like here, I always tell Seniang, across that ocean is the Philippines, we're not far from home."

"But you're alone now. It's not good to be alone," Mrs. Zafra said.

"At night I hear better. I can see the Pacific Ocean from my bedroom. It sends me to sleep. I sleep soundly like I got no debts. I can sleep all day, too, but that's bad. So I walk. I walk much before. I go out there. I let the breakers touch me. It's nice the touch. Seniang always scold me, she says I'll be catching cold, but I don't catch cold, she catch the cold all the time."

"You must miss her," Mrs. Zafra said. Monica was staring at her hands on her lap while the sister talked. Monica's skin was transparent and the veins showed on the back of her hands like trapped eels.

"I take care of Seniang. I work all day and leave her here alone. When I come home, she's smiling. She's wearing my jacket and my slippers. You look funny, I says, why do you wear my things, you're lost inside them. She chuckles, you keep me warm all day, she says, like you're here, I smell you. Oh, that Seniang. You see, we have no baby. If we have a baby. . . ."

"I think you and Carlito have the same fate. We have no baby also."

"God dictates," Alipio said, making an effort to stand. In a miraculous surge of power, Monica rushed to him and helped him up. She seemed astonished and embarrassed at what she had done.

"Thank you," said Alipio. "I have crutches, but I don't want no crutches. They tickle me, they hurt me, too." He watched Monica go back to her seat.

"You need help better than crutches," Mrs. Zafra said.

"God helps," Alipio said, walking towards the kitchen as if expecting to find the Almighty there. Mrs. Zafra followed him. "What are you preparing?" she asked.

"Let's have lunch," he said, "I'm hungry. I hope you are also."

"We'll help you," Mrs. Zafra said, turning back to where Monica sat staring at her hands again and listening perhaps for the sound of the sea. She had not noticed nor heard her sister when she called, "Monica!"

The second time she heard her. Monica stood up and went to the kitchen. "There's nothing to prepare," Alipio was saying, as he opened the refrigerator. "What you want to eat? Me, I don't eat bread so I got no bread. I eat rice. I was just opening a can of sardines when you come. I like sardines with lotsa tomato juice, it's great with hot rice."

"Don't you cook the sardines?" Mrs. Zafra asked. "Monica will cook it for you if you want."

"No! If you cook sardines, it taste bad. Better uncooked. Besides it gets cooked on top of the hot rice. Mix with onions, chopped nice. Raw not cooked. You like it?"

"Monica loves raw onions, don't you, Sis?"

"Yes," Monica said in a low voice.

"Your sister, she is well?" Alipio said, glancing towards Monica.

Mrs. Zafra gave her sister an angry look.

"I'm okay," Monica said, a bit louder this time.

"She's not sick," Mrs. Zafra said, "But she's shy. Her own shadow frightens her. I tell you, this sister of mine, she got problems."

"Oh?" Alipio exclaimed. He had been listening quite attentively.

"I eat onions, raw," Monica said. "Sardines, too, I like uncooked."

Her sister smiled. "What do you say, I run out for some groceries," she said, going back to the living room to get her bag.

"Thanks. But no need for you to do that. I got lotsa food, canned food. Only thing I haven't got is bread," Alipio said.

"I eat rice, too," Monica said.

Alipio reached up to open the cabinet. It was stacked full of canned food: corned beef, pork and beans, Vienna sausage, tuna, crab meat, shrimp, chow mein, imitation noodles, and, of course, sardines, in green and yellow labels.

"The yellow ones with mustard sauce, not tomato," he explained.

"All I need is a cup of coffee," Mrs. Zafra said, throwing her handbag back on the chair in the living room.

Alipio opened two drawers near the refrigerator. "Look," he said as Mrs. Zafra came running back to the kitchen. "I got more food to last me . . . a long time."

The sisters gaped at the bags of rice, macaroni, spaghetti sticks, sugar, dried shrimps wrapped in cellophane, bottles of soy sauce and fish sauce, vinegar, ketchup, instant coffee, and more cans of sardines.

The sight of all that foodstuff seemed to have enlivened the old man. After all, food meant life, continuing sustenance, source of energy and health. "Now look here," he said, turning briskly now to the refrigerator, which he opened, the sudden light touching his face with a glow that erased years from his eyes. With a jerk he pulled open the large freezer, cramped full of meats. "Mostly lamb chops," he said, adding, "I like lamb chops."

"Carlito, he hates lamb chops," Mrs. Zafra said.

"I like lamb chops," Monica said, still wild-eyed, but now a bit of color tinted her cheeks. "Why do you have so much food?" she asked.

Alipio looked at her before answering. He thought she looked younger than Mrs. Zafra. "You see," he said, closing the refrigerator. He was beginning to chill. "I watch the papers for bargain sales. I can still drive the car when I feel right. It's only now my legs bothering me. So. I buy all I can. Save me many trips. Money, too."

Later they sat around the enormous table in the dining room. Monica shared half a plate of boiling rice topped with a sardine with Alipio. He showed her how to place the sardine on top, pressing it a little and pouring spoonfuls of tomato juice over it.

Mrs. Zafra had coffee and settled for a small can of Vienna sausage and a little rice. She sipped her coffee meditatively.

"This is good coffee," she said. "I remember how we used to hoard Hills Bros. coffee at . . . at the convent. The sisters were quite selfish about it."

"Antonieta was a nun, a sister of mercy," Monica said.

"What?" Alipio exclaimed, pointing a finger at her for no apparent reason, an involuntary gesture of surprise.

"Yes, I was," Mrs. Zafra admitted. "When I married, I had been out of the order for more than a year, yes, in California, at St. Mary's."

"You didn't . . ." Alipio began.

"Of course not," she interrupted him. "If you mean did I leave the order to marry Carlito. Oh, no. He was already an old man when I met him."

"I see. We used to joke him because he didn't like the girls too much. He prefer the cocks." The memory delighted him so much, he reared his head up as he laughed, covering his mouth hastily, but too late. Some of the tomato soaked grains had already spilled out on his plate and on the table in front of him.

Monica looked pleased as she gathered carefully some of the grains on the table.

"He hasn't changed," Mrs. Zafra said vaguely. "It was me who wanted to marry him."

"You? After being a nun, you wanted to marry . . . Carlito? But why Carlito?" Alipio seemed to have forgotten for the moment that he was still eating. The steam from the rice touched his face till it glistened darkly. He was staring at Mrs. Zafra as he breathed in the aroma without savoring it.

"It's a long story," Mrs. Zafra said. She stabbed a chunky sausage and brought it to her mouth. She looked pensive as she chewed on it.

"When did this happen?"

"Five, six years ago. Six years ago, almost."

"That long?"

"She had to marry him," Monica said blandly.

"What?" Alipio shouted, visibly disturbed. There was the sound of dentures in his mouth. He passed a hand over his face. "Carlito done that to you?"

The coffee spilled a little as Mrs. Zafra put the cup down. "Why no," she said. "What are you thinking of?"

Before he could answer, Monica spoke in the same tone of voice, low, unexcited, saying, "He thinks Carlito got you pregnant, that's what."

"Carlito?" She turned to Monica in disbelief. "Why, Alipio knows Carlito," she said.

Monica shrugged her shoulders. "Why don't you tell him why?" she suggested.

"As I said, it's a long story, but I shall make it short," Mrs. Zafra began. She took a sip from her cup and continued, "After leaving the order, I couldn't find a job. I was interested in social work, but I didn't know anybody who could help me."

As she paused, Alipio said, "What the heck does Carlito know about social work?"

"Let me continue," Mrs. Zafra said.

She still had a little money, from home, and she was not too worried about being jobless. But there was the question of her status as an alien. Once out of the community, she was no longer entitled to stay in the United States, let alone secure employment. The immigration office began to hound her, as it did other Filipinos in similar predicaments. They were a pitiful lot. Some hid in the apartments of friends like criminals running away from the law. Of course, they were law breakers. Those with transportation money returned home, which they hated to do. At home they would be forced to invent stories, tell lies to explain away why they returned so soon. All their lives they had to learn how to cope with the stigma of failure in a foreign land. They were losers and no longer fit for anything useful. The more sensitive and weak lost their minds and had to be committed to insane asylums. Others became neurotic, antisocial, depressed in mind and spirit. Some turned to crime. Or just folded up, in a manner of speaking. It was a nightmare. Antonieta didn't want to go back to the Philippines under those circumstances. She would have had to be very convincing to prove that she was not thrown out of the order for immoral reasons. Just when she seemed to have reached the breaking point, she recalled incidents in which women in her situation married American citizens and, automatically, became entitled to permanent residency with an option to become U.S. citizens after five years. At first, she thought the idea of such a marriage was hideous, unspeakable. Perhaps other foreign women in similar situations, could do it—and have done it—but not Philippine girls. But what was so special about Philippine girls? Nothing really, but their upbringing was such that to place themselves in a situation where they had to tell a man that all they wanted was a marriage for convenience, was degrading, an unbearable shame. A form of self-destruction. Mortal sin. Better repatriation. A thousand times better.

When an immigration officer finally caught up with her, he proved to be very understanding and quite a gentleman. Yet he was firm. He was young, maybe of Italian descent, and looked like a salesman for a well-known company in the islands that dealt in farm equipment.

"I'm giving you one week," he said. "You have already overstayed by several months. If in one week's time, you haven't left yet, you might have to wait in jail for deportation proceedings."

She cried, oh, how she cried. She wished she had not left the order, no, not really. She had no regrets about leaving up to this point. Life in the convent turned sour on her. She despised the sisters and the system, which she found tyrannical, inhuman. In her own way, she had a long series of talks with God and God had approved of the step she had taken. She was not going back to the order. Anyhow, even if she did, she would not be taken back. To jail then?

But why not marry an American citizen? In one week's time? How? Accost the first likely man and say, "You look like an American citizen. If you are, indeed, and you have the necessary papers to prove it, will you marry me? I want to remain in this country."

All week she talked to God. It was the same God she had worshipped and feared all her life. Now they were *palsy walsy,* on the best of terms. As she brooded over her misfortune, He brooded with her, sympathized with her, and finally advised her to go look for an elderly Filipino who was an American citizen, and tell him the truth of the matter. Tell him that if he wished, it could be a marriage in name only. For his trouble, she would be willing to pay. How much? If it's a bit too much, could she pay on the installment plan? If he wished . . . otherwise . . . Meanwhile He would look the other way.

How she found Carlito Zafra was another story, a much longer story, more confused and confusing. It was like a miracle, though. Her friend God could not have sent her to a better instrument to satisfy her need. That was not expressed well, but it amounted to that, a need. Carlito was an instrument necessary for her good. And, as it turned out, a not too unwilling instrument.

"We were married the day before the week was over," Mrs. Zafra said. "And I've been in this country ever since. And no regrets."

They lived well and simply, a country life. True, they were childless, but both of them were helping relatives in the Philippines, sending them money and goods marked Made in U.S.A.

"Lately, however, some of the goods we've been sending do not arrive intact. Do you know that some of the good quality material we send never reach our relatives? It's frustrating."

"We got lotsa thieves between here and there," Alipio said, but his mind seemed to be on something else.

"And I was able to send for Monica. From the snapshots she sent us she seemed to be getting thinner and more sickly, teaching in the barrio. And she wanted so much to come here."

"Seniang was like you also, hiding from immigration. I thank God for her," Alipio told Mrs. Zafra in such a low voice he could hardly be heard.

The sisters pretended they didn't know, but they knew practically everything about him. Alipio appeared tired, pensive, and eager to talk so they listened.

"She went to my apartment and said, without any hesitation, marry me and I'll take care of you. She was thin then and I thought what she said was funny, the others had been matching us, you know, but I was not really interested. I believe marriage mean children. And if you cannot produce children, why get married? Besides, I had ugly experiences, bad moments. When I first arrived in the States, here in Frisco, I was young and there were lotsa blondies hanging around on Kearny Street. It was easy. But I wanted a family and they didn't. None of 'em. So what the heck, I said."

Alipio realized that Seniang was not joking. She had to get married to an American citizen; otherwise she would be deported. At that time, Alipio was beginning to feel the disadvantages of living alone. There was too much time in his hands. How he hated himself for some of the things he did. He believed that if he was married, he would be more sensible with his time and his money. He would be happier and live long. So when Seniang showed that she was serious, he agreed to marry her. It was not to be in name only. He wanted a woman. He liked her so much he would have proposed himself had he suspected that he had a chance. She was hard working, decent, and in those days, rather slim.

"Like Monica," he said.

"Oh, I'm thin," Monica protested, blushing deeply, "I'm all bones."

"Monica is my only sister. We have no brother," Mrs. Zafra said, adding more items to her sister's vita.

"Look," Monica said, "I finished everything on my plate. I've never tasted sardines this good. Especially the way you eat them. I'm afraid I've eaten up your lunch. This is my first full meal. And I thought I've lost my appetite already."

The words came out in a rush. It seemed she didn't want to stop and she paused only because she didn't know what else to say. She moved about, gaily and at ease, perfectly at home. Alipio watched her with a bemused look in his face as she gathered the dishes and brought them to the kitchen sink. When Alipio heard the water running, he stood up, without much effort this time, and walked to her saying, "Don't bother. I got all the time to do that. You got to leave me something to do. Come, perhaps your sister wants another cup of coffee."

Mrs. Zafra had not moved from her seat. She was watching the two argue about the dishes. When she heard Alipio mention coffee, she said, "No, no more, thanks. I've drunk enough to keep me awake all week."

"Well, I'm going to wash them myself later," Monica was saying as she walked back to the table, Alipio close behind her.

"You're an excellent host, Alipio." Mrs. Zafra spoke in a tone like a reading from a citation on a certificate of merit or something. "And to two complete strangers at that. You're a good man."

"But you're not strangers. Carlito is my friend. We were young together in this country. And that's something, you know. There are lotsa guys like us here. Old-timers, o.t.'s, they call us. Permanent residents. U.S. citizens. We all gonna be buried here." He appeared to be thinking deeply as he added, "But what's wrong about that?"

The sisters ignored the question. The old man was talking to himself.

"What's wrong is to be dishonest. Earn a living with both hands, not afraid of any kind of work, that's the best good. No other way. Yes, everything for convenience, why not? That's frankly honest. No pretend. Love comes in the afterwards. When it comes. If it comes."

Mrs. Zafra chuckled, saying, "Ah, you're a romantic, Alipio. I must ask Carlito about you. You seem to know so much about him. I bet you were quite a . . ." she paused because what she wanted to say was "rooster," but she might give the impression of over-familiarity.

Alipio interrupted her, saying, "Ask him, he will say yes, I'm a romantic." His voice held a vibrance that was a surprise and a revelation to the visitors. He gestured as he talked, puckering his mouth every now and then, obviously to keep his dentures from slipping out. "What do you think? We were young, why not? We wowed 'em with our gallantry, with our cooking. Boy those dames never seen anything like us. Also, we were fools, most of us, anyway. Fools on fire."

Mrs. Zafra clapped her hands. Monica was smiling.

"Ah, but that fire's gone. Only the fool's left now," Alipio said, weakly. His voice was low and he looked tired as he passed both hands across his face. Then he raised his head. The listening look came back to his face. When he spoke, his voice shook a little.

"Many times I wonder where are the others. Where are you? Speak to me. And I think they're wondering the same, asking the same, so I say, I'm here, your friend Alipio Palma, my leg is broken, the wife she's dead, but I'm okay. Are you okay also? The dead they can hear even if they don't answer. The alive don't answer. But I know. I feel. Some okay, some not. They old now, all of us, who were very young. All over the United States of America. All over the world . . ."

Abruptly, he turned to Mrs. Zafra, saying, "So. You and Carlito. But Carlito, he never had fire."

"How true, how very very true," Mrs. Zafra laughed. "It would burn him. Can't stand it. Not Carlito. But he's a good man, I can tell you that."

"No question. Dabest," Alipio conceded.

Monica remained silent, but her eyes followed every move Alipio made, straying no further than the reach of his arms as he gestured to help make clear the intensity of his feeling.

"I'm sure you still got some of that fire," Mrs. Zafra said.

Monica gasped, but she recovered quickly. Again a rush of words came from her lips as if they had been there all the time waiting for what her sister had said that touched off the torrent of words. Her eyes shone as in a fever as she talked.

"I don't know Carlito very well. I've not been with them very long, but from what you say, from the way you talk, from what I see, the two of you are very different."

"Oh, maybe not," Alipio said, trying to protest, but Monica went on.

"You have strength, Mr. Palma. Strength of character. Strength in your belief in God. I admire that in a man, in a human being. Look at you. Alone. This huge table. Don't you find it too big sometimes?" Monica paused perhaps to allow her meaning to sink into Alipio's consciousness, as she fixed her eyes on him.

"No, not really. I don't eat at this table. I eat in the kitchen," Alipio said.

Mrs. Zafra was going to say something, but she held back. Monica was talking again.

"But it must be hard, that you cannot deny. Living from day to day. Alone. On what? Memories? Cabinets and a refrigerator full of food? I repeat, I admire you, sir. You've found your place. You're home safe. And at peace." She paused again, this time to sweep back the strand of hair that had fallen on her brow.

Alipio had a drugged look. He seemed to have lost the drift of her speech. What was she talking about? Groceries? Baseball? He was going to say, you like baseball also? You like tuna? I have all kinds of fish. Get them at bargain price. But, obviously, it was not the proper thing to say.

"Well, I guess, one gets used to anything. Even loneliness," Monica said in a listless, dispirited tone, all the fever in her voice gone.

"God dictates," Alipio said, feeling he had found his way again and he was now on the right track. What a girl. If she had only a little more flesh. And color.

Monica leaned back on her chair, exhausted. Mrs. Zafra was staring at her in disbelief, in grievous disappointment. Her eyes seemed to say, what happened, you were going great, what suddenly hit you that you had to stop, give up, defeated? Monica shook her head in a gesture that quite clearly said, no, I can't do it, I can't anymore, I give up.

Their eyes kept up a show, a deaf-mute dialogue. Mrs. Zafra: Just when everything was going on fine, you quit. We've reached this far and you quit. I could have done it my way, directly, honestly. Not that what you were doing was dishonest, you were great, and now look at that dumb expression in your eyes. Monica: I can't. I can't anymore. But I tried. It's too much.

"How long have you been in the States?" Alipio asked Monica.

"For almost a year now!" Mrs. Zafra screamed and Alipio was visibly shaken, but she didn't care. This was the right moment. She would take it from here whether Monica went along with her or not. She was going to do it her way. "How long exactly, let's see. Moni, when did you get your last extension?"

"Extension?" Alipio repeated the word. It had such a familiar ring like "visa" or "social security," it broke into his consciousness like a touch from Seniang's fingers. It was quite intimate. "You mean . . ."

"That's right. She's here as a temporary visitor. As a matter of fact, she came on a tourist visa. Carlito and I sponsored her coming, filed all the necessary papers, and everything would have been fine, but she couldn't wait. She had to come here as a tourist. Now she's in trouble."

"What trouble?" Alipio asked.

"She has to go back to the Philippines. She can't stay here any longer. "

"I have only two days left," Monica said, her head in her hands. "And I don't want to go back."

Alipio glanced at the wall clock. It was past three. They had been talking for hours. It was visas right from the start. Marriages. The long years and the o.t.'s. Now it was visas again. Were his ears playing a game? They might as well as they did sometimes, but his eyes surely were not. He could see this woman very plainly, sobbing on the table. Boy, she was in big trouble. Visas. Immigration. Boy, oh, boy! He knew all about that. His gleaming dentures showed a crooked smile. He turned to Mrs. Zafra.

"Did you come here," he began, but Mrs. Zafra interrupted him.

"Yes, Alipio. Forgive us. As soon as we arrived, I wanted to tell you without much talk, I wanted to say, 'I must tell you why we're here. I've heard about you. Not only from Carlito, but from other Filipinos who know you, how you're living here in San Francisco alone, a widower, and we heard of the accident, your stay in the hospital, when you were released, everything. Here's my sister, a teacher in the Philippines, never married, worried to death because she's being deported unless something turned up like she could marry a U.S. citizen, like I did, like your late wife Seniang, like many others have done, are doing in this exact moment, who can say? Now look at her, she's good, religious, any arrangement you wish, she'd accept it.' But I didn't have a chance to say it. You welcomed us like old friends, relatives. Later every time I began to say something about why we came, she interrupted me. I was afraid she had changed her mind and then she began to talk, then stopped without finishing what she really wanted to say, that is, why we came to see you, and so forth."

"No, no!" Monica cried, raising her head, her eyes red from weeping, her face damp with tears. "You're such a good man. We couldn't do this to you. We're wrong. We started wrong. We should've been more honest, but I was ashamed. I was afraid. Let's go! Let's go!"

"Where you going?" Alipio asked.

"Anywhere," Monica answered. "Forgive us. Forgive me, Mister. Alipio, please."

"What's to forgive? Don't go. We have dinner. But first, let's have *merienda*. I take *merienda*. You do also, don't you? And I don't mean snacks like the Americans."

The sisters exchanged glances, their eyes chattering away.

Alipio chuckled. He wanted to say, talk of lightning striking the same fellow twice, but thought better of it. A bad thing to say. Seniang was not lightning. At times only. Mostly his fault. And this girl Monica . . . Moni? Nice name also. How can this one be lightning?

Mrs. Zafra picked up her purse and before anyone could stop her, she was opening the door. "Where's the nearest grocery store around here?" she asked, but she didn't wait for an answer.

"Come back, come back here, we got lotsa food," Alipio called after her, but he might just as well have been calling the Pacific Ocean.

11.2 SEÑOR PAYROLL
William E. Barrett

Larry and I were Junior Engineers in the gas plant, which means that we were clerks. Anything that could be classified as paper work came to the flat double desk across which we faced each other. The Main Office downtown sent us a bewildering array of orders and rules that were to be put into effect.

Junior Engineers were beneath the notice of everyone except the Mexican laborers at the plant. To them we were the visible form of a distant, unknowable paymaster. We were Señor Payroll.

Those Mexicans were great workmen; the aristocrats among them were the stokers, big men who worked Herculean eight-hour shifts in the fierce heat of the retorts. They scooped coal with huge shovels and hurled it with uncanny aim at tiny doors. The coal streamed out from the shovels like black water from a high-pressure nozzle, and never missed the narrow opening. The stokers worked stripped to the waist, and there was pride and dignity in them. Few men could do such work, and they were the few.

The Company paid its men only twice a month, on the fifth and on the twentieth. To a Mexican, this was absurd. What man with money will make it last fifteen days? If he hoarded money beyond the spending of three days, he was a miser—and when, Señor, did the blood of Spain flow in the veins of misers? Hence, it was the custom for our stokers to appear every third or fourth day to draw the money due to them.

There was a certain elasticity in the Company rules, and Larry and I sent the necessary forms to the Main Office and received an "advance" against a man's pay check. Then, one day, Downtown favored us with a memorandum:

"There have been too many abuses of the advance-against-wages privilege. Hereafter, no advance against wages will be made to any employee except in a case of genuine emergency."

We had no sooner posted the notice when in came stoker Juan Garcia. He asked for an advance. I pointed to the notice. He spelled it through slowly, then said, "What does this mean, this 'genuine emergency'?"

I explained to him patiently that the Company was kind and sympathetic, but that it was a great nuisance to have to pay wages every few days. If someone was ill or if money was urgently needed for some other good reason, then the Company would make an exception to the rule.

Juan Garcia turned his hat over and over slowly in his big hands. "I do not get my money?"

"Next payday, Juan. On the twentieth."

He went out silently and I felt a little ashamed of myself. I looked across the desk at Larry. He avoided my eyes.

In the next hour two other stokers came in, looked at the notice, had it explained and walked solemnly out; then no more came. What we did not know was that Juan Garcia, Pete Mendoza, and Francisco Gonzalez had spread the word, and that every Mexican in the plant was explaining the order to every other Mexican. "To get money now, the wife must be sick. There must be medicine for the baby."

The next morning Juan Garcia's wife was practically dying, Pete Mendoza's mother would hardly last the day, there was a veritable epidemic among children, and, just for variety, there was

From *Autumn Southwest Review.* Copyright © 1943 Southern Methodist University Press. Reprinted with permission.

one sick father. We always suspected that the old man was really sick; no Mexican would other-wise have thought of him. At any rate, nobody paid Larry and me to examine private lives; we made out our forms with an added line describing the "genuine emergency." Our people got paid.

That went on for a week. Then came a new order, curt and to the point: "Hereafter, employees will be paid ONLY on the fifth and the twentieth of the month. No exceptions will be made except in the cases of employees leaving the service of the Company."

The notice went up on the board, and we explained its significance gravely. "No, Juan Garcia, we cannot advance your wages. It is too bad about your wife and your cousins and your aunts, but there is a new rule."

Juan Garcia went out and thought it over. He thought out loud with Mendoza and Gonzales and Ayala, then, in the morning, he was back. "I am quitting this company for different job. You pay me now?"

We argued that it was a good company and that it loved its employees like children, but in the end we paid off, because Juan Garcia quit. And so did Gonzalez, Mendoza, Obregon, Ayala and Ortez, the best stokers, men who could not be replaced.

Larry and I looked at each other; we knew what was coming in about three days. One of our duties was to sit on the hiring line early each morning, engaging transient workers for the handy gangs. Any man was accepted who could walk up and ask for a job without falling down. Never before had we been called upon to hire such skilled virtuosos as stokers for handy-gang work, but we were called upon to hire them now.

The day foreman was wringing his hands and asking the Almighty if he was personally sup-posed to shovel this condemned coal, while there in a stolid, patient line were skilled men—Garcia, Mendoza, and others—waiting to be hired. We hired them, of course. There was nothing else to do.

Every day we had a line of resigning stokers, and another line of stokers seeking work. Our paper work became very complicated. At the Main Office they were jumping up and down. The procession of forms showing Juan Garcia's resigning and being hired over and over again was too much for them. Sometimes Downtown had Garcia on the payroll twice at the same time when someone down there was slow in entering a resignation. Our phone rang early and often.

Tolerantly and patiently we explained: "There's nothing we can do if a man wants to quit, and if there are stokers available when the plant needs stokers, we hire them."

Out of chaos, Downtown issued another order. I read it and whistled. Larry looked at it and said, "It is going to be very quiet around here."

The order read: "Hereafter, no employee who resigns may be rehired within a period of 30 days."

Juan Garcia was due for another resignation, and when he came in we showed him the order and explained that standing in line the next day would do him no good if he resigned today. "Thirty days is a long time, Juan."

It was a grave matter and he took time to reflect on it.

So did Gonzalez, Mendoza, Ayala and Ortez. Ultimately, however, they were all back—and all resigned.

We did our best to dissuade them and we were sad about the parting. This time it was for keeps and they shook hands with us solemnly. It was very nice knowing us. Larry and I looked at each other when they were gone and we both knew that neither of us had been pulling for Downtown to win this duel. It was a blue day.

In the morning, however, they were all back in line. With the utmost gravity, Juan Garcia informed me that he was a stoker looking for a job.

"No dice, Juan," I said. "Come back in thirty days. I warned you."

His eyes looked straight into mine without a flicker. "There is some mistake, Señor," he said. "I am Manuel Hernandez. I work as the stoker in Pueblo, in Santa Fe, in many places."

I stared back at him, remembering the sick wife and the babies without medicine, the mother-in-law in the hospital, the many resignations and the rehirings. I knew that there was a gas plant in Pueblo, and that there wasn't any in Santa Fe; but who was I to argue with a man about his own name? A stoker is a stoker.

So I hired him. I hired Gonzalez, too, who swore that his name was Carrera, and Ayala, who had shamelessly become Smith.

Three days later the resigning started.

Within a week our payroll read like a history of Latin America. Everyone was on it: Lopez and Obregon, Villa, Diaz, Batista, Gomez, and even San Martín and Bolívar. Finally Larry and I, growing weary of staring at familiar faces and writing unfamiliar names, went to the Superintendent and told him the whole story. He tried not to grin, and said, "Damned nonsense!"

The next day the orders were taken down. We called our most prominent stokers into the office and pointed to the board. No rules any more.

"The next time we hire you hombres," Larry said grimly, "come in under the names you like best, because that's the way you are going to stay on the books."

They looked at us and they looked at the board; then for the first time in the long duel, their teeth flashed white. "Si, Señores," they said.

And so it was.

11.3   NO ONE TO YELL AT
Ilyas Halia

Kazim Aga from Kayseri was mad as a hornet. He was cursing everything from hell to break-fast. "Damn country!" he yelled. "It's not a country, it's an insane asylum! Nobody has any brains! Something goes wrong and they don't even care! These dull, cowardly dogs, by God! The bastards have no guts! Like a bunch of blockheads. No love, no enthusiasm! If their pants caught fire, they wouldn't put it out without permission from their wives, the idiots! Everything is carefully calculated. Damn such a life! Our money disgraces us. There's no pleasure or charm! Does living here have to be like this? Man, we have everything; we should live like pashas. But we've become coolies wearing ties! In Adana, even my clerk had more pleasure and fun. At least, on holidays, I gave him some spending money and sent him to a bar to enjoy himself. And he knew how to be a clerk; on occasion he came, kissed my hand, and asked after my health. Is it like that in this damn country? Just look at that old guy sitting over there! Has anyone ever seen him grin? Not on your life!

"I go to the bank and deposit wads of money; I withdraw money. Does that insensitive fool, that so-called director, ever offer me tea or coffee, or even a Coke? Never, never!"

In Old Montreal, on a street below the great Notre Dame Cathedral, stands the business place belonging to our Kazim Aga. He wholesales imported crystal giftware from Eastern-European countries. His business seems to go well, but whenever I go to see him, he complains about the situation. Sometimes he plays backgammon with his Lebanese neighbor, a carpet man. When he loses, he's mad at losing, and when he wins, he's mad because he can't make a rural Arab angry. "I can't get a fellah mad," he complains, swallowing his anger.

It was as if the city were on fire that last week in June. The sun blazed in the sky. Narrow streets were filled with idly wandering tourists and young secretaries from neighboring banks. From time to time, the sound of steamships came from the harbor. This area is back of Old Montreal's harbor. The buildings are old and dirty, their walls thick. Wholesalers have occupied this part of the city from way back. However, now, with help from the Montreal city government, a restaurant has been opened on every corner.

A phaeton was parked at the door. It was a one-horse, pretty coach with a fold-down top. Kazim Aga rushed to the window to look at the vehicle. "I love that coach. When I look at it I'm cheered up. If I could, I'd ride it from home every day. But it's expensive! The guy drove me once and took me for fifteen dollars. I swore never to ride it again."

When I came in, Kazim Aga had stopped yelling. I go to visit him during noon-hour from time to time. He's a pleasant man, easy to talk with. Though he appears ignorant, he's really a sharp country boy with lots of common sense. When it comes to money business, or people, he rarely makes a mistake.

Upon seeing me, he said, "Come in and have a coffee. There's something I want to tell you." He sent one of the employees working beside him, to a nearby coffee man to get two Turkish coffees. The young woman left with a sour look on her face.

"Did you see that hussy?" he said, "I pay these people lots of money but they don't want to take two steps to fetch a cup of coffee. That slip of a girl complained to the accountant about me.

From *Unregulated Chicken Butts and Other Stories,* trans. Joseph S. Jacobsen (Salt Lake City: University of Utah Press, 1990), 35–38. Copyright © 1990 University of Utah Press. Reprinted by permission.

'I'm no coffee girl,' she said. 'If he's going to send me for coffee all the time I won't work here.'
I told the accountant, 'You tell that girl that I'll not only send her, but the accountant himself if I
want to.' Nonsense! If we take jobs, we all must work. If I want, I'll even have her sweep the
shop. But, after all, I don't want to judge the young woman. You see all these sons-of-bitches!
Spend a wad of money on them, give them jobs, and they all defy you. We couldn't find even one
good Moslem to hire. This is the third girl we've tried. Women don't stay long. And I pay them
plenty, too! I don't cut their pay the way those other Greek Turks do. Shall I tell you something,
sir? Life here doesn't suit me! It's empty, cheerless! As my father used to say, 'Life has to have
some charm and pleasure!'

"In Adana, I had a little store with a clerk and errand boy. I used to send my errand boy, little
Kürt Hasso, to the market to get food and vegetables for the house. Every evening, he swept the
store, too. You know, those two were the charm of my life. Sir, we worked together all those years
and I didn't offend them even once. We got along together like a big family. They knew how to
be errand boy and clerk and I knew how to be boss. On holidays, they came to kiss my hand and
I never failed to open my wallet and pay them a bonus. With that life, they were happy, I was
happy! When things went wrong, at least I had someone to yell at and curse. If I was upset, I
swore at Hasso; I yelled at Hasso. And he would say, 'Good health to you, boss, get mad at me
rather than a stranger,' and pacify me, the son-of-a-bitch. I swore at Hasso over little things. If big
things went wrong, and I needed someone bigger to curse, I yelled at the clerk, Emin Effendi. He
didn't usually answer. He didn't say 'thank you' or 'to your good health.' Perhaps the man hid his
anger. Anyway, he never forgot his gentlemanly behavior; he knew his place and, if unwillingly,
accepted the cursing with good manners. Never, at any time, did either of them abandon his
gentlemanly behavior because I got mad and cursed them. Neither ever stopped me or gave me a
cross answer. Being a well-bred man is really something, my friend! Look at the dirty fellows
around here! Do they have even a trace of courtesy? Doesn't it ever occur to them to say, 'This is
the boss, the owner; naturally he swears, he has a right to.' No one says, 'Let's be a little help to
a man who takes all these troubles on his shoulders. Let's tolerate the poor guy's being all upset.'
These infidels are ungrateful, by God! They jabber away, but I never listen! I swear the way I
know how, in Turkish! But I don't get the same flavor out of it, because they don't understand.

"You know what I decided to do? I've decided to bring Hasso over here. Yesterday, I sat down
and wrote him a letter and invited him. 'Come!' I said, 'I'll give you a good monthly salary, bed
and board is on me, and I'll pay your doctor bills. I'll pay for your clothes, too.' I told Hasso, 'It's
your day again, Hasso. You son-of-a-bitch, come over and see a little country!'

"I'm truly pleased that Hasso is coming. I'll have someone around to curse and yell at. At least,
when I swear, the guy has to know, to understand what I say. He mustn't just stare at me stupidly.
As far as I'm concerned, Hasso is used to swearing. He couldn't stand not being sworn at. One
time, I didn't curse Hasso for a whole week. Whether I was very busy or sick I can't remember.
Anyway, I hadn't found a chance to yell for a week. You'll like what Hasso told me that weekend:
'Boss, it's clear you are sick! You haven't opened your mouth and said anything all week. You
haven't sworn! Swear, swear and relax, boss, don't stay upset like that!' Have you ever seen such
an intelligent man? He can ask me for anything he wants; I'd give my life to one like that. But, he
must always know his place. . . ."

Section 12
———— Customer Service ————

12.1   A NEW CUSTOMER
Viktor Slavkin

Around four o'clock, a new customer stepped over the threshold of the second-class restaurant. "Greetings." He crossed the room diagonally and sat down at an empty table.

About twenty minutes passed. Volodia, the waiter, gave his unfinished cigarette to one of his colleagues to hold, with his right hand smoothed over the piece of a Russian folk ornament hanging off his left sleeve, and moved toward the customer. Having approached the table, he silently pointed to a napkin lying in the center of the table, on which was written, "This table is not being served."

The customer looked at the waiter with the eyes of a kind dog who had just heard from its master the words, "Time for a walk."

"Move to a table where there is already someone," Volodia explained patiently. "I won't serve you alone."

"Please do not chase me away," the customer said timidly.

"Don't you understand Russian? I said this table is not set."

"I'll wait."

"As you wish. You'll sit." Volodia lost all interest in the conversation.

"I'll sit," said the customer. "Thank you."

"Only there is no need to be rude," the waiter warned.

"I'll sit. Don't worry. It's nothing."

"Besides, how can there be accusations? Just sat down, and already . . ."

"What is your name?" asked the customer.

"Are you going to cause a scene? Watch it."

The other waiters, smoking by the manager's table, felt the trouble brewing. Their loose jackets filled out by young muscles, the lapels flared up.

"I don't want to cause a scene." It seemed as if the customer was about to cry. "I just want an introduction."

Volodia waved his friends off and their jackets loosened up once again.

"Volodia," said he.

"My name might seem strange to you."

"So, what do we want to eat?" asked the waiter and took out his writing pad.

"Don't rush, Volodia. Go, finish your cigarette. Give the other table their bill. Besides, you don't even have a menu with you . . ."

"It's not been printed yet."

"Wonderful. Then I'll just sit. The people who were at this table before me left some bread, there is mustard. What else does one need? After all, it is inconvenient for you to take care of me now."

"Inconvenient," agreed Volodia, but for some strange reason, he did not walk away.

From the *FBIS Daily Report* (Washington). Reprinted with permission from the author.

The customer took a piece of bread out of the basket, covered it with a thick layer of mustard, sprinkled it with salt, and bowed his well-groomed head over this dish, deeply inhaled the scent.

"What, you've never seen food?" the waiter snickered.

The customer choked and began coughing. Volodia hit him hard on the back.

"Volodia, I'd like to ask you . . . that is, could you promise me . . . anyway, if I admit something to you, give me your word that your benevolence towards me will not change."

"What are you coming back from, prison?" The waiter guessed.

"I am a . . . foreigner . . ." the customer said quietly. Then in a completely morbid voice he added, "from a capitalist country."

Volodia's Adam's apple bobbed as if he had swallowed an apricot pit, and he asked hoarsely: "May I be allowed to change the tablecloth?"

"I thought this might happen." The customer hung his head and his thin fingers began running spasmodically over the dirty tablecloth. "This stain reminds me of the shape of my poor country."

Volodia glanced with interest at the stains from the sauce "piquant."

"Gee, I'm not aware of such a country."

"And a good thing it is." The customer covered the stain with his hand. "It is a pygmy country with no particular significance in the world. The name is Grand-Carlo. Have you heard of it?"

"No."

"We're the richest country in the world," the customer said sadly, and bit off another piece of bread.

"But I bet you don't have mustard like this!" Professional pride spoke in the waiter.

"We have everything, except economic problems. Or any problems. None whatsoever."

"Whatever you say," said the waiter somberly. "I have to go to work." He tried walking away from the table.

The foreigner held him back by his jacket.

"Volodia, my dear! You can't imagine what it's like."

"We can. Saw it in a movie.

"Oh no! What you saw in a movie can not compare to what is happening in our country. It is awful! Awful! Our muscles wither, our brains freeze, our instincts vanish, our immune system disintegrates—the nation is becoming extinct."

Bread trembled in the customer's hand.

"Only here in your country do I feel like a human being." Suddenly the customer smiled. "You know, the moment I crossed the border, I tore off all my clothes and bought clothes made in your country in the nearest manufactured goods store. I bought a shirt, shoes, a suit . . . Volodia, buy yourself one like it; there are more. The collar cuts into the neck and under the arms, it pulls in the crotch, the waist is too tight . . . But I feel them. I am in constant contact with them, I fight them! This fills me up with energy and belief in my eventual victory. I know that you dream of getting Cardin clothes. No, Volodia. Don't. Get them only from manufactured goods store."

"Your wealth is making you mad. You know this saying that we have."

"It's not a saying, Volodia. It's a proverb." Once again the customer became sad. "In any case, such is the view of Vladimir Ivanovich Dal'."

"Are your parents Russian?"

"That's another one for you. I am a native Grand-Carlean, but the moment I expressed the desire, our travel agency in two weeks, only two weeks, instilled in me the vocabulary of four volumes of Dal' as well as the total absence of an accent. They have worked out a method. I had to make no effort. But where is the happiness that comes from work, the marvel of comprehending something new? Can one live like that, Volodia?"

"You know what," squinted the waiter, "if you are so sick of it, send all you have in excess to Africa. They'll use it there and you'll be able to relax a bit."

The customer looked at him with respect.

"You have the mind for government, Volodia. But you don't know our immoral industry. We can give away everything. Burn everything. It will all be reproduced immediately, doubled in volume."

"Well, then, I don't know what to tell you." Volodia shrugged his shoulders, and his face showed the utmost concern.

The customer began speaking excitedly.

"This is not my first time in your country. I come here not without reason. Not at all. I walk down the streets, visit stores, cafeterias, other places of communal usage, and everywhere, everywhere I see burning eyes, goal-striving faces, thought-out movements. Life is in full swing, people act, everything around is changing for the better. Man struggles, meaning he exists, damn it! I feel it myself, right now. For example, if I were to walk into one of our Grand-Carlo restaurants, immediately I would be attacked by our service sharks, our courtesy gangsters, our terrorists of communal feeding. In a moment they turn a person into a well-fed satisfied beast. Now let's take your blessed establishment, your soul-saving Greetings. I crossed its threshold experiencing a sharp pang of hunger, a feeling I haven't had in a long time. And you so keenly comprehending my state did not rush over to me. I sat at the table and with nothing to do, my stomach empty, began thinking over my life. The memories came to me by themselves. I remembered how I skinned my knee as a child. I remembered my mother, my father . . . It has been a long time since I've thought of them."

"That's not good," Volodia said strictly. "I personally always bring my mother some goodies once a week."

"And when you came up to me," the customer continued, "you did not spoil my mood. On the contrary, you obliged me with your so pleasant refusal to serve me. Thank you. But how do we teach *our* dummies to do that?"

"That's easy," said the waiter. "How do you say, 'This table is not served' in your language?"

"It's an untranslatable play on words."

"So let your dummy write this play on words on a piece of paper and put it on the table."

"And that's it?"

"That's it."

"But what is the purpose?" It was apparent that the customer had difficulty grasping the novel idea. "After all, the seat is not being used, profits are lost, the earnings . . ." He was reasoning out loud.

"Well, if you think like that, it won't work for sure."

"The kitchen is still preparing food. It must realize . . ."

"So let the kitchen staff consume what they make."

"How's that?"

"Or take it home."

"I don't understand."

"What's there not to understand? Every cook must have a bag with him. He comes in the morning with it empty and goes home with it jammed."

"Jammed? What does 'jammed' mean?"

"So much for your celebrated knowledge of Russian." The customer's head dropped onto his chest.

"Come, come now. What's the matter? What's with you? . . . Oh come now, stop crying!"

Volodia shook the customer by the shoulder, and the customer once again regained control of himself.

"These are not tears my friend. It's a type of contact lenses that we have. They have neither weight, nor thickness, just sparkle to rejuvenate a person. I am old, Volodia. It is only this physical shape that we are in. Don't believe it, Volodia, don't! I am an old and a sick man. But they, our killers in white coats, they made me young and healthy. I play tennis, I swim. I am loved by young girls. But Volodia, I want to sit in the park with people my age, play chess, stand in line for cottage cheese, and if it's not there or it has run out, to go to another one and another . . . with friends, with a crowd, with company. Or maybe to ride the bus to the other end of town during the traffic hour. How many stories we can tell each other on the way there! All of us together, jointly, all at once, in cohoots, all of us, en masse . . . Do you respect me, Volodia? Do you? Tell me, Volodia, do you respect me?"

"I respect you, pops, I do. But only . . ."

"What!!!" exclaimed the customer tragically. "What!!!"

"Be quiet." Volodia threw a glance around. The restaurant was almost empty. "I'm trying to say that the kitchen is about to close. Nobody here is hired to serve you until all hours of the night."

The customer became depressed.

"Then, Volodia," he said, "I have a last request for you. Bring me something as bad as possible."

"That we'll do." The waiter scribbled something on his pad and started toward the kitchen. He came up to the serving window and shouted:

"Vasia, one burned steak with yesterday's potatoes."

"O.K.," replied Vasia, "O.K.," and carried out the order diligently.

12.2   A BRIEF HISTORY OF CAPITALISM
Moacyr Scliar

My father was a Communist and a car mechanic. A good Communist, according to his comrades, but a lousy mechanic according to consensus. As a matter of fact, so great was his inability to handle cars that people wondered why he had chosen such an occupation. He used to say it had been a conscious choice on his part; he believed in manual work as a form of personal development, and he had confidence in machines and in their capability to liberate man and launch him into the future, in the direction of a freer, more desirable life. Roughly, that's what he meant. I used to help my father in his car repair shop. Since I was an only son, he wanted me to follow in his footsteps. There wasn't, however, much that I could do; at that time I was eleven years old, and almost as clumsy as he was at using tools. Anyhow, for the most part, there was no call for us to use them since there wasn't much work coming our way. We would sit talking and thus while away the time. My father was a great storyteller; enthralled, I would listen to his accounts of the uprising of the Spartacists, and of the rebellion led by the fugitive slave Zambi. In those moments his eyes would glitter. I would listen, deeply affected by his stories; often, my eyes would fill with tears.

Once in a while a customer appeared. Usually a Party sympathizer (my father's comrades didn't own cars), who came to Father more out of a desire to help than out of need. These customers played it safe, though: It was always some minor repair, like fixing the license plate securely, or changing the blades of the windshield wipers. But even such simple tasks turned out to be extraordinarily difficult for Father to perform; sometimes it would take him a whole day to change a distributor point. And the car would drive away with the engine misfiring (needless to say, its owner would never set foot in our repair shop again). If it weren't for the financial problems (my mother had to support us by taking in sewing), I wouldn't have minded the lack of work too much. I really enjoyed those rap sessions with my father. In the morning I would go to school; but as soon as I came home, I would run to the repair shop, which was near our house. And there I would find Father reading. Upon my arrival, he would set his book aside, light his pipe, and start telling me his stories. And there we would stay until Mother came to call us for dinner.

One day when I arrived at our repair shop, there was a car there, a huge, sparkling, luxury car. None of the Party sympathizers, not even the wealthiest among them, owned a car like that. Father told me that the monster car had stalled right in front of the shop. The owner then left it there, under his care, saying he would be back late in the afternoon. And what's wrong with it? I asked, somewhat alarmed, sensing a foul-up in the offing.

"I wish I knew." Father sighed. "Frankly, I don't know what's wrong with it. I already took a look but couldn't find the defect. It must be something minor, probably the carburetor is clogged up, but . . . I don't know, I just don't know what it is."

Dejected, he sat down, took a handkerchief out of his pocket, and wiped his forehead. Come on, I said, annoyed at his passivity, it's no use your sitting there.

He got up and the two of us took a look at the enormous engine, so clean, it glittered. Isn't it a beauty? remarked my father with the pleasure of an owner who took pride in his car.

From Moacyr Scliar, *The Enigmatic Eye,* trans. Eloah F. Giacomelli (New York: Available Press, 1989). Translation copyright © 1988 Eloah F. Giacomelli. Reprinted with permission of Ballantine Books, a division of Random House, Inc.

Yes, it was a beauty—except that he couldn't open the carburetor. I had to give him a hand; three hours later, when the man returned, we were still at it.

He was a pudgy, well-dressed man. He got out of a taxi, his face already displaying annoyance. I expected him to be disgruntled, but never for a moment did I imagine what was to happen next.

At first the man said nothing. Seeing that we weren't finished yet, he sat down on a stool and watched us. A moment later he stood up; he examined the stool on which he had sat.

"Dirty. This stool is dirty. Can't you people even offer your customers a decent chair to sit on?"

We made no reply. Neither did we raise our heads. The man looked around him.

"A real dump, this place. A sty. How can you people work amid such filth?"

We, silent.

"But that's the way everything is," the man went on. "In this country that's the way it is. Nobody wants to do any work, nobody wants to get his act together. All people ever think of is booze, women, the Carnival, soccer. But to get down to work? Never."

Where's the wrench? asked Father in a low, restrained voice. Over there, by your side, I said. Thanks, he said, and resumed fiddling with the carburetor.

"You people want nothing to do with a regular, steady job." The man sounded increasingly more irritated. "You people will never get out of this filth. Now, take me, for instance. I started at the bottom. But nowadays I'm a rich man. Very rich. And do you know why? Because I was clean, well organized, hardworking. This car here, do you think it's the only one I own? Do you?"

Tighten the screw, said Father, tighten it really tight.

"I'm talking to you!" yelled the man, fuming. "I'm asking you a question! Do you think this is the only car I own? That's what you think, isn't it? Well, let me tell you something, I own two other cars. Two other cars! They are in my garage. I don't use them. Because I don't want to. If I wanted, I could abandon this car here in the middle of the street and get another one. Well, I wouldn't get it myself; I would have someone get it for me. Because I have a chauffeur, see? That's right. I drive because I enjoy driving, but I have a chauffeur. I don't *have* to drive, I don't *need* this car. If I wanted to, I could junk this fucking car, you hear me?"

Hand me the pipe wrench, will you? said Father. The small one.

The man was now standing quite close to us. I didn't look at him, but I could feel his breath on my arm.

"Do you doubt my word? Do you doubt that I can smash up this car? Do you?"

I looked at the man. He was upset. When his eyes met mine, he seemed to come to his senses; only for a moment, though; he opened his eyes wide.

"Do you doubt it? That I can smash up this fucking car? Give me a hammer. Quick! Give me a hammer!"

He searched for a hammer but couldn't find one (it would have been a miracle had he found one; even we could never find the tools in our shop). Without knowing what he was doing, he gave the car door a kick; soon followed by another, then another.

"That's what I've been telling you," he kept screaming. "That I'll smash up this fucking car! That's what I've been telling you."

Ready, said Father. I looked at him; he was pale, beads of sweat were running down his face. Ready? I asked, not getting it. Ready, he said. You can now start the engine.

The man, panting, was looking at us. Opening the car door, I sat at the steering wheel and turned on the ignition. Incredible: The engine started. I revved it up. The shop was filled with the roar of the engine.

My father stood mopping his face with his dirty handkerchief. The man, silent, kept looking at us. How much I owe you? finally he asked. Nothing, said my father. What do you mean, nothing? Suspicious, the man frowned. Nothing, said my father, it costs you nothing, it's on the house. Then the man, opening his wallet, pulled out a bill.

"Here, for a shot of rum."

"I don't drink," said my father without touching the money.

The man replaced the bill in his wallet, which he then put into his pocket. Without a word he got into his car, and, revving the engine, drove away.

For a moment Father stood motionless, in silence. Then he turned to me.

"This," he said in a hoarse voice, a voice that wasn't his, "is capitalism."

No, it wasn't. That wasn't capitalism. I wished it were capitalism—but it was not. Unfortunately not. It was something else. Something I didn't even dare to think about.

Section 13
—————— Teams and Alliances ——————

13.1   MISTER TAYLOR
Augusto Monterroso

"Somewhat less strange, although surely more exemplary," the other man said then, "is the story of Mr. Percy Taylor, a headhunter in the Amazon jungle.

"In 1937 he is known to have left Boston, Massachusetts, where he had refined his spirit to the point at which he did not have a cent. In 1944 he appears for the first time in South America, in the region of the Amazon, living with the Indians of a tribe whose name there is no need to recall.

"Because of the shadows under his eyes and his famished appearance, he soon became known as 'the poor gringo,' and the school children even pointed at him and threw stones when he walked by, his beard shining in the golden tropical sun. But this caused no distress to Mr. Taylor's humble nature, for he had read in the first volume of William C. Knight's *Complete Works* that poverty is no disgrace if one does not envy the wealthy.

"In a few weeks the natives grew accustomed to him and his eccentric clothing. Besides, since he had blue eyes and a vague foreign accent, even the president and the minister of foreign affairs treated him with singular respect, fearful of provoking international incidents.

"He was so wretchedly poor that one day he went into the jungle to search for plants to eat. He had walked several meters without daring to turn his head when, by sheerest accident, he saw a pair of Indian eyes observing him intently from the undergrowth. A long shudder traveled down Mr. Taylor's sensitive spine. But Mr. Taylor intrepidly defied all danger and continued on his way, whistling as if he had not seen anything.

"With a leap, which there is no need to call feline, the native landed in front of him and cried: 'Buy head? Money, money.'

"Although the Indian's English could not have been worse, Mr. Taylor, feeling somewhat ill, realized the Indian was offering to sell him an oddly shrunken human head that he was carrying in his hand.

"It is unnecessary to say that Mr. Taylor was in no position to buy it, but since he pretended not to understand, the Indian felt horribly embarrassed for not speaking good English and gave the head to him as a gift, begging his pardon.

"Mr. Taylor's joy was great as he returned to his hut. That night, lying on his back on the precariously balanced palm mat that was his bed, and interrupted only by the buzzing of the passionate flies that flew around him as they made love obscenely, Mr. Taylor spent a long time contemplating his curious acquisition with delight. He derived the greatest aesthetic pleasure from counting the hairs of the beard and moustache one by one and looking straight into the two half-ironic eyes that seemed to smile at him in gratitude for his deferential behavior.

From *And We Sold the Rain: Contemporary Fiction from Central America*, trans. Edith Grossman, ed. Rosario Santos (New York: Four Walls Eight Windows, 1988), 183–190. Copyright © 1988 Edith Grossman.

"A man of immense culture, Mr. Taylor was contemplative by nature, but on this occasion he soon became bored with his philosophical reflections and decided to give the head to his uncle, Mr. Rolston, who lived in New York and who, from earliest childhood, had shown a strong interest in the cultural manifestations of Latin American peoples.

"A few days later, Mr. Taylor's uncle wrote to ask him (not before inquiring after the state of his precious health) to please favor him with five more. Mr. Taylor willingly satisfied Mr. Rolston's desire and—no one knows how—by return mail he 'was very happy to honor your request.' Extremely grateful, Mr. Rolston asked for another ten. Mr. Taylor was 'delighted to be of service.' But when in a month he was asked to send twenty more, Mr. Taylor, simple and bearded but with a refined artistic sensibility, had the presentiment that his mother's brother was making a profit off of the heads.

"And, if you want to know, that's how it was. With complete frankness Mr. Rolston told him about it in an inspired letter whose strictly businesslike terms made the strings of Mr. Taylor's sensitive spirit vibrate as never before.

"They immediately formed a corporation: Mr. Taylor agreed to obtain and ship shrunken heads on a massive scale while Mr. Rolston would sell them as best he could in his country.

"In the early days there were some annoying difficulties with certain local types. But Mr. Taylor, who in Boston had received the highest grades for his essay on Joseph Henry Silliman, proved to be a politician and obtained from the authorities not only the necessary export permit but also an exclusive concession for ninety-nine years. It was not difficult for him to convince the chief executive warrior and the legislative witch doctors that such a patriotic move would shortly enrich the community, and that very soon all the thirsty aborigines would be able to have (whenever they wanted a refreshing pause in the collection of heads) an ice cold soft drink whose magic formula he himself would supply.

"When the members of the cabinet, after a brief but luminous exercise of intellect, became aware of these advantages, their love of country bubbled over, and in three days they issued a decree demanding that the people accelerate the production of shrunken heads.

"A few months later, in Mr. Taylor's country, the heads had gained the popularity we all remember. At first they were the privilege of the wealthiest families, but democracy is democracy, and as no one can deny, in a matter of weeks even schoolteachers could buy them.

"A home without its own shrunken head was thought of as a home that had failed. Soon the collectors appeared, and with them, certain contradictions: owning seventeen heads was considered bad taste, but it was distinguished to have eleven. Heads became so popular that the really elegant people began to lose interest and would only acquire one if it had some peculiarity that saved it from vulgarity. A very rare one with Prussian whiskers, that in life had belonged to a highly decorated general, was presented to the Danfeller Institute, which, in turn, immediately donated three and a half million dollars to further the development of this exciting cultural manifestation of Latin American peoples.

"Meanwhile, the tribe had made so much progress that it now had its own path around the Legislative Palace. On Sundays and Independence Day the members of Congress would ride the bicycles the company had given them along that happy path, clearing their throats, displaying their feathers, laughing very seriously.

"But what did you expect? Not all times are good times. Without warning the first shortage of heads occurred.

"Then the best part began.

"Mere natural deaths were no longer sufficient. The minister of public health, feeling sincere one dark night when the lights were out and he had caressed his wife's breast for a little while just out of courtesy, confessed to her that he thought he was incapable of raising mortality rates to the level that would satisfy the interests of the company. To that she replied he should not worry, that he would see how everything would turn out all right, and that the best thing would be for them to go to sleep.

"To compensate for this administrative deficiency it was indispensable that they take strong measures, and a harsh death penalty was imposed.

"The jurists consulted with one another and raised even the smallest shortcoming to the category of a crime punishable by hanging or the firing squad, depending on the seriousness of the infraction.

"Even simple mistakes became criminal acts. For example: if in ordinary conversation someone carelessly said 'It's very hot,' and later it could be proven, thermometer in hand, that it really was not so hot, that person was charged a small tax and executed on the spot, his head sent on to the company, and, it must be said in all fairness, his trunk and limbs passed on to the bereaved.

"The legislation dealing with disease had wide repercussions and was frequently commented on by the diplomatic corps and the ministries of foreign affairs of friendly powers.

"According to this memorable legislation, the gravely ill were given twenty-four hours to put their papers in order and die, but if in this time they were lucky enough to infect their families, they received as many month-long stays as relatives they had infected. The victims of minor illnesses, and those who simply did not feel well, earned the scorn of the fatherland, and anyone on the street was entitled to spit in their faces. For the first time in history the importance of doctors who cured no one was recognized (there were several candidates for the Nobel Prize among them). Dying became an example of the most exalted patriotism, not only on the national level but on that even more glorious one, the continental.

"With the growth achieved by subsidiary industries (coffin manufacture in particular flourished with the technical assistance of the company) the country entered, as the saying goes, a period of great economic prosperity. This progress was particularly evident in a new little flower-bordered path on which, enveloped in the melancholy of the golden autumnal afternoons, the deputies' wives would stroll, their pretty little heads nodding yes, yes, everything was fine, when some solicitous journalist on the other side of the path would greet them with a smile, tipping his hat.

"I remember in passing that one of these journalists, who on a certain occasion emitted a downpour of a sneeze that he could not explain, was accused of extremism and put against the wall facing the firing squad. Only after his unselfish end did the intellectual establishment recognize that the journalist had one of the fattest heads in the country, but once it was shrunken it looked so good that one could not even notice the difference.

"And Mr. Taylor? By this time he had been designated as special adviser to the constitutional president. Now, and as an example of what private initiative can accomplish, he was counting his thousands by the thousands; but this made him lose no sleep, for he had read in the last volume of the *Complete Works* of William C. Knight that being a millionaire is no dishonor if one does not scorn the poor.

"I believe that this is the second time that I will say that not all times are good times.

"Given the prosperity of the business, the time came when the only people left in the area were the authorities and their wives and the journalists and their wives. Without much effort Mr. Taylor concluded that the only possible solution was to start a war with the neighboring tribes. Why not? This was progress.

"With the help of a few small cannons, the first tribe was neatly beheaded in just under three months. Mr. Taylor tasted the glory of expanding his domain. Then came the second tribe, then the third, the fourth and the fifth. Progress spread so rapidly that the moment came when, regardless of the efforts of the technicians, it was impossible to find neighboring tribes to make war on.

"It was the beginning of the end.

"The little paths began to languish. Only occasionally could one see a lady taking a stroll or some poet laureate with his book under his arm. The weeds once again overran the two paths, making the way difficult and thorny for the delicate feet of the ladies. Along with the heads the bicycles had thinned out, and the happy optimistic greetings had almost completely disappeared.

"The coffin manufacturer was sadder and more funereal than ever. And everyone felt as if they had awakened from a pleasant dream—one of those wonderful dreams when you find a purse full of gold coins, and you put it under your pillow and go back to sleep, and very early the next day, when you wake up, you look for it and find emptiness.

"Nevertheless, business, painfully, went on as usual. But people were having trouble going to sleep for fear they would wake up exported.

"In Mr. Taylor's country, of course, the demand continued to increase. New substitutes appeared daily, but nobody really believed in them, and everyone demanded the little heads from Latin America.

"It happened during the last crisis. A desperate Mr. Rolston was continually demanding more heads. Although the company's stocks suffered a sharp decline, Mr. Rolston was convinced that his nephew would do something to save the situation.

"The once daily shipments decreased to one a month, and they were sending anything: children's heads, ladies' heads, deputies' heads.

"Suddenly they stopped completely.

"One harsh, gray Friday, home from the stock exchange and still dazed by the shouting of his friends and their lamentable show of panic, Mr. Rolston decided to jump out the window (rather than use a gun—the noise would have terrified him). He had opened a package that had come in the mail and found the shrunken head of Mr. Taylor smiling at him from the distant wild Amazon, with a child's false smile that seemed to say 'I'm sorry, I won't do it again.'"

Old man Grossman was worse than a nuisance. He was a source of constant anxiety and irritation; he was a menace to himself and to the passing motorists into whose path he would step, to the children in the streets whose games he would break up, sending them flying, to the householders who at night would approach him with clubs in their hands, fearing him a burglar; he was a butt and a jest to the African servants who would tease him on street corners.

It was impossible to keep him in the house. He would take any opportunity to slip out—a door left open meant that he was on the streets, a window unlatched was a challenge to his agility; a walk in the park was as much a game of hide-and-seek as a walk. The old man's health was good, physically; he was quite spry, and he could walk far, and he could jump and duck if he had to. And all his physical activity was put to only one purpose: to running away. It was a passion for freedom that the old man might have been said to have; could anyone have seen what joy there could have been for him in wandering aimlessly about the streets, in sitting footsore on pavements, in entering other people's homes, in stumbling behind advertisement hoardings across undeveloped building plots, in toiling up the stairs of fifteen-storey blocks of flats in which he had no business, in being brought home by large young policemen who winked at Harry Grossman, the old man's son, as they gently hauled his father out of their flying-squad cars.

"He's always been like this," Harry would say when people asked him about his father. And when they smiled and said: "Always?" Harry would say, "Always. I know what I'm talking about. He's my father, and I know what he's like. He gave my mother enough grey hairs before her time. All he knew was to run away."

Harry's reward would come when the visitors would say: "Well, at least you're being as dutiful to him as anyone can be."

It was a reward that Harry always refused. "Dutiful? What can you do? There's nothing else you can do." Harry Grossman knew that there was nothing else he could do. Dutifulness had been his habit of life: it had had to be, having the sort of father he had, and the strain of duty had made him abrupt and begrudging: he even carried his thick, powerful shoulders curved inwards, to keep what he had to himself. He was a thick-set, bunch-faced man, with large bones, and short, jabbing gestures; he was in the prime of life, and he would point at the father from whom he had inherited his strength, and on whom the largeness of bone showed now only as so much extra leanness that the clothing had to cover, and say: "You see him? Do you know what he once did? My poor mother saved enough money to send him from the old country to South Africa; she bought clothes for him, and a ticket, and she sent him to her brother, who was already here. He was going to make enough money to bring me out, and my mother and my brother, all of us. But on the boat from Bremen to London he met some other Jews who were going to South America, and they said to him: 'Why are you going to South Africa? It's a wild country; the savages will eat you. Come to South America and you'll make a fortune.' So in London he exchanges his ticket. And we don't hear from him for six months. Six months later he gets a friend to write to my mother asking her please to send him enough money to pay for his ticket back to the old country— he's dying in Argentina, the Spaniards are killing him, he says, and he must come home. So my

From *The Penguin Book of Jewish Short Stories,* ed. Emanuel Litvinoff (New York: Penguin Books, 1979). Copyright © Dan Jacobson. Reprinted with permission.

mother borrows from her brother to bring him back again. Instead of a fortune he brought her a new debt, and that was all."

But Harry was dutiful, how dutiful his friends had reason to see again when they would urge him to try sending the old man to a home for the aged. "No," Harry would reply, his features moving heavily and reluctantly to a frown, a pout, as he showed how little the suggestion appealed to him. "I don't like the idea. Maybe one day when he needs medical attention all the time I'll feel differently about it, but not now, not now. He wouldn't like it, he'd be unhappy. We'll look after him as long as we can. It's a job. It's something you've got to do."

More eagerly Harry would go back to a recital of the old man's past. "He couldn't even pay for his own passage out. I had to pay the loan back. We came out together—my mother wouldn't let him go by himself again, and I had to pay off her brother who advanced the money for us. I was a boy—what was I?—sixteen, seventeen, but I paid for his passage, and my own, and my mother's and then my brother's. It took me a long time, let me tell you. And then my troubles with him weren't over." Harry even reproached his father for his myopia; he could clearly enough remember his chagrin when shortly after their arrival in South Africa, after it had become clear that Harry would be able to make his way in the world and be a support to the whole family, the old man—who at that time had not really been so old—had suddenly, almost dramatically, grown so shortsighted that he had been almost blind without the glasses that Harry had had to buy for him. And Harry could remember too how he had then made a practice of losing the glasses or breaking them with the greatest frequency, until it had been made clear to him that he was no longer expected to do any work. "He doesn't do that any more. When he wants to run away now he sees to it that he's wearing his glasses. That's how he's always been. Sometimes he recognizes me, at other times, when he doesn't want to, he just doesn't know who I am."

What Harry said about his father sometimes failing to recognize him was true. Sometimes the old man would call out to his son, when he would see him at the end of a passage, "Who are you?" Or he would come upon Harry in a room and demand of him, "What do you want in my house?"

"Your house?" Harry would say, when he felt like teasing the old man. "Your house?"

"Out of my house!" the old man would shout back.

"Your house? Do you call this your house?" Harry would reply, smiling at the old man's fury.

Harry was the only one in the house who talked to the old man, and then he didn't so much talk to him, as talk of him to others. Harry's wife was a dim and silent woman, crowded out by her husband and the large-boned sons like himself that she had borne him, and she would gladly have seen the old man in an old-age home. But her husband had said no, so she put up with the old man, though for herself she could see no possible better end for him than a period of residence in a home for aged Jews which she had once visited, and which had impressed her most favourably with its glass and yellow brick, the noiseless rubber tiles in its corridors, its secluded grassed grounds, and the uniforms worn by the attendants to the establishment. But she put up with the old man; she did not talk to him. The grandchildren had nothing to do with their grandfather— they were busy at school, playing rugby and cricket, they could hardly speak Yiddish, and they were embarrassed by him in front of their friends; and when the grandfather did take any notice of them it was only to call them Boers and *goyim* and *shkotzim* in sudden quavering rages which did not disturb them at all.

The house itself—a big single-storeyed place of brick, with a corrugated iron roof above and a wide stoep all round—Harry Grossman had bought years before, and in the continual rebuilding the suburb was undergoing it was beginning to look old-fashioned. But it was solid and prosperous, and withindoors curiously masculine in appearance, like the house of a widower. The furniture was of the heaviest African woods, dark, and built to last, the passages were lined with bare linoleum, and the few pictures on the walls, big brown and grey mezzotints in heavy frames, had not been looked at for years. The servants were both men, large ignored Zulus who did their work and kept up the brown gleam of the furniture.

It was from his house that old man Grossman tried to escape. He fled through the doors and the windows and out into the wide sunlit streets of the town in Africa, where the blocks of flats were encroaching upon the single-storeyed houses behind their gardens. And in these streets he wandered.

It was Johannes, one of the Zulu servants, who suggested a way of dealing with old man Grossman. He brought to the house one afternoon Paulus, whom he described as his "brother." Harry Grossman knew enough to know that "brother" in this context could mean anything from the son of one's mother to a friend from a neighbouring *kraal,* but by the speech that Johannes made on Paulus's behalf he might indeed have been the latter's brother. Johannes had to speak for Paulus, for Paulus knew no English. Paulus was a "raw boy," as raw as a boy could possibly come. He was a muscular, moustached and bearded African, with pendulous ear-lobes showing the slits in which the tribal plugs had once hung; and on his feet he wore sandals the soles of which were cut from old motor-car tyres, the thongs from red inner tubing. He wore neither hat nor socks, but he did have a pair of khaki shorts which were too small for him, and a shirt without any buttons: buttons would in any case have been of no use for the shirt could never have closed over his chest. He swelled magnificently out of his clothing, and above there was a head carried well back, so that his beard, which had been trained to grow in two sharp points from his chin, bristled ferociously forward under his melancholy and almost mandarin-like moustache. When he smiled, as he did once or twice during Johannes's speech, he showed his white, even teeth, but for the most part he stood looking rather shyly to the side of Harry Grossman's head, with his hands behind his back and his bare knees bent a little forward, as if to show how little he was asserting himself, no matter what his "brother" might have been saying about him.

His expression did not change when Harry said that it seemed hopeless, that Paulus was too raw, and Johannes explained what the baas had just said. He nodded agreement when Johannes explained to him that the baas said that it was a pity that he knew no English. But whenever Harry looked at him, he smiled, not ingratiatingly, but simply smiling above his beard, as though saying: "Try me." Then he looked grave again as Johannes expatiated on his virtues. Johannes pleaded for his "brother." He said that the baas knew that he, Johannes, was a good boy. Would he, then, recommend to the baas a boy who was not a good boy too? The baas could see for himself, Johannes said, that Paulus was not one of these town boys, these street loafers: he was a good boy, come straight from the *kraal.* He was not a thief or a drinker. He was strong, he was a hard worker, he was clean, and he could be as gentle as a woman. If he, Johannes, were not telling the truth about all these things, then he deserved to be chased away. If Paulus failed in any single respect, then he, Johannes, would voluntarily leave the service of the baas, because he had said untrue things to the baas. But if the baas believed him, and gave Paulus his chance, then he, Johannes, would teach Paulus all the things of the house and the garden, so that Paulus would be useful to the baas in ways other than the particular task for which he was asking the baas to hire him. And, rather daringly, Johannes said that it did not matter so much if Paulus knew no English, because the old baas, the *oubaas,* knew no English either.

It was as something in the nature of a joke—almost a joke against his father—that Harry Grossman gave Paulus his chance. For Paulus was given his chance. He was given a room in the servants' quarters in the back yard, into which he brought a tin trunk painted red and black, a roll of blankets, and a guitar with a picture of a cowboy on the back. He was given a houseboy's outfit of blue denim blouse and shorts, with red piping round the edges, into which he fitted, with his beard and physique, like a king in exile in some pantomime. He was given his food three times a day, after the white people had eaten, a bar of soap every week, cast-off clothing at odd intervals, and the sum of one pound five shillings per week, five shillings of which he took, the rest being left at his request, with the baas, as savings. He had a free afternoon once a week, and he was allowed to entertain not more than two friends at any one time in his room. And in all the particulars that Johannes had enumerated, Johannes was proved reliable. Paulus was not one of these town boys, these street loafers. He did not steal or drink, he was clean and he was honest and hardworking. And he could be gentle as a woman.

It took Paulus some time to settle down to his job; he had to conquer not only his own shyness and strangeness in the new house filled with strange people—let alone the city, which, since taking occupation of his room, he had hardly dared to enter—but also the hostility of old man Grossman, who took immediate fright at Paulus and redoubled his efforts to get away from the house upon Paulus's entry into it. As it happened, the first result of this persistence on the part of the old man was that Paulus was able to get the measure of the job, for he came to it with a willingness of spirit that the old man could not vanquish, but could only teach. Paulus had been given no instructions, he had merely been told to see that the old man did not get himself into trouble, and after a few days of bewilderment Paulus found his way. He simply went along with the old man.

At first he did so cautiously, following the old man at a distance, for he knew the other had no trust in him. But later he was able to follow the old man openly; still later he was able to walk side by side with him, and the old man did not try to escape from him. When old man Grossman went out, Paulus went too, and there was no longer any need for the doors and windows to be watched, or the police to be telephoned. The young bearded Zulu and the old bearded Jew from Lithuania walked together in the streets of the town that was strange to them both; together they looked over the fences of the large gardens and into the shining foyers of the blocks of flats; together they stood on the pavements of the main arterial roads and watched the cars and trucks rush between the tall buildings; together they walked in the small, sandy parks, and when the old man was tired Paulus saw to it that he sat on a bench and rested. They could not sit on the bench together, for only whites were allowed to sit on the benches, but Paulus would squat on the ground at the old man's feet and wait until he judged the old man had rested long enough, before moving on again. Together they stared into the windows of the suburban shops, and though neither of them could read the signs outside the shops, the advertisements on billboards, the traffic signs at the side of the road, Paulus learned to wait for the traffic lights to change from red to green before crossing a street, and together they stared at the Coca-cola girls and the advertisements for beer and the cinema posters. On a piece of cardboard which Paulus carried in the pocket of his blouse Harry had had one of his sons print the old man's name and address, and whenever Paulus was uncertain of the way home, he would approach an African or a friendly-looking white man and show him the card, and try his best to follow the instructions, or at least the gesticulations which were all of the answers of the white men that meant anything to him. But there were enough Africans to be found, usually, who were more sophisticated than himself, and though they teased him for his "rawness" and for holding the sort of job he had, they helped him too. And neither Paulus nor old man Grossman were aware that when they crossed a street hand-in-hand, as they sometimes did when the traffic was particularly heavy, there were white men who averted their eyes from the sight of this degradation, which could come upon a white man when he was old and senile and dependent.

Paulus knew only Zulu, the old man knew only Yiddish, so there was no language in which they could talk to one another. But they talked all the same: they both explained, commented and complained to each other of the things they saw around them, and often they agreed with one another, smiling and nodding their heads and explaining again with their hands what each happened to be talking about. They both seemed to believe that they were talking about the same things, and often they undoubtedly were, when they lifted their heads sharply to see an aeroplane cross the blue sky between two buildings, or when they reached the top of a steep road and turned to look back the way they had come, and saw below them the clean impervious towers of the city thrust nakedly against the sky in brand-new piles of concrete and glass and face-brick. Then down they would go again, among the houses and the gardens where the beneficent climate encouraged both palms and oak trees to grow indiscriminately among each other—as they did in the garden of the house to which, in the evenings, Paulus and old man Grossman would eventually return.

In and about the house Paulus soon became as indispensable to the old man as he was on their expeditions out of it. Paulus dressed him and bathed him and trimmed his beard, and when the old man woke distressed in the middle of the night it would be for Paulus that he would call—"*Der schwarzer*," he would shout (for he never learned Paulus's name), "*vo's der schwarzer*"—and Paulus would change his sheets and pyjamas and put him back to bed again. "Baas *Zeide*," Paulus called the old man, picking up the Yiddish word for grandfather from the children of the house.

And that was something that Harry Grossman told everyone of. For Harry persisted in regarding the arrangement as a kind of joke, and the more the arrangement succeeded the more determinedly did he try to spread the joke, so that it should be a joke not only against his father but a joke against Paulus too. It had been a joke that his father should be looked after by a raw Zulu: it was going to be a joke that the Zulu was successful at it. "Baas *Zeide*! That's what *der schwarzer* calls him—have you ever heard the like of it? And you should see the two of them, walking about in the streets hand-in-hand like two schoolgirls. Two clever ones, *der schwarzer* and my father going for a promenade, and between them I tell you you wouldn't be able to find out what day of the week or what time of day it is."

And when people said, "Still that Paulus seems a very good boy," Harry would reply:

"Why shouldn't he be? With all his knowledge, are there so many better jobs that he'd be able to find? He keeps the old man happy—very good, very nice, but don't forget that that's what he's paid to do. What does he know any better to do, a simple kaffir from the *kraal*? He knows he's got a good job, and he'd he a fool if he threw it away. Do you think," Harry would say, and this too would insistently be part of the joke, "if I had nothing else to do with my time I wouldn't be able to make the old man happy?" Harry would look about his sitting-room, where the floorboards bore the weight of his furniture, or when they sat on the stoop he would measure with his glance the spacious garden aloof from the street beyond the hedge. "I've got other things to do. And I had other things to do, plenty of them, all my life, and not only for myself." What these things were that he had had to do all his life would send him back to his joke. "No, I think the old man has just found his level in *der schwarzer*—and I don't think *der schwarzer* could cope with anything else."

Harry teased the old man to his face too, about his "black friend," and he would ask his father what he would do if Paulus went away; once he jokingly threatened to send the Zulu away. But the old man didn't believe the threat, for Paulus was in the house when the threat was made, and the old man simply left his son and went straight to Paulus's room, and sat there with Paulus for security. Harry did not follow him: he would never have gone into any of his servants' rooms least of all that of Paulus. For though he made a joke of him to others, to Paulus himself Harry always spoke gruffly, unjokingly, with no patience. On that day he had merely shouted after the old man, "Another time he won't be there."

Yet it was strange to see how Harry Grossman would always be drawn to the room in which he knew his father and Paulus to be. Night after night he came into the old man's bedroom when Paulus was dressing or undressing the old man; almost as often Harry stood in the steamy, untidy bathroom when the old man was being bathed. At these times he hardly spoke, he offered no explanation of his presence: he stood dourly and silently in the room, in his customary powerful and begrudging stance, with one hand clasping the wrist of the other and both supporting his waist, and he watched Paulus at work. The backs of Paulus's hands were smooth and black and hairless, they were paler on the palms and at the finger-nails, and they worked deftly about the body of the old man, who was submissive under the ministrations of the other. At first Paulus had sometimes smiled at Harry while he worked, with his straightforward, even smile in which there was no invitation to a complicity in patronage, but rather an encouragement to Harry to draw forward. But after the first few evenings of this work that Harry had watched, Paulus no longer smiled at his master. And while he worked Paulus could not restrain himself, even under Harry's stare, from talking in a soft, continuous flow of Zulu, to encourage the old man and to exhort him to be helpful and to express his pleasure in how well the work was going. When Paulus would at last wipe the gleaming soap-flakes from his dark hands he would sometimes, when the old man was tired, stoop low and with a laugh pick up the old man and carry him easily down the passage to his bedroom. Harry would follow; he would stand in the passage and watch the burdened, barefooted Zulu until the door of his father's room closed behind them both.

Only once did Harry wait on such an evening for Paulus to reappear from his father's room. Paulus had already come out, had passed him in the narrow passage, and had already subduedly said: "Good night, baas," before Harry called suddenly:

"Hey! Wait!"

"Baas," Paulus said, turning his head. Then he came quickly to Harry. "Baas," he said again, puzzled and anxious to know why his baas, who so rarely spoke to him, should suddenly have called him like this, at the end of the day, when his work was over.

Harry waited again before speaking, waited long enough for Paulus to say: "Baas?" once more, and to move a little closer, and to lift his head for a moment before letting it drop respectfully down.

"The *oubaas* was tired tonight," Harry said. "Where did you take him? What did you do with him?"

"Baas?" Paulus said quickly, Harry's tone was so brusque that the smile Paulus gave asked for no more than a moment's remission of the other's anger.

But Harry went on loudly: "You heard what I said. What did you do with him that he looked so tired?"

"Baas—I—" Paulus was flustered, and his hands beat in the air for a moment, but with care, so that he would not touch his baas. "Please baas." He brought both hands to his mouth, closing it forcibly. He flung his hands away. "Johannes," he said with relief, and he had already taken the first step down the passage to call his interpreter.

"No!" Harry called. "You mean you don't understand what I say? I know you don't," Harry shouted, though in fact he had forgotten until Paulus had reminded him. The sight of Paulus's startled, puzzled, and guilty face before him filled him with a lust to see this man, this nurse with the face and the figure of a warrior, look more startled, puzzled, and guilty yet; and Harry knew that it could so easily be done, it could be done simply by talking to him in the language he could not understand. "You're a fool," Harry said. "You're like a child. You understand nothing, and it's just as well for you that you need nothing. You'll always be where you are, running to do what the white baas tells you to do. Look how you stand! Do you think I understood English when I came here?" Harry said, and then with contempt, using one of the few Zulu words he knew: "*Hamba!* Go! Do you think I want to see you? "

"*Au* baas!" Paulus exclaimed in distress. He could not remonstrate; he could only open his hands in a gesture to show that he knew neither the words Harry used, nor in what he had been remiss that Harry should have spoken in such angry tones to him. But Harry gestured him away, and had the satisfaction of seeing Paulus shuffle off like a schoolboy.

Harry was the only person who knew that he and his father had quarrelled shortly before the accident that ended the old man's life took place; this was something that Harry was to keep secret for the rest of this life.

Late in the afternoon they quarrelled, after Harry had come back from the shop out of which he made his living. Harry came back to find his father wandering about the house, shouting for *der schwarzer,* and his wife complaining that she had already told the old man at least five times that *der schwarzer* was not in the house: it was Paulus's afternoon off.

Harry went to his father, and when his father came eagerly to him, he too told the old man, "*Der schwarzer*'s not here." So the old man, with Harry following, turned away and continued going from room to room, peering in through the doors. "*Der schwarzer*'s not here," Harry said. "What do you want him for?"

Still the old man ignored him. He went down the passage towards the bedrooms. "What do you want him for?" Harry called after him.

The old man went into every bedroom, still shouting for *der schwarzer.* Only when he was in his own bare bedroom did he look at Harry. "Where's *der schwarzer*?" he asked.

"I've told you ten times I don't know where he is. What do you want him for?"

"I want *der schwarzer.*"

"I know you want him. But he isn't here."

"I want *der schwarzer.*"

"Do you think I haven't heard you? He isn't here."

"Bring him to me," the old man said.

"I can't bring him to you. I don't know where he is." Then Harry steadied himself against his own anger. He said quietly: "Tell me what you want. I'll do it for you. I'm here, I can do what *der schwarzer* can do for you.*"

"Where's *der schwarzer*?"

"I've told you he isn't here," Harry shouted, the angrier for his previous moment's patience. "Why don't you tell me what you want? What's the matter with me—can't you tell me what you want?"

"I want *der schwarzer.*"

"Please," Harry said. He threw out his arms towards his father, but the gesture was abrupt, almost as though he were thrusting his father away from him. "Why can't you ask it of me? You can ask me—haven't I done enough for you already? Do you want to go for a walk?—I'll take you for a walk. What do you want? Do you want—do you want—?" Harry could not think what his father might want. "I'll do it," he said. "You don't need *der schwarzer.*"

Then Harry saw that his father was weeping. The old man was standing up and weeping, with his eyes hidden behind the thick glasses that he had to wear: his glasses and his beard made his face a mask of age, as though time had left him nothing but the frame of his body on which the clothing could hang, and this mask of his face above. But Harry knew when the old man was weeping—he had seen him crying too often before, when they had found him at the end of a street after he had wandered away, or even, years earlier, when he had lost another of the miserable jobs that seemed to be the only one he could find in a country in which his son had, later, been able to run a good business, drive a large car, own a big house.

"Father," Harry asked, "what have I done? Do you think I've sent *der schwarzer* away?" Harry saw his father turn away, between the narrow bed and the narrow wardrobe. "He's coming—" Harry said, but he could not look at his father's back, he could not look at his father's hollowed neck, on which the hairs that Paulus had clipped glistened above the pale brown discolorations of age—Harry could not look at the neck turned stiffly away from him while he had to try to promise the return of the Zulu. Harry dropped his hands and walked out of the room.

No one knew how the old man managed to get out of the house and through the front gate without having been seen. But he did manage it, and in the road he was struck down. Only a man on a bicycle struck him down, but it was enough, and he died a few days later in the hospital.

Harry's wife wept, even the grandsons wept; Paulus wept. Harry himself was stony, and his bunched, protuberant features were immovable; they seemed locked upon the bones of his face. A few days after the funeral he called Paulus and Johannes into the kitchen and said to Johannes: "Tell him he must go. His work is finished."

Johannes translated for Paulus, and then, after Paulus had spoken, he turned to Harry. "He says, yes baas." Paulus kept his eyes on the ground; he did not look up even when Harry looked directly at him, and Harry knew that this was not out of fear or shyness, but out of courtesy for his master's grief—which was what they could not but be talking of, when they talked of his work.

"Here's his pay." Harry thrust a few notes towards Paulus, who took them in his cupped hands, and retreated.

Harry waited for them to go, but Paulus stayed in the room, and consulted with Johannes in a low voice. Johannes turned to his master. "He says, baas, that the baas still has his savings."

Harry had forgotten about Paulus's savings. He told Johannes that he had forgotten, and that he did not have enough money at the moment, but would bring the money the next day. Johannes translated and Paulus nodded gratefully. Both he and Johannes were subdued by the death there had been in the house.

And Harry's dealings with Paulus were over. He took what was to have been his last look at Paulus, but this look stirred him again against the Zulu. As harshly as he told Paulus that he had to go, so now, implacably, seeing Paulus in the mockery and simplicity of his houseboy's clothing, to feed his anger to the very end Harry said: "Ask him what he's been saving for. What's he going to do with the fortune he's made?"

Johannes spoke to Paulus and came back with a reply: "He says, baas, that he is saving to bring his wife and children from Zululand to Johannesburg. He is saving, baas," Johannes said, for Harry had not seemed to understand, "to bring his family to this town also."

The two Zulus were bewildered to know why it should have been at that moment that Harry Grossman's clenched, fistlike features should suddenly seem to have fallen from one another, nor why he should have stared with such guilt and despair at Paulus, while he cried, "What else could I have done? I did my best," before the first tears came.

13.3   ONLY APPROVED INDIANS CAN PLAY: MADE IN USA
Jack Forbes

The all-Indian basketball tournament was in its second day. Excitement was pretty high, because a lot of the teams were very good or at least eager and hungry to win. Quite a few people had come to watch, mostly Indians. Many were relatives or friends of the players. A lot of people were betting money and tension was pretty great.

A team from the Tucson Inter-Tribal House was set to play against a group from the Great Lakes region. The Tucson players were mostly very dark young men with long black hair. A few had little goatee beards or mustaches though, and one of the Great Lakes fans had started a rumor that they were really Chicanos. This was a big issue since the Indian Sports League had a rule that all players had to be of one-quarter or more Indian blood and that they had to have their BIA roll numbers available if challenged.

And so a big argument started. One of the biggest, darkest Indians on the Tucson team had been singled out as a Chicano, and the crowd wanted him thrown out. The Great Lakes players, most of whom were pretty light, refused to start. They all had their BIA identification cards, encased in plastic. This proved that they were all real Indians, even a blonde-haired guy. He was really only about one-sixteenth but the BIA rolls had been changed for his tribe so legally he was one-fourth. There was no question about the Great Lakes team. They were all land-based, federally-recognized Indians, although living in a big midwestern city, and they had their cards to prove it.

Anyway, the big, dark Tucson Indian turned out to be a Papago. He didn't have a BIA card but he could talk Papago so they let him alone for the time being. Then they turned towards a lean, very Indian-looking guy who had a pretty big goatee. He seemed to have a Spanish accent, so they demanded to see his card.

Well, he didn't have one either. He said he was a full-blood Tarahumara Indian and he could also speak his language. None of the Great Lakes Indians could talk their languages so they said that was no proof of anything, that you had to have a BIA roll number.

The Tarahumara man was getting pretty angry by then. He said his father and uncle had been killed by the whites in Mexico and that he did not expect to be treated with prejudice by other Indians.

But all that did no good. Someone demanded to know if he had a reservation and if his tribe was recognized. He replied that his people lived high up in the mountains and that they were still resisting the Mexicanos, that the government was trying to steal their land.

"What state do your people live in," they wanted to know. When he said that his people lived free, outside of the control of any state, they only shook their fists at him. "You're not an official Indian. All official Indians are under the whiteman's rule now. We all have a number given to us, to show that we are recognized."

Well, it all came to an end when someone shouted that "Tarahumaras don't exist. They're not listed in the BIA dictionary." Another fan yelled, "He's a Mexican. He can't play. This tournament is only for Indians."

From *Earth Power Coming: Short Fiction in Native American Literature,* ed. Simon J. Ortiz (Tsaile, AZ: Navajo Community College Press, 1983). Copyright © 1983 Jack Forbes. Reprinted with permission from the author.

The officials of the tournament had been huddling together. One blew his whistle and an announcement was made. "The Tucson team is disqualified. One of its members is a Yaqui. One is a Tarahumara. The rest are Papagos. None of them have BIA enrollment cards. They are not Indians within the meaning of the laws of the government of the United States. The Great Lakes team is declared the winner by default."

A tremendous roar of applause swept through the stands. A white BIA official wiped the tears from his eyes and said to a companion, "God Bless America. I think we've won."

Section 14
—————— Managerial Insights ——————

14.1   FOREIGN KNOWLEDGE WORKERS AS A STRATEGIC STAFFING OPTION
Lawrence A. West, Jr., and Walter A. Bogumil, Jr.

WHO WILL DO THE WORK?

The robust U.S. economy of the 1990s placed increasing demands on a workforce that isn't growing the way it once was. . . .

The greater-than-average growth in demand for knowledge workers has already resulted in widely publicized shortages of certain professionals. One study, for example, has found that 10 percent of all U.S. computer programmer/systems analyst positions and 17 percent of all computer engineer positions were vacant in 1998. The U.S. has seen cyclical shortages of nursing talent with a new shortage expected, and, while the overall number of physicians is adequate for the population, their distribution leaves many rural areas with insufficient healthcare coverage. Industries of all sorts are looking for increased technical skills in their workforces at the same time that many school districts are experiencing severe shortages of math, science, and technology teachers. . . .

This article presents an analysis of one of the options available to employers experiencing a shortage of technically trained professionals—using U.S. immigration programs to bring qualified workers to the U.S. for temporary or permanent residence. These programs have been used for nearly 100,000 professional employees per year for the past several years. Recent industry pressures have prompted Congress to nearly double the quota on one important program from 65,000 to 115,000 for two years, and to possibly revise the cap further to 195,000 for three years. We show that hiring foreign professionals is one of several options available to companies and highlight the managerial implications of this staffing option. . . .

TRADITIONAL STAFFING OPTIONS

Traditional staffing programs operated by companies and governments work through a variety of mechanisms. Some seek to expand the qualifications of existing professionals into new areas. A number of school districts offer retraining programs to qualify credentialed teachers to teach math and technology classes. They also use creative credentialing programs to bring technically qualified professionals into the classroom. One program brings retiring military officers—many with advanced degrees in math, science, computers, and engineering—into the classroom with temporary credentials, and provides summer and other programs to attain full credentials.

Excerpted from *The Academy of Management Executive* 14, no. 4 (November 2000): 71–83. Copyright © 2000 Academy of Management Executive. Reprinted with permission.

Other programs are broader attempts to increase the supply of key skills in the overall labor force. Microsoft has initiated the Skills 2000 program to provide information, training, and financial resources to attract people to the information technology field. A special program teams Microsoft, the Department of Labor, and a consortium of technical recruiting firms to recruit retiring and separating military personnel for information technology positions. The U.S. Federal Government has sponsored efforts to increase technology training for displaced workers.

Still other programs address shortages by redefining and extending job descriptions. The number of colleges with nurse practitioner programs doubled from 101 in 1990 to 202 by 1995, and graduates of these programs can perform about 80 percent of the tasks previously performed only by general practice physicians.

Finally, outsourcing and offshoring can be solutions to labor shortages by making the shortage someone else's problem. While there are many reasons for outsourcing everything from janitorial services to information systems development and operation, a key feature is that the outsourcer agrees to provide a service for a fee and then faces the burden of staffing the activity. We will return to the issue of outsourcing in our discussion of strategic implications of foreign hiring later in the article.

There are drawbacks to each of these approaches. First, many of these programs have public good characteristics. For example, if an employer sponsors a training program to address a specific labor shortage, it is difficult to be sure that the newly trained employee will remain with the sponsoring company. The companies that invest in education, on-the-job training, or other skill-enhancing programs may not reap the benefits of the outlay, and will therefore be reluctant to gamble on these investments. Instead, as public goods theory argues, federal, state, and local governments step in to implement many of these initiatives in collaboration with employment services, colleges, and other programs. Companies and government agencies needing specific targeted skills are, for the most part, left with traditional recruiting activities. These include conventional and Internet advertising and raiding competitor workforces by bidding up compensation.

Second, many of these programs take from six months to 10 years before producing results. One does not produce cardiologists (even from trained physicians) with a short on-the-job retraining program. It is similarly difficult to bypass the intensive education and licensing process for engineers, nurse practitioners, and other professionals. Finally, outsourcing surrenders a degree of control over the employee's activities. If the activities involve the creation of knowledge or the organization's core competency, then the firm risks losing control over these activities.

FOREIGN-RECRUITING ADVANTAGES

While foreign-recruiting options are not free of cost or risk, they do address some of the problems inherent in traditional staffing programs. Choosing to hire foreign professionals, for example, allows companies to target specific skills, recruit foreign professionals with those skills, and bring them to the U.S. for the purpose of practicing those skills for the recruiting company. The time lag can be a matter of days to hire Canadian or Mexican citizens, or a few weeks when recruiting foreign students already located in the U.S.

The foreign-staffing option also reduces the public good problem through three mechanisms. First, while the most popular of the employment-based immigration programs does not prohibit employees from changing jobs, potential new employers must repeat the sponsorship application process, which slightly reduces the incentive for job changing. Second, the same law further reduces employees' incentive to leave by requiring that their wages be at the prevailing market rate throughout the employment period. Finally, because foreign employees already have the requisite skills, employers invest only in the immigration process and do not subsidize employees' entire training program. . . .

However, foreign staffing is not a costless panacea. . . . Understanding these program features is essential to the discussion of managerial implications that follows. [*Editor's note:* Details can be found in the original article.]

U.S. IMMIGRATION POLICY AND OPTIONS

U.S. immigration law currently allows for several different types of visas, five of which are based on employment: the H-1B temporary professional visa, the L-1 intracompany transferee visa, the TN NAFTA visa, the second preference employment-based visa, and the third preference employment-based visa. Each visa is distinguished from the others along four dimensions:

- employee characteristics or qualifications;
- number of visas available;
- employer certifications and fees needed to hire workers;
- whether the visa leads to temporary or potential permanent U.S. residence. . . .

ORGANIZATIONAL IMPLICATIONS

The section presents a framework to help decision makers determine if hiring under one of the available visa programs might be in the best interests of the organization. Because the issue presents itself differently to managers at different levels, the discussion is presented by managerial level: strategic planning (top management), management control (middle management), and operational control (first-line management). We show how decisions made at the top two levels influence actions at lower levels.

Strategic Management Decisions

Top managers are concerned with decisions that affect the long-range success of the organization. Several writers specifically mention setting broad human-resources policies as a strategic management function, and it makes intuitive sense that broad staffing policies fall into the realm of top management.

Establishing a Corporate Infrastructure

A key role for top management with respect to the shortage of knowledge workers is to determine its strategic impact on the organization. If the firm is not highly dependent on knowledge workers, if the required skills are widely available in the labor market, or if outsourcing is a viable option, then the need for strategic attention may be slight. However, if the firm is highly dependent on a skill, if the skill provides the firm with key competitive advantages, and if staff turnover in the field or new technologies require the regular infusion of new labor, then the strategic consequences of a shortage may be more serious. For example, a firm with a strategy of providing cutting-edge engineering in its products will be vulnerable to a shortage of engineering talent. A consulting firm will be vulnerable to a shortage of consultants. Firms with broad dependency on production, clerical, or sales staff with basic computer skills could be in trouble if the supply of these workers is diminished.

Top managers may address a strategically important shortage of skilled professionals by allocating resources to attract skilled professionals. Resources may include salary and hiring bonuses, training or retraining programs, outsourcing, and supporting international hires through the visa programs described earlier.

If foreign knowledge workers are to be integrated into the workforce on a large scale, top management should establish additional policies that facilitate and reduce the cost of hiring foreign workers. These policies may include the percentage of foreign workers, especially those on temporary visas, to include in the workforce, and whether the firm will actively sponsor foreign workers for permanent resident (green card) status. The firm should also decide whether to outsource the immigration processing to immigration attorneys or to develop the internal infrastructure to perform this function.

One major technology company relies extensively on knowledge workers in many fields to provide consulting services to clients, perform R&D, and design and manufacture a wide range of equipment and software products. This company has developed a corporate-wide policy that encourages the recruitment and retention of technically trained immigrants and has developed an infrastructure to support these efforts. The company has regional centers that support the administrative aspects of the immigrant hiring process and contracts with immigration attorneys in major cities. The company has also established a policy that immigrants hired under the temporary H-1B visa will automatically be sponsored for permanent resident status. The company picks up the cost (up to $10,000) of the application and supports the process with administrative assistance.

A major entertainment and hospitality company has also established top-level policies that support the employment of foreign workers. This company uses both knowledge workers and less-skilled employees and has requirements for individuals from specific cultural backgrounds in some positions. Because this company's activities are quite centralized, it made sense for the firm to establish its own immigration-processing and compliance office. This office includes immigration attorneys as well as personnel specialists who deal with reporting requirements and other personnel needs unique to foreign employees.

Both of these firms see hiring immigrant workers as a critical success factor. Further, the technology firm recognizes that the continuous availability of qualified professionals gives it a competitive advantage over firms that have trouble staffing consulting engagements or delivering products to market. Finally, both firms have recognized the early-bird-gets-the-worm aspect of the immigration quota system, and prepare to get as many hiring applications as possible processed early in the federal fiscal year.

Another area for top management involvement is in establishing corporate diversity programs. A recent study contrasted two organizations with different levels of CEO support for ensuring that the organization hires and effectively employs a diverse workforce. The organization with the stronger diversity program sought to be the employer of choice in the area. It had less than half the turnover rate of the other organization, and the diversity programs were specifically tied to the organization's profit and performance goals.

Influencing the Environment

Another role of strategic managers is to influence the environment in which their organizations operate. Microsoft Chairman Bill Gates, for example, has initiated a major effort, Skills 2000, to increase the technical proficiency of thousands of workers through technical training programs. Because this action serves to increase the market for Microsoft products, Microsoft is able to support training for workers without concern for where they work. In another example, a consortium of information industry CEOs lobbied Congress in support of the recent increases in the H-1B visa quota, and the Information Technology Association of America uses its blue ribbon board to support lobbying activities at the state and national levels.

Economies of Scale and Outsourcing

The employment of foreign knowledge workers has implications for the choice between outsourcing work and performing it in-house. Consider an industry with a shortage of knowledge workers where the ability to attract and retain these workers is a critical success factor. Three sources of competitive advantage may accrue from this situation:

- Economies of scale advantage: A large firm with a need for many immigrant knowledge workers may realize economies of scale in recruiting and processing visa-related paperwork. If the volume of applications is large enough to warrant in-house specialists and immigration attorneys, the firm will realize savings on each application processed; it will be able to prioritize applications to move more critical hires through the system faster; and is likely to be more efficient at attracting immigrant employees. Larger-scale immigration hiring should also produce a learning effect in which staff members make fewer mistakes on applications, reduce exposure to penalties or sanctions, recognize earlier when an applicant is not likely to meet immigration standards, make personal contacts in the processing agencies, and lower the time and cost needed to move an application through the system.
- Early bird advantage: Even small firms have been able to realize advantages in previous years if they were nimble and did their immigrant recruiting early in the federal fiscal year, before quotas are exhausted. Top managers can emphasize hiring, including early processing of foreign national hires, when foreign workers are needed to address a strategic personnel shortage.
- Outsourcing advantage: Economies of scale and other factors may cause the widespread need for foreign knowledge workers to increase the advantages realized by firms providing outsourcing services. One reason for outsourcing is to acquire services for a limited period, such as to augment in-house staff during peak periods or to provide software construction services. The extra time and expenses of hiring immigrant labor under these conditions increases the average cost of these workers when they are assigned to short-term projects. An outsourcing-services firm, though, may realize economies of scale and shift workers from project to project. With one investment in hiring an H-1B visa worker, for example, the outsourcing-services firm could employ the worker on three one-year projects for different clients.

In contrast, the same clients would pay the hiring expenses three times if each were to hire the foreign worker in succession.

Middle-Management Decisions

Strategic managers establish the organization's objectives. First-line managers accomplish activities. Middle managers bridge these levels by planning the allocation of resources in support of strategic objectives, exercising oversight, and creating systems that support managers in the execution of organizational objectives. Anthony called this activity "management control."

There are distinct management control activities associated with the use of foreign labor to close the skilled-labor gap. Consider a national or regional HMO for which the shortage of a particular medical specialist is not seen as a strategic problem. If there are still local shortages of qualified practitioners, however, a hospital administrator might authorize hiring under the H-1B visa program to make up the shortfall.

Different activities for middle managers exist in organizations where the shortage is more serious and where top management has determined that systematic foreign hiring will be implemented to close the gap. These activities may include:

- Organizing the recruiting process. This may include finding an international placement agency or publicizing the openings.
- Monitoring salary and benefits equity. The H-1B visa program requires that salary and benefits for foreign employees be equal to those of domestic workers in the same position, and the firm must be able to document and justify its pay rates. It will probably be a middle-management responsibility to ensure that programs for monitoring compliance are established.
- Documenting unsuccessful domestic hiring efforts. Managers must create programs to ensure that open positions are advertised sufficiently and to document these efforts to satisfy regulatory requirements. The Department of Labor scrutinizes employers' efforts to fill jobs with U.S. workers, and the recruiting employer must provide details of the recruitment and selection process.
- Monitoring foreign employment rates. Companies are generally restricted to having 15 percent of employees hired under the provisions of the H-1B program, so hiring statistics need to be monitored.
- Supporting employee immigration administration. Foreign employees have administrative challenges that domestic workers do not face, including immigration and travel for their families, permanent resident applications, and visa renewals. If the firm supports these activities, then middle managers will be charged with establishing appropriate programs.
- Supporting foreign employees' personal concerns. Newly arrived workers often encounter issues that are not problematic for other new hires. These issues include opening a bank account, paying taxes, arranging short- and long-term housing, and obtaining credit cards and driver's licenses. Our research showed that surprisingly few companies provide this kind of support for immigrant employees, though some immigration attorneys provide guidance to their clients. Middle managers will probably need to decide whether to provide this support.
- Developing promotion policies. Workers hired under the provisions of the H-1B and TN programs have, by definition, only a limited future in the organization. Unless they are sponsored for permanent residence status, these workers are required by statute to leave the country by the end of their authorized stay. Firms must therefore decide how promotions should be handled when the best candidate is a foreign worker with only a few months remaining on his or her work visa.
- Developing training and acculturation programs for arriving workers. Many training activities or acculturation programs will be of value in any organization that seeks to accommodate an increasingly diverse workforce. Making a specific decision to hire foreign workers may highlight the need for such programs, but many may be desirable in their own right. Training foreign workers in organizational values and understanding cultural differences will be beneficial and should include policies on preventing sexual harassment, as well as the status of women in the workplace.

First-Line Management Activities

First-line managers are responsible for the day-to-day execution of the organization's activities, including the direction of production workers and the expenditure of resources. Managers at the operational control level are unlikely to make the decision to hire foreign professionals, but decisions in this regard made at higher levels do impose new requirements on the first-line managers. Because the law limits foreign workers to 15 percent of the workforce employed in similar positions, there is guaranteed to be diversity in the labor pool, and first-line managers may need new skills to operate effectively.

First-Line Human Resource Managers

First-line human resource managers have responsibility for processing newly arrived foreign workers and for managing personnel issues throughout their stays. Since work practices, benefits, and the relationships between workers and employers vary widely across the globe, the HR staff may be faced with particular challenges. Managers in this area will need to be involved with:

- Explaining benefits. Some employees come from cultures where medical, retirement, and other benefit plans are not traditionally provided, or are provided in radically different ways. In Brazil, for example, many employees work multiple part-time jobs and receive fringe benefits from none of them. In Iceland, most workers are covered by the same government benefit plan and would not be used to differing benefit structures, cafeteria plans, or other flexible benefits.
- Managing discipline and terminations. Workers in some countries are used to different ways of handling discipline and terminations. Russian workers, for example, are rarely fired. They are much more acculturated to being offered the opportunity to resign. The HR staff may also be in the front lines with regard to explaining disciplinary actions (e.g., for chronic tardiness or sexual harassment) to employees whose cultures do not consider these issues as problems.

In addition, first-line HR professionals are likely to be charged with implementing programs uniquely related to foreign workers. These actions may include:

- Completing necessary immigration documents and reports,
- Collecting data to monitor and comply with salary requirements and the mix of foreign workers in the labor force,
- Completing the Department of Labor's Labor Condition Application,
- Documenting the need for the foreign workers and efforts to recruit local workers.

First-Line Functional Supervisors

First-line functional supervisors are responsible for the day-to-day activities of foreign professionals. They assign them to projects and project teams, provide performance reports, and make recommendations for raises and other personnel actions. They interact personally with these workers on a daily basis and are aware of the personal interactions of the foreign workers with the rest of the team.

Assuming that the foreign workers are technically qualified for their new positions, one of the biggest challenges for first-line managers with respect to foreign workers is dealing with different expectations for everything from personal communication styles to work assignments to evaluating job performance.

- Rules of polite behavior. Rules of polite behavior vary widely from one culture to another. In the U.S., Argentina, and Korea it is considered correct to make and maintain eye contact during face-to-face communications, but workers from other cultures will often not look at the person with whom they are speaking. They may unintentionally seem inattentive or disrespectful. Americans are about in the middle of the continuum of personal space. In some cultures, people routinely stand much closer than an American would find comfortable, while people from other cultures may appear aloof to Americans because of the greater distance they keep.
- Unexpected social rivalries. A diverse workforce may include social relationships other than those between the foreign worker and the predominant culture of the organization. In particular, employees from the same country do not necessarily come from homogeneous backgrounds. Indians may bring prejudices from the caste system to the workplace. Consider regions such as Ireland, the former Yugoslavia, the Kurdish areas of Turkey and Iraq, parts of Africa, or Cambodia, where simmering hostility or even open warfare may exist within the same society. One organization assigned two Vietnamese workers to the same project with the assumption that they would work well together. One team member, however, was Catholic and the other Buddhist. One was from a rural area and the other from a city. The two could not get along and eventually had to be reassigned.
- Relationships with workers. Workers from some cultures treat persons in positions of authority quite differently from the average American worker. Western managers in Russia often find it difficult to obtain information from their Russian employees as many Russian workers are uncomfortable talking to authority figures. Many immigrants from Latin cultures would never consider addressing a supervisor by his or her first name, even though this practice is the norm in many U.S. workplaces.
- Managing project teams. First-line managers responsible for incorporating foreign workers into project teams may find themselves managing their own relationships with foreign workers while also raising the cultural awareness of other team members. Cultural misunderstandings can severely reduce the effectiveness of cross-cultural teams, such as computer programmers.
- Individual and contextual differences. Cultural stereotypes do not always hold up, and managers will be well served to look for a richer set of explanations for behaviors by members of a foreign culture. In particular, contextual circumstances may lead to paradoxical behavior. For example, many Japanese dislike uncertainty but routinely adopt vague contracts. Cultural mentors and adopting a learning organization focus are useful for dealing with a multicultural staff.

IMPLICATIONS FOR THE HOME COUNTRIES

Skilled foreign professionals hired in the U.S. bring with them language and professional skills acquired elsewhere and leave gaps in the workforces of their native countries. If the position a worker is hired for requires specialized education, the immigrant's home country is essentially exporting its educational resources to the U.S.

In some cases, there is an elegant match between supply and demand. India has a large English-speaking population with many well-educated professionals. While local positions are available for most of these individuals, a labor surplus in some professions and regions made immigration to the U.S., Canada, or the U.K. a logical alternative for some mobile Indian professionals. In 1998, New York City hired 20 Austrian math and science teachers to address a 200-teacher shortfall in these disciplines. A surplus of teachers in Austria helped generate 300 applicants and the district selected the 20 based on needed skills and English-language proficiency. Similarly, the demise of Communist governments in Eastern Europe resulted in a surplus of computer professionals formerly working on government projects. Many of these professionals have helped alleviate the estimated 510,000-worker shortfall in information technology workers in Western Europe.

In other cases, differential wage rates, working conditions, or educational opportunities promote temporary or permanent immigration to the U.S., resulting in the depletion of key skills and educational investments in the worker's home country. America's neighbors in the western hemisphere, for example, deplore the exodus of information technology professionals to the higher wages of the U.S. In particular, the TN visa provided by NAFTA for Mexican and Canadian citizens makes it possible for these professionals to obtain a visa at the border with minimal documentation.

One consequence of this situation is the potential for other nations to protest what may be seen as United States labor imperialism. If, for example, the flow of knowledge workers from Mexico and Canada improves the U.S. economy at the expense of the workers' countries of origin, international objections may result in policy changes. If these changes restrict the supply of knowledge workers, managers who rely on these workers would need to anticipate and react to the changes. These same managers would need to monitor economic conditions in regions that have served as a supply of knowledge workers in order to gauge the impact on their own operations.

ASSESSING OPPORTUNITIES AND CONSTRAINTS

Hiring foreign workers has been and continues to be viewed as a partial solution to a wide range of labor problems in the United States, and is currently seen as particularly pertinent to shortages in the supply of knowledge workers.

This practice has implications at several levels, however. International issues such as surpluses and shortages of labor and differences in wages and standards of living can lead to supplies of labor seeking to fill demand elsewhere. National issues such as immigration policy and economic performance affect the demand for and supply of foreign knowledge workers. Strategic managers assess the vulnerability of their firms to labor shortages and may establish policies and directions for the use of immigrant labor. Managers at the operational-control and management-control levels carry out these policies and manage foreign knowledge workers as they carry out the firm's operations.

In their ongoing assessment of the organization's status and prospects, strategic managers must identify when personnel shortages create a strategic threat to the organization. When this happens, they may consider institutionalizing the use of foreign professionals to meet the organization's needs. This decision must consider the factors discussed here.

Finally, strategic managers, especially top executives of large firms, can influence national immigration policy, as has been seen in America's technology industry. This leadership function at the national level may be the most significant role for strategic managers to play in the immigration arena.

Many companies have used foreign labor to reduce workforce shortages so successfully that they have used up all available allocations, and have had to lobby for increased quotas under the H-1B program. Administrative hurdles also must be overcome when hiring workers under the available programs, but these hurdles are not nearly as burdensome as they may at first appear. Many companies have found that carefully selecting an immigration attorney can result in cost-effective outsourcing of the most difficult part of the process.

Deciding to use foreign labor to satisfy key professional shortages introduces new requirements at different levels of management. These issues differ according to the scope of managerial responsibility, with top management dealing with broader issues, and the level of involvement becoming increasingly detailed closer to the operational-control level. It is important to recognize, though, that many of the issues presented here for middle- and first-line managers are similar to those that will arise in any organization employing a diverse workforce. Since the U.S. working population is becoming increasingly heterogeneous, many companies will be faced with these and similar issues, even without hiring foreign workers directly.

National immigration policy is influenced by, and influences, a multitude of national and international issues. Organizations must be aware of the issues that affect immigration policy, as this policy directly affects the availability and retainability of immigrant workers. A shortage of professional workers in the U.S. has had a direct impact on immigration policy, resulting in a temporary doubling of available visas for skilled labor. It remains to be seen, however, what will happen to these increased quotas after the 2001 expiration of the current legislation.

14.2 FOUR SEASONS GOES TO PARIS
Roger Hallowell, David Bowen, and Carin-Isabel Knoop

THE LINKAGE BETWEEN SERVICE CULTURE AND COMPETITIVE ADVANTAGE

. . . Corporate culture has been linked to competitive advantage in companies, for better or worse, and in service companies, in particular. Culture is so important in service companies because of its effect on multiple factors affecting customer value, factors as critical as employee behavior and as mundane (but important) as facility cleanliness. . . .

UNDERSTANDING CORPORATE CULTURE

Our model of corporate culture, which uses Schein as a point of departure, consists of the following four components: underlying assumptions, values, employee perceptions of management practices, and cultural artifacts.

Underlying Assumptions

These are basic assumptions regarding the workplace, such as the assumption that subordinates should fulfill their job requirements as a condition of employment.

Values

These are those things that are viewed as most important in an organizational setting, such as cost control, customer satisfaction, and teamwork.

Values exist in two forms in organizations. The first is what can be termed "espoused values," which are what senior managers or company publications *say* the values are.

The second form is "enacted values," which are what employees infer the values to be. Although enacted values, *per se,* are invisible, employees infer what they are by examining the evidence found in the next two components of culture: management practices and cultural artifacts. These two components are more readily observed than assumptions and values.

Employee Perceptions of Management Practices (particularly relating to human resources): Policies and Behaviors

Employees' views of practices such as selection, training, performance appraisal, job design, reward systems, supervisory practices, and so on shape their perceptions of what values are actually being enacted in a setting. For example, although customer service may be an espoused value, if job applicants are not carefully screened on service attitude, or if employees who provide great service are not recognized and rewarded, then employees will not believe that management truly values service. In short: culture is what employees perceive that management believes.

Excerpted from *The Academy of Management Executive* 16, no. 4 (November 2002): 7–24. Copyright © 2002 Academy of Management Executive. Reprinted with permission.

Cultural Artifacts

These include heroes, rituals, stories, jargon, and tangibles like the appearance of employees and facilities. Again, given the espoused value of customer service, if jargon used to characterize customers is usually derogatory, then a strong service culture is unlikely to emerge.

In contrast, if espoused values are enacted—and thus reflected in policies, management behaviors, and cultural artifacts—then a culture may emerge in which senior management and employees share similar service-relevant thoughts, feelings, and patterns of behavior. This behavior has the potential to enhance customer value and contribute to competitive advantage.

EXPORTING CORPORATE CULTURE: CAN CULTURE TRAVEL ACROSS BORDERS?

If a company succeeds in creating a corporate culture that contributes to competitive advantage in its home country, can it successfully "export" that corporate culture to another country—particularly if that country's national culture is strongly distinct, as is the case in France?

The Issue of Flexibility versus Consistency

Will an organization's corporate culture "clash" or "fit" with a different *national* culture? The key consideration here is what components of corporate culture link most tightly to competitive advantage and, as a consequence, must be managed *consistently* across country borders—even if they seem to clash with the culture of the new country. Alternatively, are there components of culture that are not critical to the linkage? If so, *flexibility* may enhance the competitiveness of the corporate culture given the different national culture. . . .

FOUR SEASONS HOTELS AND RESORTS: OVERVIEW

In 2002, Four Seasons Hotels and Resorts was arguably the world's leading operator of luxury hotels, managing 53 properties in 24 countries. Being able to replicate "consistently exceptional service" around the world and across cultures was at the heart of the chain's international success and sustained advantage.

For Four Seasons, "consistently exceptional service" meant providing high-quality, truly personalized service to enable guests to *maximize the value of their time*, however guests defined doing so. Corporate culture contributed to the firm's success in two ways. First, through the values that the organization espoused. For Four Seasons, these were personified in the Golden Rule: "Treat others as you wish they would treat you." Second was the set of behaviors that employees and managers displayed, in effect the enactment of the firm's values. The organizational capability of translating core values into enacted behaviors created competitive advantage at Four Seasons. Doing so required managers to address a central question as they expanded into new countries: What do we need to keep consistent, and what should be flexible, i.e., what should we adapt to the local market?

Performance

Four Seasons generally operated (as opposed to owned) mid-sized luxury hotels and resorts. From 1996 through 2000 (inclusive), Four Seasons increased revenues from $121 million to

$347.5 million and earnings from $55.7 million to $125.8 million, a 22.6 percent compounded annual growth rate (CAGR). Operating margins increased from 58.8 percent to 67.9 percent during the same period. . . .

Four Seasons entered the French market by renovating and operating the Hotel George V, a historic Parisian landmark. The hotel was renamed the Four Seasons Hotel George V Paris (hereafter, "F.S. George V").

International Structure

Each Four Seasons property was managed by a general manager responsible for supervising the day-to-day operations of a single property. Compensation was in part based on the property's performance. Hotel general managers had a target bonus of 30 percent of base compensation. Twenty-five percent of the bonus was based on people measures (employee attitudes), 25 percent on product (service quality), and 50 percent on profit. . . .

Management

Four Seasons' top management team was noted for its longevity, many having been at the firm for over 25 years. Characteristics which executives attributed to their peers included an international flair, a respect for modesty and compassion, and a "no excuses" mentality.

Italian in Italy, French in France

The firm's top managers were very comfortable in a variety of international settings. Antoine Corinthios, President, Europe, Middle East and Africa, for example, was said to be "Italian in Italy, French in France." Born and educated in Cairo, Corinthios then spent 20 years in Chicago but described himself as a world citizen. . . .

No Bragging, No Excuses

Modesty, compassion, and discipline were also important. A manager who stayed with Four Seasons from the prior management of the George V described the Four Seasons due diligence team that came to the property as "very professional and not pretentious; detail oriented; and interested in people. They did not come telling me that all I did was wrong," he remembered, "and showed a lot of compassion. The people are good, but still modest—many people in the industry can be very full of themselves." Importantly, excuses were not tolerated at Four Seasons. "Oh, but we have just been open a year" or "The people here do not understand" were not acceptable statements.

Strong Allegiance to the Firm

Both corporate and field managers often referred to the firm as a "family," complete with rules, traditions, and tough love. There was a strong "one-firm sentiment" on the part of managers in the field; they worked for the firm, not for the individual property to which they were assigned. For example, a general manager explained, "We are happy to let stars go to other properties to help them."

Service Orientation

Customer service extended to all levels in the organization. Managers sometimes assisted in clearing restaurant tables in passing. "If I see that something needs to get done," a manager explained, "I do it."

FOUR SEASONS' APPROACH TO INTERNATIONAL GROWTH

. . .

Diversity and Singularity

One of the things Four Seasons managers were wary about was being perceived as an "American" company. They found it useful in Europe to position Four Seasons as the Canadian company it was. One noted, "The daughter of a property owner once told us, 'I do not want you to be the way Americans are.' She assumed that Americans say 'Do it my way or take the highway.' Canadians are seen as more internationally minded and respectful of other value systems."

According to Corinthios, "Our strength is our diversity and our singularity. While the essence of the local culture may vary, the process for opening and operating a hotel is the same everywhere." . . .

Globally Uniform Standards

The seven Four Seasons "service culture standards" expected of *all* staff *all* over the world at *all* times were:

1. **S**MILE: Employees will actively greet guests, smile, and speak clearly in a friendly manner.
2. **E**YE: Employees will make eye contact, even in passing, with an acknowledgment.
3. **R**ECOGNITION: All staff will create a sense of recognition by using the guest's name, when known, in a natural and discreet manner.
4. **V**OICE: Staff will speak to guests in an attentive, natural, and courteous manner, avoiding pretension and in a clear voice.
5. **I**NFORMED: All guest contact staff will be well informed about their hotel, their product, will take ownership of simple requests, and will not refer guests elsewhere.
6. **C**LEAN: Staff will always appear clean, crisp, well-groomed, and well-fitted.
7. **E**VERYONE: Everyone, everywhere, all the time, show their care for our guests.

In addition to its service culture standards, Four Seasons had 270 core worldwide operating standards. . . . Arriving at these standards had not been easy; until 1998 there were 800. With the firm's international growth, this resulted in an overly complex set of rules and exceptions. The standards were set by the firm's senior vice presidents and Wolf Hengst, President, Worldwide Hotel Operations, who explained: "We had a rule about the number of different types of bread rolls to be served at dinner and number of bottles of wine to be opened at lounges. But in countries where no bread is eaten at dinner and no wine is consumed, that's pretty stupid."

"While 270 standards might seem extensive," Richey noted, "if there are only 270, there are thousands of things that are not covered over which the general manager and local management team have a lot of control."

In addition, exceptions to the standards were permitted if they made local sense. For example, one standard stated that the coffee pot should be left on the table at breakfast so that guests could choose to refill their cups. This was perceived as a lack of service in France, so it was amended there. Standards were often written to allow local flexibility. While the standards require an employee's uniform to be immaculate, they do not state what it should look like. In Bali, uniforms were completely different from uniforms in Chicago. Managers underlined the fact that standards set *minimum expectations*: "If you can do something for a client that goes beyond a standard," they told staff, "do it." As a result, stories about a concierge taking a client to the hospital and staying with that person overnight were part of Four Seasons lore, contributing to cultural artifacts.

To evaluate each property's performance against the standards, Four Seasons used both external and internal auditors in its measurement programs. . . . "When you talk to a Four Seasons person," Richey concluded, "they are so familiar with each of the standards, it is astonishing. With many managers at other firms this is not the case." . . .

Delivering Intelligent, Anticipatory, and Enthusiastic Service Worldwide

A manager stated: "We decided many years ago that our distinguishing edge would be exceptional, personal service—that's where the value is. . . ." Another manager added, "Service like this, what I think of as 'intelligent service,' can't be scripted. As a result, we need employees who are as distinguished as our guests—if employees are going to adapt, to be empathetic and anticipate guests' needs, the 'distance' between the employee and the guest has to be small." . . .

Human Resources and The Golden Rule

Four Seasons' managers believed that human resource management was key to the firm's success. According to one senior manager, "People make the strength of this company. Procedures are not very varied or special. What we do is fairly basic." Human resource management started and ended with "The Golden Rule," which stipulated that one should treat others as one would wish to be treated. Managers saw it as the foundation of the firm's values and thus its culture. . . .

GOING TO PARIS

However it developed its approach and philosophy, Four Seasons management knew that entering France would be a challenge.

The George V Opportunity

The six hotels in Paris classified as "Palaces" were grand, historic, and luxurious. Standard room prices at the F.S. George V, for example, ranged from $400 to $700. Most palaces featured award-winning restaurants, private gardens, and expansive common areas. . . .

Observers of the Paris hotel scene noted that by the 1980s and 1990s, the George V, like some of its peers, was coasting on its reputation. In December 1996, H.R.H. Prince Al Waleed Bin

Talal Bin Abdulaziz al Saud purchased the hotel for $170 million. In November 1997, Four Seasons signed a long-term agreement to manage the hotel. . . .

In order to transform the George V into a Four Seasons, however, an extensive amount of effort had to be placed into both the tangible and experiential service which the property and its people could deliver.

Physical Renovations

Four Seasons' challenge was to preserve the soul of the legendary, almost mythical, George V Hotel while rebuilding it for contemporary travelers. Four Seasons closed the hotel for what ended up being a two-year, $125 million total renovation. . . .

While Four Seasons decided to build to American life-safety standards, it also had to adhere to local laws, which affected design and work patterns. For example, a hygiene law in France stipulates that food and garbage cannot travel the same routes: food and trash have to be carried down different corridors and up/down different elevators. Another law involved "right to light," stipulating that employees had the right to work near a window for a certain number of hours each day. As a result, employees in the basement spa also worked upstairs in a shop with a window for several hours a day, and as many windows as possible had to be programmed into the design.

The new Four Seasons Hotel George V opened on December 18, 1999 at 100 percent effective occupancy (occupancy of rooms ready for use). . . .

BECOMING A FRENCH EMPLOYER

Entering the French hospitality market meant becoming a French employer, which implied understanding French labor laws, business culture, and national idiosyncrasies.

Rules

. . . The country was known for its strong unions. "In France, one still finds a certain dose of antagonism between employees and management," a French manager underlined. The political party of the Force Ouvrière, the union that was strongest at the F.S. George V, garnered nearly 10 percent of the votes in the first round of the 2002 French presidential election with the rallying cry, "Employees fight the bosses!" . . .

The law did give employers some flexibility, allowing them to work someone a little more during peak business periods and less during a lull. A housekeeper, for example, might work 40-hour weeks in the summer in exchange for a few 30-hour weeks in the late fall. Furthermore, French employers could hire 10 percent to 15 percent of staff on a "temporary," seasonal basis. . . .

National and Organizational Culture

Geert Hofstede's seminal work, *Culture's Consequences,* indicates a great disparity between North American (U.S. and Canadian) national culture and that of France. . . . Further, Hofstede's work and that of other scholars indicate that the differences between North American and French organizational culture are large. Corinthios identified attitudes surrounding performance evaluation as one difference:

European and Middle Eastern managers have a hard time sitting across from people they supervise and talking about their weaknesses. The culture is not confrontational. It is more congenial and positive. It is very important to save face and preserve the dignity of the person being reviewed. Some Four Seasons managers using standard forms might even delete certain sections or questions or reprogram them in different languages.

For Didier Le Calvez, General Manager of the F.S. George V and recently appointed Regional Vice President, another significant difference was the degree to which middle and front-line managers felt accountable. "The greatest challenge in France is to get managers to take accountability for decisions and policies," he said. "In the French hierarchical system there is a strong tendency to refer things to the boss."

Le Calvez was also surprised by managers' poor understanding of human resource issues. In France, when a manager has a problem with an employee, the issue generally gets referred to the human resources department. "We, at Four Seasons, on the other hand, require that operating managers be present, deal with the issue, and lead the discussion."

"Seeing Is Believing"

When reflecting on their experiences with employees in France, several Four Seasons managers mentioned Saint Thomas ("doubting Thomas"). "They must see it to believe it," Le Calvez explained. "They do not take things at face value. They also tend to wait on the sidelines—once they see that something works, they come out of their shells and follow the movement." A Four Seasons manager continued: "Most of the workforce in France did not know what Four Seasons was all about. For example, they did not think we were serious about the Golden Rule. They thought it was way too American. Initially there were some eyebrows raised. Because of this skepticism, when we entered France, we came on our tip toes, without wanting to give anyone a lecture. I think *how* we came in was almost as important as *what* we did."

More Differences

For several Four Seasons managers, working in France required a "bigger cultural adjustment" than had been necessary in other countries. "In France, I always knew that I would be a foreigner," a manager explained. "It took me a while to adjust to the French way." "There is simply an incredible pride in being French," added another. "The French have a very emotional way to do things," an F.S. George V manager explained. "This can be good and bad. The good side is that they can be very joyous and engaging. On the bad side, sometimes the French temper lashes out."

According to Four Seasons managers, what was referred to in the cultural research literature as the French "logic of honor" was strong. While it would be degrading to be "in the service of" (*au service de*) anybody, especially the boss, it was honorable to "give service" (*rendre service*), with magnanimity, if asked to do so with due ceremony. In this context, management required a great deal of tact and judgment.

Managing differing perceptions of time could also be a challenge for North Americans in France. North Americans have been characterized as having a "monochronic" culture based on a high degree of scheduling and an elaborate code of behavior built around promptness in meeting obligations and appointments. In contrast, the French were "polychronic," valuing human relationships and interactions over arbitrary schedules and appointments. . . .

An example of differences in employee-manager relationships can be found in the French managerial practice of being extremely cautious in providing employee feedback to the degree that, according to Four Seasons managers, the practice is unusual. In contrast, Four Seasons management practice involved a great deal of communication, including feedback on an individual employee's performance, which managers believed critical to solving problems and delivering superior service.

Cultural Renovation at the F.S. George V

Awareness and management of French cultural patterns were especially important to Four Seasons managers in Paris because a significant portion of the former operator's management and staff remained. . . .

Managers uniformly noted that the cultural renovation necessary to enable Four Seasons to be able to deliver its world-class service was on par with the extent of the physical renovation. [Exevutive Vice President John] Young provided an example. "During the due diligence process, the former general manager went to lunch with one of our senior staff. Even though guests were waiting, the maitre d' immediately tried to escort the general manager and his party to the general manager's customary table. At Four Seasons this is seen as an abuse of privilege. For us, 'the guest always comes first.'" . . .

Apples and Oranges

Young described the firm's approach to cultural transformation in acquired properties with existing staffing:

> [. . .] If one rotten apple can ruin the barrel, then you have to seed the organization with oranges that cannot be spoiled by the apples. As a result, a departing old-guard employee is *very* carefully replaced. Concurrently, individuals with the right culture and attitude are promoted. That creates a new culture, bit by bit by bit. At the F.S. George V, we also appealed to the national pride of our staff to help us restore a French landmark—to restore the pride of France.

"Un Boss Franco-Français"

To effect this cultural change, Four Seasons picked Le Calvez to be general manager. Le Calvez was described as both demanding and "Franco-Français," an expression used in France to describe someone or something "unequivocally French." At the same time, Le Calvez brought extensive Four Seasons and North American experience. Prior to opening the Regent Hotel in Singapore, he spent 25 years outside France, including 11 years at The Pierre. . . .

An F.S. George V manager noted, "The hotel's culture is embodied in the general manager—he shows a lot of love and respect for others and promotes social and cultural and ethnic integration." In a country where people typically referred to each other as Monsieur and Madame with their last name, Le Calvez encouraged the use of the first name. "It is more direct, relaxed, and straightforward. It represents the kind of relationship I want to have with my staff," he stated. . . .

The Task Force—"Culture Carriers"

To help Le Calvez and his team "Four Seasonize" the F.S. George V staff and ensure a smooth opening, Four Seasons assigned a 35-person task force, as it did to every new property. . . .

"The task force is truly a human resource, as well as a strong symbol," a manager explained. . . . Most task force members, who typically stayed three weeks for an opening, stayed seven to eight weeks at the F.S. George V.

Strong Tides

After working 25 years abroad, Le Calvez admitted that he was hesitant to return to work in France in light of the general tension he sensed between labor and management. However, he was encouraged by what he had seen at The Pierre, where Four Seasons managers noted that they had fostered a dialogue with the New York hospitality industry union. Le Calvez felt he could do the same in Paris. . . .

Le Calvez communicated this commitment by openly discussing the 35-hour work week, the Four Seasons retirement plan, and the time and attendance system, designed to make sure that staff would not work more than required.

At the outset of negotiations, in preparation for the reopening, Le Calvez took the representatives of the various unions to lunch. As work progressed, he organized tours of the site so that union representatives could see what was being done and "become excited" about the hotel. He noted that "Touring the property in hard hats and having to duck under electric wires builds bonds. Witnessing the birth of a hotel is exciting." Managers stated that the unions were not used to such an inclusive approach in France. . . .

RUNNING THE F.S. GEORGE V

Recruitment and Selection

Four Seasons wanted to be recognized as the best employer in each of its locations. In Paris, F.S. George V wages were among the top three for hotels. Salaries were advertised in help wanted ads, a first in the industry in Paris according to F.S. George V managers, who believed doing so would help them attract high quality staff.

At the F.S. George V, as across the firm, every potential employee was interviewed four times, the last interview with the General Manager. According to one executive, "In the selection process, we try to look deep inside the applicant. I learned about the importance of service from my parents—did this potential employee learn it from hers?" "What matters is attitude, attitude, attitude," Corinthios explained. . . .

To spread the culture and "de-demonize" the United States, the new F.S. George V management recruited staff with prior Four Seasons and/or U.S. experience to serve as ambassadors. A manager noted, "Staff with U.S. experience share with other staff what the United States is about and that it is not the terrible place some French people make it out to be." Several managers had international experience. About 40 individuals had prior U.S. experience.

"Anglo-Saxon" Recognition, Measurement, and Benefits

Le Calvez and his team launched an employee-of-the-month and employee-of-the-year program. "This had been controversial at Disney. People said it could not be done in France, but we manage to do it quite successfully. It all depends how it is presented," Le Calvez noted. "We explained that the program would recognize those who perform. Colleagues can tell who is good at their job."

Le Calvez used the same spirit to introduce annual evaluations, uncommon in France:

> People said evaluations would be unpopular, but the system seems to work. We told the staff that it would be an opportunity for open and constructive dialogue so that employees can know at all times where they stand. This allows them to adapt when need be. We wanted to make clear that there would be no favoritism, but rather that this would be a meritocracy. Here your work speaks for itself. The idea that your work is what matters could be construed as very Anglo Saxon!

In another "Anglo Saxon" action, a *"Plan d'Epargne d'Entreprise"* was set up for George V employees. This was a combination tax-deferred savings account and 401(k) type retirement plan. "This is totally new in France," Le Calvez claimed. Employees could contribute up to 4 percent of their salary, and the hotel would match it with 2 percent, to be raised based on profitability. The unions signed the agreement, although they were opposed to the principle of a non-government-sponsored retirement plan.

IMPLEMENTING THE GOLDEN RULE

The Golden Rule was at work at the F.S. George V, as its human resource director illustrated: "Cooks, before joining Four Seasons, used to have very long days starting in the morning to prepare for lunch, having a break during the afternoon, and coming back to prepare dinner. Today they work on either the morning or afternoon shift, enabling a better organization of their personal lives."

"All these gestures take time to work," Le Calvez summarized. "At first employees do not think we mean it. Some new hires think it's artificial or fake, but after a few months they let their guard down when they realize we mean what we say." . . .

Communication

To promote communication and problem solving, the F.S. George V management implemented a "direct line." Once a month the general manager met with employees, supervisors, and managers in groups of 30. The groups met for three consecutive months so that issues raised could be addressed, with results reported to the group. Managers believed that the F.S. George V was the only palace hotel in France with such a communication process. It was important to note that the groups met separately—that is, employees met separately from supervisors—because subordinates in France did not feel comfortable speaking up in front of superiors.

French law mandated that a *comité d'entreprise* (a staff committee) be established in organizations with more than 50 employees. It represented employees to management on decisions that affected employees (e.g., salaries, work hours). At the F.S. George V, Le Calvez chaired the committee's monthly meeting, which included union representatives. "We would do these things anyway, so it is easy to adjust to these laws," Corinthios said. "We do it in France because it is required by law. But we do the same around the world; it just has a different name."

Every morning the top management team gathered to go over glitches—things that may have gone wrong the day before and the steps that had been, or were being, taken to address the problem. "Admitting what went wrong is not in the French culture," a French Four Seasons manager explained. "But the meetings are usually very constructive."

Finally, about three times a year, Le Calvez and his team hosted an open-door event inviting employees and their families to spend some time at the hotel. "This is to break down barriers," he explained. "We take people around the hotel, into the back corridors. Try to remind people of a notion that is unfortunately being lost—that of the *'plaisir du travail'*—or enjoying one's work. Furthermore, we celebrate achievement. Good property rankings, for example, are recognized with special team celebrations."

The property also cultivated external communication with the press in a way that was culturally sensitive. Le Calvez and his team felt that they had been very open and responsive to the press (which they stated was unusual in France) and that as a result, "Not a single negative article had been written about Four Seasons Hotel George V since its opening." A colleague added, "The press appreciated that they were dealing with locals. It was not like Disney where everyone was American."

CULINARY COUP D'ETAT

In a significant diversion from typical Four Seasons practice, a non-Four Seasons executive chef was hired. "In France having a serious chef and serious food is important," the F.S. George V food and beverage director noted. . . .

Despite Legendre's success (earning two Michelin stars), a colleague added that "bringing in such an executive chef was problematic. The challenge is that with this chef you have someone with extraordinary talent, but who must still adjust to the way service is delivered at Four Seasons." Coexistence was not always easy. Legendre described a situation illustrating miscommunication and cultural differences that required tremendous patience on the part of the restaurant, guests, and management:

> Recently a man ordered an omelet and his wife ordered scrambled eggs. The man returned the omelet because he decided he wanted scrambled eggs. We made them. Then he sent them back because they did not meet his expectations. Of course, we realize that our oeufs brouillés are different from scrambled eggs, which don't contain cream. Because we are Four Seasons we cooked the eggs as he wanted them, like American scrambled eggs, and didn't charge for them. But cooking is about emotion—if you want to please someone, you have to do it with your heart. *We live differently in France.*

RESULTS

A Cultural Cocktail

The F.S. George V was, in effect, a cultural cocktail. Le Calvez explained, "The F.S. George V is not *only* a French hotel—it is French, but it is also very international. . . ."

The cultural cocktail also contained a number of elements unusual in France. At the time of the opening, journalists asked about the "American" smiling culture, which was referred to in France as "la culture Mickey Mouse." Le Calvez replied, "If you tell me that being American is being friendly and pleasant, that is fine by me. People tell me everyone smiles at the Four Seasons George V."

. . . Another departure from French standard was the decision to hire women as concierges and men in housekeeping. These were viewed by managers as revolutionary steps in Paris.

Service Quality

Richey summarized the results of the first F.S. George V service quality audit in October 2000, identifying some differences between French and North American business culture:

> Keep in mind that this occurred less than one year after opening, and it takes at least a year to get things worked out. There were three things we talked to Four Seasons' executives about, mostly related to employee attitude. First, the staff had an inability to apologize or empathize. I think that could be construed as typically European, and especially French. Second, the team had a very tough time doing anything that could be described as selling. This is also typically European. For example: say your glass is empty at the bar. In Paris, they may not ask you if you want another drink. Third, the staff were rules and policy oriented. If something went wrong, they would refer to the manual instead of focusing on satisfying the guest.

Things had changed considerably by Richey's second audit in August 2001, when "they beat the competitive market set." The scores showed a significant improvement, raising the property to the Four Seasons system average.

More good news came in July 2002 with the results of an Employee Opinion Survey, in which 95 percent of employees participated. The survey yielded an overall rating of 4.02 out of 5. The questions that ranked the highest were: "I am proud to work for Four Seasons Hotels and Resorts" (4.65) and "I would want to work here again" (4.61). . . .

CONCLUSION: CULTURE, CONSISTENCY, AND FLEXIBILITY

The Four Seasons Hotel George V case illustrates how a service firm with a strong, successful organizational culture expanded internationally into a country with a distinct, intense national culture. When Four Seasons entered France, some elements of organizational culture were held constant, while others were treated flexibly. . . .

Managers in widely diverse service industries can benefit from Four Seasons' approach to global management when entering countries with distinct, intense national cultures. To do so they must understand their own organizational culture: What are their (1) underlying assumptions, (2) values, (3) employee perceptions of management practices (policies and behaviors), and (4) cultural artifacts? Managers must then ask what elements of their culture are essential to competitive advantage in existing environments, and how the new environment will change that linkage. When there is a change, does the element of culture itself need to change (coffee pot no longer left on the table), or does the way the element is implemented, the way a value is enacted, need to change, such as the implementation "on tip toes" of an employee-of-the-month recognition program. In general, *values core to the organization's "value proposition" (what customers receive from the firm relative to what they pay for it) will not change, but elements of how they are enacted may.* . . .

[Referenced book:] Hofsteade, G. 1982. *Culture's Consequences: International Differences in Work-related Values.* Thousand Oaks, CA: Sage.

14.3   KEYS TO EFFECTIVE VIRTUAL GLOBAL TEAMS
Elizabeth Kelley

The globalization of business and the trend toward leaner, flatter organizations, combined with ubiquitous access to information technology, have spawned the growth of a different type of work unit, the virtual team. While a considerable amount of practitioner literature deals with virtual-team management and effectiveness, the empirical research is not so abundant. Clearly, as firms establish teams whose work is done completely or partially in a virtual environment, organizational success may hinge on understanding how to enhance virtual-team effectiveness.

In their study of global virtual teams, Martha Maznevski, of the University of Virginia, and Katherine Chudoba, of Florida State University, have made a significant contribution to that understanding. Virtual teams have been defined in many ways, with the virtual component ranging from occasional to total reliance on technology as the medium for interaction. In focusing on global virtual teams, Maznevski and Chudoba examined teams that were responsible for making and/or implementing decisions important to their organization's global strategy, used technology-supported communication substantially, and whose members worked and lived in different countries.

The authors conducted an intensive 21-month study of three global virtual teams in an eastern United States company and two of its strategic partners. The company, one of the top producers of technological manufacturing equipment in North America, was in the process of becoming a strong global competitor. Structured by product group, with a very flat hierarchy, it was designed to ensure rapid and strong links to customers. Within this environment, three teams were selected for study. Those teams differed on three critical structural characteristics—task, composition, and length of time working together. Of the three teams, two were eventually judged to be effective on decision outcomes, while the third was clearly ineffective and ultimately disbanded. Access to these three teams provided the researchers with an opportunity to compare team effectiveness and the factors that may affect team outcomes.

Maznevski and Chudoba uncovered two pivotal themes relating to global virtual-team processes and performance. First, global virtual-team dynamics consist of a series of interaction incidents. Second, there is a rhythm to these incidents that are sequenced in a repeating pattern over time.

The incidents and the rhythms of both the effective and ineffective teams were examined in terms of the relationship between technology use, primarily choice of medium, and group outcomes. The researchers looked at how structural characteristics such as task, organization culture, and group characteristics, interacted with technology use and led to various decision outcomes, including decision quality, action quality, and team commitment and cohesion.

Within the interaction incident itself, effectiveness appeared to be determined by a fit between the decision process required and the complexity of the message, and the form chosen for the interaction (medium and duration). For example, building commitment requires a high level of involvement in the decision process, and inevitably involves complex messages. An effective interaction would involve a rich medium, such as a face-to-face meeting or a conference call, and would last a fairly long time. Lower levels of complexity and simpler stages of the decision process, such as pure information sharing, could be effectively handled by a medium

From *Academy of Management Executive* 15, no. 2 (May 2001): 132–133. Copyright © 2001 Academy of Management Executive. Reprinted with permission.

such as e-mail. The unsuccessful team exhibited inappropriate fit in their interactions; for example, discussion of complex strategic issues was attempted with brief e-mails.

In effective teams, choice of medium and message characteristics was influenced by the nature of the task or group itself. As task interdependence increased, so did interaction frequency; as task complexity increased, so did message complexity. In turn, these factors influenced the choice of media. Similarly, as the number of cultural, professional, company, or country borders spanned within the group increased, richer media were required. The successful virtual global teams focused specifically on building relationships to increase trust and develop shared views across these borders, while the ineffective team did not. These relationship-building activities were typically conducted through face-to-face or telephone interactions. However, as trust and shared views were built, the message complexity decreased and choice of medium was again affected.

Contrary to what might be expected, the successful teams used only a limited number of interaction configurations: coordinating meetings, regularly scheduled conference calls, and impromptu conference calls. A more loosely defined category of interactions also existed, which team members called day-to-day stuff and involved communication between meetings.

Effective teams also exhibited a strong, repeating temporal pattern to their interaction incidents. The basic rhythm was set by intense face-to-face meetings, with the interaction between meetings defined by a response to previous meetings or anticipation of the next. The researchers characterized the face-to-face meetings as "a heartbeat, rhythmically pumping new life into the team's processes, before members circulated to different parts of the world and task, returning again at a predictable pace."

Task or team characteristics strongly influenced the rhythm. The beats grew closer if, for example, the task became more complex or required a greater level of interdependence or stronger group relationships. When tasks were unambiguous and roles well defined, the frequency of meetings was considerably slower. In one effective team, when frequent face-to-face meetings were not required, scheduled conference calls provided a secondary rhythm that supported the meetings.

The rhythm appeared to be absolutely critical to the ability of effective teams to function. It provided long-term stability and helped to structure expectations and response times. It also performed a control function, preventing inadvertent transitions, and seemed to provide a level of comfort and predictability that enabled individual members to carry out their roles within the group.

Maznevski and Chudoba offer some very practical advice for managers of virtual teams. They highlight the importance of face-to-face meetings, if possible, particularly in the early stages of a team's life and for teams faced with tasks that require a high degree of interdependence. Face-to-face meetings can facilitate strong relationships between team members and minimize potential conflict that may arise in the future.

The researchers also suggest that any scheduled rhythm should be structured around the most difficult performance challenge facing the team. This implies that rhythms must be consciously scheduled and managed, as in the two effective teams studied, and should not be allowed to emerge spontaneously.

Finally, the study indicates the importance of choosing appropriate communication media to fit the requirements of the task and the message. Rich media, such as meetings or conference calls, are necessary when a high level of interdependence defines the task or the message is complex. Under less demanding conditions, a less rich medium, such as e-mail, is quite acceptable.

[Referenced article:] Maznevski, M.L., and K.M. Chudoba. 2000. "Bridging Space Over Time: Global Virtual-team Dynamics and Effectiveness." *Organization Science* 11: 473–492.

14.4   CULTIVATING A GLOBAL MINDSET
Anil K. Gupta and Vijay Govindarajan

. . . [H]ow multinational companies and their managers perceive and interpret the global social and economic environment around them has a major impact on the strategies that they pursue and the success of these strategies. Building on this premise, our goal in this article is to explore the concept of global mindset, differentiate it from alternatives such as parochial or diffused mindsets, discuss why a global mindset is important in the business world of today, and present guidelines regarding what managers and companies can and should do to cultivate a global mindset.

WHAT IS A GLOBAL MINDSET?

The Concept of Mindset

In order to understand the meaning of the term global mindset, it is important first to achieve clarity regarding the underlying core concept of mindset. Generically, the mindset concept has had a long history in the fields of cognitive psychology and, more recently, organization theory, where scholars have focused on the question of how people and organizations make sense of the world with which they interact. The basic research findings can be summarized as follows:

1. As human beings, we are limited in our ability to absorb and process information. Thus, we are constantly challenged by the complexity, ambiguity, and dynamism of the information environment around us.
2. We address this challenge through a process of filtration. We are selective in what we absorb and biased in how we interpret it. The term mindset refers to these cognitive filters.
3. Our mindsets are a product of our histories and evolve through an iterative process. Our current mindset guides the collection and interpretation of new information. To the extent that this new information is consistent with the current mindset, it reinforces that mindset. From time to time, however, new information appears that is truly novel and inconsistent with the existing mindset. When this happens, we either reject the new information or change our mindset. The likelihood that our mindsets will undergo a change depends largely on how explicitly self-conscious we are of our current mindsets: the more hidden and subconscious our cognitive filters, the greater the likelihood of rigidity.
4. Every organization is a collectivity of individuals. Each individual has a mindset which continuously shapes and is shaped by the mindsets of others in the collectivity. How this shaping and reshaping of mindsets occurs depends crucially on who has how much power and who interacts with whom, in what context, for what purpose, and so forth. Hence, how the firm is organized and how decision-making power and influence are distributed within the organization play a decisive role in the shaping of the collective mindset.
5. Organizational mindsets can change and evolve in four primary ways: (1) new experiences which cause a change in the mindsets of organizational members, (2) a change in the relative power of different individuals, (3) a change in the organizational and social

Excerpted from *The Academy of Management Executive* 16, no. 1 (February 2002): 116–126. Copyright © 2002 Academy of Management Executive. Reprinted with permission.

processes through which members meet and interact with each other, and (4) a change in the mix of members comprising the firm such that the mindsets of new members differ from those departing. As illustrated by the mid-1990s shift from John Akers to Lou Gerstner at IBM, the need for a different mindset is one of the most common reasons for involuntary changes in CEO positions.

Mindsets as Knowledge Structures

Research in cognitive psychology has also revealed that mindsets exist in the form of knowledge structures and that the two primary attributes of any knowledge structure are differentiation and integration.

Differentiation in knowledge structures refers to the narrowness vs. breadth of knowledge that the individual or organization brings to the particular context. Consider, for example, the proverbial functional expert with almost no exposure outside the functional area. In colloquial terms, we would say that this person has tunnel vision—a classic case of low differentiation in knowledge structure. In contrast, a manager with significant experience in multiple functional areas has a more highly differentiated knowledge structure and is unlikely to exhibit the tunnel-vision syndrome.

Integration in knowledge structures refers to the extent to which the person or organization can integrate disparate knowledge elements. For organizations or people with low differentiation, integration is not an issue; there is no need to integrate if the knowledge is not differentiated. Integration is a critical attribute of mindsets in those contexts where differentiation is high.

Each of us, at one time or another, probably has met someone who appears to swing from one position to another as a result of being heavily influenced by whoever the person happens to meet last. Using our terminology, such a person is exhibiting a combination of high differentiation coupled with low integration (High D-Low I). In contrast, a person who seeks and values multiple opinions but then is able to develop an integrative perspective has a combination of high differentiation and high integration (High D-High I).

At the organizational level, consider a team of technical experts strongly focused on new product development. The mindset of such a team, operating in the silo of its members' expertise, would be Low D-High I. Compare this team to a cross-functional team whose composition includes experts from several functional areas such as R&D, manufacturing, marketing, after-sales service, and accounting but that has no strong leadership. The mindset of such a diffused/unfocused team would be High D-Low I. Finally, consider another team that in addition to being multifunctional has a strong leader who helps the team synthesize the diverse perspectives. The mindset of such a team would be High D-High I.

The Concept of Global Mindset

Building on the language of differentiation and integration, we define global mindset as a High D-High I mindset in the context of different cultures and markets. More concretely, we would define a global mindset as one that combines an openness to and awareness of diversity across cultures and markets with a propensity and ability to synthesize across this diversity. The simultaneous focus on developing a deep understanding of diversity and an ability to synthesize across diversity is illustrated well by Home Décor Inc. (disguised name), a U.S.-based household accessories company. Founded barely five years ago, the company is one of the fastest growing manufacturers of household accessories, with a five-star customer base that includes some of the most prestigious retail chains in the United States. The CEO, an immigrant from China, summarizes the company's strategy succinctly as "combining Chinese costs with Japanese quality, European design, and American marketing. There are other Chinese competitors in the market, but along with Chinese costs, what they bring is Chinese quality. On the other hand, our American competitors have excellent product quality but their costs are too high. We can and do beat both of them."

As depicted in Figure 1, it is useful to compare and contrast a global mindset (High D-High I situation) with two alternative mindsets regarding the global economic environment: a parochial mindset (Low D-High I situation), and a diffused mindset (High D-Low I situation). As an illustration of a parochial mindset, consider the situation at Ikea, the world's largest furniture retailer. Until as recently as a decade ago, Swedish nationals constituted virtually the entire top management team of the company. Fluency in the Swedish language was considered essential at the senior levels. And, when the company entered foreign markets, for example, the United States, it replicated its traditional Swedish concepts such as no home delivery, a Swedish cafeteria, beds that required sheets conforming to Swedish rather than U.S. standards, and so forth. In short, Ikea saw the world through a Swedish filter; it was almost blind to alternative views of market reality. Not surprisingly, the outcome was a very disappointing performance and unambiguous feedback that this mindset would be a major barrier to success in the U.S. market.

As Ikea re-examined its format for U.S. operations, it faced two challenges: first, to develop a better understanding of how the needs and buying behavior of American customers differed from those it had served in the past, and second, to synthesize this understanding with its beliefs and competencies pertaining to the furniture business. Without the former, the company would continue to suffer from a misalignment between its product and service offerings and market needs; without the latter, it would be unable to develop competitive advantage over incumbent players. For Ikea, the shift from a parochial to a more global mindset required an understanding of differences between Europe and the U.S. and, equally important, also a commitment to synthesize these differences and develop a more integrative perspective on the global furniture retailing industry.

In contrast to a parochial mindset, we have observed a diffused mindset most often in the case of professional service firms (e.g., in accounting, advertising, and management consulting). These firms are often structured as networks of local partner-owned organizations. In such contexts, the power of the CEO and even the senior management team is severely constrained. While certain individual executives at the top may have highly developed global mindsets, the firm as a whole behaves as if it has a diffused mindset. The appreciation for and understanding of local issues and local differences is great, but often the ability to see the bigger global picture is inadequate.

Figure 2 presents sets of diagnostic questions that managers and organizations can use to assess the extent to which they have a global mindset.

The Value of a Global Mindset

The central value of a global mindset lies in enabling the company to combine speed with accurate response. It is easy to be fast, simplistic, and wrong. It also is easy to become a prisoner of diversity, get intimidated by enormous differences across markets, and stay back, or if the company does venture abroad, to end up reinventing the wheel in every market. The benefit of a global mindset derives from the fact that, while the company has a grasp of and insight into the needs of the local market, it is also able to build cognitive bridges across these needs and between these needs and the company's own global experience and capabilities.

These benefits can manifest themselves in one or more of the following types of competitive advantage:

Figure 1   **Alternative Mindsets: A Conceptual Framework**

High	Parochial mindset	Global mindset
Low	Not applicable	Diffused mindset
	Low	High

Integration
(Ability to integrate diversity across cultures and markets)

Differentiation
(Openness to diversity across cultures and markets)

- An early-mover advantage in identifying emerging opportunities;
- Greater sophistication and more fine-grained analysis regarding the trade-off between local adaptation and global standardization;
- Smoother coordination across complementary activities distributed across borders;
- Faster roll-out of new product concepts and technologies; and
- More rapid and efficient cross-border sharing of best practices across subsidiaries.

As an illustration of how valuable a global mindset can be, let us examine how its presence or absence might affect Microsoft's strategy regarding the Chinese market. In China, there is obviously a huge market for software today with an even larger market tomorrow. However, the promise of the Chinese market is accompanied by perils. Software piracy has been rampant. Public policy tends to be unpredictable and often favors local over foreign enterprises. The market's sophistication level lags a few years behind that of the more economically developed countries, but this gap is closing. And, the use of Chinese characters requires, at the very least, a major adaptation of the software's user interface and possibly even the internal code. We would contend that when Microsoft formulates and reformulates its strategy for China, it will not be successful if its mindset vis-à-vis China is lacking along either of the two dimensions: if it is shallow in its understanding of what is happening in China and/or if it is not sufficiently able to see events in China from a more integrative global perspective. China is not the only country where Microsoft faces dedicated pirates, nor is it the only one with a nationalistic public-policy regime.

Can Microsoft bring to bear lessons learned from other markets as it analyzes China? Alternatively, might lessons from China be relevant in other markets? What does Microsoft's experience in other countries say about the rate at which the sophistication of the Chinese market might evolve and about how quickly the company should bring leading-edge products and services to China? Might China be one of the best global centers for Microsoft's research into voice and character recognition technologies? Given a global mindset, these are just some of the fundamental questions that would be raised in the process of developing the company's China strategy. In the absence of a global mindset, on the other hand, few if any of these questions would be identified or addressed.

Figure 2   **Assessing the Global Mindset of Individuals and Organizations**

Assessing Individuals

1. In interacting with others, does national origin have an impact on whether or not you assign equal status to them?

2. Do you consider yourself as open to ideas from other countries and cultures as you are to ideas from your own country and culture of origin?

3. Does finding yourself in a new cultural setting cause excitement, or fear and anxiety?

4. When you are in another culture, are you sensitive to the cultural differences without becoming a prisoner of these differences?

5. When you interact with people from other cultures, what do you regard as more important: understanding them as individuals or viewing them as representatives of their national cultures?

6. Do you regard your values to be a hybrid of values acquired from multiple cultures as opposed to just one culture?

Assessing Organizations

1. Is your company a leader or a laggard in your industry in discovering and pursuing emerging market opportunities in all corners of the world?

2. Do you regard all customers wherever they live in the world as important as customers in your own domestic market?

3. Do you draw your employees from the worldwide talent pool?

4. Do employees of every nationality have the same opportunity to move up the career ladder all the way to the top?

5. In scanning the horizon for potential competitors, do you examine all economic regions of the world?

6. In selecting a location for any activity, do you seek to optimize the choice on a truly global basis?

7. Do you view the global arena as not just a "playground" (i.e., market to exploit) but also a "school" (i.e., source of new ideas and technology)?

8. Do you perceive your company as having a global identity with many homes, or do you instead perceive your company as having a strong national identity?

THE QUEST FOR A GLOBAL MINDSET

In thinking about how to achieve a global mindset, it is critical to remember that the key word is cultivation and that the quest for a global mindset is a ceaseless journey. Living in a complex and dynamic world as we do, the extent to which one could continue to explore the world's diversity as well as the linkages across this diversity has no upper limit. No matter how developed the global mindset of a Nokia, a Toyota, or a Cisco Systems may appear today, twenty years from now their current mindsets are, in relative terms, likely to appear quite limited.

Building on ideas from cognitive psychology and organization theory regarding development of knowledge, we would contend that the speed with which any individual or organization can cultivate a global mindset is driven by four factors: (1) curiosity about the world and a commitment to becoming smarter about how the world works, (2) an explicit and self-conscious articulation of current mindsets, (3) exposure to diversity and novelty, and (4) a disciplined attempt to develop an integrated perspective that weaves together diverse strands of knowledge about cultures and markets. We shall explore these factors in turn.

Cultivating Curiosity About the World

Curiosity and openness about how the world works reflect an attitude, an element of the individual's personality makeup. Like other elements of personality, it is shaped heavily by early childhood experiences and becomes more resistant to change with age. Thus, while a company does have some maneuvering room in further cultivating curiosity among its existing employees, its greatest degrees of freedom lie at the point of employee selection and in managing the company's demographic makeup.

In situations where a company has the luxury of hiring a younger workforce (e.g., Nokia, where the average age across the entire company is around 30), it may be able to develop an inherent corporate advantage in the degree to which its employees will strive to develop a global mindset. In any case, every company has a good deal of discretion in hiring people who are curious about diverse cultures and markets and in promoting those who have shown this desired curiosity.

These considerations appeared to lie behind DaimlerChrysler's appointment of Andreas Renschler as the head of executive management development in 1999, a role which gave him broad power to help shape the careers of the top 2000–3000 managers in the merged corporation. Renschler came to this job not with a background in human resource management but with a track record of having successfully managed the launch of Daimler-Benz's M-class sports utility vehicle out of a newly built Alabama car plant, a challenge that required effectively melding a team of managers from diverse national and corporate backgrounds. According to Renschler, what he looked for was "people who were willing to change."

Promoting people to senior executive levels who place high value on global experience and global mindsets sends strong signals regarding the importance of openness to diverse cultures and markets. As an example, consider the case of Douglas N. Daft who was appointed as the chairman and CEO of Coca-Cola Company in February 2000. Born in Australia, Daft had worked outside the company's U.S. operations for almost his entire career prior to being selected for the CEO position. Daft's predecessor, Douglas Ivester, was forced out by the board partly because of insensitivity to diversity issues both outside and within the U.S. Reflecting his own background, Daft has started to steer Coca-Cola strongly in the direction of a local focus and greater regional- and country-level autonomy. The company's emphasis is more along the lines of "think local, act local," hoping to take advantage of country-level differences in areas such as consumer preferences for carbonated soft drinks versus other beverages, the way products are sold and distributed, pack sizes, and the sovereign risk.

Articulating the Current Mindset

Mindsets evolve through a process of interaction between people and the environment. Our current mindsets shape our interpretations of the world around us; in turn, these interpretations affect whether or not our mindsets change or remain unaltered. Unless this iterative process allows for new learning, it is easy to get trapped in one's own mental web. A powerful way to reduce the likelihood of this entrapment is to cultivate self-consciousness about one's mindset. Doing so requires accepting the possibility that our view of the world is just one of many alternative interpretations of reality. Accepting this possibility significantly enhances the likelihood of new learning.

How might an individual manager or team of managers cultivate self-consciousness regarding their current mindsets? In our experience, two approaches work best. The first approach is to ask managers or teams to articulate their beliefs about the subject domain (e.g., at Hewlett-Packard, what are our beliefs regarding the structure of the personal computer market in Europe?). In contrast, the second approach is to conduct a comparative analysis of how different people or companies appear to interpret the same reality (e.g., at Hewlett-Packard, how does our view of the European personal computer industry compare with that of Compaq, IBM, Intel, and Microsoft?). Since the comparative-analysis approach rests on the premise that any particular mindset is just one of several possibilities, our experience has been that it is the more effective of the two approaches for helping a manager, a team, or a company to uncover their often deeply buried current mindsets.

Consider, for example, the experience of one company where we succeeded in persuading the CEO that, at least once every quarter, the agenda for the board meeting must include a strategic review of why a different competitor behaves the way that it does. After a year of this relatively simple exercise, the quality of discussions in the board meetings changed dramatically. It became clear that the company's own perspective on the market potential of different countries and on whether or not joint ventures were a sensible entry mode in this particular industry were not necessarily shared by some of the industry's key players. As a byproduct, board deliberations on action issues facing the company became more comprehensive and even led to the abandonment of what the CEO had earlier believed to be some of the seemingly "obvious" rules of this industry. In fact, this comparative-analysis approach resulted in the CEO becoming a proponent rather than an opponent of strategic alliances in this industry.

Cultivating Knowledge Regarding Diverse Cultures and Markets

Companies can cultivate exposure to and increase knowledge of diverse cultures and markets in two ways: (1) facilitate such knowledge building at the level of individuals, and (2) build diversity in the composition of the people making up the company. These approaches complement each other: the former focuses on building cognitive diversity inside the mindsets of individuals, and the latter focuses on assembling a diverse knowledge base across the organization's members. Both approaches are essential for every multinational company. Cultivating a global mindset at the level of individuals is a slow process that can take years of learning through experience in multiple cultures; thus, relying exclusively on the globalization of individual mindsets would be woefully inadequate vis-à-vis industry and competitive imperatives.

Building on the widely accepted idea that people learn through both formal education and on-the-job experience, we describe and illustrate below several mechanisms that companies can use to cultivate literacy about and enthusiasm for diverse cultures and markets at the individual level.

Formal Education

Formal education (language skills and knowledge building regarding diverse cultures and markets) can take place through self-study courses, university-based education, or in-company seminars and/or management development programs. For example, at its Global Management Development Institute, South Korea's Samsung Group has routinely offered substantive courses in international business management; country histories, cultures, and economies; and foreign languages. In-company programs have the added advantage that the learning occurs at multiple levels—not only in the classroom but through interactions with colleagues from other locations around the world as well.

Participation in Cross-Border Endeavors

Companies can participate in cross-border business teams and projects. Consider, for example, a leading U.S. bank creating a "Euro" team to coordinate the company's response to the introduction of the new European currency. Should such a team be composed only of selected managers from the company's European units, or should the team also include a very small number of Americans from the company's U.S. operations? The latter approach, in our view, can be extremely effective in building in-depth knowledge regarding diverse cultures and markets—in addition to the obvious benefits of byproducts such as development of interpersonal ties.

Utilization of Diverse Locations for Team and Project Meetings

This approach has been used successfully by VeriFone, a global market leader in the automation and delivery of secure payment and payment-related transactions. In the late 1990s, the company had nearly 3000 employees based at more than 30 facilities around the world. As one of several mechanisms to become more attuned to the global environment, the company's top-management team instituted a policy of meeting for five days every six weeks at a different location around the globe. This generic approach can be implemented easily at any level of the corporate hierarchy, from the board of directors to a multinational R&D team within one of the business units.

Immersion Experiences in Foreign Cultures

Immersion experiences can range from two- to three-month training assignments to more extensive cultural learning programs. Standard Chartered, a London-based global bank, has used the former approach, sending trainees recruited in London to Singapore and those recruited in Singapore to London. The Overseas Area Specialist Course, initiated by South Korea's Samsung Group in 1991, is an example of an extensive program. Every year, over 200 carefully screened trainees selected one country of interest, underwent three months of language and cross-cultural training, and then spent a year in the chosen country devoted solely to understanding it. Trainees had no specific job assignment and were forbidden to make contact with the local Samsung office. While abroad, they were even encouraged to use modes of travel other than airlines, to achieve a deeper immersion in the local culture. At the end of the immersion period, trainees returned to headquarters in Seoul and reported on their experiences during a two-month debriefing period.

Expatriate Assignments

Multi-year expatriate assignments are by far the most intensive mechanism through which employees can learn about another culture and market. However, this mechanism can be the most expensive for cultivating a global mindset—for the company and, given the increasing preponderance of dual-career marriages, often for the individual. Accordingly, companies need to target expatriate assignments toward high-potential managers (as distinct from the common practice of selecting people that you don't want to see too much of) and also to ensure that their stay abroad fosters cultural learning rather than cultural isolation. . . .

Cultivating Geographic and Cultural Diversity Among the Senior Management Ranks

Notwithstanding the value of the various mechanisms discussed above, limits do exist on the speed with which a company can cultivate a global mindset among its employees, the number of employees that it can efficiently target for this objective, and the rate of success in cultivating their global mindsets. Accordingly, virtually all multinational companies must also expand the cognitive map of the organization by creating geographic and cultural diversity among senior management. Such efforts can be targeted at many executive levels, from the composition of the board of directors and the office of the CEO to the composition of business-unit management teams. For example, in recent years, IBM elected Minoru Makihara, the president of Mitsubishi, to its board, and General Motors elected Sweden's Percy Barnevik, first president and CEO of ABB, to its board. Similarly, in the early 1990s, of the 22 people on Dow Chemical's senior-most management committee, 10 were born outside the U.S. and 17 had had significant international experience. At the level of individual lines of business, Hoechst, the German pharmaceutical company, serves as a good example of diversity. In the late 1990s, Hoechst's pharmaceutical business was led by an American CEO, a French CFO, and a Canadian COO.

Location of Business-Unit Headquarters

By dispersing business-unit headquarters to carefully selected locations around the world, companies can also further the differentiation of their organizational mindset (i.e., their knowledge about diverse cultures and markets). Among major corporations, ABB was perhaps the pioneer in dispersing the locations of business-area headquarters away from the corporate center. Other more recent examples would include Eaton Corporation, which has shifted the worldwide headquarters of its light/medium truck transmission business to Amsterdam, Holland and moved the world headquarters of its automotive controls business to Strasbourg, France.

Cultivating the Ability to Integrate Diverse Knowledge Bases

Notwithstanding the fact that cognitive diversity is critical for navigating in today's complex and dynamic global environment, it also can be paralyzing. A management team composed of seven people representing four nationalities adds value only when the diverse perspectives can be integrated into a coherent vision and a coherent set of decisions and actions. Otherwise, what you get is conflict, frustration, delay, and at best either a forced or a compromise decision.

In order to cultivate the ability to integrate diverse knowledge bases, the organization needs to act on two fronts: one, ensure that people will view such integration as a rewarding endeavor, and two, ensure that people will be given ample opportunity to engage in such integration as a part of their on-the-job responsibilities. The following are some of the mechanisms that companies can use to accomplish both of these goals.

Definition and Cultivation of a Set of Core Values Throughout the Corporation

By definition, core values are those values that cut across subsidiaries no matter where located. A set of deeply ingrained and widely shared core values (as in the case of companies such as Marriott, GE, Unilever, and Honda) can serve as an organizational as well as a social integrating mechanism. Belief in a set of core values implicitly requires people to make sense of their local observations from the perspective of the company's global agenda. And, on a social level, shared values give people with diverse cultural backgrounds and knowledge bases a common mindset on which to build a constructive rather than unproductive, conflict-ridden dialog.

Widespread Distribution of Ownership Rights on a Global Basis

Ownership rights in the global parent are a powerful mechanism to ensure that every employee, regardless of location or nationality, will be inclined to look at local opportunities, local challenges, and local resources from a global perspective. Companies such as Eli Lilly (which issues stock options to every employee worldwide through the company's GlobalShares program) significantly increase the likelihood that every employee will be more cosmopolitan, more global in mindset.

Cultivation of an Internal Labor Market Driven by Pure Meritocracy

Companies such as Cisco, McKinsey, and Ford, which are committed to using merit rather than nationality as the prime driver of career mobility right up to the CEO level, create an environment in which all managers see themselves as global resources. Such an environment goes a long way toward removing the tendency to view local knowledge as idiosyncratic and of only local value, and building a global mindset.

Job Rotation Across Geographic Regions, Business Divisions, and Functions

Job rotations across countries have long served as an effective mechanism to promote openness to and knowledge about diverse cultures and markets. If well planned, they also help cultivate an ability to integrate across this diversity. Consider the approach adopted by Nokia. CEO Jorma Ollila systematically and periodically switches the jobs of his key managers right up to very senior levels. In 1998 Sari Baldauf, formerly the head of Nokia's Asia-Pacific operations, was appointed the new head of corporate R&D. Similarly, Olli-Pekka Kallasvuo, the former head of Nokia's U.S. operations, became the new corporate chief financial officer. From a management-development perspective, one major outcome of these shuffles is to cultivate a thorough understanding of diversity (through regional responsibilities for Asia or North America) as well as an ability to integrate across this diversity (through global responsibilities for R&D or finance).

Cultivation of Interpersonal and Social Ties Among People Based in Different Locations

Typically, the frequency and openness of interaction between two people is a function of how strong their interpersonal and social ties are. Accordingly, the more successful a company is at cultivating interpersonal and social ties among people based in different subsidiaries, the more effective it should be at integrating their diverse perspectives and knowledge bases. For instance, in France's Rhone-Poulenc Group, the top 50 managers from across the world meet three to four times every year to socialize as well as to discuss business issues. In addition, people from various subsidiaries meet with each other through their involvement in cross-border business teams. . . .

EMERGING OPPORTUNITIES AND A GLOBAL MINDSET

The world's economic landscape is changing rapidly and becoming increasingly global. For virtually every medium- to large-size company in developed as well as developing economies, market opportunities, critical resources, cutting-edge ideas, and competitors lurk not just around the corner in the home market but increasingly in distant and often little-understood regions of the world as well. How successful a company is at exploiting emerging opportunities and tackling their accompanying challenges depends crucially on how intelligently it observes and interprets the dynamic world in which it operates. Creating a global mindset is a central requirement for building such intelligence. The conceptual framework and mechanisms provided in this article can guide companies in moving systematically toward this goal.

ABOUT THE EDITOR

Sheila M. Puffer is a professor of international business at Northeastern University in Boston, Massachusetts. She is also a fellow at the Davis Center for Russian Studies at Harvard University and recently served as program director of the Gorbachev Foundation of North America. She has been recognized internationally as the #1 scholar in business and management in Russia. Dr. Puffer has more than 100 publications, including the books *Behind the Factory Walls: Decision Making in Soviet and US Enterprises, The Russian Management Revolution, Managerial Insights From Literature, Management International, Business and Management in Russia, The Russian Capitalist Experiment,* and *Corporate Governance in Russia.* She was editor of *The Academy of Management Executive* and a member of the Academy's Board of Governors from 1999–2002. She worked for six years as an administrator in the Government of Canada and has consulted for a number of private and nonprofit organizations. Dr. Puffer earned a diploma from the Plekhanov Institute of the National Economy in Moscow and holds a BA (Slavic Studies) and an MBA from the University of Ottawa, Canada, and a PhD in business administration from the University of California, Berkeley.